Differential Psychology

A Study of Individual Differences

Edited by Lynn Ourth and Stephanie Metzler
University of Tennessee at Chattanooga

KENDALL/HUNT PUBLISHING COMPANY
4050 Westmark Drive   Dubuque, Iowa 52002

ISBN 978-0-7872-9725-1

Printed in the United States of America
10 9 8 7 6 5 4 3

Contents

Acknowledgements

There are four people that I would like to thank: Shelly Ansel, Renae Heacock, Billee Jo Hefel and Stephen Perry. They have been truly professional. They are gracious, responsive, and long-suffering. They have been most helpful and have made this undertaking a really pleasant one. I have worked with two previous publishers, and there is simply no comparison. In fact, it is painful to even make the comparisons. Thank all of you so much.

An Introduction to Differential Psychology

Almost everyone has some interest in people. And especially when they are different from themselves. Everyone has interest in how people see them. And especially when different people see them differently. Upon becoming an adult, most are somewhat surprised and puzzled that their brother/sisters are as different as they are from themselves. It usually takes a bit longer to discover that some of the troublesome things going on between their parents and themselves are related to the real differences between them. All have discovered, sooner or later, that there are differences between their friends and lovers and themselves. They may wish that some of those differences weren't there, but more often what they want is to understand those differences.

There are some differences around which strong prejudices have developed and been maintained. The most pervasive and the longest standing prejudice is that regarding gender. In our American culture, the second most pervasive is that regarding African-American vs. Caucasian differences. It seems, though, that in our culture that most interpersonal differences evoke judgemental rather than neutral or positive responses. Interpersonal similiarities evoke initial and often sustained positive feelings.

Typical comments a person might make when dealing with another whom she/he perceives to be different are "I don't understand her" or "I don't know where he is coming from". With one who is perceived to be similar, the comments are more likely to be "I liked him right off the bat" or "We understand each other". In both sets, the issue is understanding. Where understanding is lacking, the typical response is to move away, to avoid, to be cautious; at times, it is to move against, to attack. Where understanding is present, the usual response is to move forward, to maintain contact.

Is understanding individual differences a key ingredient in determining how people regard and interact with each other? It is that dissimilarity makes understanding difficult to achieve and similarity makes it easy to accomplish? To what extent is it true that once sufficient understanding is achieved, people make decisions regarding extent of involvement with others independent of dissimilarity or similarity as such? These are the kind of questions we will be addressing in this discourse on individual differences.

The sequence of selections will hopefully reflect how a sound understanding of individual differences is developed: Understanding causes; looking at the early manifestations of these causes through temperament, early interests and abilities; studying how the interaction of these three with certain specified environments creates the fabric of adult structure and functioning. The book concludes by taking one set of individual differences—gender and seeing how these differences influence the development of dyadic intimacy.

We are glad that you are aboard and that we can share in this endeavor.

PART 1

The Causes of Individual Differences

There are three primary causes of individual differences in behavior: Heredity, non-shared environment and shared environment.

Declarations like "David got his temper from his Uncle John" or "Susie got her fear of spiders from her dotty old Grandma Lucille" occur daily, are often strongly felt and are certainly pro-heredity remarks. Likewise, an assertion like "It is no wonder that Tom turned to a life of crime; look at how he was raised" focuses on the potential impact of home environment on behavioral outcomes. There is truth in both kinds of observations. The challenge is in precisely determining the mix that is involved in each identifiable behavior or class of behaviors. Fortunately, the field of behavioral genetics has made some real progress in doing this, and in Chapter One we will consider the methods and findings of this field.

Dividing environmental influences into shared and non-shared is a relatively recent occurrence. The earlier, usually implicit, assumption was that if persons lived in the same environment at the same times, they would turn out to be much the same. However, when a closer look started being taken at all of the siblings in an intact family, the most striking discovery was just how different siblings are. This led to investigators taking more seriously both the idea that siblings are not treated in the same fashion and the idea that the same self-same environment could be perceived differently. Together, these two define the nature of non-shared environment. Seeking to identify what generates different experiences for siblings in the same family at the same time led to identifying three major contributors: Birth order, gender and degree of similarity in parent-child temperaments. All three of these, plus siblings' treatment of each other, lead to much greater differences than similarities in siblings' interests, abilities and personalities.

In Chapter Two the relative impact of birth order will be assayed. The powerful influence of gender will be rather extensively examined in Part Three. The influence that parent-child dissimilarity will be looked at in installments in most of the chapters.

What about shared environment? It plays a much lesser role than had been assumed for a long time. It appears that it accounts for values development and little else. Thus it will not be pursued further.

CHAPTER

1

Genetic Influences

An astounding pronouncement was made in the mid-80s by several behavioral geneticists: On the whole, human behaviors are predisposed by genetic influences as much as bodily structural characteristics. Conventional wisdom in our culture has granted the latter, and has had opposite views of the former. Well, bad behavior might come from bad seed, but good behavior is wholly learned.

The next fifteen years of work has strongly confirmed the mid-80s position. From gestures to intelligence, from interests to personality structures, and from normalcy to disorders, genes play an equal part to environment in giving shape to these behaviors.

How have behavioral geneticists arrived at these findings? A discussion of their methods is offered first. Next, Clare Mead Rosen puts the twinning approach "in the flesh" as she discusses real twins who were separated at birth and came together as adults for the first time. In the next selection, D.T. Lykken and colleagues explore the concept of emergenesis, an unusual genetic occurrence. Emergenesis accounts for extraordinary feats that don't 'run in the family'. Finally, Jay S. Efran discusses a series of practical implications that grow out of the most recent behavioral genetics research.

The Eerie World of Reunited Twins

Clare Mead Rosen

Clare Mead Rosen, formerly a writer and reporter for Time, *is now a freelance journalist based in Minneapolis.*

Jerry Levey was uncomfortable. The New Jersey volunteer fire captain was ending a weekend at a local firefighters' convention and had stopped into a pub for a beer and a sandwich. From across the room, however, a conventioneer he had never met was staring at him curiously. Uneasy, Levey looked away. But each time he looked back, the stranger continued to gaze. Finally the man approached him. "He told me his name was Jim Tedesco," Levey recalls, "and then he asked me if I had a twin brother." Levey assured him he did not, but Tedesco persisted. There was a man in Paramus, he explained—another fire captain it so happened—who, except for a few extra pounds, could be Levey's double. Levey laughed it off. If he had a twin he'd certainly know it.

Tedesco wasn't swayed. Later he phoned Levey with more information: his Paramus friend was born on April 15, 1954. Was there anything special about that date? "I nearly dropped the phone," Levey recalls. "That's my birthday."

Tedesco arranged for the two men to meet. When his mysterious friend entered Levey's firehouse, Levey went silent with wonder. "Lop off the extra pounds and I was looking in the mirror," he says. "We had the same mustache, same sideburns, even the same glasses." For a long moment the Paramus twin stared skeptically back at him. Suddenly the fire chiefs whooped in concert.

Later, sharing beers in a local bar, Levey and his brother—Mark Newman was the twin's name—began to assemble the jigsaw of their past. Each man already knew his biological parents had put him up for adoption, but neither had ever suspected that a sibling had been given up at the same time. As they talked and drank, the brothers discovered that they had more than looks and work in common. Both men drank only Budweiser; both held the bottle with the little finger stretched awkwardly beneath the bottom. Both were bachelors, both compulsive flirts, both raucously good-humored. "We kept making the same remarks at the same time and using the same gestures," says Jerry. "It was spooky."

In the months following the reunion the spookiness began to fade, but the behavioral parallels continued to emerge. Though Mark and Jerry saw their strange history, and their even stranger similarities, as nothing more than wondrous curiosities, the scientific community sees things very differently. For behavioral researchers grappling with the old and stubborn question of whether it is our homes or our chromosomes that make us what we are, Jerry Levey and Mark Newman, and a tiny population of siblings like them, have always represented a rare research treasure: identical twins with perfectly matching genetic hardware but perfectly different lifetime programming.

> "I used to feel something was missing. Now it's back."

Tantalizing though such subjects are, few researchers have ever attempted the painstaking job of tracking them down and bringing them in for a look. For close to half a century, only three studies—one in 1937 and two in the 1960s—tried to explore the mystery of twins reared apart. And even those surveys were, at best, cursory: the largest of the three tested 44 pairs of identical twins; the smallest investigated only 12 pairs.

But in 1979 all that began to change. That year Thomas Bouchard, Jr., a psychologist working at the University of Minnesota, Minneapolis, read an article about a pair of separated twins who had been reunited. Almost casually, he decided to contact them for study. After working with the pair, however, Bouchard grew hooked, and his goal gradually changed: he would study more reared-apart twins—not just a dozen sets, or even a *dozen* dozen—but all he could find. Twins reared together would also be studied, in a companion project, to serve as a basis for comparison.

The work has been under way for eight years. Bouchard's research crew has swelled from 3 to 18 and includes psychologists, psychiatrists, pathologists, geneticists, and dentists. Many of the twins who serve as subjects

From *Discover,* September 1987, pp. 36–46.

had already reunited before they volunteered for the program or were recruited by the researchers. Others have come individually to Minnesota hoping for help in locating a twin they know is out there. Once in the program, all the twins engage in a six-day testing marathon. They are wired with electrodes, placed on treadmills, hooked to round-the-clock portable devices that monitor temperature and activity. They are X-rayed, videotaped, and probed for everything from high blood pressure to heart murmurs to anxieties. In written tests and oral interviews they recount their sexual history, life stresses, schooling, and family history. They will answer 15,000 written questions alone.

To date, 77 sets of reunited twins—including Jerry Levey and Mark Newman—and 4 sets of reunited triplets have traveled to the Twin Cities to serve science and learn more about themselves. Several hundred sets of reared-together twins have also been studied. "The reared-apart pairs are coming in at about eight or ten per year." says psychophysiologist and team member David Lykken. "Since twins who are put up for adoption aren't being separated anymore at birth, we have a finite pool. I guess we'll study the ones there are until we retire."

Results, however, are beginning to appear. The team has already published some of its findings in professional journals, and other papers have been written and are awaiting publication. Boudchard and colleague Nancy Segal are at work on a book due to be published in 1989. With their work quickly coming to public light, the researchers have grown increasingly eager to talk about what they've discovered so far. The stories they tell are remarkable indeed.

There were the Jim twins of Ohio. That they had the same name was obviously a fluke. But the Jims also smoked the same brand of cigarettes, drove the same kind of car, held the same jobs, and engaged in the same hobby: woodworking. In fact, they had built identical white wood benches around trees in their yards. The Jims were both nervous nail-biters and both developed migraines at the same age.

Then there was Jack, a Jew who lived variously in Trinidad, California, and Israel. His twin, Oskar, grew up as a Catholic in Germany and belonged to the Hitler Youth. Despite their dramatically different backgrounds, the twins showed dramatically similar personalities when tested in Minnesota. They even shared the same eccentricities: both flushed the toilet before and after use, and both thought it funny to fake a sneeze in a crowded elevator.

Also fascinating were Daphne and Barbara, a bubbly pair of Finnish twins. Despite growing up in opposite socioeconomic circumstances, they were both penny-pinchers. And both were stingy not just with their money but also with their opinions, refusing to take stands on even the most innocuous issues. Both had suffered miscarriages during their first marriage but went on to have three healthy children. The women shared a fear of heights. Shortly after meeting for the first time, they began finishing each other's sentences and answering questions in unison.

But such dramatic, even freakish similarities are by no means all the Minnesota team is after. Indeed, while the researchers understand the appeal of such anecdotes, they consider them little more than that—colorful stories that dress up their work but don't accurately represent it. The true focus of their studies, they explain, lies in the genes. What they hope to discover is the heritability of countless thousands of human traits and characteristics. "Heritable," they stress, does not mean "*in*heritable." What heritability addresses is percentages—how much of, say, our intelligence is bequeathed to us in our genes and how much we pick up from our upbringing and our surroundings.

To help answer these questions, Bouchard's group had made it a point to include fraternal twins as well as identical twins in the study. Both superficially and genetically, the difference between the two twin types is considerable. At the cellular level the conception of identical twins is a routine matter, taking place just like the conception of any singleton (as the rest of us are called): a solitary sperm fertilizes a solitary egg, creating a zygote. Ordinarily, the zygote immediately begins the nine-month process of maturing into a human being. But in the case of identical twins one step is added first: the zygote divides in two. Since both of the new cells originated from the same egg and the same sperm, they are perfectly identical, sharing 100 percent of their genetic material. The infants who appear nine months later—dubbed monozygotic (MZ) twins—will therefore usually be similarly indistinguishable.

Fraternal twins are a different matter. There, a glitch in the ovulation process causes not one egg to be released into the mother's fallopian tube, but two. This pair of completely separate ova are then fertilized by a pair of completely separate sperm, creating two completely discrete zygotes. Fraternal, or dizygotic (DZ), twins thus have an average of half of their genetic material in common, no more or less than any other pair of singleton siblings. With their often identical upbringing, however, they serve as a valuable control group against which the *genetic* similarities of identical twins can be measured.

Twin types are not taken for granted. A 20-part blood analysis is the ultimate test of whether a pair is monozygotic or dizygotic. There have been some surprises. One pair assumed to be fraternal because of their differing appearances and abilities turned out to be identical. Their differences came about because one was found to have had an environmentally induced neurological problem. This, says Bouchard, was a case of "environment overwhelming nature." Another case of mistaken zygosity involved two young women who were so physically similar that they first discovered each other when one was mistaken for the other. But their blood tests proved them fraternal.

The most puzzling case, however, involved two Japanese-born women reared by separate families in

California. Though the twins looked almost indistinguishable, a few key markers, like the shape of their ears and face, were just different enough to get researchers wondering. Examinations and interviews revealed that both twins shared split nails on the same toes; both had had miscarriages; both suffered from a similar intestinal ailment. Yet one twin wore glasses and the other did not; one had a phobia of flying and the other did not; and one was reserved and traditional, the other more outgoing. It was not until the blood tests were completed that the answer was known: the twins were indeed identical. What then could account for the differences between them? "A whole host of things," says Lykken. "Environment, perhaps nutrition. Twins are also susceptible to all sorts of birth stresses, including the 'transfusion effect,' where one twin gets more than his share of blood. Twins are thus more likely than singletons to suffer from congenital birth anomalies that could distinguish them from each other."

Despite such occasional zygosity muddles, the Minnesota study is yielding a wealth of hard, empirical data—and not just on twins, but on the heritability of characteristics for the population at large. Most of the least controversial findings involve not psychological or temperamental traits, but physical ones. The researchers have observed that our capacity to ward off illness, for example, seems highly heritable. Monozygotic twins reared apart (MZA's) appear to have remarkably similar immune systems; researchers looked for nine key antibodies in the blood and found that these twins usually had at least seven in common. Dizygotic twins reared apart (DZA's) and singleton siblings share, on the average, only four. Genes also seem to govern susceptibility to heart and lung disease, as shown by the almost identical cardiac and pulmonary histories of the Minnesota MZA's.

More remarkable, however, is that not just the absence or presence of disease appears to be genetically encoded but also its timing. MZA's have developed everything from pancreatitis to diabetes to heart attacks within a short time of each other. Jerry and Mark both underwent a hernia operation during early childhood.

MZA's also seem to share the tendency to have or not have periodic disorders like cold sores or ear infections. William Knobloch, the chief ophthalmologist in the study, has found that identical twins are highly concordant in the timing of their need for glasses as well as in the onset of other eye problems like glaucoma.

The most striking example of biological timing Knobloch has seen was in the case of MZA triplets. "The men were in their fifties when they were reunited," he says. "One had just been diagnosed with glaucoma when he came to Minnesota. We then found that the other two were also glaucoma suspect. At the same time, one triplet had lost some vision in one eye from a different degenerative problem. And sure enough we found the same deterioration was beginning in the other brothers."

The Minnesota twin-researchers never use the word *inheritable.* They speak instead of "heritability"—the degree to which a trait or characteristic is caused by our genes rather than our environment.

The heritability of a specific characteristic—say, height—can be judged by looking at pairs of monozygotic twins reared apart (MZA's). Since these siblings share 100 percent of their genetic material, any height difference must be due to environment. By comparing the typical amount of variation between one pair of twins and another with the typical amount of variation within a pair, the researchers come up with a ratio. In the case of height that ratio is 0.9, meaning that 90 percent of the variation in people's height is genetic and the remaining 10 percent is environmental. Researchers stress that the 0.9 figure applies not to individuals but to the population as a whole.

"We don't say that ninety percent of *your* height is influenced by genetic factors and the other ten percent by environmental factors," says Minnesota psychologist Nancy Segal. "Rather, that ratio represents the proportion of differences among the people that can be explained by genes or by environmental influences."

Monozygotic twins reared together (MZT's) have an even closer height correlation—0.94. From this number, researchers conclude that an additional 4 percent of stature similarity can be caused by environmental experiences the siblings share—say, the balanced diet mom provided both her twins.

And what of the remaining 6 percent *difference* in height that can distinguish MZT's from each other? This can be attributed to experiences unique to each sibling even when they're reared under the same roof. Maybe one twin poured his milk down the sink, while the other drank extra in hopes of making the basketball team. "Just because a characteristic is genetically influenced does not mean it can't be modified," says Segal. "By altering elements of our environment, we can alter genetic expression in any number of ways."

Researchers stress, that, in many cases, MZ twins do not simply inherit disease time bombs, set to go off at unchangeable, preset ages. Rather, like the rest of us, they inherit predispositions to illness. Other research suggests that a nonsmoking twin with a family history of lung cancer will still have a better chance of staying healthy than his identical sibling with a pack-a-day habit. Similarly, no matter what two twins' genes say about their hearts, the sibling who favors red meat and eggs is still at greater risk than the one who eats fish and salad. Indeed, even physical characteristics as seemingly predetermined as height can be profoundly influenced by environment: Identical twins reared apart may vary in stature if only one receives proper nourishment.

Other Minnesota findings suggest that predispositions to both severe and mild mental disorders might also have some genetic component. Schizophrenia, for instance, has long been known to be heritable; but the Minnesota study now suggests that such subtler problems as antisocial leanings, depression, and alcoholism might also involve genes. MZ's tend to share these problems far more frequently than do DZ's or singleton siblings. Many MZA's even display identical anxieties and phobias. One set of twins, for example, shared a terror of water that neither could trace to any triggering trauma. But both had learned to cope with their fear in the same unusual way: they always backed into a pool or lake.

It is in these areas of so-called soft science—personality and intelligence—that the Minnesota team has earned its most vocal critics. And perhaps understandably. Although blood type, immune function, and cardiac health can all be measured empirically, no one has ever been able to assign an irrefutable number to such vague characteristics as social skills, anxiety levels, and problem-solving abilities. Admits Lykken: "Psychological research is not exactly high-tech stuff."

Lykken's specialty is psychophysiology, meaning he deals with simple physiological responses that reflect psychological causes. He has found that identical twins reared apart have very similar brain-wave patterns, react alike to stimuli, and process information with comparable speed. MZA's also perform alike on tests of spatial perception, verbal fluency, and IQ. All this indicates that genes are at work, but no one seems to know just how.

"Genes do not fashion IQ or personality, they make proteins," Lykken says. "And those proteins are many biochemical steps removed from the complex traits and abilities we see in a person. Our study and others show that a good deal of what we are is heritable. But don't forget that heritability figures are estimates, not absolutes. Subsequent experience can sometimes overcome nature."

Nonetheless, Lykken believes that the testing techniques the Minnesota group uses come as close as any can to providing an accurate measure of twin intelligence and personality. The IQ methodology is a good example. "In the past," he says, "a single IQ test would sometimes be given by a single tester to both twins in turn." Bouchard and his team determined that just one day of testing was insufficient to judge IQ accurately. They also knew that the use of a single examiner could bias whatever scores the tests did yield.

So the Minnesota scientists do things differently. On one day of testing, the twins are taken into separate rooms by separate researchers who administer what is known as the WAIS (Wexler Adult Intelligence Scale), the standard method of evaluating IQ. On another day the subjects are given a second test, this one administered not by a psychologist but by a computer. A third test is also included, designed to evaluate such cognitive skills as spatial reasoning. Over the remaining week the twins participate in no fewer than 20 tests or interviews designed to measure other aspects of intellectual ability.

The grueling sessions have yielded some remarkable number, most supporting the findings of twin and adoption studies of the last half century. Identical twins reared in the same family usually have about an 86 percent level of correspondence. Fraternal twins hover at about 60 percent. But identical twins reared apart are generally much more similar than same-nest fraternals, with a 72 percent match. By contrast, garden-variety siblings reared together score 47 percent, and adopted children have only a 32 percent correspondence with their nonblood siblings.

Though the Minnesota researchers believe these findings indicate that mental ability is strongly affected by the genes, they do concede that there is no way to separate the development of an inherited trait from its environmental history. They stress, however, that if the environment does influence intellectual talents, the effect is subtle. Time after time in the Minnesota study, twins with very different schooling opportunities came out only a few points apart in intelligence. One memorable case involved two British twins with a lifetime of unequal opportunity behind them. "One had a cockney accent and the other one spoke like the queen," Lykken recalls.

The more privileged of the sisters was the daughter of a wealthy lawyer and had attended posh private schools; her sister was the daughter of a lower-middle-class East Londoner and had to give up formal education at age 16 in order to take a job. But when their scores were tallied, the two women were found to be just a single point apart in IQ. Lykken concludes that the upbringing of the disadvantaged twin was "plenty good enough" to allow her mind to flower. "Just because your father is from the lower middle class," he says, "doesn't mean he doesn't like books."

Most twins in the Minnesota study have come from the white Western world with backgrounds that meet Lykken's "plenty good enough" criterion. The Minnesota team acknowledges that its findings are therefore valid for only that segment of the population. But there is disagreement from other researchers about the findings from even this relatively thin demographic slice.

In 1981 psychologist Susan Farber of Columbia University reanalyzed the data from three smaller twin studies that preceded the Minnesota work and from a number of individual case studies. While she agrees generally with Bouchard's work, she feels more attention must be paid not just to how much genes affect the IQ of separated twins but also to the length and the timing of the separation. The earlier the siblings are taken from each other and the more years they spend apart, she suggests, the more dissimilar some of their IQ skills might be.

Bouchard disagrees. Working with the scores from the same studies, he found no such effect: Twins who had been "highly separated" had similar or identical IQ's an astonishing 76 percent of the time, while, paradoxically, "little separated" twins showed a far lower 65 percent correlation. Bouchard attributes these upside-down results to what researchers call the differentiation phenomenon, a theory to which Farber herself subscribes. Differentiation suggests that MZ's reared together may often try to distinguish themselves from their partners and thus—either consciously or unconsciously—create intellectual or personality differences. When reared under separate roofs, however, they feel no such pressure to differentiate themselves and so are more likely to become what they are genetically inclined to be.

Some of the controversies that bedevil the study of twin IQ also show up in the study of twin personality. Like intelligence, personality appears to be determined by a complicated interplay of both genes and upbringing. *Un*like intelligence, however, temperament traits do not appear to be rooted in the genes and merely influenced by environment. Rather, according to Minnesota psychologist Auke Tellegen, the formation of personality is closer to a fifty-fifty affair, with genetics and experience both holding considerable sway over what we become.

Though the twins under study go through a number of interviews and written tests during their stay in Minnesota, the most telling exam they take is a 300-question survey Tellegen developed, called the Multi-dimensional Personality Questionnaire. The MPQ is designed to provide a deep, 11-layer core sample of a twin's personality. Subjects are evaluated for impulsiveness; aggressiveness; need for achievement; traditionalism; stress reaction; sense of well-being; social potency, which includes such traits as leadership; social closeness or bonding ability; alienation; harm avoidance; and even absorption, or "proneness to imaginative activities."

In each of these areas, Tellegen found a heritability of about half. The figures range from 39 percent for achievement to 55 percent for harm avoidance; but Tellegen stresses that the significance of his findings is that heritabilities were found at all, and that they all hover at about 50 percent.

The other half of the psychological diversity—the half not accounted for by genetic diversity—is, of course, environmental. But it's environment broken down into two parts. One part is common family environment; the other is experiences unique to the individual. While in some areas all siblings may react in the same fashion to lessons taught by mom and dad, in other areas they may go their own way. The desire for achievement, for example, could be molded less by parental example than by the personal

---

Twins come in two varieties, right? Wrong. Geneticists have now proven that a third type of twin certainly exists and a fourth may be out there as well.

The two most common twin types are identical twins, who share 100 percent of their genetic material, and fraternal twins, who share about 50 percent. However, a quirk in the way human eggs are manufactured makes a 75 percent twin at least a biological possibility.

An immature ovum begins life as a 46-chromosome cell called an oocyte. During its development, the oocyte divides once, shedding a cell with enough genetic material for 46 chromosomes. This cell soon disintegrates; the surviving partner then divides again into a pair of 23-chromosome cells.

Sometimes, though, the cell that *should* die, doesn't. Known as a polar body, this unusual egg is genetically identical to the ovum from which it separated. If both the ovum and the polar body are released during ovulation, and if both are fertilized by separate sperm (which usually have about half their genes in common), a pair of three-quarter twins could result.

It is difficult to identify polar-body twins. However, Frederick Bieber, a geneticist at Harvard Medical School, reports one case in which a woman gave birth to a healthy twin with a normal 46 chromosomes and a badly deformed stillborn twin with 69 chromosomes. The stillborn baby, Bieber concludes, was the result of the fertilization of the first polar body shed by the oocyte, which contributed 46 chromosomes.

"This tells us that fertilization of healthy, twenty-three-chromosome polar bodies is also theoretically possible," he says. "It is, however, probably rare, since a human polar body contains less cytoplasm than a mature ovum and is therefore less viable."

Just as remarkable as polar-body twinning is an observed phenomenon known as heteropaternal dizygotic twinning—the conception of fraternal twins by separate fathers. "Sperm can survive for up to forty-eight hours in the female genital tract," says Bieber. "If a woman ovulates twice—as she would ordinary fraternal twins—and has sex with two men within this period, the eggs can be fertilized by different men."

Ordinarily, it takes a blood test to identify these unusual half-twins, but sometimes all that's needed is a simple look. "We've seen some cases," Bieber reports, "in which one twin was white and the other one black."

triumph of pitching a no-hitter in a Little League game or by winning a school election.

Tellegen examined the common family environment and found that social closeness was the only personality trait that could really be attributed to it. Other traits seemed to depend on individual experiences. "Our findings don't show that families have no influence over their children," Tellegen says. "What we looked for was the 'common' family effect, the ways in which parents try to move all their children in the same direction. Families undoubtedly affect children, but not uniformly."

But Tellegen concedes that the architecture of personality—and the factors that shape it—can be only approximated by tests like his. Says psychiatrist Leonard Heston, another member of the Minnesota team: "It is utterly frustrating to try to pinpoint the environmental. We simply haven't got the tools to measure such effects."

Such caveats notwithstanding, the team has put forward a provocative hypothesis about an always controversial subject: the roots of homosexuality. So far, the findings suggest that while homosexuality may be heritable to a degree in males, it is probably based more on environment among females. Heston, along with psychiatrist Elke Eckert, was largely responsible for this branch of the research. Of the 55 separated MZ twins the two of them studied, six sets have contained homosexual or bisexual members. In one male pair, both brothers were homosexual; in another, only one was. In contrast with the men, none of the three female twins who said they were lesbian, nor a fourth who said she was bisexual, had an identical twin with a matching sexual orientation.

Curiously, the bisexual woman and the three lesbians were all taller and heavier than their heterosexual twins and all had started menstruation two years later than their sisters. Eckert thus speculates that lesbianism or female bisexuality may stem from a non-genetic endocrine change. She hastens to add, however, that this is just a possibility, since so few lesbian twins have been studied.

Though the Minnesota project is the first to investigate homosexual twins reared apart, a number of earlier studies have looked at the profiles of homosexual twins reared together. All these studies were of men, and all suggested that genetics plays a substantial role in the emergence of homosexuality. The largest previous survey showed a 100 percent sexual correlation in identical twins reared together, compared with only a 12 percent similarity in fraternal twins reared under the same roof. Heston himself, in a 1968 study, found a less striking but still significant 40 to 50 percent concordance in identical male twins reared together.

Until the Minnesota study is complete, most of the findings—from those regarding homosexuality to those that touch on personality and IQ—must remain indicators rather than answers. "We are in the long, arduous process of collecting data," Bouchard says. And data, he recognizes, can often lead to controversy. Bouchard recalls an argument he had with psychologist Leon Kamin of Princeton University over Kamin's claim that the similar environment of same-sex fraternal twins—particularly females, because they often share bedrooms—gives them IQ scores closer than those of ordinary siblings. Kamin cited a study showing that male fraternals showed an impressive 51 percent IQ concordance, and females a staggering 70 percent. Bouchard countered by citing 41 separate IQ studies embracing 3,670 same-sex fraternal pairs and 1,592 opposite-sex fraternal pairs. The statistics showed that same-sex fraternals had about the same IQ correlation (62 percent) as did opposite-sex fraternals (57 percent). While Bouchard insists the numbers are conclusive, Kamin points out that data are not accepted unless they fit the bias of the day.

"You can use data to prove anything you want," he says. "When I went to school, schizophrenia was laid to 'family dynamics.' Now we know genes play a part. But the new data are no better than the old, they're just better accepted."

And so the war between biology and culture grinds on. Lykken insists that the very concept of nature versus nurture is artificial because the two are totally interdependent: "I like to think of it as 'nature via nurture.'"

To the twins themselves, the whole debate seems pretty esoteric. They have something more fundamental on their minds: the sometimes easy, other times taxing job of readjusting to a world in which a living carbon of themselves has suddenly appeared after three or four decades of absence. Before even joining the study Mark and Jerry were comfortable declaring: "I'm him and he's me." And yet just as often they need their distance. Toward the end of their week in Minnesota, both said: "When this is over, we'll take a vacation from each other."

But like most twins who have gone to Minnesota, these two count their reunion as the greatest good luck of their lives. Again and again, twins who have found each other tell researchers that their only sadness is that they lost so many years together.

"I used to feel something was missing," Mark Newman confided in one of his interviews. "Now, it's back in place."

Emergenesis

Genetic Traits That May Not Run in Families

D. T. Lykken, M. McGue, A. Tellegen, and T. J. Bouchard, Jr.
University of Minnesota

Traits that are influenced by a configuration—rather than by a simple sum—of polymorphic genes may not be seen to be genetic unless one studies monozygotic twins (who share all their genes and thus all gene configurations) because such "emergenic" traits will tend not to run in families. Personal idiosyncrasies that have been found to be surprisingly concordant among MZ twins separated in infancy and reared apart may be emergenic traits. More speculatively, important human traits like leadership, genius in its many manifestations, being an effective therapist or parent, as well as certain psychopathological syndromes may also be emergenic. These ideas reemphasize the importance of the role played in human affairs by genetic variation.

It is a common observation that monozygotic (MZ) twins tend to be remarkably similar, not just in appearance and aptitude but also in those idiosyncrasies of habit, taste, and style that constitute what we think of as human individuality. When the twins have grown up together in the same home, one is inclined to attribute these similarities to common experience, mutual modeling, and the strong attachment that is commonly seen in MZ twins from earliest infancy. Twin studies of metrical traits (e.g., IQ, personality, and interest traits), however, have found surprisingly little evidence for such effects of shared environment; the residual variance remaining in most of these traits after the genetic variance has been removed consists primarily of nonshared variance of environmental origin (i.e., unshared *threptic* variance; Cattell, 1982), plus components due to measurement error (e.g., Plomin & Daniels, 1987) and to the unsystematic secular variation that is characteristic of psychological traits (e.g., McGue, Bacon, & Lykken, in press). Moreover, studies of MZ twins who have been separated in infancy and reared apart (MZA twins) have also noted idiosyncratic similarities similar to those seen in MZ twins reared together (MZTs; e.g., Juel-Nielsen, 1965; H. H. Newman, Freeman, & Holzinger, 1937; Shields, 1962).

In the Minnesota Study of Twins Reared Apart (Bouchard, Lykken, McGue, Segal, & Tellegen, 1990; Lykken, Bouchard, McGue, & Tellegen, 1992b), we too have been struck by the similarities in personal style within many of the MZA pairs whom we have studied over the past 12 years. While videotaping an interview with one twin, we discovered that he was an accomplished raconteur with a fund of amusing anecdotes, so, while interviewing the co-twin, we asked him if he knew any funny stories. "Why, sure," he said, leaning back with a practiced air, "I'll tell you a story" and proceeded to demonstrate his concordance. A pair of British MZAs, who had met for the first time as adults just a month previously, both firmly refused in their separate interviews to express opinions on controversial topics; since long before they discovered each other's existence, each had resolutely avoided controversy. Another pair were both habitual gigglers, although each had been raised by adoptive parents whom they described as undemonstrative and dour, and neither had known anyone who laughed as freely as she did until finally she met her twin. Both members of another pair independently reported that they refrained from voting in political elections on the principle that they did not feel themselves well enough informed to make wise choices. A pair of male MZAs, at their first adult reunion, discovered that they both used Vademecum toothpaste, Canoe shaving lotion, Vitalis hair tonic, and Lucky Strike cigarettes. After

Samuel M. Turner served as action editor for this article.

This research was supported by grants from the Pioneer Fund, the Seaver Institute, the Koch Charitable Foundation, the Spencer Foundation, the University of Minnesota Graduate School, the National Institute of Mental Health (MH37860), the National Science Foundation (BNS-7926654), the National Institute on Aging (AG06866), and the Harcourt Brace Jovanovich Publishing Company.

Correspondence concerning this article should be addressed to D. T. Lykken, Psychology Department, Elliott Hall, University of Minnesota, Minneapolis, MN 55455.

that meeting, they exchanged birthday presents that crossed in the mail and proved to be identical choices, made independently in separate cities.

There were two "dog people" among the MZA individuals; one showed her dogs, and the other taught obedience classes—they were an MZA pair. Only two of the more than 200 individual twins reared apart were afraid to enter the acoustically shielded chamber used in our psychophysiology laboratory, but both separately agreed to continue if the door was wired open—they were a pair of MZA twins. When at the beach, both women had always insisted on entering the water backwards and then only up to their knees; they were thus concordant, not only in their phobic tendencies but also in the specific manifestations of that timidity. There were two gunsmith hobbyists among the group of twins; two women who habitually wore seven rings; two men who offered a (correct) diagnosis of a faulty wheel bearing on Bouchard's car; two who obsessively counted things; two who had been married five times; two captains of volunteer fire departments; two fashion designers; two who left little love notes around the house for their wives. . . . in each case, an MZA pair.

Some of these similarities were surely coincidence; for example, one pair of twins had both divorced women named Linda and then married women named Betty. When any two biographies are avidly compared, at least some overlap is likely to be found. These same men discovered that, for several years before they met one another, they had both vacationed in Florida on the same stretch of beach, driving down there in the same model Chevrolet. They both had named their sons "James Alan" (one "Allan") and both chain-smoked Salems with nail-bitten fingers while at work in their basement woodshops. The dizygotic separated in infancy and reared apart (DZA) twins whom we have studied, in contrast, seldom produced similar "coincidences"; the one striking exception was a pair of DZA men who both had prison records and histories of drug abuse and who both were decorated with numerous tattoos.

These anecdotal observations are suggestive in the "context of discovery," and what they suggest is the existence of genetic traits that do not run in families. That is, if these idiosyncratic similarities of MZA twins are not all mere coincidence, then it is likely that they are related to the genome common to both twins (i.e., that these similarities are of genetic origin). Because they are seldom seen in DZA twins, it is doubtful that these similarities would be often seen in other pairs of first-degree relatives (i.e., it is unlikely that they are familial). The standard models of behavior genetics require that genetic traits must also be familial. As we review below, however, there is other evidence of qualitative genetic traits that do not run in families. The standard polygenic-additive model for continuous or metrical traits predicts that pairs of relatives will be correlated in proportion to their genetic correlation. Yet, as we show, there is also evidence of metrical traits for which the MZ correlation is high, indicating a genetic basis, whereas the DZ correlation is insignificant, indicating that the usual family or adoption studies would be unlikely to reveal the genetic understructure.

The existence of genetic traits that are not (or are only weakly) shared by first-degree relatives would be evidence for a neglected mechanism of non-additive or configural genetic determination (Eaves, 1987; Grayson, 1989; Heath, Martin, Eaves, & Loesch, 1984; Li, 1987; Lykken, 1982; Lykken, Tellegen, & Iacono, 1982). Before developing this argument, however, we will review the standard model.

Genetic Variation: The Standard Doctrine

The genome, the entire collection of genes arranged on their 46 chromosomes, can be thought of as a blueprint or, better, a very large book of instructions, each of the approximately 100,000 pages representing a different gene. Nearly three fourths of these pages are identical for all normal individuals (Lewontin, 1967); because they do not vary within species, we can all these *monomorphic* genes. Some of them we share with other mammals, and most of them we share with the higher apes. Only a relative handful of our full set of monomorphic genes cause us to develop into the primate called *Homo sapiens* rather than the ones called *Pan troglodytes* or *Gorilla gorilla.* The remaining pages of our instruction book represent *polymorphic* genes. As we look across the population, we find from 2 to as many as 20 or more variations of each page—different forms or *alleles* of each polymorphic gene. It is the polymorphic genes that are responsible for individual (genetic) differences within a species.

Mendelian traits, such as the red blood cell antigens or blood types, are determined by which of the possible alleles are present in one particular gene locus on a pair of homologous chromosomes. Scores on metrical traits, traits like stature or IQ in humans or milk production in cows, are thought to be determined—to the extent that they are *genetically* determined—by the combined action of many genes. Such traits are expected to fit a *polygenic-additive* model. This model assumes that each participating polygene contributes its fungible bit to the total result. These genes are on different chromosomes, or far apart on the same chromosome, so that they segregate independently when the parental genome divides into two approximately random halves to form the nucleus of an egg or sperm.

Thus, the father passes on to each offspring a random half of all his genes and maybe less, maybe more, than half of all his "tall" genes. This paternal contribution combines with whatever fraction of the mother's tall genes happens to be included in the ovum, and the sum of these components determines genetic stature. MZ twins have identical *genotypic* stature. (As a result of environmental differences such as marked differences in placental nutrition, some MZ twins differ by several inches in *phenotypic* height; nonetheless, MZ twins correlate approximately .94 in stature even after correction for age and sex.) DZ co-twins (and other sib pairs), who represent two different random samples from the same parental gene pool, share by common descent approximately 50 percent of their polymorphic genes (as distinguished from the monomorphic genes shared by all normal members of the species). The fraction of the parental tall genes apportioned to each DZ twin—his or her genetic height—will be about half as similar within pairs as for MZ twins (a little more than half, actually, because of assortative mating for stature). Indeed, same-sex DZ twins correlate about .50 in height (e.g., Lykken, 1982, p. 365).

This rule, that pairs of relatives correlate in proportion to their genetic correlation, applies generally to polygenic-additive traits. A polygenic-additive model explains why these familiar genetic traits tend to run in families. And that is why polygenic-additive traits are easily recognized as features of interest to geneticists: They run in families. But this is not the *only* way in which genes contribute to the quantitative variation within a species, to individual differences. Indeed, the polygenic-additive model seems a very curious way of describing the way in which genes actually work (see Murphy, 1979).

The mammalian eye and the hominid hand with its opposable thumb are multigenic, but they are not constructed additively. If, at conception, one is short-changed on eye genes, one does not develop a smaller but otherwise normal eye. Like all the organs specified in the species plan, eyes and hands are fabricated in a complex, sequential process, an assembly line in which each stage depends on the one preceding and in which every worker—every gene—plays a pivotal role. This process is not additive but, rather, *configural:* all of the components are essential, and the absence of, or a change in, any one (i.e., in any gene) can produce a qualitative or a large quantitative change in the result. The familiar Mendelian genetic abnormalities can be attributed to single genes not because one gene orchestrates the entire syndrome but because, in the polygenic configuration that manufactures the normal system, a one-gene change makes a qualitative difference in the product. Dawkins (1982b, pp. 22–26) made the same point.

These organs and attributes are emergent properties of configurations of monomorphic genes, configurations that we all share as part of being human. Polymorphic genes, the ones responsible for individual differences, can also behave configurally. Human lymphocyte antigens (HLA) are a nice example. Most body cells are marked by a group of special proteins, antigens, that function as a kind of brand or code, identifying your cells as yours and someone else's tissue as foreign. Each HLA antigen is coded for by a gene that is highly polymorphic—has many allelic forms—so the chances that two friends have any particular antigen may be only 1 in 10 or 20. The probability that they match on the whole set of HLA antigens is vanishingly small because there are hundreds of millions of different combinations. This *histocompatibility* code is configural in the same sense as a telephone number: Change even one digit in a phone number and you get the wrong party; change just one antigen in the histocompatibility code and the transplanted kidney may be rejected.

It happens that the antigens most important in tissue rejection are coded for by genes close together on the same chromosome so that they do not segregate independently but are usually passed from parent to offspring as a package. For this reason, one has a reasonable chance of finding a close relative whose tissues match well enough to risk a transplant. Traits that depend on configurations of polymorphic genes that *do* segregate independently will be shared by MZ twins, who share all their genes and hence all gene configurations, but are much less likely to be shared by DZ twins, siblings, or parents and offspring. Such traits, although genetic, would not tend to run in families.

Genetic Traits That Do Not Run in Families

Frequency of the Alpha Rhythm

The spectrum of the resting electroencephalogram (EEG; i.e., the graph of the relative amount of brain wave activity at each frequency from, say, 0.1 hz to 20.0 hz) is rather like a fingerprint in that its shape varies from person to person but is quite constant for the same person over time. In two experiments (Lykken, Tellegen, & Thorkelson, 1974; Lykken et al., 1982), we obtained EEG spectra from a total of 147 pairs of adult MZ twins and 53 pairs of DZs. We analyzed each spectrum into its five main components: the amount of EEG activity in the four classical EEG frequency bands, called delta, theta, alpha, and beta; and the midfrequency of the alpha component, a parameter that we called phi. Then we computed the within-pair correlations for each of these parameters. The MZ twins correlated about .80 for all five, and the DZ correlations averaged .40 for the first four parameters, as would be expected with polygenic-additive variables. But the DZ correlation for phi was .13, only about one sixth rather than half of the MZ value. The midfrequency of the alpha rhythm, because it is so weakly correlated in DZ co-twins, is unlikely to be strongly correlated among first-degree relatives generally. Yet, because the MZ correlation is very high even among MZA twins (see Table 1), phi must

TABLE 1
Examples From the Minnesota Twin Studies of Metrical Traits for Which the MZ Correlations are Substantial and the DZ Correlations Weak, Suggesting That the Traits are Emergenic*

Variable	MZT	MZR	MZA	DZT	DZR	DZA
EEG spectrum parameters						
No. of pairs	89		.38	.53		
Alpha midfrequency	.81		.80	.13		
Personality traits						
No. of pairs	553	131	52	459	74	33
MPQ Well-being	.44	.68	.53	.11	.12	−.04
Electrodermal habituation						
No. of pairs	36		43	42		
Rate of habituation	.72		.54	.05		
Interests and talents						
No. of pairs	503	102		390	96	
Arts and crafts	.51	.63		.14	.07	
Self-ratings						
No. of pairs	503	102		390	96	
Well-adjusted	.44	.53		.10	.02	

Note. MZ = monozygotic; MZT = Adult MZ twins reared together; MZR = MZT twins retested after 2–10 years, mean scores correlated; MZA = MZ twins reared apart; DZ = dizygotic; DZT = DZ twins reared together; DZR = DZT twins retested after 2–10 years; DZA = DZ twins reared apart; EEG = electroencephalagraph; MPQ = Multidimensional Personality Questionnaire. Data updated from Lykken, 1982; Lykken, Iacono, Haroian, McGue, & Bouchard, 1988; Lykken, Bouchard, McGue, & Tellegen, 1990; Tellegen, et al., 1988; Waller, Lykken, & Tellegen, in press.

be strongly genetic, even though it does not tend to run in families.[1]

This is interesting because, although no one knows exactly how the alpha frequency is determined biologically, it probably involves some sort of resonance phenomenon (e.g., Fedotchev, Bonda, & Konovalov, 1990). Resonance is a classic example of a non-additive configural phenomenon. In electronics, for example, the resonant frequency of a circuit is a function of the *product* of inductance and capacitance. The pitch and timbre of the human voice is determined by the resonant characteristics of the vocal apparatus, the shape and musculature of the vocal chords, the glottis, the hard palate, the nasopharynx, and so on. The properties of each of these components are genetically, and largely independently, determined. For this reason MZ twins, whether reared together or apart, have very similar voices and can easily substitute for one another on the telephone. In her review of the MZA literature, Farber (1981) said, "The pitch, tone, and overall characteristics of the twins' voices were so stunningly alike that almost all investigators made mention of the similarity" (p. 85). Ordinary siblings, however, seldom have really similar voices. A recent study by Stearns and VanderWoude (1991) found that students of voice, like music students generally, more often have musically talented parents than do arts college students not majoring in music. The proportion of parents who are gifted singers, however, was no greater for vocal students than for instrumentalists. Serious singers need to be musical, a trait that seems to run in families, but they also need a mellifluous voice, a trait that may be emergenic.

Beauty

Facial beauty (or handsomeness; there is no gender-neutral term in English) similarly is a function not of the sum but of the configuration of facial features. Admittedly from time to time one sees individual features that would spoil almost any face, but as a rule the attractiveness of a given nose or chin or pair of ears depends to an important extent

[1]Stassen, Lykken, Propping, & Bomben (1988) confirmed that the EEG spectra of MZA twins are about as similar within pairs as between retests of the same individuals. Propping (1977) also found that the correlation within 24 pairs of DZ twins for amount of alpha and beta activity was approximately half the MZ value. Propping's twins then consumed a standard dose of ethanol, and the EEG was repeated after two hours when the EEG effects of alcohol were at a peak. The MZ correlations for beta and alpha activity were still high (.74 and .80), whereas the DZ correlations had decrease to zero (−.09 and −.01). Thus it appears that the electrocortical response to alcohol challenge is an emergenic trait.

on the context of the other features. This is easily demonstrated by asking an artist to imagine a mating of two conventionally beautiful people; our artist used two television actors. When she had sketched these two faces, we asked her to construct the faces of possible male and female offspring of this mating by arbitrarily reassorting the features of the imagined parents. A reasonable conclusion, based on the results of this experiment is that comeliness is emergenic.

A Psychiatric Example

Abrams (1986), a psychoanalyst, described a pair of female twins who were separated in early infancy and separately placed in rather different but equally promising adoptive homes. After an unexceptional first year, problems began to develop in both children. By age 10, both children were said to have "serious disorders," albeit rather nonspecific ones. "The two are *equivalently* pathological: they share a limited development; they share a timetable of emergence, an excess of expression, and a channelization of symptoms; they share character disturbances; they share a quality of shallowness and a limited self-definition; they are poorly integrated; they share comparable cognitive deficiencies" (p. 43).

What is especially interesting about this report is the author's acknowledgement that, if the children had been studied as singletons, most clinicians would have found it easy to explain their problems in terms of their different family environments. Indeed,

> They might even have speculated along these lines: If Beth had only had the dominant features of Amy's family—the confrontative mother, the strong father, the successful brother, the value of academic achievement—or if Amy had only had the dominant features of Beth's family—the overly accepting mother, the evenly attentive father, the less successful brother, the lack of concern about education—how much better each would have fared! (Abrams, 1986, pp. 52–53)

Only the fact that these girls were MZA twins forced this research team to the realization that they were dealing with a syndrome that had genetic roots, a novel *configuration* of disabilities that manifested itself in both girls, not because of but in spite of the differences in their family environments, environmental features that these clinicians would otherwise have regarded as significant and even causal.

Emergenesis

It is useful to have a name for this odd type of trait, a trait that is an emergent property of a configuration of genes or perhaps a configuration of more basic traits that are themselves partly genetic in origin. Lykken (1982) proposed the term *emergenic* for this purpose.

> **emergenic** (*adj*) Arising as a novel or emergent property resulting from the interaction of more elementary and partly genetic properties. An emergenic trait might be determined by a configuration of independently segregating polygenes interacting in the sensè of epistasis, or, at a more molar level, an emergenic trait might be a property of a configuration of independent traits that are themselves in part genetically determined. In some instances (see *Impact Traits,* below) situational factors may figure as configural components. The distinctive feature of emergenesis is the notion of configurality, which implies that any change of any one component may result in a qualitative, or a large quantitative, change in the emergenic trait. Emergenic traits may—but are likely not to—run in families. On the other hand, marked MZ similarity combined with weak similarity of DZ twins is strongly suggestive of an emergenic trait.

What we suggest now is that perhaps many complex human psychological traits (e.g., many of the idiosyncrasies of personal style that we have observed in twins), as well as traits like extraversion; the ability to stop reacting to a meaningless repeating stimulus (*habituation*); more familiar traits like leadership, artistic ability, selling ability, teaching ability, creativity, parenting ability—and also many examples of human genius—are emergenic traits. Because these attributes do not tend to run in families, the possibility of their having a genetic basis has been overlooked. As we have seen, we will not discover the emergenic character of such traits unless we study twins. Until this idea is more broadly accepted, we will not *believe* what we discover unless we study twins reared apart.

Metrical Emergenic Traits

Extraversion

In the case of metrical traits, emergenesis is suggested when the intraclass correlation of MZ twins is substantially greater than twice the DZ correlation, as is true of the mid-frequency of the EEG alpha rhythm discussed above. This is also true for the trait Eysenck (1952) identified as extraversion. Cattell (1956) as exvia–invia, and Block (1965) as ego control. Extraversion is one of the small set of temperament traits or superfactors that are found in factor analyses of personality traits or first-order factors. Jinks and Fulker (1970) attempted to fit a polygenic-additive model to extraversion data and found that the too-weak DZ similarity caused their model to yield nonsensical results. To account for their findings, Jinks and Fulker proposed that, while growing up together, DZ twins tend to "react against each other in such a way as to develop opposite characteristics with respect to a trait" (p. 333). Eaves

(1976) proposed a competitive model with somewhat different properties. In their study of 850 sets of twins recruited from students who took the National Merit Scholarship test, Loehlin and Nichols (1976) subjected the contrast hypothesis to a number of empirical tests and found it wanting. In particular, of course, this hypothesis cannot explain why DZA twins would be much less than half as similar in extraversion as are MZA twins. Using a population-based sample of Swedish twins, including 315 pairs reared apart since age 10, Pederson, Plomin, McClearn, and Friberg (1988) administered a nine-item version of the Extraversion scale from the Eysenck Personality Inventory (EPI), obtaining MZA and MZT correlations of .30 ± .09 and .54 ± .06, respectively, compared with .04 ± .07 and .06 ± .07 for DZAs and DZTs. The Well-Being scale of the Multidimensional Personality Questionnaire (MPQ: Tellegen & Waller, in press) measures a facet of extraversion. Lykken et al. (1992b) reported correlations for Well-Being of .44 ± .03 in MZT twins (.53 ± .14 in 52 pairs of MZAs) but only .11 ± .04 in DZT twins (−.04 ± .18 in DZAs; see Table 1).

Electrodermal Response and Habituation

Lykken, Iacono, Haroian, McGue, and Bouchard (1988) subjected 121 pairs of adult twins, some reared together and others reared apart, to a series of 17 relatively unpredictable 105-db tones while measuring their electrodermal responses (EDRs) in a habituation paradigm. Both the MZT and the MZA twins were strongly correlated (.72 ± .17 and .54 ± .16, respectively) in the slope of the curves describing their habituation to these tones. The combined group of 42 pairs of DZT and DZA twins, however, was negligibly correlated (.05 ± .16) on these variables (see Table 1).

Interests and Talents

Inventories of occupational and recreational interests and of self-rated talents, a total of 291 Likert-type items, were administered to more than 4,000 middle-aged participants of the Minnesota Twin Registry; in some 900 pairs, both twins completed all the inventories (Lykken, Bouchard, McGue, & Tellegen, 1992a). Factor analyses of the 291 items for men and women separately yielded 39 factors congruent in both sexes. After three years, 198 twin pairs were retested, of which 53 pairs were female MZs, 52 were female DZs, 49 were male MZs, and 44 were male DZs. By testing twins twice over a lengthy time span, one can obtain improved estimates of within-pair similarity with respect to the *stable* component of their self-rated traits, partly disattentuated by both measurement error and also by the unsystematic variation about the stable setpoint that we believe to be characteristic of psychological traits. Some improvement is achieved by correlating the mean of the scores obtained at Time 1 and Time 2 as shown in Table 1.

These twins, who had been reared in the same families, had similar interest (or lack of interest) in hunting and fishing and in visiting casinos or race tracks, playing poker, and engaging in other forms of gambling. The DZ similarity was actually more than half the MZ value for both gambling and blood sports, suggesting that shared rearing environment influenced these interests. These middle-aged MZ twins were also very similar in the factor we called arts and crafts; the correlation for 503 pairs of MZ twins tested once was .51 (±.04), and for 102 pairs tested twice three years apart, the mean arts and crafts score correlated .63 (±.10). The DZ similarity, however, was much weaker for this factor (which combined interests and self-rated talents); .14 (±.05) for 390 DZ pairs and only .07 (±.10) for the mean of two testings of 96 pairs (see Table 1). Assuming other first-degree relatives are no more alike than DZ twins, we conclude that, among adults, interest in arts and crafts is only faintly familial at best. Noting that MZA twins are nearly as similar on these interest and talent traits as MZTs are (Lykken et al., 1992a), we can say that at least half the stable variance in arts and crafts was based on genetic factors. This interest/talent factor therefore, appears to qualify as an emergenic trait.

Among the most clearly emergenic of the self-rated traits in this study was what we called the well-adjusted factor. The MZ correlation was .44 (±.04) compared with the .10 (±.04) for DZ twins tested once and .53 (±.10) versus .02 (±.10) for the mean of two testings (see Table 1). The Likert-type items that make up the well-adjusted scale ask about optimistic outlook, contentment, sense of personal worth, emotional control, coolness under stress, affability, and capacity for happiness. This scale appears to be related to the ubiquitous extraversion superfactor, which as we have seen is itself emergenic.

Structure of Metrical Emergenic Traits

As we have defined *emergenesis* above, any nonlinear function of two or more partially genetic traits is emergenic (whether a given variable, thus defined, is a trait unity, a natural or useful parameter of the individual, is a separate question). But it is not the case that all nonlinear functions of several independent genetic traits yield variables that are not familial. Thus, for example, if we measure stature (S), fingerprint ridge count (R), and IQ (Q) on a large sample of twins, convert each variable to standard-score form, and take the product, then E = SRQ is emergenic. If, however, we let the variables take on only positive values, say, with a mean of 50 and a standard deviation of 10, then the MZ correlation for E will be substantial, and the DZ correlation will still be approximately half the MZ value. That is, the linear-additive model can often closely approximate the effects of an underlying structure that is nonlinear. As Anderson and Shanteau (1977) pointed out, merely showing that a linear regression equation can make accurate estimates cannot be taken as evidence that the predictor variables actually combine additively. Thus, the fact that E is emergenic (configural) would not be deduced even from twin data because E behaves like a familial trait.

We know from the examples cited earlier, however, that some emergenic traits do not run in families. One simple nonlinear function that may yield such a result is the squared difference (SQD) of two underlying traits. For instance, using data from some 1,200 pairs of adult twins from the Minnesota Registry, we converted both height (HT) and weight (WT) to age- and sex-corrected *T*-score units ($M = 50$, $SD = 10$) and then computed $SQD = (HT - WT)^2$ for each individual. SQD is low for people whose weight is proportionate to their height, high for those who are tall and thin or short and fat. The MZ correlation for SQD is $0.64 \pm .02$, and the DZ value is $0.15 \pm .04$. Therefore, we can reasonably conclude that SQD is an emergenic trait. Whether it has scientific interest, of course, remains to be seen. It is not unreasonable to suppose that psychologically interesting traits of this type do exist, traits that depend on the balance between two or more component traits.

Nonfamilial metrical traits can also result from an aggregate or sum of threshold traits. For example, if X_i is the *i*th component trait, and if W_i, the *i*th weight, equals 1.0 if $X_i >$ threshold and zero otherwise, then

$$Y = W_1X_1 + W_2X_2 + \cdot \cdot \cdot W_kX_k$$

will be a nonfamilial additive trait, provided that the X_is are heritable and $P(X_i > \text{threshold})$ is small. If W_i depends, say, on X_j rather than on X_i, then the aggregate will be configural—emergenic—as well as nonfamilial. To illustrate this idea, an American child's potential for becoming a football running back might be an aggregate of strength, running speed, balance, fearlessness, and resistance to injury, but with each variable contributing to the total only if the next-listed variable is above some relatively high threshold.

Child development seems to involve many threshold situations—fighting versus backing off, yielding to temptation versus not yielding, succeeding versus failing, daring versus not daring, and so on. The child whose aggressiveness, impulsiveness, talent, or fearlessness is just slightly above the threshold level may subsequently have qualitatively different experiences from—and become emergenically different from—his or her siblings. To the extent that the genome tends to determine the child's effective environment—the experiences, that is, that create these threshold situations (Lykken et al., 1992b)—to that extent will MZ twins, and even MZA twins, tend to develop the same emergenic traits.

Emergenesis Versus Epistasis

Geneticists would say that emergenic traits result from *epistasis,* defined as the nonreciprocal interaction of nonallelic genes. But it is customary to subsequently disregard this component in applications of the general model, either on the assumption that epistatic effects will be minimal (e.g., Jinks & Fulker, 1970) or in the frank recognition of the difficulties of testing for epistasis in human family data (Cavalli-Sforza & Bodmer, 1971). Murphy (1979) remarked that the inclusion, in the partitioning of the phenotypic variance, of a term identified as "epistasis, etc., the chief property of which is that it fills a hole in a balance sheet" (p. 132) provides the biometrical geneticist with an illusory sense of having covered all the bases. "What results is not science but devious accountancy" (p. 132). Heath et al. (1984) published what they believed to be "the strongest evidence so far for polygenic epistasis in man" (p. 719). This evidence, involving counts of the number of fingerprint tri-radii, consists of high (.90) correlations in 110 pairs of MZ twins combined with lower (from .24 to .41) correlations in 111 pairs of DZ twins and in hundreds of sibling and parent–child pairs. Heath et al. pointed out that the effects of dominance and Additive × Additive Epistasis can be resolved with the addition of parent–child data to the data for twins. The examples of non-additivity in psychophysiological, interest, and personality variables that we have reported have all involved similar or larger ratios of MZ to DZ correlations, although still larger samples and the addition of twin family data will be needed to confirm these findings.

However, the idea of a configural relationship conveys more than interaction, and some of the emergenic traits discussed herein are more naturally described at the molar level, as configurations of partly genetic traits, than at the level of interacting polygenes (although see Li, 1987). Most phenotypic traits, and certainly most psychological traits, are many steps removed from genetic activity, so far removed that attempts to understand any surface (metrical) trait in terms of specific gene action seem premature if not presumptuous. It is more plausible to suppose that the behavior genetics of the future will assume a hierarchical structure in which surface traits are seen to be functions of source traits that are, in turn, determined by dispositions at a lower level, and so on. If one is interested in the trait of leadership, for example, it seems sensible to analyze it in terms of other more basic psychological variables rather than to start searching for enzymatic correlates.

Impact Traits

Charismatic leadership, selling ability, parenting success, interpersonal attractiveness, entrepreneurial ability, and many other important dimensions of individual difference are difficult, perhaps impossible, to define solely in terms of characteristics of the actor without reference to the impact of his or her actions on the (primarily social) environment (Lykken, 1991, p. 18). Measures of such traits must often be configural, rather than additive, functions of the relevant intrapsychic and environmental components. Suppose, for example, two great leaders like Gandhi and Churchill could by some magic have undergone a random interchange of certain salient traits; surely both would then have been diminished in their leadership ability, just as two prize-winning cakes might be ruined by a random exchange of certain ingredients (e.g., one egg vs. six). The recipes for leadership, like the recipes for cakes, seem likely to be configural rather than additive. Even a total exchange of psychological characteristics might have been disastrous; Gandhi's simplicity and saintliness might not have dealt effectively with Hitler's war machine, and Churchill's bombast and epicurean self-indulgence would not have endeared him to the Indian masses.

Because it encompasses configurations, not just of polygenes but of partly genetic component traits and even of situational factors in the case of impact traits, *emergenesis* seems to have a broader and psychologically more useful scope than *epistatic.*

Qualitative Emergenic Traits

Secretariat

Old-fashioned hereditarians used to make much of the notion of breeding, a concept that has been pushed to the extreme by exponents of the sport of horse racing. Through careful breeding in the early part of the last century, the thoroughbred race horse became steadily stronger and faster, and the record times recorded at old English race courses steadily fell. Along about the turn of this century, however, this curve leveled off as the initial additive variance was bred out of the line (e.g., Cunningham, 1991). The modest improvements in performance over the next 70 years or so are largely attributed to better training, nutrition, and veterinary techniques.

And then along came Secretariat, a great red stallion who lay down and took a nap on the day of his Kentucky Derby and then got up and broke the course record, not by just a whisker but by seconds. He did the same thing at Pimlico and then won the Belmont—and the Triple Crown—by more than 30 lengths. Put out at once to stud, where only the most promising mares could afford his fees, Secretariat sired more than 400 foals—most of them disappointments, none of them remotely in their sire's class. Secretariat had a distinguished lineage, of course, although none of his forebears could have run with him, but whatever he received at the great lottery of his conception could not be easily passed on in random halves. It seems a reasonable conjecture that Secretariat's qualities were configural, emergenic.

At last, in 1988, one of Secretariat's sons, Risen Star, finished third in the Kentucky Derby, won the Preakness, and then won the Belmont by some 14 lengths, albeit a full two seconds behind his sire's record pace. After more than 400 attempts, Secretariat managed to produce a winner; although emergenic traits do not run in families, they are more likely to reappear in a carrier family than in a random lineage. No doubt Risen Star's dam contributed key elements of the emergenic configuration.

It may be in this chancy way that evolution sometimes makes its qualitative steps onward after periods of stasis; it may be that Secretariat was one of Goldschmidt's (1940) "hopeful monsters" awaiting a similarly configured mate with whom he might breed true. For such an emergenic trait to play a role in equine evolution requires the occurrence of a critical mass of traited individuals in the same time and place, at least one stallion and two or several mares who, by interbreeding, might have the chance to found a race of superior horses. If the S (Secretariat) trait were based on a five-locus, homozygous-recessive configuration (as in Li's example, discussed below), then such a stallion would occur only once in 20 million random matings. But, if a million ancestral horses roamed the steppes of Central Asia during the early Pleistocene, producing 2×10^5 foals each year, the odds would favor the appearance of a traited stallion approximately every 70 years. Ancestral horses probably traveled like wild horses do today, either in bands of bachelor males or in harems of mares headed by a single stallion (Anthony, Telegin, & Brown, 1991). We shall assume that S-traited horses would be substantially stronger and faster and thus able to compete successfully and that patriarchs of harems were able to sire, say, 200 foals over the course of their reigns.

A traited stallion would be likely to become a harem patriarch. The offspring of an affected sire would carry at least one of the required recessive genes at each of the five loci. Each 120 matings between such half-sibs would be likely to produce the emergenic trait. Moreover, at least one in 11 patriarchs would (with $p > .5$) produce a traited foal in the first filial generation. A traited filly produced in this way, if she remained in the paternal harem, would produce only traited foals. If a traited foal of the patriarch (or of his daughter) was a colt, he would be destined to become a patriarch himself and, at minimum, to start the lottery again without another 70-year wait. He might also produce carrier offspring contiguous in time and place to the harem of their affected grandsire. Any aged traited patriarch might in time be replaced as harem leader by one of his untraited sons who, interbreeding with his paternal half-sisters, would be likely to produce several traited offspring during his regnancy.

Not every contiguous appearance of traited mating partners will suffice to found a dynasty, of course, but each appearance of a traited stallion would generate a reasonable chance of such an outcome, through breeding with or among his offspring, and this chance would recur at least every 100 years or so. This dependence on inbreeding, with its perils of deleterious recessive traits, might reduce the competitive advantage of some traited offspring, although the mating of half-sibs carries only the slight genetic risk of cousin matings.

Note that the qualitative evolutionary step we are describing requires merely a novel recombination of existing alleles rather than an unlikely macromutation (see Dawkins, 1982a). Like the accepted mechanism of accumulating micromutations (which it would supplement and not replace), emergenic evolution also requires long spans of evolutionary time. Yet it may be that important saltations, like the appearance of the hominid opposable thumb, occurred in just such a way.

Although running speed is, of course, a metrical variable, Secretariat so far exceeded the limits of the normal distribution as to suggest a qualitative difference, a new natural class or taxon (see Meehl, 1992). The arena of human achievement appears to offer many similar examples, individuals whose accomplishments so far exceed the norm that we classify them separately from the common herd. An important example of such a class includes those people we call *geniuses.*

Genius

How did it come about that a man born poor, losing his mother at birth and soon deserted by his father, afflicted with a painful and humiliating disease, left to wander for twelve years among alien cities and conflicting faiths. . . . suspected of crime and insanity, and seeing, in his last months, the apotheosis of his greatest enemy—how did it come about that this man, after his death, triumphed over Voltaire, revived religion, transformed education, elevated the morals of France, inspired the Romantic movement and the French Revolution, influenced the philosophy of Kant and Schopenhauer, the plays of Schiller, the novels of Goethe, the poems of Wordsworth, Byron, and Shelly, the socialism of Marx, the ethics of Tolstoy, and, altogether, had more effect upon posterity than any other writer or thinker of that eighteenth century in which writers were more influential than they had ever been before? Here, if anywhere, the problem faces us: What is the role of genius in history? (Durant & Durant, 1967, p. 1)

In these celebrated first sentences of their *Rousseau and Revolution,* Will and Ariel Durant posed as well the psychological problem of genius itself, its mysterious irrepressibility, and its ability to arise from the most unpromising of lineages and to flourish even in the meanest of circumstances.

Human genius has always been a problem for both environmentalists and hereditarians to understand (Galton, 1869; Kroeber, 1944; Simonton, 1988.) There have been families of genius, of course—the Bernoullis and the Bachs, the Darwins and the Huxleys, the musical Marsalis family—but it is the solitary genius, rising like a great oak in a forest of scrub and bramble, who challenges our understanding. Carl Friedrich Gauss, ranked with Archimedes and Newton as one of the "princes of mathematics," had uneducated parents. His mother was illiterate, yet the boy had taught himself to read and to do simple arithmetic by the time he was 3 years old (Buhler, 1981). When Gauss was 10, the village schoolmaster thought to keep his large class occupied by writing down the integers from one to 100 and then finding their sum. Moments later he was startled to see little Carl at his desk with just a single number on his slate. "There 'tis," said the boy and then sat with his hands folded while the rest of the class toiled on. In the end, only Carl had the correct answer (Dunnington, 1955). The boy had at once perceived that the problem reduced to $(1 + 100) + (2 + 99) + \cdots + (50 + 51) = 50(101) = 5{,}050$. To believe that some extraordinary accident of experience created this prince out of ordinary clay is to believe in magic.

The great Hindu mathematician, Srinivasa Ramanujan, whom Mark Kac called a magical genius (Kolata, 1987), was reared in a one-room adobe hut in southern India, and his mathematical education consisted primarily of two books, both in a foreign language (Borwein & Borwein, 1988). In 1913, with the help of a better educated friend, Ramanujan wrote from Madras to the great G. H. Hardy at Cambridge, asking his opinion of some 120 theorems that were enclosed. Hardy reported that some of these were classical although obscure; others were in Hardy's own area, and he managed to prove them himself,

> though with a good deal more trouble than I had expected. . . . The formulae 110–113 are on a different level and obviously both difficult and deep. . . . I had never seen anything the least like them before. A single look at them is enough to show that they could only be written down by a mathematician of the highest class. They must be true because, if they were not true, no one would have had the imagination to invent them. (Hardy, cited in J. R. Newman, 1956)

Suppose that Gauss or Ramanujan had been born with a healthy MZ twin who was spirited away to be reared by some country parson in Oxfordshire. Barring cholera or other accident, is it not likely that the parson's surname too would now be immortal? Ramanujan died young without offspring; his parents and one brother apparently were unexceptional. Although Gauss provided rich stimulation and opportunity for his six offspring (by two different and highly cultivated wives), none of them distinguished themselves.[2] But if the genius of these men was prefigured in their genes, why was it never manifested elsewhere in their

[2]Gauss's second son, Eugene, emigrated to the United States in 1830, enlisted in the army, and later went into business in Missouri. Eugene is said to have had some of his father's gift for languages and the ability to perform prodigious arithmetic calculations, which he did for recreation after his sight had failed him in old age.

lineage? The answer is, we think, that genius consists of unique configurations of attributes that cannot be transmitted in half helpings.

Michael Faraday, the premier experimental scientist of his generation, was the self-taught son of a humble blacksmith (Thomas, 1991). Knight (1985) referred to Faraday's "curious mixture, or perhaps we should say compound, of humility and pride" (p. 35); biographers of people of genius often allude in this way to interactions or configurations of their subjects' attributes. We know that Shakespeare, too, came from undistinguished stock, that this foremost wordsmith in our history had numerous siblings and several children, none of whom left any trace—or any word—behind them (Parrott, 1938). An American genius, Benjamin Franklin, was one of a large family and sired two children of his own, all of them members of the common generality of humankind (Garfield, 1982). The configurality of genius is dramatically illustrated in the life's work of another extraordinary American, Gutzon Borglum, the sculptor, engineer, inventor, and entrepreneur who carved Mount Rushmore (Shaff, 1985). However one evaluates the aesthetic or ecological impact of transforming a mountain into a frieze of presidential heads, this prodigious monument will survive the millennia because of the configuration of prodigious talents, each of them essential to the project, that were combined in this singular individual. One of the luminaries of twentieth-century science, John von Neumann, was capable of such extraordinary intellectual feats that some of his colleagues were led to suggest that von Neumann's brain "might be an emergent organ, of a different order of complexity than those of ordinary mortals" (Campbell, 1988, p. 103.) Genius of this caliber seems to be not just an abundance of one or several components such as IQ but rather a harmony of attributes, a compound rather than merely a mixture.

Some More Mundane Examples

Electrodermal nonresponding. Some psychiatric patients, during remission of their symptoms when they are relatively normal, are EDR nonresponders in the habituation situation referred to above; they do not react electrodermally even to the first loud tones (Bernstein et al., 1988). About 15% of the individuals in our sample of normal twins (Lykken et al., 1988) also were EDR nonresponders. None of them had psychiatric histories, but we think it possible that these people might have had the genetic "talent" for one of the major psychiatric disorders (Iacono, 1982, 1985; Iacono et al., 1983). At least one member of 16 of the 79 MZ pairs was a nonresponder, and 12 of their 16 co-twins (75%) were nonresponders also. Eight of the smaller group of 42 DZ pairs contained a nonresponder, but only one pair (13%) was concordant (Lykken et al., 1988).

Striped flight and blotched belligerence. It is well known that morphological and behavioral traits are often correlated across related species. For example, in snakes, species whose coats are longitudinally striped "tend to be more active, wide-foraging, and flee when threatened, whereas species with broken color patterns (blotches or crossbands) are more secretive and rely on crypsis or aggression as their primary defense" (Brodie, 1989, p. 542). This same heterogeneity in color pattern and behavior has also been observed within a single species, the Northwest garter snake, and Brodie has shown that vulnerability to predation is a configural function of color pattern together with the tendency to freeze or flee. "It is more difficult for the vertebrate eye to detect motion or judge the speed of a moving stripe than a moving heterogeneous pattern, so that flight may be a more effective antipredator behavior for striped snakes than for blotched ones" (Brodie, p. 544). Among most snake species, configurations of coat markings and behavior tendencies that yield higher vulnerability to predators have disappeared through natural selection; in the garter snake, two different configurations, two mutually exclusive emergenic traits—what Tooby and Cosmides (1990) call "heritable alternative strategies"—have proved adaptive and have survived. Note that such heritable alternative configurations, although emergenic, may tend to run in families.

The Structure of Qualitative Emergenic Traits

Li (1987) has examined in detail a *multiple homozygosis* model for qualitative emergenic traits. Li assumes as an example a trait that is produced by a configuration of two recessive alleles in each of $k = 5$ independently segregating loci, each allele having a moderate gene frequency of 0.20. The frequency in the population of such a trait would be approximately 10^{-7}, so this is a truly rare anomaly, talent, or idiosyncrasy. A mating with one affected parent has only about 3 chances in 10,000 of producing an affected child, whereas the probability of concordance in a pair of DZ twins with one affected proband is less than 1%. As Li points out, any of the $3^5 = 243$ different genotypic configurations possible with five loci might be the one that effects the trait in question and moreover, it is biologically plausible that other closely related genotypes (e.g., aaBbccddee as well as aabbccddee) might effect an approximation of the emergenic trait. "This situation is analogous to that of man-made growth hormones or insulin molecules, which, though not perfect, may still have some biological activities" (Li, 1987, p. 523).

A relatively simple example of multiple homozygosis is dactylaplasia, the absence of phalangial bones in the middle digits of each foot, which is due (at least in mice) to a mutant autosomal dominant gene, M, that is epistatically inhibited by a dominant gene, X, at another locus (Chai,

1981). Although all MZ twins will be concordant for this trait, concordance among sib pairs will be only 12.5%, if the frequency of the X gene, *P*(X), equals 0.5, and only 0.5% if *P*(X) = 0.9. Because it is configural, dactylaplasia is an emergenic trait; because it is strongly genetic but only weakly familial, it is a trait that might not be seen to be genetic had one not observed it in MZ twins or inbred strains.

Threshold Traits

A threshold trait can be defined as a qualitative phenotype that is observed when the individual's susceptibility or risk exceeds some threshold value. The threshold is normally considered to be determined by the environment (or even by convention, as in psychiatric diagnosis), whereas the metrical risk is at least partly heritable. Fitting threshold models to concordance data for various kinship pairings has been popular since Falconer (1960). A number of qualitative psychopathological traits that are definitely familial, traits like schizophrenia and antisocial personality, do not seem to fit any simple Mendelian model. For example, bipolar affective disorder is approximately 70% concordant in MZ twins but less than 15% in DZs and other sib pairs (Novitski, 1982, p. 377). When such a phenotype can be fitted to the Falconer model, it is commonly assumed that the underlying genetic mechanism is polygenic-additive.

Chai (1981) pointed out, however, that threshold models can be (and commonly are) fitted to the statistics of such congenital malformations as dactylaplasia, where the model is now known to be wrong. He argued that the threshold model "is not a useful concept since it cannot be experimentally disproved . . . [and it] has practically frozen research in congenital malformations ever since the concept was adopted" (p. 237). (Because Chai himself experimentally disproved the threshold model in the case of dactylaplasia, we interpret his criticism to be that the threshold model too easily appears to fit cases where it in fact is false.) The dactylaplasia example illustrates the possibility that other qualitative traits for which the MZ concordance is much higher than the DZ value, including dysfunctional traits like schizophrenia and antisocial personality, may in fact be emergenic.

Schizophrenia

Manfred Bleuler's view was that "hereditary dispositions to schizophrenia consist in *disharmonic* tendencies for personality development" (quoted in Rosenthal & Kety, 1968, p. 12, italics added). *Harmony* is a configural concept; in suggesting that the schizophrenic diathesis involves a dysfunctional or disrupted configuration, Bleuler seems to be implying an emergenic model. The fact that the concordance for schizophrenia (as for bipolar affective psychosis) is much higher in MZ twins (44%–58%) than in DZ twins or siblings (8%–14%; Gottesman & Shields, 1982; Rosenthal, 1970) tends to encourage this view. But schizophrenia *is* familial. The incidence even in second-degree relatives is clearly higher than in the general population. Therefore, if this trait is configural, the number of independent loci involved must be no greater than two or three (configurations of four or more loci yield nonfamilial traits unless the gene frequencies are very high). We have made a preliminary study of two-locus models but have not found adequate fits to the available data on the morbid risk among relatives of probands. A dominant–recessive model, however, with the right choice of gene frequencies, penetrance, and fertility assumptions, comes close enough so that we feel confident that a similar three-locus model, with its still greater degrees of freedom, could produce an excellent fit. The protean character of such models, of course, detracts from their value; Chai did not merely show that a two-locus model *could* fit dactylaplasia but rather that a particular two-locus model was correct. Because one cannot do back-cross experiments with human subjects, showing that a three-locus emergenic model is "correct" for schizophrenia, if possibly it is, will be difficult; but, like the polygenic threshold model and the idea that "schizophrenia" conflates several etiologically distinct disorders, the emergenic model remains a possibility.

The Game of Life

The educational pastime known as poker provides a useful analogy that may help clarify the idea of emergenesis. At conception, each of us received a very large number of "cards" containing a very large number of potential "hands," probably more than one could hope to play out in the course of the typical life. In one form of poker, each player is dealt seven cards and then must select three to be passed to his or her neighbor on the right. This game is interesting for configural reasons; the cards you receive from the person on your left were of little value in the context of his or her other cards, but they just might be exactly what you need to create a winning hand.

At conception, each of us received an approximately random half of the cards dealt out originally to each of our parents. Your tall mother held four queens, and she passed three of them along to you. Combining them (additively) with a queen from the paternal line, you can stand as tall as Mom. Your handsome father held a royal flush in hearts. Your half of his cards included the king, queen, and jack of hearts, but your mirror tells you that a three-card approximation of a royal flush looks merely "interesting," not handsome. The exciting thing about emergenesis is that you *might* receive the 10 and king of spades from Dad, and the jack, queen, and ace of spades from Mom, cards that had never counted for much in either family tree but whose combination in you might produce a Ramanujan, a new Olympic record—or a True Crime miniseries for television.

Summary and Conclusion

Species-specific traits are assuredly produced by configurations of monomorphic polygenes, interacting with each other and with the environment in roughly the same sense that specialized construction workers interact with the supply stocks and with the elaborating structure. It is plausible to assume that some polymorphic traits of psychological interest, similarly, are produced by configurations of polymorphic genes, similarly interacting with the environment both embryologically and during subsequent development. Such configural polymorphisms can be labeled *emergenic* traits. This configural emergenic model provides a possible explanation of those metrical traits for which MZ twins are substantially more than twice as similar as DZ twins and other first-degree relatives. Examples of putatively emergenic metrical traits include extraversion, EEG alpha frequency, electrodermal habituation, certain recreational and occupational interests, and facial and vocal beauty. Other interesting possibilities, for which no relevant data exist to our knowledge, include complex competencies such as leadership, selling ability, being an effective teacher or parent, and so on.

Taxonic or qualitative traits that show high concordance in MZ twins may also be emergenic. These may include developmental anomalies, idiosyncrasies of taste and style, various psychopathological syndromes, and some examples of human genius. One frequent (but not inevitable) feature of an emergenic trait is that it may tend not to run in families. This is because traits resulting from rare configurations of polygenes, or from unusual configurations of component traits, are unlikely to be passed on intact from parent to offspring. Genetic traits that do not run in families are unlikely to be seen to be genetic (i.e., to have an important part of their variance associated with genetic variance) unless one is studying monozygotic twins.

We conjecture that the most interesting emergenic psychological traits will turn out to be taxonic or qualitative. There is a strong tradition in psychology to eschew categorical in favor of dimensional thinking, a tradition in psychometrics that runs unbroken from Spearman to Eysenck (1986). But taxonomy, the classification of types of entities, is an integral part of all of the natural sciences from biology to astronomy. Meehl (1992) made a strong case for the existence of taxa not only in psychopathology but also in relation to those individual differences that we regard as normal. To the extent that some of these taxa (for the discovery of which Meehl provided powerful statistical tools) will turn out to be genetically influenced, we would expect them to be also emergenic.

The suggestion that genius may be emergenic should be understood to include what is called evil genius. Even those who tend to reject the Great Man theory of history find it hard to defend the proposition that the history of Europe in this century would not have been vastly different if Adolf Hitler had been killed by an English bullet in 1918. If Hitler had been one of 10 brothers, 9 of whom survived the First World War, it is unlikely that any one of the brothers would have become chancellor of the Third Reich. But if Hitler had left behind an MZ twin, who then would be prepared to deny the possibility that events might have developed much as, in fact, they did?

It is worth considering whether the competencies listed above as metrical traits might not be more accurately classified as qualitative traits. We obviously can rank salespeople, teachers, scientists, psychotherapists, or leaders on continua of competence, but they are already self-selected members of what may be taxonic groupings. If 1,000 people at random are put to work selling used cars or commanding military units, psychoanalyzing or behavior modifying, doing research or teaching sixth-grade civics, we would find a J-curve and, quite possibly, a bimodal distribution of competence: just a few good salespeople (some better than others), just a few charismatic leaders, a few born teachers, and a handful of truly effective therapists. Even compared with other scientists, some 5% publish 50% of the papers (Price, 1962). Suppose we could truly assess parenting, not merely measuring effort or dedication but *effectiveness*—given the raw material with which a parent had to work, how good was his or her product (measured by some reasonable standard of parental success) in comparison with an average parent working with the same raw material (e.g., the MZA co-twin)? Might not our evaluations of parenting ability also be bimodal, with just a few gifted parents and the majority merely providers, relatively ineffectual in actually shaping in some intended way?

It seems hardly speculative to contend that great competence in any area, competence for good or for ill, is likely to involve a *configuration* rather than a mere aggregation of component traits. In their discussion of exceptional performance, Walberg, Strykowski, Rouai, and Hung (1984) concluded that the J-curve of performance output or impact results from many factors interacting in a multiplicative, rather than an additive, manner. Because there is much evidence that a substantial portion of the variance in nearly all human psychological traits is genetic variance (in the broad sense of nature *via* nurture), then it seems likely that great competence is also emergenic.

The rare occurance of extraordinarily adaptive configurations (e.g., Secretariats or other hopeful monsters) among other species will have lasting consequences only when chance conspires to produce a critical mass of traited individuals able to found a new subspecies. For our humankind, however, culture provides a mechanism through which individuals of extraordinary competence, although unable to pass on their configurated talents to succeeding generations, can nonetheless leave behind works of art or invention or political upheaval that do have lasting consequences.

Finally, the concept of emergenesis has obvious, albeit speculative, evolutionary implications. Goldschmidt's (1940) hopeful monster proposal could be interpreted as a conjecture that saltation or even speciation is sometimes a consequence of a new genetic configuration with emergent properties. Although the evidence is somewhat indirect, it is now widely believed that the human monomorphic genome differs from that of some of the great apes to the extent of only a few percent of its constituent genes. If the book of instructions that produces a human being shares nearly all of its pages with the book that yields a chimpanzee, then is it not likely that the books must differ in some other way, perhaps in the sequence (i.e., configuration) in which many of the pages are arranged? We propose that emergenic differences exist within all species of living things, including *Homo sapiens,* and that such configural diversity has contributed to the evolution of diversity both within and among species.

REFERENCES

Abrams, S. (1986). Disposition and environment. *The Psychoanalytic Study of the Child, 41,* 41–60.

Anderson, N. H. & Shanteau, J. (1977). Weak inference with linear models. *Psychological Bulletin, 64,* 115–117.

Anthony, D., Telegin, D. V., & Brown, D. (1991). The origins of horseback riding. *Scientific American, 265,* 94–100.

Bernstein, A. S., Riedel, J., Graae, F., Seidmen, D., Steele, H., Connolly, J., & Lubowsky, J. (1988). Schizophrenia is associated with altered orienting activity; depression with electrodermal (cholinergic?) deficit and normal orienting response. *Journal of Abnormal Psychology, 97,* 3–12.

Block, J. (1965). *The challenge of response sets.* New York: Appleton-Century-Crofts.

Borwein, J. M., & Borwein, P. B. (1988). Ramanujan and pi. *Scientific American, 258,* 112–117.

Bouchard, T. J., Jr., Lykken, D. T., McGue, M., Segal, N. L., & Tellegen, A. (1990). Sources of human psychological differences: The Minnesota Study of Twins Reared Apart. *Science, 250,* 223–228.

Buhler, W. K. (1981). *Gauss: A biographical study.* Berlin: Springer-Verlag.

Brodie, E. D., III. (1989). Genetic correlations between morphology and antipredator behavior in natural populations of the garter snake *Thamnophis ordinoides, Nature, 342,* 542–543.

Campbell, J. (1988). *Grammatical man.* New York: Simon & Schuster.

Cattell, R. B. (1956). Second-order personality factors in the questionnaire realm. *Journal of Consulting Psychology, 20,* 411–418.

Cattell, R. B. (1982). *The inheritance of personality and ability.* San Diego, CA: Academic Press.

Cavalli-Sforza, L. L., & Bodmer, W. F. (1971). *The genetics of human populations.* New York: Freeman.

Chai, C. K. (1981). Dactylaplasia in mice. *The Journal of Heredity, 72,* 234–237.

Cunningham, P. (1991). The genetics of thoroughbred horses. *Scientific American, 265,* 92–98.

Dawkins, R. (1982a). *The blind watchmaker.* Essex, England: Longman.

Dawkins, R. (1982b). *The extended phenotype.* Oxford, England: Oxford University Press.

Durant, W., & Durant, A. (1967). *Rousseau and revolution.* New York: Simon & Schuster.

Dunnington, G. W. (1955). *Carl Friedrich Gauss: Titan of science.* New York: Hafner.

Eaves, L. J. (1976). The effect of cultural transmission on continuous variation. *Heredity, 37,* 41–57.

Eaves, L. J. (1987). Dominance alone is not enough. *Behavior Genetics, 18,* 27–34.

Eysenck, H. J. (1952). *The scientific study of personality.* London: Kegan Paul, Trench, & Trubner.

Eysenck, H. J. (1986). A critique of contemporary classification and diagnosis. In T. Millon & G. L. Klerman (Eds.), *Contemporary directions in psychopathology* (pp. 73–78). New York: Guilford Press.

Falconer, D. S. (1960). *Introduction to quantitative genetics.* New York: Ronald Press.

Farber, S. L. (1981). *Identical twins reared apart: A reanalysis.* New York: Basic Books.

Fedotchev, A. I., Bonda, A. T., & Konovalov, V. F. (1990). Stability of resonance EEG reactions to flickering light in humans. *International Journal of Psychophysiology, 9,* 189–194.

Galton, F. (1869). *Hereditary genius.* London: Macmillan.

Garfield, E. (1982). Benjamin Franklin: Philadelphia's scientist extraordinaire. *Current Contents, 40,* 5–12.

Goldschmidt, R. B. (1940). *The material basis of evolution.* New Haven, CT: Yale University Press.

Gottesman, I. I., & Shields. J. (1982). *Schizophrenia: The epigenetic puzzle.* Cambridge, England: University of Cambridge Press.

Grayson, D. A. (1989). Twins reared together: Minimizing shared environmental effects. *Behavior Genetics, 19,* 593–604.

Health, A. C., Martin, B. G., Eaves, L. J., & Loesch, D. (1984). Evidence for polygenic epistatic interactions in man. *Genetics, 106,* 719–727.

Iacono, W. G. (1982). Bilateral electrodermal habituation-dishabituation and resting EEG in remitted schizophrenics. *Journal of Nervous and Mental Disease, 170,* 91–101.

Iacono, W. G. (1985). Psychophysiological markers of psychopathology: A review. *Canadian Psychology, 26,* 96–112.

Iacono, W. G., Lykken, D. T., Peloquin, L. J., Lumry, A. E., Valintine, R. H., & Tuason, V. (1983). Electrodermal activity in euthymic patients with affective disorders: A possible marker of depression. *Archives of General Psychiatry, 40,* 557–565.

Jinks, J. L., & Fulker, D. W. (1970). Comparison of the biometrical genetical, MAVA, and classical approaches to the analysis of human behavior. *Psychological Bulletin, 73,* 311–349.

Juel-Nielson, N. (1965). Individual and environment: A psychiatric and psychological investigation of monozygous twins raised apart. *Acta Psychiatrica et Neurologica Scandinavica* (Suppl. 183).

Knight, D. M. (1985). Davey and Farraday: Fathers and sons. In D. Gooding & F. A. J. L. James (Eds.). *Faraday rediscovered* (pp. 33–50). New York: Stockton.

Kolata. G. (1987). Remembering a "magical genius." *Science, 236,* 1519–1521.

Kroeber, A. H. (1944). *Configurations of culture growth.* Berkeley: University of California Press.

Lewontin, R. C. (1967). An estimate of average heterozygosity in man. *American Journal of Human Genetics, 19,* 681–685.

Li, C. C. (1987). A genetical model for emergenesis. *American Journal of Human Genetics, 41,* 517–523.

Loehlin, J. C., & Nichols, R. C. (1976). *Heredity, environment, and personality.* Austin: University of Texas Press.

Lykken, D. T. (1982). Research with twins: The concept of emergenesis. *Psychophysiology, 19,* 361–373.

Lykken, D. T. (1991). What's wrong with psychology anyway? In D. Cicchetti & W. M. Grove (Eds.), *Thinking clearly about psychology* (Vol. 1, pp. 3–39). Minneapolis: University of Minnesota Press.

Lykken, D. T., Bouchard, T. J., McGue, M., & Tellegen, A. (1990). The Minnesota Twin Registry: Some initial findings. *Acta Geneticae Medicae et Gemmellologiae, 39,* 35–70.

Lykken, D. T., Bouchard, T. J., McGue, M., & Tellegen, A. (1992a). *The heritability of interests: A twin study.* Manuscript submitted for publication.

Lykken, D. T., Bouchard, T. J., McGue, M., & Tellegen, A. (1992b). *Nature via nurture: The implications of recent twin research.* Manuscript submitted for publication.

Lykken, D. T., Iacono, W. G., Haroian, K. McGue, M., & Bouchard, T. J. (1988). Habituation of the EDR to strong stimuli: A twin study. *Psychophysiology, 25,* 4–16.

Lykken, D. T., Tellegen, A., & Iacono, W. G. (1982). EEG spectra in twins: Evidence for a neglected mechanism of genetic determination. *Physiological Psychology, 10,* 60–65.

Lykken, D. T., Tellegen, A., & Thorkelson, K. (1974). Genetic determination of EEG frequency spectra. *Biological Psychology, 1,* 245–259.

McGue, M., Bacon, S., & Lykken, D. T. (in press). Personality stability and change in early adulthood: A behavioral genetic analysis. *Developmental Psychology.*

Meehl, P. E. (1992). Factors and taxa, traits and types, differences of degree and differences in kind. *Journal of Personality, 60,* 117–174.

Murphy, E. A. (1979). Quantitative genetics: A critique. *Social Biology, 26,* 126–141.

Newman, H. H., Freeman, F. N., & Holzinger, K. J. (1937). *Twins: A study of heredity and environment.* Chicago: University of Chicago Press.

Newman, J. R. (1956). Srinivasa Ramanujan. In Newman, J. R. (Ed.), *The world of mathematics* (Vol. 1, pp. 368–380). New York: Simon & Schuster.

Novitski, E. (1982). *Human genetics* (2nd ed.). New York: Macmillan.

Parrott, T. M. (1938). *Shakespeare.* New York: Scribner.

Pederson, N. L., Plomin, R., McClearn, G. E., & Friberg, L. (1988). Neuroticism, extraversion, and related traits in adult twins reared apart and reared together. *Journal of Personality and Social Psychology, 55,* 950–957.

Plomin, R., & Daniels, D. (1987). Why are children in the same family, so different from one another? *Behavioral and Brain Sciences, 10,* 1–16.

Price, D. J. (1962). The exponential curve of science. In B. Barber & W. Hirsch (Eds.). *The sociology of science* (pp. 112–131). New York: Free Press.

Propping, P. (1977). Genetic control of ethanol action on the central nervous system. *Human Genetics, 35,* 309–334.

Rosenthal, D. (1970). *Genetic theory and abnormal behavior.* New York: McGraw-Hill.

Rosenthal, D., & Kety, S. S. (Eds.). (1968). *The transmission of schizophrenia.* Oxford, England: Pergamon Press.

Shaff, H. (1985). *Six wars at a time: The life and times of Gutzon Borglum.* Darien, CT: Permelia.

Shields, J. (1962). *Monozygotic twins brought up apart and brought up together.* London: Oxford University Press.

Simonton, D. K. (1988). *Scientific genius: A psychology of science.* Cambridge, England: Cambridge University Press.

Stassen, H. H., Lykken, D. T., Propping, P., & Bomben, G. (1988). Genetic determination of the human EEG. *Human Genetics, 80,* 165–142.

Stearns, S., & VanderWoude, A. (1991). *Musical talent among first-degree relatives of university students majoring, or not majoring, in instrumental or vocal music.* Unpublished student research report, University of Minnesota, Department of Psychology, Minneapolis.

Tellegen, A., Lykken, D. T., Bouchard, T. J., Wilcox, K., Segal, N., & Rich, S. (1988). Personality similarity in twins reared apart and together. *Journal of Personality and Social Psychology, 54,* 1031–1039.

Tellegen, A., & Waller, N. (in press). Exploring personality through test construction: Development of the Multidimensional Personality Questionnaire. In S. R. Briggs & J. M. Cleek (Eds.), *Personality measures: Development and evaluation* (Vol. 1). Minneapolis: University of Minnesota Press.

Thomas, J. M. (1991). *Michael Faraday and the Royal Institution: The genius of man and place.* New York: American Institute of Physics.

Tooby, J., & Cosmides, L. (1990). On the universality of human nature and the uniqueness of the individual: The role of genetics and adaptation. *Journal of Personality, 58,* 17–68.

Walberg, H. J., Strykowski, B. F., Rouai, E., & Hung, S. S. (1984). Exceptional performance. *Review of Educational Research, 54,* 87–112.

Waller, N., Lykken, D. T., & Tellegen, A. (in press). Occupational interests, leisure time interests, and personality: Three domains or one? In R. Dawes & D. Lubinsky (Eds.), *Assessing individual differences in human behavior: New methods, concepts and findings.* Minneapolis: University of Minnesota Press.

RESPONSE SHEET

for D. T. Lykken: Emergenesis

1. Just exactly what is emergenesis? What difference does it make that we now know about it?

2. Write one question regarding this article that can be used for class discussion.

3. Describe one application of the information in this article. It can be:

1) A next research step to take.
2) An educational, clinical/counseling or rearing application
3) A personal application

CHAPTER

2

Non-shared Environmental Influences

As was mentioned above, there are three main influences: Birth order, gender and parent-child temperament fit. Each of these leads to differential parental treatment of offspring who live in the same home at the same time.

One of the most powerful instigators of differential treatment is the birth position that the child holds. Much of this is organized around the first born position. To a great extent, those born later experience a default treatment. That is, they are treated differently precisely because they are *not* first born, rather than that they have certain attributions.

Geoffrey Cowley examines these attributions to the first born, and also the effects of such attributions.

Richard W. Bradley pursues the effects in school settings, and makes some prescriptions regarding the impact of birth order.

The third selection is a summary of characteristic birth order findings, regarding both differential treatment and differential outcomes (characteristics). Both are found about 70% of the time.

First Born, Later Born

Rebel or Reactionary? A New Book Says It's Due to Your Place in the Family Structure

By Geoffrey Cowley

When 22-year-old Charles Darwin set out in 1831 to circle the globe on the HMS Beagle, his mind lay squarely in the mainstream. He assumed that life forms were fixed entities, each one handcrafted by God for its special place in nature. But during his travels, Darwin started noticing things that didn't fit the paradigm. Why, he wondered, would finches and iguanas assume distinct but related forms on adjacent islands? And when Darwin proposed a revolutionary solution—that all nature's variety stems from a simple process that preserves useful variations and discards harmful ones—the authorities were appalled. "A scientific mistake," thundered Louis Agassiz, then the world's leading naturalist—"untrue in its facts . . . and mischievous in its tendency."

What drives people like Darwin to stick pins in conventional wisdom? And why do radical innovations so enrage people like Agassiz? *To Frank Sulloway,* a science historian at MIT, it's no coincidence that Darwin was the fifth of six kids in his family, or that Agassiz was the firstborn in his. Sulloway has spent two decades gathering data on thousands of people involved in historic controversies—from the Copernican revolution to the Protestant Reformation—and running statistical tests to see what sets rebels apart from reactionaries. His findings, due out this month in a new book titled "Born to Rebel" *(640 pages. Pantheon Books. $30),* suggest that "the foremost engine of historical change" is not the church, state or economy but family structure. Sulloway makes a compelling case that firstborns, whatever their age, sex, class or nationality, specialize in defending the status quo while later-borns specialize in toppling it. Indeed, he says, people with the same birthranks have more in common with each other than they do with their own siblings.

It's an audacious claim (Sulloway himself is a laterborn), and not one that social scientists will flock to embrace. Birth-order research, for all its intuitive appeal, has a reputation for flakiness. "Both laypeople and experts tend to overinterpret the importance of birth order," says Joseph Rodgers, a psychologist at the University of Oklahoma. "There are very few birth-order effects." In a 1983 review of 2,000 studies dating to the 1940s, the Swiss psychologists Cecile Ernst and Jules Angst declared that since most had failed to control for variables like social class and family size, none could be taken seriously. Sulloway agrees that much of the past research has been marred by weak hypotheses and poor methods. But his own study tackles many of the issues left unresolved by earlier ones, and some experts are raving about it. "It's a monumental work of scholarship," says Sarah Blaffer Hrdy, an anthropologist at the University of California, Davis. "I think it will change the way all of us think about ourselves and our families."

Most of us already have a seat-of-the-pants sense of how birthrank affects personality. Firstborns are by reputation the list makers and control freaks. "Show me a librarian who's not a firstborn," says pop psychologist Kevin Leman, author of "The Birth Order Book" and "Growing Up First Born." "They live by the Dewey Decimal System." Firstborns are supposedly at home in trades like accounting and architecture—and maybe airline piloting. Walter Cronkite, Peter Jennings and Ted Koppel are all firstborns or only children. Chevy Chase, Danny DeVito and Jay Leno are last-borns. Psychologists have theorized about sibling differences since the 1920s, when Freud's estranged disciple Alfred Adler alleged that firstborns spend their lives getting over their displacement by

Bill Clinton

Firstborn: He's ambitious, extroverted and status-conscious. In private, he's famously short-tempered. Flirted with rebellion, but says he didn't inhale.

younger brothers and sisters. But the models have been vague enough to accommodate almost any real-world observation—or its opposite. Adler, for example, argued that last-borns are often spoiled and lazy because they don't have younger siblings challenging them. He also characterized them as go-getters, hardened by incessant competition with their elders. Take your pick.

Sulloway starts not by spinning random hypotheses but by thinking about the Darwinian pressures that foster sibling competition throughout the natural world. Parental support is often the key to a youngster's survival—and siblings are often the primary obstacle. When food is scarce, chicks in a nest may gang up to murder the youngest member of the brood, without a peep of parental protest. Humans harbor similar propensities. Many societies accord firstborns higher status than later-borns, and some still condone killing a newborn in times of scarcity, just to ensure an older child's survival. Sibling competition may take different forms in the New Jersey suburbs than it does among peasants facing starvation. But firstborns and later-borns still confront very different pressures and opportunities. And by Sulloway's reckoning, their experiences should foster very different qualities of character.

How, exactly, should they differ? Firstborns, who grow up knowing they're "bigger, stronger and smarter than their younger siblings," should be more assertive and dominant. They should also be more jealous and status-conscious, having seen their untrammeled turf invaded by newcomers. Their early experience as parents' lieutenants should make them more conscientious than later-borns. And the favoritism they enjoy should leave them more closely wedded to their parents' values and standards. Later-borns, since they can't get their way by force or bluster, should be more sociable and agreeable. And their lesser stake in the established family order should leave them more open to novelty and innovation.

Sulloway has found ingenious ways of testing these hypotheses. By sifting through the 2,000 studies that Ernst and Angst discarded in 1983, he found 196 in which researchers had factored out differences in social class and family size before looking for birth-order effects. And those studies, which included nearly 121,000 participants, supported his predictions about each of the five personality dimensions that psychological tests look for. Birth order was a lousy predictor of extroversion, a category so broad that it could encompass both a firstborn's assertiveness and a later-born's backslapping sociability. But most studies found that firstborns were more neurotic than were later-borns, and more conscientious (as in responsible, organized and achievement-oriented). Later-borns were consistently deemed more agreeable, and they were overwhelmingly more open to experience. People without siblings fell somewhere between firstborns and later-borns on most personality measures, but they were no more open to experience than were firstborns.

Howard Stern

Later-born: A professional rebel, the shock jock uses humor to get attention and subvert the status quo. 'Butt Bongo Fiesta' does not a president make.

So far, so good. But did these psychological tests say anything about how people would behave out in the world? That's where Sulloway's historical surveys come into play. To get at the roots of real-life radicalism, he compiled biographical data on 6,566 people who have played public roles in scientific or political controversies over the past five centuries. By having panels of historians rate these players on their resistance or receptivity to the innovations they confronted, he was able to plot their "openness to experience" in relation to everything from birth order to age, sex, race, temperament, social class, family size and even the tenor of their family relationships.

In one case after another, the influence of birth order is remarkable. Later-borns were more likely than firstborns were to support each of the 61 liberal causes Sulloway surveyed, from the Protestant Reformation to the American civil-rights movement. Indeed birth order rivaled race as a predictor of who would support the abolition of slavery during the mid-1800s. Firstborns and later-borns differ more in their styles of thought than in their core beliefs—liberals can be rigidly doctrinaire and conservatives can be open to new ways of thinking. But the last-borns in Sulloway's survey were 18 times more likely to take up left-wing causes than to get involved in conservative ones, such as the temperance movement. Not surprisingly, Mahatma Gandhi and Martin Luther King Jr. were all later-borns, as were Leon Trotsky, Fidel Castro, Yasir Arafat and Ho Chi Minh. Rush Limbaugh, George Wallace and Newt Gingrich are all firstborns.

The pattern was just as clear when Sulloway examined 28 scientific controversies. Later-borns were five times more likely than firstborns were to support the Copernican and Darwinian revolutions—and nine times more likely to embrace phrenology, a wacky 19th-century fad that involved divining character from the shape of a person's skull. By contrast, Sulloway found that "conservative innovations," such as the eugenics movement, have consistently been spearheaded by firstborns and opposed by later-borns.

This isn't to say that birth order is all that counts in life, or even in the contentious worlds of science and politics. "These are statistical patterns, not physical laws," says Harvard evolutionist Ernst Mayr. "There are always exceptions." Isaac Newton was a firstborn, for example, and

Adolf Hitler wasn't. Sulloway is the first to admit that the effects of birth order can be offset, exaggerated or even overridden by other factors. Indeed, he devotes much of the new book to plotting the ways in which different influences interact. Gender has a huge and obvious impact on personality. But studies have found that firstborn girls are typically more confident, assertive and verbally aggressive than their younger brothers or sisters are. By the same token, age makes most people less open-minded, regardless of their birthrank. Within Sulloway's sample, young later-borns were more than twice as likely as elderly ones were to embrace the idea of evolution during the 19th century. But 80-year-old later-borns were still more receptive than 30-year-old firstborns.

Like age, certain features of a person's innate temperament can mask the effects of birth order. Congenital shyness, for example, tends to minimize birth-order differences. By placing a damper on other aspects of character, it makes firstborns less arch and later-borns less outwardly subversive. Likewise, extroversion tends to magnify the contrast. It might lead a firstborn to become a drill sergeant instead of a bank teller, and a last-born to do stand-up comedy instead of writing poems. Conflict with a parent can also offset a firstborn's conformist ways. Once estranged from the familial status quo and pushed into the underdog role, says Sulloway, anyone becomes more radical.

Sulloway's findings are sure to strike a chord with lay readers, but social scientists may not appreciate his chutzpah. In the years since Ernst and Angst declared birth order meaningless, few researchers have bothered to look at it, and many of those who have tried have been disappointed. In a recent book titled "Birth Order and Political Behavior," Alfred University political scientist Steven Peterson and two colleagues describe how they analyzed a huge list of eminent figures to see if it was dominated by firstborns. When they came up dry, they assumed there was nothing left to study. "There are always some people who are going to say, 'Gee, you just didn't look at enough variables'," says Peterson's collaborator Alan Arwine. "It's like trying to kill a vampire." But Arwine and Peterson's findings don't contradict Sulloway's. They merely answer a less interesting question. "The question isn't whether firstborns are more eminent than later-borns," Sulloway insists. "Eminence isn't even a personality trait. It's an outcome. What's interesting is that firstborns and later-borns become eminent in different ways."

Other critics will dismiss Sulloway's whole approach. "From what I read, it's not scientific," says Toni Falbo, a professor of educational psychology at the University of Texas at Austin. "He looks at special cases. If you're looking at special cases, particularly in history, you can find a case that fits almost any hypothesis you want." By her logic, history is just an endless series of special cases, not a lawful process that can be illuminated through hypothesis testing. Sulloway's real accomplishment is to show that's not the case. His "special cases" span five centuries and many countries, yet they repeatedly confirm his predictions. "Frank attacks questions that could not be more contingent," says John Tooby, an anthropologist at the University of California, Santa Barbara—"why some countries ended up Protestant, why France resisted Darwinism, who ended up in which faction in the French National Assembly—and shows that they fit into larger patterns."

Sulloway doesn't claim to have solved any ultimate questions. He plans to expand his database, test new predictions and publish a revised edition of the book every five years or so. "The publisher put that in my contract," he says. "It was the only way I could make myself stop and publish this." Anyone who can stomach a revolution should be glad that he did.

With KAREN SPRINGEN

RESPONSE SHEET

Geoffrey Cowley: First Born, Later Born

1. Cowley reviews researcher Frank Sulloway's work on Birth Order, especially the last born. What is Sulloway's central argument (thesis, contention)?

2. Write one question regarding this article that can be used for class discussion.

3. Describe one application of the information in this article. It can be:

1) A next research step to take
2) An educational, clinical/counseling or rearing application
3) A personal application

PSY 241. HO: BIRTH ORDER

Introduction

We have been discussing heritability, one of the main causes of behavioral individual differences. Non-shared familial environment is the other main cause. There are three primary determinants of differential treatment of siblings: Birth order, female-male sex and temperament differences. We will look at birth order first, then temperament, and late in the course gender effects.

A good deal of research has been devoted to birth order effects. Two sets of variables are at focus in these studies: Treatment and resulting behavioral characteristics. Most of the work has compared first borns with later borns. The characteristics associated with first and later birth positions occur about 70% of the time.

The differential treatments and characteristics for first and later borns are summarized below.

FIRST BORNS

Treatment:

____ Perfection expected
____ Family duties assigned, incl. care of siblings
____ Have to 'live up to. . .'
____ Strict
____ Parents protective of
____ Parents attentive to
____ When sick, parents hover
____ Parents use punishment
____ pushed, not left off hook
(9)

Characteristics:

____ Achievement-oriented
____ Task-oriented
____ Making good grades
____ Competitive
____ Rule-oriented
____ Cautious
____ Conformist
____ Nervous, anxious
____ Performance-approval oriented
____ More likely to excel in science, business, policy-making, nonfiction writing, law
(10)

LATER BORNS

Treatment:

____ Relaxed with
____ making choices encouraged
____ social contacts encouraged
____ given a good deal of affection
____ allowed personal freedom
____ mother favors
____ teased by oldest
____ coached by oldest
(8)

Characteristics:

____ Interpersonally skillful
____ independent
____ uninhibited
____ friendly
____ socially popular
____ not very judgemental
____ charismatic, manipulative at times
____ excel in performing and graphic arts, athletics, fiction, promotion, youth activity work
(8)

And, now, the few comments that can be made about middle-borns. Treatment-wise, it is true that they are less-attended than either FB or LB; they are 'taken for granted'. Teachers are more likely to compare them to their FB siblings. They are not encouraged as much as other siblings. Behaviorally, they are more persistent, thoughtful and perceptive. And sensitive. They have a more vulnerable self-esteem. They excel in teaching, personal help work, clinical work, advocacy programming. They make the 'best' spouses!

Psy 241. HO: Birth Order

Introduction

We have been discussing heritability, one of the main causes of behavioral individual differences. Non-shared familial environment is the other main cause. There are three primary determinants of differential treatment of siblings: Birth order, female-male sex and temperament differences. We will look at birth order first, then temperament, and late in the course gender effects.

A good deal of research has been devoted to birth order effects. Two sets of variables are at focus in these studies: Treatment and resulting behavioral characteristics. Most of the work has compared first borns with later borns. The characteristics associated with first and later birth positions occur about 70% of the time.

The differential treatments and characteristics for first and later borns are summarized below.

FIRST BORNS

Treatment:

____ Perfection expected
____ Family duties assigned, incl. care of siblings
____ Have to 'live up to. . .'
____ Strict
____ Parents protective of
____ Parents attentive to
____ When sick, parents hover
____ Parents use punishment
____ pushed, not left off hook
(9)

Characteristics:

____ Achievement-oriented
____ Task-oriented
____ Making good grades
____ Competitive
____ Rule-oriented
____ Cautious
____ Conformist
____ Nervous, anxious
____ Performance-approval oriented
____ More likely to excel in science, business, policy-making, nonfiction writing, law
(10)

LATER BORNS

Treatment:

____ Relaxed with
____ making choices encouraged
____ social contacts encouraged
____ given a good deal of affection
____ allowed personal freedom
____ mother favors
____ teased by oldest
____ coached by oldest
(8)

Characteristics:

____ Interpersonally skillful
____ independent
____ uninhibited
____ friendly
____ socially popular
____ not very judgemental
____ charismatic, manipulative at times
____ excel in performing and graphic arts, athletics, fiction, promotion, youth activity work
(8)

And, now, the few comments that can be made about middle-borns. Treatment-wise, it is true that they are less-attended than either FB or LB; they are 'taken for granted'. Teachers are more likely to compare them to their FB siblings. They are not encouraged as much as other siblings. Behaviorally, they are more persistent, thoughtful and perceptive. And sensitive. They have a more vulnerable self-esteem. They excel in teaching, personal help work, clinical work, advocacy programming. They make the 'best' spouses!

PART 2

Personality Differences

Probably unfortunately, the word personality is used both specifically and to refer to all adult domains of function. We will use it both ways, too. First, generically: It includes interests, abilities, and personality dimensions, traits, types. It also includes any developmental preliminaries, such as temperament. The word early in front of any of the three domains means preliminary version.

The differences that are featured in this division of the book are those of temperament, interests, abilities and personality traits/types. Temperament is virtually 100% heritable; abilities are the next highest with 60–77% heritability; interests and personality traits are about 50% heritable. Non-shared environmental impact is greatest upon personality traits. The heritability of interests is the most surprising to those not in this field; there has been a fairly strongly held view that interests develop through what people are exposed to, or in other words, it is predominantly environmentally determined.

For any of you who are undergoing career sorting, planning or deliberating, be sure that you are gathering data from all three domains: Interests, abilities and work-related personality assessments. Many costly career changes occur because one of these has been left out!

And now, on to temperament.

CHAPTER 3

Early Temperament

Forty-eight years ago, three investigators launched a longitudinal study of temperament (which are unlearned behaviors). Alexander Thomas, Stella Chess and Herbert Birch had identified nine dimensions, that showed sufficient independence from each other, and which taken together could define early temperament. They started by measuring these nine dimensions in almost 500 three months olds. They would periodically reassess these almost 500 subjects, first every six months, then annually. Over half of the original participants are still in the study. It is truly a unique study, and what has been learned about the stability of these dimensions, and how they combine to form certain personality constellations, and what level of environmental force is required to bring about change, and what dispositions to the environment are generated are just a few of the developmental issues addressed by this monumental study.

The first selection describes each of the nine dimensions.

In the second selection Jerome Kagan discusses one of the dispositions-to-environment that is central to our utilizing our environment.

Temperament and the Reactions to Unfamiliarity

Jerome Kagan

The behavioral reactions to unfamiliar events are basic phenomena in all vertebrates. Four-month-old infants who show a low threshold to become distressed and motorically aroused to unfamiliar stimuli are more likely than others to become fearful and subdued during early childhood, whereas infants who show a high arousal threshold are more likely to become bold and sociable. After presenting some developmental correlates and trajectories of these 2 temperamental biases, I consider their implications for psychopathology and the relation between propositions containing psychological and biological concepts.

INTRODUCTION

A readiness to react to events that differ from those encountered in the recent or distant past is one of the distinguishing characteristics of all mammalian species. Thus, the events with the greatest power to produce both an initial orienting and sustained attention in infants older than 3 to 4 months are variations on what is familiar, often called discrepant events (Fagan, 1981; Kagan, Kearsley, & Zelazo, 1980). By 8 months of age, discrepant events can produce a vigilant posture of quiet staring and, occasionally, a wary face and a cry of distress if the event cannot be assimilated easily (Bronson, 1970). That is why Hebb (1946) made discrepancy a major basis for fear reactions in animals, why a fear reaction to strangers occurs in the middle of the first year in children growing up in a variety of cultural settings, and, perhaps, why variation in the initial behavioral reaction to novelty exists in almost every vertebrate species studied (Wilson, Coleman, Clark, & Biederman, 1993).

Recent discoveries by neuroscientists enrich these psychological facts. The hippocampus plays an important role in the detection of discrepant events (Squire & Knowlton, 1995). Projections from the hippocampus provoke activity in the amygdala and lead to changes in autonomic function and posture and, in older children, to reflection and anticipation (Shimamura, 1995). Because these neural structures and their projections are influenced by a large number of neurotransmitters and neuromodulators, it is reasonable to expect inherited differences in the neurochemistry of these structures and circuits and, therefore, in their excitability. Variation in the levels of, or receptors for, corticotropin releasing hormone, norepinephrine, cortisol, dopamine, glutamate, GABA, opioids, acetylcholine, and other molecules might be accompanied by differences in the intensity and form of responsivity to unfamiliarity (Cooper, Bloom, & Roth, 1991). This speculation is supported by research with infants and children (Kagan, 1994). This article summarizes what has been learned about two temperamental types of children who react in different ways to unfamiliarity, considers the implications of these two temperamental categories for psychopathology, and comments briefly on the relation between psychological and biological constructs.

INFANT REACTIVITY AND FEARFUL BEHAVIOR

About 20% of a large sample of 462 healthy, Caucasian, middle-class, 16-week-old infants became both motorically active and distressed to presentations of brightly colored toys moved back and forth in front of their faces, tape recordings of voices speaking brief sentences, and cotton swabs dipped in dilute butyl alcohol applied to the nose. These infants are called high reactive. By contrast, about 40% of infants with the same family and ethnic background remained motorically relaxed and did not fret or cry to the same set of unfamiliar events. These infants are called low reactive. The differences between high and low reactives can be interpreted as reflecting variation in the excitability of the amygdala and its projections to the

From *Child Development,* February 1997, pp. 139–143.

ventral striatum, hypothalamus, cingulate, central gray, and medulla (Amaral, Price, Pitkanen, & Carmichael, 1992; Davis, 1992).

When these high and low reactive infants were observed in a variety of unfamiliar laboratory situations at 14 and 21 months, about one-third of the 73 high reactives were highly fearful (4 or more fears), and only 3% showed minimal fear (0 or 1 fear) at both ages. By contrast, one-third of the 147 low reactives were minimally fearful at both ages (0 or 1 fear), and only 4% displayed high levels of fear (Kagan, 1994).

The profiles of high and low fear to unfamiliar events, called inhibited and uninhibited, are heritable, to a modest degree, in 1- to 2-year-old middle-class children (DiLalla, Kagan, & Reznick, 1994; Robinson, Kagan, Reznick, & Corley, 1992). Further, high reactives show greater sympathetic reactivity in the cardiovascular system than low reactives during the first 2 years (Kagan, 1994; Snidman, Kagan, Riordan, & Shannon, 1995).

As children approach the fourth and fifth years, they gain control of crying to and reflex retreat from unfamiliar events and will only show these responses to very dangerous events or to situations that are not easily or ethically created in the laboratory. Hence, it is important to ask how high and low reactive infants might respond to unfamiliar laboratory situations when they are 4–5 years old. Each species has a biologically preferred reaction to novelty. Rabbits freeze, monkeys display a distinct facial grimace, and cats arch their backs. In humans, restraint on speech seems to be an analogue of the immobility that animals display in novel situations (Panksepp, Sacks, Crepeau, & Abbott, 1991), for children often become quiet as an initial reaction to unfamiliar situations (Asendorpf, 1990; Kagan, Reznick, & Gibbons, 1989; Kagan, Reznick, & Snidman, 1988; Murray, 1971). It is also reasonable to expect that the activity in limbic sites provoked by an unfamiliar social situation might interfere with the brain states that mediate the relaxed emotional state that is indexed by smiling and laughter (Adamec, 1991; Amaral et al., 1992). When the children who had been classified as high and low reactive were interviewed at 4½ years of age by an unfamiliar female examiner who was blind to their prior behavior, the 62 high reactives talked and smiled significantly less often (means of 41 comments and 17 smiles) than did the 94 low reactives (means of 57 comments and 28 smiles) during a 1 hour test battery: $F(1, 152) = 4.51$, $p < .05$ for spontaneous comments; $F(1, 152) = 15.01$, $p < .01$ for spontaneous smiles. Although spontaneous comments and smiles were positively correlated ($r = 0.4$), the low reactives displayed significantly more smiles than would have been predicted from a regression of number of smiles on number of spontaneous comments. The high reactives displayed significantly fewer smiles than expected. Every one of the nine children who smiled more than 50 times had been a low reactive infant.

However, only a modest proportion of children maintained an extreme form of their theoretically expected profile over the period from 4 months to 4½ years, presumably because of the influence of intervening family experiences (Arcus, 1991). Only 19% of the high reactives displayed a high level of fear at both 14 and 21 months (>4 fears), together with low values (below the mean) for both spontaneous comments and smiles at 4½ years. But not one low reactive infant actualized such a consistently fearful and emotionally subdued profile. By contrast, 18% of low reactive infants showed the opposite profile of low fear (0 or 1 fear) at both 14 and 21 months together with high values for both spontaneous smiles and spontaneous comments at 4½ years. Only one high reactive infant actualized that prototypic, uninhibited profile. Thus, it is uncommon for either temperamental type to develop and to maintain the seminal features of the other type, but quite common for each type to develop a profile that is characteristic of the less extreme child who is neither very timid nor very bold.

The 4½-year-old boys who had been high reactive infants had significantly higher resting heart rates than did low reactives, but the differences between high and low reactive girls at this older age took a different form. The high reactive girls did not show the expected high negative correlation (-0.6 to -0.8) between heart rate and heart rate variability. It is possible that the greater sympathetic reactivity of high reactive girls interfered with the usual, vagally induced inverse relation between heart rate and heart rate variability (Porges, Arnold, & Forbes, 1973; Richards, 1985).

Honest disagreement surrounds the conceptualization of infant reactivity as a continuum of arousal or as two distinct categories. The raw motor activity score at 4 months formed a continuum, but the distribution of distress cries did not. Some infants never fretted or cried; others cried a great deal. A more important defense of the decision to treat high and low reactivity as two distinct categories is the fact that within each of the two categories variation in motor activity and crying was unrelated to later fearfulness or sympathetic reactivity. If reactivity were a continuous trait, then a low reactive infant with extremely low motor and distress scores should be less fearful than one who showed slightly more arousal. But that prediction was not affirmed. Second, infants who showed high motor arousal but no crying or minimal motor arousal with frequent crying showed developmental profiles that were different from those who were categorized as low or high reactive. Finally, high and low reactives differed in physical and physiological features that imply qualitatively different genetic constitutions. For example, high reactives have narrower faces than low reactives in the second year of life (Arcus & Kagan, 1995). Unpublished data from our laboratory reveal that the prevalence of atopic allergies among both children and their parents is significantly greater among high than low reactive infants. Studies of monozygotic and dizygotic same-sex twin pairs reveal significant heritability for inhibited and uninhibited behavior in the second year of life (Robinson et al., 1992). These facts imply that the two temperamental groups represent qualitatively different types and do not lie on a continuum of arousal or reactivity to stimulation.

The decision to regard individuals with very different values on a construct as members of the discrete categories or as falling on a continuum will depend on the scientists' purpose. Scientists who are interested in the relation, across families and genera, between brain size and body mass treat the two measurements as continuous. However, biologists interested in the maternal behavior of mice and chimpanzees regard these two mammals as members of qualitatively different groups. Similarly, if psychologists are interested in the physiological foundations of high and low reactives, it will be more useful to regard the two groups as categories. But those who are giving advice to mothers who complain about the ease of arousal and irritability of their infants may treat the arousal as a continuum.

IMPLICATIONS

The differences between high reactive-inhibited and low reactive-uninhibited children provoke speculation on many issues; I deal briefly with implications for psychopathology and the relation between psychological and biological propositions.

Anxiety Disorder

The high reactive infants who became very inhibited 4-year-olds—about 20% of all high reactives—have a low threshold for developing a state of fear to unfamiliar events, situations, and people. It is reasonable to expect that these children will be at a higher risk than most for developing one of the anxiety disorders when they become adolescents or adults. The childhood data do not provide a clue as to which particular anxiety profile will be most prevalent. However, an extensive clinical interview with early adolescents (13–14 years old), who had been classified 11 years earlier (at 21 or 31 months) as inhibited or uninhibited (Kagan et al., 1988), revealed that social phobia was more frequent among inhibited than among uninhibited adolescents, whereas specific phobias, separation anxiety, or compulsive symptoms did not differentiate the two groups (Schwartz, personal communication). This intriguing result, which requires replication, has interesting theoretical ramifications.

Research with animals, usually rats, suggests that acquisition of a fear reaction (e.g., freezing or potentiated startle) to a conditioned stimulus (light or tone) that had been paired with electric shock is mediated by a circuitry that is different from the one that mediates the conditioned response to the context in which the conditioning had occurred (LeDoux, 1995).

Davis (personal communication) has found that a potentiated startle reaction in the rat to the context in which light had been paired with shock involves a circuit from the amygdala to the bed nucleus of the stria terminalis and the septum. The potentiated startle reaction to the conditioned stimulus does not require that circuit. A phobia of spiders or bridges resembles an animal's reaction of freezing to a conditioned stimulus, but a quiet, avoidant posture at a party resembles a fearful reaction to a context. That is, the person who is extremely shy at a party of strangers is not afraid of any particular person or of the setting. Rather, the source of the uncertainty is a situation in which the shy person had experienced anxiety with other strangers. Thus, social phobia may rest on a neurophysiology that is different from that of specific phobia.

Conduct Disorder

The correlation between social class and the prevalence of conduct disorder or delinquency is so high it is likely that the vast majority of children with these profiles acquired their risk status as a result of life conditions, without the mediation of a particular temperamental vulnerability. However, a small proportion—probably no more than 10%—who began their delinquent careers before age 10, and who often committed violent crimes as adolescents, might inherit a physiology that raises their threshold for the conscious experience of anticipatory anxiety and/or guilt over violating community standards for civil behavior (Tremblay, Pihl, Vitaro, & Dubkin, 1994). Damasio (1994) and Mountcastle (1995) have suggested that the surface of the ventromedial prefrontal cortex receives sensory information (from the amygdala) that originates in the peripheral targets, like heart, skin, gut, and muscles. Most children and adults who think about committing a crime experience a subtle feeling that accompanies anticipation of the consequences of an antisocial act. That feeling, which might be called anticipatory anxiety, shame, or guilt, provides an effective restraint on the action. However, if a small proportion of children possessed a less excitable amygdala, or a ventromedial surface that was less responsive, they would be deprived of the typical intensity of this feeling and, as a result, might be less restrained than the majority (Kochanska, Murray, Jacques, Koenig, & Vandegeest, 1996; Zahn-Waxler, Cole, Welsh, & Fox, 1995). If these children are reared in homes and play in neighborhoods in which antisocial behavior is socialized, they are unlikely to become delinquents; perhaps they will become group leaders. However, if these children live in families that do not socialize aggression consistently and play in neighborhoods that provide temptation for antisocial behavior, they might be candidates for a delinquent career.

Biology and Psychology

The renewed interest in temperament has brought some psychologists in closer intellectual contact with neuroscientists. Although this interaction will be beneficial to both disciplines, there is a tension between traditional social scientists who describe and explain behavioral and emotional events using only psychological terms and a smaller group who believe that an acknowledgment of biological events is theoretically helpful. The recent, dramatic advances in the neurosciences have led some scholars to go further and to imply that, in the future, robust generalizations about psychological processes might not be possible without study of the underlying biology (LeDoux, 1995).

Although some neuroscientists recognize that the psychological phenomena of thought, planning, and emotion are emergent—as a blizzard is emergent from the physics of air masses—the media suggest, on occasion, that the biological descriptions are sufficient to explain the psychological events. This publicity creates a misperception that the biological and psychological are competing explanations when, of course, they are not. Vernon Mountcastle notes that although "every mental process is a brain process, . . . not every mentalistic sentence is identical to some neurophysiological sentence. Mind and brain are not identical, no more than lung and respiration are identical" (Mountcastle, 1995, p. 294).

Some neuroscientists, sensing correctly the community resistance to a strong form of biological determinism, are emphasizing the malleability of the neuron's genome to environmental events. A few neurobiologists have come close to declaring that the human genome, like Locke's image of the child's mind, is a tabula rasa that is subject to continual change. This position tempts citizens unfamiliar with neuroscience to conclude that there may be a linear cascade that links external events (e.g., loss of a loved one) directly to changes in genes, physiology, and, finally, behavior, with the psychological layer (e.g., a mood of sadness) between brain physiology and apathetic behavior being relatively unimportant. This error is as serious as the one made by the behaviorists 60 years ago when they assumed a direct connection between a stimulus and an overt response and ignored what was happening in the brain. Both corpora of evidence are necessary if we are to understand the emergence of psychological qualities and their inevitable variation. "The phenomena of human existence and experience are always simultaneously biological and social, and an adequate explanation must involve both" (Rose, 1995, p. 380).

ACKNOWLEDGMENTS

This paper represents portions of the G. Stanley Hall Lecture delivered at the annual meeting of the American Psychological Association, New York City, August 1995. Preparation of this paper was supported, in part, by grants from the John D. and Catherine T. MacArthur Foundation, William T. Grant Foundation, and NIMH grant 47077. The author thanks Nancy Snidman and Doreen Arcus for their collaboration in the research summarized.

ADDRESS AND AFFILIATION

Corresponding author: Jerome Kagan, Harvard University, Department of Psychology, Cambridge, MA 02138; e-mail: JK@WJH.HARVARD.EDU.

REFERENCES

Adamec, R. E. (1991). Anxious personality and the cat. In B. J. Carroll & J. E. Barrett (Eds.), *Psychopathology in the brain* (pp. 153–168). New York: Raven.

Amaral, D. J., Price, L., Pitkanen, A., & Carmichael, S. T. (1992). Anatomical organization of the primate amygdaloid complex. In J. P. Aggleton (Ed.), *The amygdala* (pp. 1–66). New York: Wiley.

Arcus, D. M. (1991). *Experiential modification of temperamental bias in inhibited and uninhibited children.* Unpublished doctoral dissertation, Harvard University.

Arcus, D. M., & Kagan, J. (1995). Temperament and craniofacial variation in the first two years. *Children Development, 66,* 1529–1540.

Asendorpf, J. B. (1990). Development of inhibition during childhood. *Developmental Psychology, 26,* 721–730.

Bronson, G. W. (1970). Fear of visual novelty. *Developmental Psychology, 2,* 33–40.

Cooper, J. R., Bloom, F. E., & Roth, R. H. (1991). *Biochemical basis of neuropharmacology.* New York: Oxford University Press.

Damasio, A. (1994). *Descartes' error.* New York: Putnam.

Davis, M. (1992). The role of the amygdala in conditioned fear. In J. P. Aggleton (Ed.), *The amygdala* (pp. 256–305). New York: Wiley.

DiLalla, L. F., Kagan, J., & Reznick, J. S. (1994). Genetic etiology of behavioral inhibition among two year olds. *Infant Behavior and Development, 17,* 401–408.

Fagan, J. F. (1981). Infant intelligence. *Intelligence, 5,* 239–243.

Hebb, D. O. (1946). The nature of fear. *Psychological Review, 53,* 259–276.

Kagan, J. (1994). *Galen's prophecy.* New York: Basic.

Kagan, J., Kearsley, R. B., & Zelazo, P. R. (1980). *Infancy.* Cambridge, MA: Harvard University Press.

Kagan, J., Reznick, J. S., & Gibbons, J. (1989). Inhibited and uninhibited types of children. *Child Development, 60,* 838–845.

Kagan, J., Reznick, J. S., & Snidman, N. (1988). Biological bases of childhood shyness. *Science, 240,* 167–171.

Kochanska, G., Murray, K., Jacques, T. Y., Koenig, A. L. & Vandegeest, K. A. (1996). Inhibitory control in young children and its role in emerging internalization. *Child Development, 67,* 490–507.

LeDoux, J. E. (1995). In search of an emotional system in the brain. In M. S. Gazzinaga (Ed.), *The cognitive neurosciences* (pp. 1049–1062). Cambridge, MA: MIT Press.

Mountcastle, V. (1995). The evolution of ideas concerning the function of the neocortex. *Cerebral Cortex, 5,* 289–295.

Murray, D. C. (1971). Talk, silence, and anxiety. *Psychological Bulletin, 75,* 244–260.

Panksepp, J., Sacks, D. S., Crepeau, L. J., & Abbott, B. B. (1991). The psycho and neurobiology of fear systems in the brain. In M. R. Denny (Ed.), *Fear, avoidance, and phobias* (pp. 17–59). Hillsdale, NJ: Erlbaum.

Porges, S. W., Arnold, W. R., & Forbes, E. J. (1973). Heart rate variability: An index of attention responsivity in human newborns. *Developmental Psychology, 8,* 85–92.

Richards, J. E. (1985). Respiratory sinus arrhythmia predicts heart rate and visual responses during visual attention in 14 to 20 week old infants. *Psychophysiology, 22,* 101–109.

Robinson, J. L., Kagan, J., Reznick, J. S., & Corley, R. (1992). The heritability of inhibited and uninhibited behavior: A twin study. *Developmental Psychology, 28,* 1030–1037.

Rose, R. J. (1995). Genes and human behavior. In J. T. Spence, J. M. Darley, & D. P. Foss (Eds.) *Annual review of psychology* (pp. 625–654). Palo Alto, CA: Annual Reviews.

Shimamura, A. P. (1995). Memory and frontal lobe function. In M. S. Gazzinaga (Ed.), *The cognitive neurosciences* (pp. 803–814). Cambridge, MA: MIT Press.

Snidman, N., Kagan, J., Riordan, L., & Shannon, D., (1995). Cardiac function and behavioral reactivity in infancy. *Psychophysiology, 31,* 199–207.

Squire, L. R., & Knowlton, B. J. (1995). Memory, hippocampus, and brain systems. In M. S. Gazzinaga (Ed.), *The cognitive neurosciences* (pp. 825–838). Cambridge, MA: MIT Press.

Tremblay, R. E., Pihl, R. O., Vitaro, F., & Dubkin, P. L. (1994). Predicting early onset of male antisocial behavior from preschool behavior. *Archives of General Psychiatry, 51,* 732–739.

Wilson, D. S., Coleman, K., Clark, A. B., & Biederman, L. (1993). Shy-bold continuum in pumpkinseed sunfish (*Lepomis gibbosus*): An ecological study of a psychological trait. *Journal of Comparative Psychology, 107,* 250–260.

Zahn-Waxler, C., Cole, P., Welsh, J. D., & Fox, N. A. (1995). Psychophysiological correlates of empathy and prosocial behavior in preschool children with behavioral problems. *Development and Psychopathology, 7,* 27–48.

RESPONSE SHEET

for Jerome Kagan: Temperament

1. What is Jerome Kagan's thesis regarding discrepant events?

2. Write one question regarding this article that can be used for class discussion.

3. Describe one application of the information in this article. It can be:
1) A next research step to take
2) An educational, clinical/counseling or rearing application
3) A personal application

Descriptions of the Nine Temperament Dimensions

Lynn Ourth

Introduction

There are wide individual differences within all of these dimensions. An ordinal estimate is that the highest/greatest is five times more than the lowest/least. It is not unusual for people to account for this variation by making motivational attributions to individuals that are at either end (e.g., low activity, "he's lazy"; high activity, "he must be on something"). These studies offer an alternative approach to understanding very important human differences: These levels are natural levels of functioning, and although departures from them are possible, they are effortful and not easy to sustain. If such a change is either desired or required, it is much more likely to be achieved if approached from an individual differences perspective, than from a motivational one (which makes the assumption that we are all alike). In these descriptions the within dimension treatment will not usually be even. It will reflect those aspects that are more significant in our culture, either positively or negatively. Some of these dimensions are linear (unidirectional) and some are bipolar (go in opposite directions from the center).

Activity Level (Linear)

This refers to differences in motor activity levels. Those who have very high levels are constantly in motion. They are tireless; they do sleep less. They are high energy. They are usually involved with several tracks at once. The motor energy does not originate from being stimulated; it comes from within, it is endogenous. Stimulation can raise the level, but they don't need it to go full blast. Those who have the highest levels are hyperactive; just as is true for any of the other levels, this level becomes apparent in very early childhood. A distinction needs to be made, however. There are also hyperreactive children and adults. The motor activity level for these is dependent upon the pervasiveness and intensity of stimulation the person is experiencing. Though the motor outcome can be quite similar, how the person gets there is very different. Diagnostically, knowing which is which can make a crucial difference in whether the treatment/management program is effective. Mania also reflects extremely high activity; it involves another temperament, though, which will be discussed below.

As is true for all of these temperaments, knowing about the real individual differences in activity can prevent you from thinking something is wrong about you, or that something is wrong with another person with whom you are connected in some fashion.

Approach-Withdrawal (Bipolar)

This refers to the initial response to a new stimulus/set. Some individuals approach a new s/s, some neither approach or withdraw, and some retreat to a safe (for them) distance. These s/s can be objects, events or ideas. Those who approach, are experiencing interest, curiosity and at least a minimal level of pleasantness. Those who don't do either are experiencing cautiousness. Those who pull back are experiencing fearfulness. The core individual difference involved in this is our brain's disposition to new stimuli. The work done with Schema Theory can help us understand what is going on here.

The Tenets of Schema Theory

1. Each time an s/s is presented, our brain scans its memory banks to see if there is a schema (a representation of the s/s) present. If there is, we recognize (re-cognize) it, and would say that it is familiar.
2. If the s/s has no representation, our brain starts constructing a schema for it. We would say that it is strange, that we don't recognize it. *Those who have withdrawal tendencies will also experience this new/strange s/s as having some degree of threat/danger/warning.* They have at least a residual of negative

emotion attached, which carries on for an indefinite time. This reduces the probability that they will explore those stimuli, which could lead to neutralizing the fearful aura.

It takes several exposures to fully develop a schema. That is why, when this is in progress, a person cannot be recognized if she alters one significant aspect of her appearance.

3. Once a schema has been reasonably fully developed, we can recognize the s/s from any angle, coming toward us or going away from us, and even if there are embellishments. We can also recognize it although there are structural, color or sequential alterations, as long as there is framing integrity or some highly distinctive characteristic still present. However, even though there is recognition, we also realize there is something different about the s/s. We know that it has been altered. This is called a violation of schema. There are four levels of violation; as the extent of violation increases, the degree of fearfulness also increases. Here are the levels and their typical effects:

Violation Levels	Effects
1. Mild. A political cartoon	Curiosity. Humor. Approach
2. Moderate. An arm missing	Staring. Uneasiness. Maintain some distance
3. Considerable. Hunchback of N. Dame	Revulsion. Fear. Avoidance. Elimination
4. Severe. Complete, multimodal alteration of highly familiar phenom. Halloween time. Earthquake.	Panic, if the alteration continues for more than a few minutes. Run or freeze.

Those who have withdrawal tendencies experience violations with greater apprehension. Slight changes evoke uneasiness. In the table above, they start out at level two, so their responses are always a level higher, compared to their non-withdrawing colleagues.

As can readily be seen, the Withdrawer has a double whammy. Both new stimuli and violated s/s put him on the alert and arouse uneasiness. But the withdrawer isn't consigned to this for life with no reprieve. There are desensitization and other training programs that can bring this native tendency into manageable limits.

Perhaps the key consideration relating to this approach-withdrawal dimension is that we must be able to utilize our environment. We must engage it on our behalf. The approacher's natural orientation is to do this. The withdrawer needs help in doing this. Once beyond these initial binding responses, though, these persons can engage as well as anyone.

Adaptability (Linear)

This refers to how a person responds to a s/s after the first exposure. The approacher is also adaptable. So, this dimension refers to how long it takes for those who are from low approach to high withdrawal to feel comfortable with a strange s/s or to deal with change (violation). There is not a high correlation between degree of withdrawal and difficulty in adapting, though. This suggests that there is another process that is associated with adaptability that needs to be identified. One candidate is the tendency to what behavioral geneticists call emotionality, which refers to the degree to which emotion is automatically linked to each perception the person has. The greater this is, the longer the initial reaction continues, regardless of the nature of the emotion. This in turn keeps the individual from being adaptable.

Anyone who says that he or she doesn't like change is reflecting what is involved in adaptability. The irony is that our society has increased its demands for adaptability, but has not provided any increased means for doing it.

Quality of Mood (Bipolar)

This ranges from highly positive to highly negative. This refers to moods that are generated from within, that are endogenous. They are not being caused by some outside circumstances. Outside circumstances can influence the situational level of expression, but cannot determine the quality over time. Positive individuals were positive as babies; cheerful from the outset. Negative individuals were grumps when they were babies. There is now pretty good evidence that there is a central brain site that is involved in this. In the early fifties, a psychologist named James Olds was doing studies on reinforcements with rats. He was using the quite new procedure of microelectrode probing, which could detect how rat's individual cortical neurons were responding to varying kinds of reinforcement. This was done by inserting microdes into various parts of the brain, and linking these to the rat's own exploratory behaviors in the booths they were exploring. One portion of the brain that Olds was linking was the limbic region. It had already been established as central coordinator of emotional processes, so seemed to Olds to be a relevant region to explore. One fateful morning he launched the limbic studies. As mentioned, these rats were stimulating their own brains, by simply striking a bar that was inserted in the booth. There was one small portion of the brain that the rats singled out, and they were engaging it virtually nonstop. They would keep pressing the bar until they became exhausted. It was entirely evident that this was a most pleasurable experience. This led Olds to precisely establish the location and boundaries of this portion of the brain, to do comparative studies and to name the entity. He called it the pleasure center of the brain. His comparative studies led him to discover a counterpart. This he called the pain center of the brain.

Those who have naturally occurring positive moods show higher linkages to the pleasure centers in their brains. Those who have naturally occurring negative moods show higher linkages to the pain centers of their brains.

There are those who experience the simple pleasures of life. But there are also those who experience the simple displeasures. Their negativity is not from untoward early life; it is from their neurology.

As if this is not enough, there are combinations that have been found: Positive approach and negative withdrawal. These combine the bipolar ends of Temperament #2 and #4. Positive approach individuals are some of the most naturally effective people to be found.

Negative withdrawal individuals are some of the most problematic. They are not very easy to like. They get caught up in downward spirals, in which their negative behaviors lead others to become negative with them, which confirms what they thought in the first place: The world isn't a very good place to be.

It sounds like some people get a better shake, from early on. It's true. They do.

Threshold of Responsiveness (linear)

Threshold is a neurological concept. All cortical neurons have minimums; they won't respond unless that minimum is met. Minimum refers to the amount of bioelectrical energy needed to activate the neuron. The bioelectrical energy is carried by neurotransmitters. This dimension refers to the wide individual differences in the minimum needed. There are individuals who are impervious to a bomb exploding right beside them; there are others who can hear a whisper one hundred feet away. These differences are found in all of our senses: hearing, seeing, smelling, tasting, proprioceptive and touching. Also, there are within person differences. A person may be able to hear the whisper, but can't smell a dead mouse if she/he stepped on it.

These differences have major implications for occupational choices. A wine taster has to have very low thresholds for both tasting and smelling. A park ranger has to have acute hearing and smelling. Any attending medical person must have low thresholds for touch. A professional athlete must have finely honed proprioceptive (muscle and joint) senses. One of the things that defines occupations is differential sensory thresholds.

Intensity of Reaction (linear)

Once the threshold is crossed, the next individual difference is how strongly an individual responds to the s/s. We will use seeing a mouse in one's house. The low intensity respondent says "shoo, go away". The high intensity respondent jumps up on a chair, screams at the top of her/his voice and throws the closest utensil. People are forever counseling with the high I, saying such things as calm down, you are overreacting, get ahold of yourself. The lower I (not lowest) is considered a cool dude. So, there are motivational attributions assigned for this dimension as well. Finally, a pair of occupations that draw heavily on this temperament dimension: Police-lower I; Actresses/actors-Hi I.

Distractibility/Persistence (bipolar) and Attention Span (linear)

First, attention span. This refers to how long a person can focus on a task, when there are no distractions. Distractibility/Persistence refers to how long a person can stay focused (persist) on a task when there are distractions present. These two are not the same. There are those whose AS is short even when there are no distractions. That is coming from within the person. The second one—D/P—is wholly determined from without; the person is at the mercy of the immediate environment. These two are not diagnosed well for a number of the children who are classified as ADHD. Neurogenic etiology-AS-is very different from stimulogenic (D/P). Both pharmacological and environmental treatment is different. Finally, motivational attributions rear their ugly heads. D/P is seen as a total lack of discipline and/or willful. Low AS may be seen in the same fashion and/or as not caring, not taking responsibility for the tasks they know they have to do.

Rhythmicity (linear)

There are several segments of the gastrointestinal tract that use peristaltic (rhythmic) contractions to do their jobs; these run the length of the GI tract. There are great differences in just how rhythmic they are. When they are, we hardly know they are there. When they are not, they cause painful distress. Swallowing difficulties (reflux), digestive difficulties (heartburn, indigestion), small intestine difficulties (colitis) and bowel difficulties (constipation) are all related to irregular rhythms. So are certain breathing and cardiac difficulties. Babies and young children who have these are on their way to being difficult children to raise. If the child gets hungry in two hours in the morning, then three hours in the afternoon, and then the next day this reverses, what's a mother to do? It doesn't take long for mothers to start attributing motives to her young child. The only thing that can keep that from happening is for the mother to gain extraordinary knowledge of her child.

I trust that you can see how crucial understanding is for any of these temperaments. Our culture does not provide that for us.

I made reference to combinations earlier. Thomas, Chess, and Birch engaged in considerable studies with varying combinations of the nine. One of particular moment is what they called the difficult child. This child shows high activity, negative mood, high intensity, high distractibility and low rhythmicity. 75% of these children had come to the attention of mental health professionals by the time they were 14 years old. They also were able to do another sort: those who act out and those who act in. The former were significantly higher in negative mood and activity level. The latter were very high in withdrawing and intensity of reaction (high). Please appreciate that these data were gathered when these individuals were 3 mos, 6 mos and a year old, and show predictive strength 8 to 12 years later.

TEMPERAMENT DIMENSIONS

		Earlies					Recents						
Temperament Dimensions	**Self**	**E1**	**E2**	**E3**	**EAV**	**E:Self**	**R1**	**R2**	**R3**	**RAV**	**R-Self**	**RAV-EAV**	**E&R Totals**
1. Activity Level													
2. Approach-Withdrawal													
3. Adaptability													
4. Quality of Mood													
5. Threshold of Response													
6. Intensity of Reaction													
7. Distractability/Persistence													
8. Attention Span													
9. Rhythmicity													

Legend:
EAV: earlies rating average for each dimension
E-self: the difference between the earlies rating average and your rating on each dimension
RAV: recents rating average, for each dimension
R-self: the difference between the recents' rating average and your rating on each dimension
RAV-EAV: the difference between these two averages on each dimension
E & R Totals: Adding up the 3 earlies and 3 recents ratings on each dimension. Use the sums, not averages for this column.

Rater's name ______________________ Ratee's name ______________________

The Temperament Rating Scale

Please rate the person named as accurately as you can on each of the nine dimensions. Please make each rating by marking through the line exactly at that point which you think best characterizes how the person usually acts. Thank you.

1. Activity level. The level of activity the person usually maintains.

1	2	3	4	5
Low		Moderate		High

2. Approach-withdrawal. Does the person move toward or away from new/strange stimuli? (R)

1	2	3	4	5
Approach		Variable		Withdraw

3. Adaptability. Is it easy or does it take some time for this person to adjust to new situations, after the initial approach or withdrawal? (R)

1	2	3	4	5
Quickly		Average time		Slow

4. Quality of mood. To what extent is the person spontaneously cheerful or cranky? (R)

1	2	3	4	5
Positive		Variable		Negative

5. Threshold of responsiveness. Amount of stimulus energy to evoke a response.

1	2	3	4	5
Low		Moderate		High

6. Intensity of reaction. Strength of response to a stimulus/situation.

1	2	3	4	5
Mild		Variable		Strong

7. Distractibility/persistence. To what extent can an external stimulus set divert the person from an activity in which he/she is already engaged?

1	2	3	4	5
Distractible		Variable		Persistent

8. Attention span. The extent to which a person stays focused on a task.

1	2	3	4	5
Short		Variable		Long

9. Rhythmicity. To what extent are cyclic bodily processes (e.g., hunger, sleep) regular?

1	2	3	4	5
Irregular		Variable		Regular

Rater's name ______________________ Ratee's name ______________________

The Temperament Rating Scale

Please rate the person named as accurately as you can on each of the nine dimensions. Please make each rating by marking through the line exactly at that point which you think best characterizes how the person usually acts. Thank you.

1. Activity level. The level of activity the person usually maintains.

1	2	3	4	5
Low		Moderate		High

2. Approach-withdrawal. Does the person move toward or away from new/strange stimuli? (R)

1	2	3	4	5
Approach		Variable		Withdraw

3. Adaptability. Is it easy or does it take some time for this person to adjust to new situations, after the initial approach or withdrawal? (R)

1	2	3	4	5
Quickly		Average time		Slow

4. Quality of mood. To what extent is the person spontaneously cheerful or cranky? (R)

1	2	3	4	5
Positive		Variable		Negative

5. Threshold of responsiveness. Amount of stimulus energy to evoke a response.

1	2	3	4	5
Low		Moderate		High

6. Intensity of reaction. Strength of response to a stimulus/situation.

1	2	3	4	5
Mild		Variable		Strong

7. Distractibility/persistence. To what extent can an external stimulus set divert the person from an activity in which he/she is already engaged?

1	2	3	4	5
Distractible		Variable		Persistent

8. Attention span. The extent to which a person stays focused on a task.

1	2	3	4	5
Short		Variable		Long

9. Rhythmicity. To what extent are cyclic bodily processes (e.g., hunger, sleep) regular?

1	2	3	4	5
Irregular		Variable		Regular

Rater's name ______________________ Ratee's name ______________________

The Temperament Rating Scale

Please rate the person named as accurately as you can on each of the nine dimensions. Please make each rating by marking through the line exactly at that point which you think best characterizes how the person usually acts. Thank you.

1. Activity level. The level of activity the person usually maintains.

1	2	3	4	5
Low		Moderate		High

2. Approach-withdrawal. Does the person move toward or away from new/strange stimuli? (R)

1	2	3	4	5
Approach		Variable		Withdraw

3. Adaptability. Is it easy or does it take some time for this person to adjust to new situations, after the initial approach or withdrawal? (R)

1	2	3	4	5
Quickly		Average time		Slow

4. Quality of mood. To what extent is the person spontaneously cheerful or cranky? (R)

1	2	3	4	5
Positive		Variable		Negative

5. Threshold of responsiveness. Amount of stimulus energy to evoke a response.

1	2	3	4	5
Low		Moderate		High

6. Intensity of reaction. Strength of response to a stimulus/situation.

1	2	3	4	5
Mild		Variable		Strong

7. Distractibility/persistence. To what extent can an external stimulus set divert the person from an activity in which he/she is already engaged?

1	2	3	4	5
Distractible		Variable		Persistent

8. Attention span. The extent to which a person stays focused on a task.

1	2	3	4	5
Short		Variable		Long

9. Rhythmicity. To what extent are cyclic bodily processes (e.g., hunger, sleep) regular?

1	2	3	4	5
Irregular		Variable		Regular

Rater's name ____________________ Ratee's name ____________________

The Temperament Rating Scale

Please rate the person named as accurately as you can on each of the nine dimensions. Please make each rating by marking through the line exactly at that point which you think best characterizes how the person usually acts. Thank you.

1. Activity level. The level of activity the person usually maintains.

1	2	3	4	5
Low		Moderate		High

2. Approach-withdrawal. Does the person move toward or away from new/strange stimuli? (R)

1	2	3	4	5
Approach		Variable		Withdraw

3. Adaptability. Is it easy or does it take some time for this person to adjust to new situations, after the initial approach or withdrawal? (R)

1	2	3	4	5
Quickly		Average time		Slow

4. Quality of mood. To what extent is the person spontaneously cheerful or cranky? (R)

1	2	3	4	5
Positive		Variable		Negative

5. Threshold of responsiveness. Amount of stimulus energy to evoke a response.

1	2	3	4	5
Low		Moderate		High

6. Intensity of reaction. Strength of response to a stimulus/situation.

1	2	3	4	5
Mild		Variable		Strong

7. Distractibility/persistence. To what extent can an external stimulus set divert the person from an activity in which he/she is already engaged?

1	2	3	4	5
Distractible		Variable		Persistent

8. Attention span. The extent to which a person stays focused on a task.

1	2	3	4	5
Short		Variable		Long

9. Rhythmicity. To what extent are cyclic bodily processes (e.g., hunger, sleep) regular?

1	2	3	4	5
Irregular		Variable		Regular

Rater's name ____________________ Ratee's name ____________________

The Temperament Rating Scale

Please rate the person named as accurately as you can on each of the nine dimensions. Please make each rating by marking through the line exactly at that point which you think best characterizes how the person usually acts. Thank you.

1. Activity level. The level of activity the person usually maintains.

1	2	3	4	5
Low		Moderate		High

2. Approach-withdrawal. Does the person move toward or away from new/strange stimuli? (R)

1	2	3	4	5
Approach		Variable		Withdraw

3. Adaptability. Is it easy or does it take some time for this person to adjust to new situations, after the initial approach or withdrawal? (R)

1	2	3	4	5
Quickly		Average time		Slow

4. Quality of mood. To what extent is the person spontaneously cheerful or cranky? (R)

1	2	3	4	5
Positive		Variable		Negative

5. Threshold of responsiveness. Amount of stimulus energy to evoke a response.

1	2	3	4	5
Low		Moderate		High

6. Intensity of reaction. Strength of response to a stimulus/situation.

1	2	3	4	5
Mild		Variable		Strong

7. Distractibility/persistence. To what extent can an external stimulus set divert the person from an activity in which he/she is already engaged?

1	2	3	4	5
Distractible		Variable		Persistent

8. Attention span. The extent to which a person stays focused on a task.

1	2	3	4	5
Short		Variable		Long

9. Rhythmicity. To what extent are cyclic bodily processes (e.g., hunger, sleep) regular?

1	2	3	4	5
Irregular		Variable		Regular

Rater's name ______________________ Ratee's name ______________________

The Temperament Rating Scale

Please rate the person named as accurately as you can on each of the nine dimensions. Please make each rating by marking through the line exactly at that point which you think best characterizes how the person usually acts. Thank you.

1. Activity level. The level of activity the person usually maintains.

1	2	3	4	5
Low		Moderate		High

2. Approach-withdrawal. Does the person move toward or away from new/strange stimuli? (R)

1	2	3	4	5
Approach		Variable		Withdraw

3. Adaptability. Is it easy or does it take some time for this person to adjust to new situations, after the initial approach or withdrawal? (R)

1	2	3	4	5
Quickly		Average time		Slow

4. Quality of mood. To what extent is the person spontaneously cheerful or cranky? (R)

1	2	3	4	5
Positive		Variable		Negative

5. Threshold of responsiveness. Amount of stimulus energy to evoke a response.

1	2	3	4	5
Low		Moderate		High

6. Intensity of reaction. Strength of response to a stimulus/situation.

1	2	3	4	5
Mild		Variable		Strong

7. Distractibility/persistence. To what extent can an external stimulus set divert the person from an activity in which he/she is already engaged?

1	2	3	4	5
Distractible		Variable		Persistent

8. Attention span. The extent to which a person stays focused on a task.

1	2	3	4	5
Short		Variable		Long

9. Rhythmicity. To what extent are cyclic bodily processes (e.g., hunger, sleep) regular?

1	2	3	4	5
Irregular		Variable		Regular

CHAPTER

4

Interests

It can be argued that interests are the single most important component of the human being. They are the most consistent aspect. They are the most powerful sustained motivators. They require no external rewards. They may be the least complex in unfolding and reach fruition. They are at least as equal in bringing pleasure to the person as any other experience or process. Almost invariably their pursuit results in productive outcomes.

Individual differences in interests probably evidence a wider span than any other human characteristics. Thus, they are the best reminder for us of what we must understand, if we are going to truly appreciate our fellow humans.

Given the above, it is probably not a difficult task to appreciate the challenge of effectively measuring interests. Robert J. Gregory helps us out with this, in his discussion of various assessments and how they are used.

Vocational and Values Assessment

History, Principles, and Applications

Robert J. Gregory
Wheaton College, Wheaton, Illinois

In this chapter we examine approaches to the assessment of interests and values, broadly defined. Because they are formative in everything from work to worship, interests and values are fundamental to the identity of each individual. It is no accident that the adolescent who values aesthetic harmony later reveals an interest in literature and then pursues a vocation as English teacher. Nor is it surprising when a shy teenager with an analytic bent shows a passion for mathematics and becomes a computer scientist. The values held by persons shape their interests in life which, in turn, shape career choices. Lives possess a coherency that is explained, in part, by the influence of interests and values.

Values not only link the individual to the world of work, they are intertwined in moral, spiritual, and religious matters as well. Whether we favor or oppose capital punishment, whether we find life meaningful or merely chaotic, whether we seek or avoid religious practice—these matters we resolve based upon personal values. In sum, the choices we make in matters of work, spiritual life, and personal conduct are not random, they are bound together by common threads that we call interests and values.

Assessment of Interests and Work Values

A problem faced by many young adults is that their values are unstated and their interests are unexplored. Furthermore, they lack knowledge about career options. In these cases, career selection can arouse anxiety, and perhaps it should. Lowman (1991) has noted that the process of finding a vocation can be as complex and as difficult as choosing a mate. The dilemma of career choice is not limited to young adults entering the job market, but also vexes older workers who are dissatisfied with their careers. Fortunately, a large array of tests and guidance approaches are available to help individuals identify values, interests, and potential career choices, as reviewed in this topic.

In Topic 12A, Assessment of Interests and Work Values, we survey the measurement of interests and work-related values. The focus here is on the world of work and the use of specialized tests for career assessment and advising. In Topic 12B, Values in Moral, Spiritual, and Religious Development, we introduce the reader to methods and concerns in the assessment of moral, spiritual, and religious dimensions of the individual.

An Overview of Interest Assessment

In most applications of psychological testing, the goals of assessment are reasonably clear. For example, intelligence testing helps predict school performance; aptitude testing foretells potential for accomplishment; and personality testing provides information about social and emotional functioning. But what is the purpose of interest assessment? Why would a psychologist recommend it? What can a client expect to gain from a survey of his or her interests?

Interest assessment promotes two compatible goals: life satisfaction and vocational productivity. It is nearly self-evident that a good fit between individual interests and chosen vocation will help foster personal life satisfaction.

After all, when work is interesting we are more likely to experience personal fulfillment as well. In addition, persons who are satisfied with their work are more likely to be productive. Thus, employees and employers both stand to gain from the artful application of interest assessment. Several useful instruments exist for this purpose, and we will review the most widely used interest inventories later.

In the selection of employees, the consideration of personal interests may be of great practical significance to employers and therefore circumstantially relevant to the job candidates as well. We may sketch out a rough equation as follows: productivity = ability × interest. In other words, high ability in a specific field does not guarantee success; neither does high interest level. The best predictions are possible when both variables are considered together. Thus, employers have good reason to determine if a potential employee is well matched to the position; the employee should like to know as well.

We begin this section with a critical examination of major interest tests. The six instruments chosen for review include the following:

- The Strong Interest Inventory (SII), the latest revision of the well-known Strong Vocational Interest Blank (SVIB).
- The Jackson Vocational Interest Survey (JVIS), a test that embodies modern methods for scale construction
- The Kuder General Interest Survey (KGIS), an instrument that incorporates a divergent philosophy of test construction
- The Vocational Preference Inventory (VPI), which measures six widely used vocational themes
- The Self-Directed Search (SDS), a self-administered and self-scored guide to exploring career options
- The Campbell Interest and Skill Survey (CISS), a recent and appealing test that is simple in format but sophisticated in execution

The review of prominent interest tests is followed by the related topic of assessment in career and work values.

INVENTORIES FOR INTEREST ASSESSMENT

Strong Interest Inventory (SII)

The Strong Interest Inventory (SII) is the latest revision of the Strong Vocational Interest Blank (SVIB), one of the oldest and most prominent instruments in psychological testing (Hansen, 1992). We can best understand the SII by studying the history of its esteemed predecessor, the SVIB. In particular, we need to review the guiding assumptions used in the contruction of the SVIB which have been carried over into the SII.

The first edition of the SVIB appeared in 1927, eight years after E. K. Strong formulated the essential procedures for measuring occupational interests while attending a seminar at the Carnegie Institute of Technology (Campbell, 1971; Strong, 1927). In constructing the SVIB, Strong employed two little-used techniques in measurement. First, the examinee was asked to express liking or disliking for a large and varied sample of occupations, educational disciplines, personality types, and recreational activities. Second, the responses were *empirically keyed* for specific occupations. In an empirical key, a specific response (e.g., liking to roller skate) is assigned to the scale for a particular occupation only if successful persons in that occupation tend to answer in that manner more often than comparison subjects.

Although Strong did not express his underlying assumptions in a simple and straightforward manner, it is clear that the theoretical foundation for the SVIB derives from a *typological, trait-oriented conception of personality.* Tzeng (1987) has identified the following basic assumptions in the development and application of the SVIB:

1. Each occupation has a desirable pattern of *interests and personality characteristics* among its workers. The ideal pattern is represented by successful people in that occupation.
2. Each individual has relatively stable interests and personality traits. When such interests and traits match the desirable interest patterns of the occupation the individual has a high probability to enter that occupation and be more likely to succeed in it.
3. It is highly possible to differentiate individuals in a given occupation from others-in-general in terms of the desirable patterns of interests and traits for that occupation.

Strong constructed the scales of his inventory by contrasting the responses of several specific occupational criterion groups with those of a people-in-general group. The subjects for each criterion group were workers in that occupation who were satisfied with their jobs and who had been so employed for at least three years. The items which differentiated the two groups, keyed in the appropriate direction, were selected for each occupational scale. For example, if members of a specific occupational group disliked "buying merchandise for a store" more often than people-in-general, then that item (keyed in the dislike direction) was added to the scale for that occupation.

The first SVIB consisted of 420 items and a mere handful of occupational scales (Strong, 1927). Separate editions for men and women followed shortly. The inventory has undergone numerous revisions over the years (Tzeng, 1987), culminating in the modern instrument known as the Strong Interest Inventory (Campbell, 1974; Hansen, 1992; Hansen & Campbell, 1985).

TABLE 12.1
Characteristic Items From the Strong Interest Inventory

Mark *Like, Indifferent,* or *Dislike* next to the following items.

1. Driving a truck	______
2. Being a fish and game officer	______
3. Chemistry	______
4. Doing applied research	______
5. Acting in a drama	______
6. Magazines about music	______
7. Sociology	______
8. Fundraising for charities	______
9. Buying goods for a store	______
10. People who are leaders	______
11. Regular work hours	______
12. Assertive people	______

Although the Strong Interest Inventory (SII) was fashioned according to the same philosophy as the SVIB, the latest revision departs from its predecessors in three crucial ways:

1. The SII merges the men's and women's forms into a single edition.
2. The SII introduces a theoretical framework to guide the organization and interpretation of scores, as discussed below.
3. The SII incorporates a substantial increase in the number of occupational scales, particularly in the vocational/technical areas underrepresented in the SVIB.

The SII consists of 317 items grouped into seven sections. In the first five sections, the examinee records "Like," "Indifferent," or "Dislike" for occupations, school subjects, activities, leisure activities, and contact with different types of persons (Table 12.1). A sixth part requires the examinee to express a preference between paired items (e.g., dealing with things versus dealing with people). The seventh section consists of self-descriptive statements which the examinee marks "Yes," "No," or "?".

The SII can only be scored by prepaid answer sheets or booklets that are mailed or faxed to the publisher, or through purchase of a software system that provides on-site scoring for immediate results. The results consist of a lengthy printout which is organized according to several themes. All scores are expressed as standard scores with a mean of 50 and an SD of 10. Normative results for men and women are reported separately, but cross-sex comparisons can be achieved by simple visual transposition.

At the most global level are the six General Occupational Theme Scores, namely, Realistic, Investigative, Artistic, Social, Enterprising, and Conventional. These theme scores were based upon the theoretical analysis of Holland (1966, 1985ab) whose work we discuss later. Each theme score pertains to a major interest area which describes both *a work environment and a type of person.* For example, persons scoring high on the Realistic theme are generally quite robust, have difficulty expressing their feelings, and prefer to work outdoors with heavy machinery. Within the theme scores can be found *25 Basic Interest Scales* such as Adventure, Mathematics, and Social Science. The interest scales are empirically derived and consist of substantially intercorrelated items.

The most specific results consist of *211 scores* for the Occupational Scales. In the 1985 revision of the SII, these scales were constructed in the usual manner by comparing responses of persons employed in the given occupation versus samples of men-in-general and women-in-general (Hansen, 1992; Hansen & Campbell, 1985). Sample sizes for the criterion groups ranged from 60 to 420, with most groups containing 200 or more persons. The criterion groups consisted of persons between the ages of 25 and 60, satisfied with their occupation, meeting certain minimum standards of successful employment, and employed in the given occupation for at least three years. Standardization of the 1985 version involved the testing of over 140,000 persons, of whom only 50,000 met the criteria for scale development.

A recent innovation on the SII is the addition of personal style scales (Harmon, Hansen, Borgen, & Hammer, 1994). These are designed to measure preferences for broad styles of living and working. These scales assist in vocational guidance by showing *level of comfort with distinctive styles.* The four style scales are:

1. *Work Style,* on which a high score indicates a preference to work with people and a low score signifies an interest in ideas, data, and things;
2. *Learning Environment,* on which a high score indicates a preference for *academic* learning environments and a low score indicates a preference for more *applied* learning activities;
3. *Leadership Style,* on which a high score indicates comfort in taking charge of others and a low score indicates uneasiness; and
4. *Risk Taking/Adventure,* on which a high score indicates a preference for risky and adventurous activities as opposed to safe and predictable activities.

The personal style scales each have a mean of 50 and a standard deviation of 10. Note that these are truly bipolar scales where each pole is distinct and meaningful.

Evaluation of the SII

The SII represents the culmination of over 50 years of study, involving literally thousands of research reports and hundreds of thousands of respondents. In evaluating this instrument, we can only outline basic trends in the research, referring the reader to other sources for details (Tzeng, 1987; Campbell, 1971; Campbell & Hansen, 1981; Hansen, 1984, 1987, 1992; Hansen & Campbell, 1985). We should also point out that evaluations of the reliability and validity of the SII are based in part upon its similarity to the SVIB, for which a huge amount of technical data exists.

Based upon test-retest studies, the reliability of the SII-SVIB has proved to be exceptionally good in the short run, with one- and two-week stability coefficients for the occupational scales generally in the .90s. When the test-retest interval is years or decades, the correlations drop to the .60s and .70s for the occupational scales, except for respondents who were older (over age 25) upon first testing. For younger respondents first tested as adolescents, the median test-retest correlation after 15 years is around .50 (Lubinski, Benbow, & Ryan, 1995). But for older respondents, first tested after the age of 25, the median test-retest correlation 10 to 20 years later is a phenomenal .80 (Campbell, 1971). Apparently, by the time we pass through young adulthood, personal interests become extremely stable. The questions on the SII-SVIB capture that stability in the occupational scores, providing support for the trait conception of personality upon which these instruments were based.

The validity of the SII-SVIB is premised largely on the ability of the initial occupational profile to predict the occupation eventually pursued. Strong (1955) reported that the chances were about two in three that people would be in occupations predicted by high occupational scale scores, and about one in five that respondents would be in occupations for which they had shown little interest when tested. Although other researchers have quibbled with the exact proportions (Dolliver, Irvin, & Bigley, 1972), it is clear that the SII-SVIB has impressive hit rates in predicting occupational entry. The instrument functions even better in predicting the occupations that an examinee will *not* enter. In a recent study, Donnay and Borgen (1996) provide evidence for construct validity by demonstrating strong overall differentiation between 50 occupational groups on the SII:

> The big picture is that people in diverse occupations show large and predictable differences in likes and dislikes, whether in terms of vocational interests or in terms of personal styles. And the Strong provides valid, structural, and comprehensive measures of these differences (p. 290).

The SII is used mainly with high school and college students, and adults seeking vocational guidance or advice on continued education. Because most students' interests are undeveloped and unstabilized prior to age 13 or 14, the SII is not recommended for use below high school level. As evident in the reliability data reported above, the SII becomes increasingly valuable with older subjects, and it is not unusual to see middle-aged persons use the results of this instrument for guidance in career change. Although rarely used, the forced-choice item format has the advantage of reducing the impact of social desirability upon test results. A second distinctive feature of the JVIS is that Jackson used a rational and theory-guided method in the derivation of scales, as opposed to the empirical approach found in most other instruments. As a result of these two features, the JVIS scales possess a greater independence from one another than found on other instruments and are also quite factorially pure. As evidence of factorial homogeneity of the scales, biserial correlations between item endorsements and scale scores are typically in the high .60s and low .70s.

The JVIS is normed on a very large sample—approximately 8,000 high school and college students. However, these subjects consist mainly of students from Pennsylvania and the Province of Ontario, so their representation of the general population is questionable. Reliability is excellent, at least in the short range, with one- to two-week test-retest coefficients typically in the mid-.80s. Based on an eclectic group of studies reported in the *Manual,* concurrent and predictive validity appear promising, but additional studies are needed to bolster confidence in this instrument (Shepard, 1989).

Kuder General Interest Survey

The KGIS is unique among interest inventories in that its target population is restricted to adolescents in grades *six through twelve* (Kuder, 1975). The test requires only a sixth-grade reading level and may be administered by the classroom teacher and hand-scored on site. Thus, the KGIS is well suited to the development of educational and vocational goals in the early formative years of adolescence.

The KGIS is also unusual in its methodology: The inventory uses a forced-response triad format to measure interests. Specifically, each item on the test requires the examinee to indicate most- and least-liked alternatives from three statements. This forced-choice approach is particularly suited to identifying examinees who have not answered the items sincerely.

The 168-item inventory produces 10 interest scores that are largely ipsative in nature. The reader will recall that scores on an ipsative test reflect intraindividual variability rather than interindividual variability. With the KGIS, comparison to an external reference group is of secondary importance in determining scores.[1] Thus, a high score in one interest area mainly means that the examinee pre-

[1]In truth, the KGIS is only partially ipsative. Some of the item triads are scored for more than one scale.

ferred that area more often than the others in the forced-choice items.

The 10 scales reflect broad areas of interest: Outdoor, Mechanical, Computational, Scientific, Persuasive, Artistic, Literary, Musical, Social Service, and Clerical. An eleventh scale, the Verification Scale, is designed to determine the sincerity of the responses. The manual reports extensive test-retest, internal consistency, and stability data based on a sample of 9,819 students in grades 6 through 12. The six-week test-retest and internal consistency data are generally acceptable, with the older students showing higher test-retest correlations. The possible exception to good reliability is the Persuasive Scale (pertinent to sales positions), which shows test-retest correlations of .69 and .73, respectively, for boys and girls in grades 6 through 8.

Stability data over a four-year follow-up are less impressive. The mean stability coefficient is only .50, and for low-IQ subjects (below 100) it is even lower, as low as .19 for the Clerical Scale. This is unfortunate because low-IQ adolescents would be more likely to enter clerical fields than high-IQ adolescents. Yet, measurement of clerical interests is highly unstable for precisely this group.

Comment on the KGIS and Other Interest Inventories

Considering the difficulty of the task it undertakes—measuring the broad interest patterns of adolescents—the KGIS performs at an acceptable level. In grades 6 through 8, results of the KGIS may spur students to explore new experiences pertinent to their measured interests; in grades 9 and 10, results may help students plan high school courses; and in grades 11 and 12, the results can help students make tentative vocational choices.

But the KGIS suffers the same pivotal shortcoming of all existing interest inventories, a total inattention to opportunity. Williams and Williams (1985) have expressed this point well:

> . . . for those specifically looking for a measure of interest, the Kuder is definitely an acceptable measure. But interest is only one prong in the triumvirate of interest-ability-opportunity. The most important prong, opportunity, has generated the least psychometric interest. That this would be so is not surprising. Opportunity is by far the hardest construct to define, but those who deal in career counseling should never ignore it, regardless of the difficulty in measurement and definition.

We remind the reader that the inattention to opportunity is common to all interest measures, although it is perhaps a more serious problem for the KGIS because this instrument is used with persons who have not yet entered the job market.

Vocational Preference Inventory

The Vocational Preference Inventory is an objective, paper-and-pencil personality interest inventory used in vocational and career assessment (Holland, 1985c). The VPI measures eleven dimensions, including the six personality-environment themes of Realistic, Investigative, Artistic, Social, Enterprising, and Conventional, and five additional dimensions of Self-Control, Masculinity/Femininity, Status, Infrequency, and Acquiescence. The test items consist of 160 occupational titles toward which the examinee expresses a feeling by marking *y* (yes) or *n* (no). The VPI is a brief test (15 to 30 minutes) and is intended for persons 14 years and older with normal intelligence.

Holland proposes that personality traits tend to cluster into a small number of vocationally relevant patterns, called types. For each personality type there is also a corresponding work environment best suited to that type. According to Holland, there are six types: Realistic, Investigative, Artistic, Social, Enterprising, and Conventional. This is sometimes known as the **RIASEC model,** in reference to the first letters of the six types. The types are idealizations which few people (or environments) fit completely. Nonetheless, Holland believes that most individuals tend to resemble one type more than the others. In addition, individuals show a lesser degree of resemblance to a second and third type as well.

We can summarize the personality-environment types as follows:

- *Realistic:* athletic, lacks verbal and interpersonal skills, and prefers "hands-on" or outdoors vocations such as mechanic, farmer, or electrician
- *Investigative:* task-oriented thinker with unconventional attitudes who fits well in scientific and scholarly positions such as chemist, physicist, or biologist
- *Artistic:* individualistic, avoids conventional situations, and prefers aesthetic pursuits
- *Social:* uses social competencies to solve problems, likes to help others, and prefers teaching or helping professions
- *Enterprising:* a leader with good selling skills who fits well in business and managerial positions
- *Conventional:* conforming and prefers structured roles such as bank teller or computer operator

The six themes in the RIASEC system can be arranged in a hexagon with similar themes side-by-side and dissimilar themes opposite one another, as depicted in Figure 12.1.

Test-retest reliability coefficients for the six major scales range from .89 to .97. VPI norms are based upon large convenience samples of college students and employed adults from earlier VPI editions. The characteristics of the standardization sample are not well defined which makes the norms somewhat difficult to interpret (Rounds, 1985).

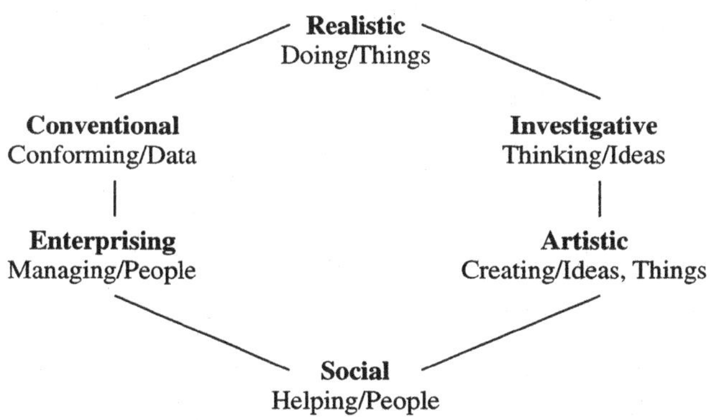

FIGURE 12.1
Holland's Hexagonal Model of Occupational Themes
Source: Reprinted with permission from Lowman, R. L. (1991). *The clinical practice of career assessment: Interests, abilities, and personality.* Washington, DC: American Psychological Association. Copyright © 1991 by the American Psychological Association.

The validity of the VPI is essentially tied to the validity of Holland's (1985a) hexagonal model of vocational interests. Literally hundreds of studies have examined this model from different perspectives. We will cite trends and representative studies. The reader is referred to Holland (1985c) and Walsh and Holland (1992) for more details.

Several VPI studies have investigated a key assumption of Holland's theory—that individuals tend to move toward environments which are congruent with their personality types. If this assumption is correct, then the real-world match between work environments and personality types of employees should be substantial. We should expect to find that Realistic environments have mainly Realistic employees, Social environments have mainly Social employees, and so on. Research on this topic has followed a straightforward methodology: Subjects are tested with the VPI and classified by their Holland types (using up to six letters); the work environments of the subjects are then independently classified by an appropriate environmental measure; finally, the degree of congruence between persons and environments is computed. In better studies, a correction for chance agreement is also applied.

Using his hexagonal model, Holland has developed occupational codes as a basis for classifying work environments (Gottfredson & Holland, 1989; Holland, 1966, 1978, 1985c). For example, landscape architect is coded as RIA (Realistic, Investigative, Artistic) because this occupation is known to be a technical, skilled trade (Realistic component) that requires scientific skills (Investigative component) and also demands artistic aptitude (Artistic component). The Realistic component is listed first because it is the most important for landscape architect, whereas the Investigative and Artistic components are of secondary and tertiary importance, respectively. Some other occupations and their codes are taxi driver (RSE), mathematics teacher (ISC), reporter (ASE), police officer (SRE), real estate appraiser (ECS), and secretary (CSA). In a similar manner, Holland has also worked out codes for different college majors.

One approach to congruence studies is to compare VPI results of students or workers with the Holland codes which correspond to their college majors or occupations. For example, VPI Holland codes for a sample of police officers should consist mainly of profiles that begin with S and should contain a larger-than-chance proportion of specifically SRE profiles. Furthermore, the degree of congruence should be related to the degree of expressed satisfaction with that line of work or study.

Research with college students provides *strong support for the congruence prediction:* Students tend to select and enter college majors which are congruent with their primary personality types (Holland, 1985a; Walsh & Holland, 1992). Thus, Artistic types tend to major in art, Investigative types tend to major in biology, and Enterprising types tend to major in business, to cite just a few examples. These results provide strong support for the VPI and the theory upon which it is based.

This short review has barely touched the surface of supportive validity studies with the VPI. Walsh and Holland (1992) cite several additional lines of research which buttress the validity of this test. But not all studies of the VPI affirm its validity. Furnham, Toop, Lewis, and Fisher (1995) failed to find a relationship between person-environment (P-E) "fit" and job satisfaction, a key theoretical underpinning of the test. According to Holland's theory, the better the P-E fit, the greater should be job satisfaction. In three British samples, the relationships were weak or nonexistent, suggesting that the VPI does not "travel well" in cultures outside of the United States.

Although we have emphasized mainly the strengths of the VPI up to this point, even the authors of the test acknowledge that there is room for improvement. For example, Walsh and Holland (1992) cite the following weaknesses of the VPI: (1) the notions about vocational environments are only partially tested; (2) the hypotheses about the person-environment interactions need considerable additional research work; (3) the formulations about personal development have received some support but need more comprehensive examinations; (4) the classification of occupations may differ depending on the device used to assess the personality types; and (5) there are personal and environmental contingencies that are currently outside the scope of the theory.

The last weakness is perhaps the most serious. After all, the VPI assessment approach does not currently recognize any role for education, intelligence, and special aptitudes, except insofar as these factors might indirectly bear upon personality and vocational interests. Yet, common sense dictates that intellectual ability will have a great deal to do with vocational satisfaction for some professions, independent of the match between personality type and work environment. For further discussion of the VPI and the theory upon which it is based, the interested reader is referred to Gottfredson (1990), Holland (1990), and Holland and Gottfredson (1990).

Self-Directed Search

Holland has always shown a keen interest in the practical applications of his research on vocational development. Consistent with this interest, he developed the Self-Directed Search, a highly practical, brief test that is appealing in its simplicity (Holland, 1985ab). As the name suggests, the Self-Directed Search is designed to be a self-administered, self-scored, and self-interpreted test of vocational interest. The SDS measures the six RIASEC vocational themes described previously.

The SDS consists of dichotomous items which the examinee marks "like" or "dislike" (or "yes" or "no") in four sections: (1) Activities (six scales of 11 items each); (2) Competencies (six scales of 11 items each); (3) Occupations (six scales of 14 items each); and (4) Self-Estimates (two sets of six ratings). For each section, the face-valid items are grouped by RIASEC themes. For each theme, the total number of "like" and "yes" answers is combined with the self-estimates of ability to come up with a total theme score. The SDS takes 30 to 50 minutes for completion and is intended for persons 15 years and older.

The RIASEC themes on the SDS showed test-retest reliabilities that range from .56 to .95 and internal consistencies that range from .70 to .93. Norms for SDS scales and codes are reported for pooled convenience samples of 4,675 high school students, 3,355 college students, and 4,250 employed adults ages 16 through 24 (Holland, 1985ab). However, SDS results are typically interpreted in an individualized, ipsative manner ("Is this occupation a good fit for this client?"), so normative data are of limited relevance.

The SDS is available in a hand-scored paper-and-pencil version and a computerized version as well. Unfortunately, the paper-and-pencil version is prone to a 16 percent clerical error rate when used by high school students (Holland, 1985ab). The user-friendly microcomputer test is probably the preferred version because of the ease of administration and the error-free scoring and interpretation.

When a subject takes the SDS, the three highest theme scores are used to denote a summary code. For example, a person whose three highest scores were on Investigative, Artistic, and Realistic would have a summary code of IAR. In a separate booklet distributed with the text—the *Occupations Finder*—the examinee can look up his or her summary code and find a list of occupations which provide the best "fit." For example, an examinee with an IAR summary code would learn that he or she most closely resembles persons in the following occupations: anthropologist, astronomer, chemist, pathologist, and physicist. The test booklet contains additional information which helps the examinee explore relevant career options.

The SDS serves a very useful purpose in providing a quick and simple format for prompting young persons to examine career alternatives. By eliminating the time-consuming process of administration, scoring, interpretation, and counselor feedback, the test makes it possible for a wide audience to receive an introductory level of career counseling. Holland (1985ab) proposes that the SDS is appropriate for up to 50 percent of students and adults who might desire career guidance. Presumably, the other 50 percent would find the SDS an insufficient basis for career exploration. Holland (1985ab) rightfully warns users to consider many sources of information in career choice and not to rely too heavily on test scores per se. Levinson (1990) discusses the integration of SDS data with other psychoeducational data to make specific vocational recommendations for high school students.

The validity of the SDS is linked to the validity of the hexagonal model of personality and environments upon which the test is based. One aspect of validity, then, is whether the model makes predictions which are confirmed by SDS results in the real world. In general, the results from over 400 studies support the construct validity of the SDS (Dumenci, 1995; Holland, 1985ab, 1987).

One approach to construct validity is to determine whether the relationships between SDS scales make theoretical sense. As is true of the VPI, the six RIASEC themes of the SDS can be arranged in a hexagon with similar themes side by side and dissimilar themes opposite one another. For example, in Figure 12.2, Artistic and Investigative themes are adjacent. It is not difficult to imagine one person combining these two themes in personality and work environment, so we would predict a moderate positive correlation between them. In a general reference sample of 175 women ages 26 to 65, Holland (1985ab) found that scores on these two themes correlated modestly, $r = .26$, as would be expected. The reader will also notice that the Investigative and Enterprising themes are opposite one another, signifying the huge disparities in these two occupational motifs. These themes should be uncorrelated. In fact, scores on these two themes correlated very little, $r = -.02$. In general, the correlations found in Figure 12.2 make theoretical sense; these findings support the construct validity of the SDS.

The predictive validity of the SDS has been investigated in several dozen studies which are summarized by Holland (1985ab, 1987). The typical methodology for these studies is that SDS high-point codes for large samples of students are compared with the first letter of their occupational choices (or aspirations) one to three years later. Overall, the findings indicate that the SDS has moderate to high predictive efficiency, depending upon the age

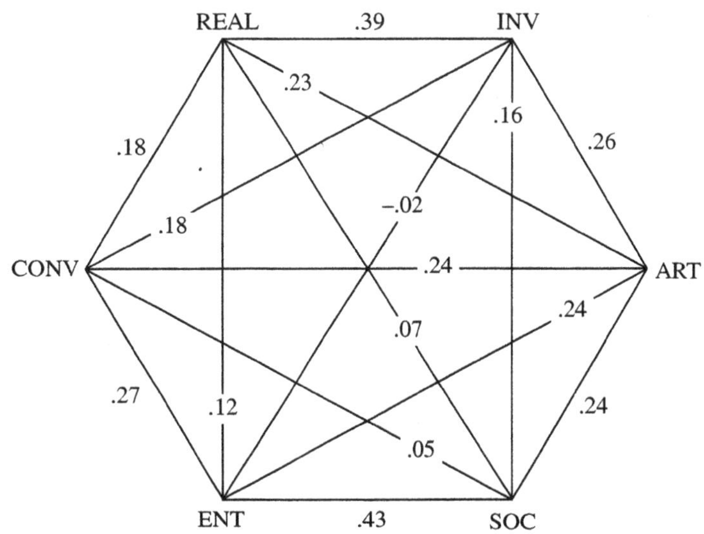

FIGURE 12.2
SDS Hexagonal Model and Correlations between Scales for 175 Women Ages 26–65
Source: Adapted from the *Self-Directed Search Professional Manual* by John L. Holland, Ph.D.

of the sample (hit rates go up with age), the length of the time interval (hit rates go down with time), and the specific category predicted (hit rates are better for Investigative and Social predictions) (Gottfredson & Holland, 1975).

Correlations between SDS scales and a wide range of other psychological measures (e.g., personality, aptitudes, and values) also serve to define the meaning of SDS scales and therefore help to validate the test (Holland, 1985ab, 1987). For example, a study by Costa, McCrae, and Holland (1984) investigated the relationship between SDS scales and the NEO Personality Inventory for a sample of 217 men and 144 women ages 21 to 89. The Investigative and Artistic scales from the SDS showed strong positive correlations with the NEO Openness scale—a measure of openness to experience in the areas of fantasy, feelings, actions, and ideas. The Social and Enterprising scales from the SDS showed strong correlations with the NEO Extraversion scale—a measure of outward-directness and sociability. The Realistic and Conventional scales from the SDS revealed only trivial correlations with the NEO scales. Overall, the observed correlations were consistent with the interpretation of the I, A, S, and E scales and provide a good support for their validity. Although results for this study failed to support the validity of the R and C scales, many other investigations have yielded confirmatory findings (Holland, 1985ab). Schinka, Dye, and Curtiss (1997) provide a thoughtful analysis and discussion of the relationship between NEO dimensions and the SDS scales.

CHAPTER

5

Adult Personality I: Robert Ornstein

Ornstein wanted to accomplish four things, in writing about adult personality differences:

1. He wanted to integrate temperament data with adult personality dimensions.
2. He wanted to directly incorporate relevant brain-behavior linkages into personality theory.
3. He wanted to use as few dimensions as possible (he wound up with three bipolar dimensions).
4. He wanted to show that personality abnormalities (disorders) were much more a continuous extension from normal functioning than a discontinuous departure. For each bipolar personality dimension, when extended, would be one of the six major disorders.

The following are his three bipolar dimensions and their extensions. The dimensions are in the center, and the associated disorders flank on either side of the three:

Hysteria: Low Gain vs High Gain: Anxiety
Obsessive compulsive: Deliberator vs Liberator: Schizophrenia
Mania: Positive Approach vs Negative Withdrawal: Depression

Each of these are highlighted in the following summary.

ORNSTEIN'S BIPOLAR PERSONALITY DIMENSIONS

DIMENSION #1: HIGH GAIN vs. LOW GAIN

(amount of needed external stimulation)

HIGH GAIN	LOW GAIN
• need less stimulation • lower thresholds for stimulation • more proficient RAS • prefer internal stimulation • cognitive introvert • quiet	• need more stimulation • higher thresholds for stimulation • less proficient RAS • prefer external stimulation • social extrovert • boisterous
Dimensions of stimulation (Maddi): • introceptive (generated internally, exercise, eating) • cortical (generated in the brain, reading, thinking)	• prefers extroceptive (other people, drugs, reading, risk taking) • likes intensity • likes variation

ASSOCIATED DISORDERS **ANXIETY**	**HYSTERIA**
• always worried • catatonia (extreme reaction to overload) • dysthemia • stupor	• increasing denial • direct disassociate repression

DIMENSION #2: DELIBERATOR vs. LIBERATOR

(caudate nucleus - sorts input/gatekeeper)

DELIBERATOR	LIBERATOR
• regulates activity • plans • difficulty in free association • can wall off judgments associated to goals • must have order • fear of safety • only answer to stress and fear is more order	• free spirits • easily free associates • changeable • fluid • more creative • disorganized structure to perceptions

ASSOCIATED DISORDERS **OBSESSIVE COMPULSIVE DISORDER**	**SCHIZOPHRENIA**
Caused when caudate nucleus breaks down • frontal lobes participate in process of checking action worry circuit stays on • degree of checking is extreme • extreme version of normal behavior • caudate nucleus acts as data input controller • highly deliberate restriction of thought	Caused when overwhelmed by excess experiences • severe disorganization of one's mental abilities • delusions (often of being spied upon) • hallucinations • overinclusion • no separation between self and world (skinlessness) • always distracted

ORNSTEIN'S BIPOLAR PERSONALITY DIMENSIONS
DIMENSION #3: POSITIVE APPROACH vs. NEGATIVE WITHDRAWAL
(positive/negative - quality of mood temperament)
(approach/withdrawal temperament)

POSITIVE APPROACH	NEGATIVE WITHDRAWAL
• enthusiastic • lifelong characteristics • durable • internal orientation • brings out positive responses in others	• cynical • self-fulfilling prophecy • external orientation • brings out worst in others
ASSOCIATED DISORDERS **MANIA**	**DEPRESSION**
• non-stop movement and thinking (flight) • in extreme situations, includes motor connections • uncontrolled euphoria • unbounded enthusiasm • no limits recognized	• triggered by significant loss (including loss of self) • overwhelming immobility • sadness • pain centers increasingly activated pain centers—thalamus and cortex segments in brain

CHAPTER 6

Adult Personality II: Myers-Briggs

Isabel Briggs Myers was a student of Carl Jung who was a student of Sigmund Freud. Based upon some of Freud's ideas regarding personality structure, Jung developed the concept of Introversion-Extraversion. This dimension is now considered the most universal one, having been found in every tribe and society so far studied, Myers in turn, retranslated this dimension into a personality assessment component, and it became a part of the Myers-Briggs Type Indicator. She developed two others of Jung's conceptual dimensions (Sensing-Intuition and Thinking-Feeling) and incorporated them into the MBTI. Finally, Isabel and her mother, Kathryn Briggs, designed a fourth bipolar dimension: Judging-Perceiving. The MBTI is now the most widely used personality assessment in the world (over 3,000,000 took it in 2001). It has been found most useful in looking at individual differences in relationships and in group development.

Since all of you will be taking it for use in one of your projects, the manual entitled *Introduction to Type,* by Isabel Briggs Myers, is included in the course as one of the required texts. As she points out, it identifies different kinds of people who are interested in different things, are drawn to different fields, and often find it hard to understand each other.

PART 3

Gender Differences: Primitive Gender Roles, Brain Lateralization, Gender Rearing and Contemporary Gender Roles

There are some fascinating structural differences in females' and males' brains. The linkages between these structural and behavioral differences have now been rather well established. Some of these behavioral differences are present at birth, and they become stimuli for differential treatment. The cultural view of what constitutes femaleness and maleness is activated by simply knowing which the newborn is. These brain and cultural influences work together to create a 'manifest destiny' for whichever sex the infant happens to be.

But how did these brain differences and cultural gender views come to be? Cultural anthropologists suggest that gender roles came first, developing somewhere in the mid-Pleistocene period, and were tied to simple functional differences between males and females. These, in turn, provided a basis for a strict division of labor between the two sexes. Those individuals who did not do their gender jobs very well either did not survive or did not give birth. Survival of the fittest was a Gender-differentiated survival. This differentiation was anchored in lateralization of the brain hemispheres, with left female orientation and right male orientation.

It appears that the gender process started with the formation of primitive gender roles, which over several thousand years led to hemispheric lateralization, which increased the probability of gender differentiation, aided by the ongoing cultural gendered orientation. Quite stable (traditional) gender roles found a cultural home, and were perpetrated through gender training and brain dispositions. Though there have been behavioral changes, the basic system is still essentially intact.

CHAPTER

7

Gender Differences: General

There is general consensus that for around 15,000 years, early homo sapiens engaged in quite stable and strongly sanctioned roles for men and women. For women, there were three primary roles: homemaker, health manager and helpmeet. For men, there were two primary roles: provider and protector. These roles will be defined and discussed in the first selection.

In the second selection, John Pfeiffer explores how gender differences are reflected in the ways that men and women talk with each other. Nesbitt does a check to see if anything has changed, gender-outlook wise, from 1968 to 1998.

Girl Talk ⇄ Boy Talk

In an Average Conversation, Women Ask 70 Percent of the Questions and Men Interrupt 96 Percent of the Time.

JOHN PFEIFFER

An investigator, pencil in hand, is transcribing two minutes of an "unobtrusively" recorded coffee-shop conversation between two university students, male and female—listening intently, making out words and pronunciations, noting hesitations, timing utterances. The tape whirs in reverse for a replay and then again, eight replays in all. Part of the final transcript:

Andrew: *It's about time uh that my family* really *went on a vacation* (pause) *y'know my father goes places all the time* (prolonged syllable) *but he y'know goes on business like he'll go ta' Tokyo for the afternoon 'n he'll get there at* (stammer) *at ten in the morning 'n catch a nine o'clock flight leaving . . .*

(two-second pause)

Betsy: *That sounds fantastic* (pause) *not everybody can jus' spend a day in someplace-* (interruption)

Andrew: *Well, we've already established the fact that um y'know he's not just* anyone.

(eight-second pause)

Betsy: *Don't you I* (stammer) *well it seems to me you you you probably have such an um interesting background that you must y'know have trouble finding um people uh like to talk to if you-* (interruption)

Andrew: *Most definitely . . .*

Candace West and Don Zimmerman, the researchers who analyzed these recordings, were particularly interested in the interruptions. The pattern is typical. According to these University of California sociologists, it held for all 11 two-person, cross-sex conversations recorded mainly in public places: Males accounted for some 96 percent of the interruptions. In same-sex conversations males also cut off males and females cut off females, but in 20 recorded encounters, interruptions were equally distributed between the speakers.

This study is part of an active and rapidly expanding field of language research—the role of gender in speech, with the accent primarily on how, under what conditions, and why the sexes talk differently. A 1983 bibliography of relevant publications includes some 800 titles, compared with about 150 titles in a bibliography published eight years before. The boom started little more than a decade ago, inspired by the women's movement. A new generation of investigators began taking hard looks at some of the things that had been written about women's talk by earlier investigators, mainly male. They encountered a number of statements like the following from Otto Jespersen, a Danish linguist who has earned a prominent place in the feminist rogues' gallery: "[W]omen much more often than men break off without finishing their sentences, because they start talking without having thought out what they are going to say."

Such belittlement of female conversation may be somewhat less frequent nowadays. But it lives on in everyday contexts, hardly surprising since it involves attitudes imbedded in thinking that get passed on like bad genes from generation to generation. The latest issue of a women-and-language newsletter notes items involving sexism in everything from the *New England Journal of Medicine* and Maidenform bra ads to campaign speeches and government offices in Japan.

Work focused on interruption contributes to understanding who controls conversations and how. To check on their original observations in a more casual context, West and Zimmerman conducted an experiment in which students meeting for the first time were told to "relax and get to know one another," with familiar results. Males again turned out to be the chief culprits, although they made only 75 percent of the interruptions, compared with that 96 percent figure for previously acquainted pairs—perhaps because they were more restrained among new acquaintances.

Men not only do the lion's share of the interrupting (and the talking) but often choose what to talk about. This can be seen in a study conducted by public relations consultant Pamela Fishman. Her subjects were three couples, a social worker and five graduate students, who consented to having tape recorders in their apartments, providing some 52 hours of conversation, 25 of which have been transcribed.

Fishman's first impression: "At times felt that all the women did was ask questions . . . I attended to my own speech and discovered the same pattern." In fact, the women asked more than percent of the questions. Dustin Hoffman put this speech pattern to use in the motion picture *Tootsie,* using the questioning intonation frequently when impersonating a woman and rather less frequently when acting unladylike.

In her study, Fishman discovered that a particular question was used with great frequency: "D'ya know what?" Research by other investigators had described how children frequently use this phrase to communicate with their elders. It serves as a conversation opener, calling for an answer like "What?" or "No, tell me," a go-ahead signal that they may speak up and that what they have to say will be heeded.

Pursuing this lead, Fishman found out why women need such reassurances when she analyzed the 76 efforts in taped conversations to start conversations or keep them going. Men tried 29 times and succeeded 28 times. That is, in all but a single case the outcome was some discussion of the topic broached. Women tried 47 times, sometimes for as long as five minutes, with dead-end results 30 times, an unimpressive .362 batting average. (It could have been worse. Each of the male subjects in this experiment professed sympathy for the women's movement.)

Other actions that control conversation (and often power) are more complicated, less open to statistical analysis. Cheris Kramarae, professor of speech communication at the University of Illinois in Urbana-Champaign, tells what happened when, as the only woman member of an important policy-shaping committee, she tried to communicate with the chairman before the start of a meeting. She suggested that certain items be added to the agenda, apparently to no effect. "He paid no attention to me, and I gave up." Once the meeting got under way, however, he featured her ideas in a review of the agenda and, turning to a male colleague, commented: "I don't remember who suggested these changes. I think it was Dick here."

Kramarae cites such instances of being heard but not listened to, "as if you were speaking behind a glass," as the sort of thing women must cope with every day. Other examples of everyday difficulties include being first-named by people who address males by last names plus "Mr." and "Dr.," hearing men discuss hiring a "qualified" woman, and looking a block around to see whether men are around who might make catcalls or pass out compliments.

These sorts of affronts lead women to way of life that fosters sensitivity to biases in the King's English. There is the intriguing record of efforts to abolish generic masculine where *man* means not just males but all humans (as in "Man is among the few mammals in which estrus has disappeared entirely," from *Emergence of Man* by John Pfeiffer). *Woman* is used only in reference to a female, a rule established by male grammarians some 250 years ago.

At first the move to a more generalized language was widely opposed, mainly on the grounds of triviality and the inviolability of language. Critics included some feminists, the linguistic faculty at Harvard, and *Time* magazine, the latter exhibiting its usual delicate touch in an essay entitled "Sispeak: A Msguided Attempt to Change Herstory." Then a number of psychologists, among them Donald MacKay and Wendy Martyna of the University of California, ran tests showing that, whatever the speaker or writer intended, most people associate *man* and the matching pronoun *he* with a male image and that the generic masculine could hurt the way *boy* hurts blacks. Today it is common practice to edit such references out of textbook manuscripts and other writings.

Meanwhile research continues along a widening front, trying to cope with unconscious attitudes, sexist and otherwise, which distinguish women and men—"two alien cultures, oddly intertwined," in the words of Barrie Thorne of Michigan State University. Recent studies of the American male culture by and large support previous findings. Men spend considerable time playing the dominance game, either at a joking level or for real. The telling of a tall tale, followed by a still taller tale in an I-can-top-that atmosphere, seems to be typically male.

In this game, keeping cool commands the respect of the other players, with an occasional flash of emotion commended, providing it has to do with politics or sports or shop talk—practically anything but personal feelings. Elizabeth Aries of Amherst College, who has recorded 15 hours of conversation among newly acquainted male students, reports that certain males consistently dominated the conversation. Her subjects addressed the entire group rather than individuals at least a third of the time, nearly five times more often than women interacting under similar conditions.

Detailed studies of women's conversations are rare, mainly conducted in the past few years. Aries discovered that leaders in all-female groups tend to assume a low profile and encourage others to speak, while leaders among men tend to resist the contributions of others. Mercilee Jenkins of San Francisco State University studied the conversation of mothers in a discussion group over a five-month period. She was interested in subject matter as well as conversational style. She found that the young mothers discussed a broad range of subjects—much beyond domestic problems.

Storytelling makes up a large proportion of conversational encounters, with narrative styles that reflect other gender differences. "The universe is made of stories, not atoms," said poet Muriel Rukeyser, and linguistic analysis confirms her insight. As a rule, the women in the Jenkins study avoided first-person narratives. In 26 out of 57 transcribed stories, the narrator played no role at all, while men frequently shine in their own stories. The women listening became heavily involved in the incidents recounted and chimed in with stories supporting the narrator, challenging the preceding story in only about five percent of the cases.

Mixing sexes conversationally produces some interesting reactions, at least among newly acquainted Harvard students in the Aries study. The men softened, competing less among themselves and talking more about their personal lives. (This may be a kind of instinctive mating or courting display, an attracting mechanism discarded upon closer acquaintance when the male usually reassumes his impersonal ways.) Women students responded with a pattern of their own, becoming more competitive. Aries notes that "the social significance of women for one another in a mixed group was low." They maintained a supportive style in talking with men, but it was every woman for herself as they spoke disproportionately more to the men than to each other.

The "music" of conversation may be as meaningful as the words. Women not only have higher voices, but the pitch is notably higher than can be explained solely by the anatomy of the female vocal apparatus. Moreover, Sally McConnell-Ginet of Cornell University finds that women's voices are more colorful—they vary more in pitch and change pitch more frequently than do men's voices. In one experiment, women immediately assumed a monotone style when asked to imitate men's speech. McConnell-Ginet regards speaking tunefully as an effective strategy for getting and holding attention, a strategy used more often by women than men, perhaps because they are more often ignored.

No one has a workable theory that accounts for all these differences. Even the longest running, most thorough searches for the root causes of differences between the sexes raise more questions than they answer. Carol Nagy Jacklin of the University of Southern California and Eleanor Maccoby of Stanford University have been tracking the development of 100 children from birth to age six. These children have been observed at several stages, in various settings. When this group reached 45 months of age, the researchers focused on how 58 of them interacted with their parents during playtime.

A surprising conclusion emerged: Discrimination by gender originates mainly outside the home. "Mothers do little behavior stereotyping," Jacklin summarizes. "They appear to treat [their own] little boys and little girls much the same." (While fathers tend to treat their children in more gender-stereotyped ways during playtimes, they ordinarily have less influence on childrearing and on actually creating the home environment.)

The implication is intriguing. If it is true that outsiders are largely responsible, and since most outsiders are also parents, it follows that parents have gender-based preconceptions more often about other people's children than about their own. In any event, school is one place where highly significant changes take place. In the beginning, teacher is "home base," a surrogate parent to whom children come for reassurance and support, and that holds for all children—until second grade.

At that point boys but not girls begin increasingly to turn away from teacher and toward one another. The stress is more and more on hierarchy, jockeying for position in speech as well as action, in talking as well as playing cowboy, soldier, Star Wars, and so on. All this is part of a constellation of changes. In playgrounds girls tend to go around in pairs, usually near teachers and the school building; boys form groups of half a dozen or so, usually as far away as possible. Boys may get more attention than girls because they are often more disruptive.

In discussing such patterns Thorne cites the classic psychoanalytic theory that boys, being raised mainly by women at home, feel the need at school to assert themselves as "not female." Also, teachers may have biased expectations about boys. But, according to Raphaela Best of the Montgomery County school system in Maryland, a high price may be paid for early male-male competition. She suggests that the resulting tensions may help account for the fact that reading disabilities are at least five times more frequent among boys than among girls.

Though the study of gender-based differences is relatively new, significant steps have been taken. Furthermore—a totally unexpected development—gender-related work has helped spark renewed interest in general language use. The ways in which men talk to men and women talk to women have come under scrutiny, as have the speech differences between people of different cultures and professional backgrounds.

West, for example, is currently interested in exchanges between doctors and patients. This work demands looking as well as listening, analyzing a kind of choreography of nonverbal as well as verbal behavior. Her raw data consist of videotapes complete with sound tracks. So far she has spent more than 550 hours transcribing seven hours of conversation in 21 patient-physician meetings at a family-practice center in the southern United States. Preliminary analysis indicates that doctors out-interrupt their patients, male and female, by a two-to-one margin—except when the doctor is a woman. In that case, the situation is reversed, with patients—both male and female—out-interrupting by the same margin.

Similar studies are tuning in on the finer points of speech and behavior. An outstanding and continuing analysis by Marjorie Harness Goodwin of the University of South Carolina shows that girls as well as boys form social groups, except that the girls tend to form exclusive "coalitions," whereas boys form all-inclusive hierarchies. With the girls not everyone gets to play, while with the boys everyone, even the nerds, can play as long as they respect rank. Girls also are far less direct in arguing with one another, and their debates may simmer for weeks, in contrast to male arguments, which generally end within a few minutes.

These findings are based on taped observations of black children at play in an urban setting. Other observations hint that the same points might apply more widely, a possibility that remains to be probed. What holds true for one culture or society may not for another. Male dominance in speech seems to be a global phenomenon. But the most notable exception cries for analysis: Sexism is probably at a lower level in Bali, where to vote or be otherwise active as a citizen, one must be part of a couple.

While most of the recent research has revealed conflict between the sexes, Carole Edelsky of Arizona State University has discovered a trend worth noting. She has studied five "very informal" meetings of a standing faculty committee consisting of seven women and four men—7.5 hours of taped conversation. It started as a "fishing expedition" project—a search for sexisms, and there were plenty. As usual, men talked longer and interrupted more, appearing to hold the floor longer.

But Edelsky also recognized a second method of holding the floor. She identified short interludes, between the more formal addresses, that featured mutual support and "greater discourse equality." (These episodes were most informal and laughter-filled.) At first Edelsky had the impression that the women were doing most of the talking during these periods. But actual counts of words and time per turn revealed an equal-time situation (thus supporting the observation that a "talkative" woman is one who talks as much as the average man). These episodes made up less than 20 percent of total talk time, but such encounters as these may reflect a change in communication between the sexes.

The future may see great change in our current perception of a conversational gap between the sexes. It may also see a correction of imbalance in present day research—a shift in the gender composition of the researchers. Today in the United States there are about 200 investigators of language and gender, and all but a dozen of them are women. Many of the researchers believe that as more enter the field the "two alien cultures" will draw closer together.

RESPONSE SHEET

for John Pfeiffer: Girl Talk, Boy Talk

1. What three findings give the strongest support for Pfeiffer's position that males and females talk differently to each other?

2. Write one question regarding this article that can be used for class discussion.

3. Describe one application of the information in this article. It can be:
1) A next research step to take
2) An educational, clinical/counseling or rearing application
3) A personal application

Gender Stereotypes After Thirty Years: A Replication of Rosenkrantz, et al. (1968)[1]

Muriel N. Nesbitt and Nolan E. Penn
The Fielding Institute
University of California, San Diego

Summary.—This study is a partial replication of the 1968 investigation by Rosenkrantz, Vogel, Bee, Broverman, and Broverman of gender stereotypes among college students. Like the students studied 30 years ago, male and female participants in this study showed very high agreement about the typical characteristics of men and women. However, current participants identified significantly fewer gender stereotypes than did those in the earlier study. In contrast to the participants in the original study, current participants judged the traits they associated with women to be significantly more socially desirable, in general, than the traits they associated with men.

Gender stereotypes are generally held beliefs about the psychological and behavioral traits of men and women. Categorization of individuals by sex seems to be fundamental to the cultural rules governing interpersonal interactions (West & Zimmerman, 1987). Interest among psychologists in the content of gender stereotypes burgeoned in the 1960s and 1970s, and an important contribution to the understanding of gender stereotypes and their implications was made by the Brovermans and their collaborators (Rosenkrantz, Vogel, Bee, Broverman, & Broverman, 1968; Broverman, Broverman, Clarkson, Rosenkrantz, & Vogel, 1970; Broverman, Vogel, Broverman, Clarkson, & Rosenkrantz, 1972). The 1968 study by Rosenkrantz, *et al.* on the gender stereotypes of college students showed that: (1) male and female college students agreed about what traits typify men and women in general; (2) male and female students generally agreed about which of the traits were socially desirable and which not; (3) regardless of gender, students attributed more socially desirable traits to men than to women; and (4) both male and female students rated themselves as less different from the opposite sex than the typical man and woman are different.

In the thirty years since the work reported by Rosenkrantz, *et al.* (1968) there have been a number of societal changes which, it would seem, could have operated to modify gender stereotypes. Economic changes have brought more women into the workforce. Women have entered previously male-dominated jobs and professions (Reskin & Roos, 1990, pp. 17–18). Discrimination against women has become an openly discussed issue, and "sexism" and "sexual harassment" are terms which are now widely understood and used. Are the societal changes since the 1960s reflected in changed perceptions and stereotypes about gender? Several studies done before or soon after the time of Rosenkrantz, *et al.* (1968) (e.g., Sherriffs & Jarrett, 1953; McKee & Sherriffs, 1957; Sherriffs & McKee, 1957; Broverman, *et al.*, 1970; Broverman, *et al.*, 1972; Wolff & Taylor, 1979) reported similar stereotypes and the greater valuation of male-associated traits by both male and female participants. Der Karabetian and Smith (1977), however, suggested changes were occurring when they found that, although male and female students agreed about gender stereotypes, women assigned higher social desirability to the traits associated with their own sex, while men valued the traits associated with men and women equally.

[1]We dedicate this work to the memory of Inge Broverman, mentor, colleague, and friend. This study was partially supported by a grant from the Fielding Institute, Santa Barbara, CA. We thank Karen Huffman, Barbara Schnelker, Linda Locklear, Terry Humphries, Roland Phelps, and James Evans for their assistance in obtaining participants. Please send correspondence to Muriel N. Nesbitt, Ph.D., Department of Biology 0355, University of California at San Diego, La Jolla, CA 92193 or e-mail (mnesbitt@ucsd.edu).

In the 1980s and 1990s a number of studies examined the existence of gender stereotypes and differences in the perceived social desirability of male- and female-associated traits, with somewhat conflicting results which might be interpretable in terms of a trend toward fewer stereotypes and less relative valuation of traits associated with men. Studies done in the 1990s have reported more perceived similarity of men and women (de Lisi & Soundranayagam, 1990) and less perceived social desirability of traits associated with men (Beckwith, 1993; Fiebert & Meyer, 1997) than studies done in the 1970s and before. Studies done in the 1980s yielded inconsistent results. Williams and Best (1990, pp. 87–90) found female-associated traits to be rated more favorably than male-associated traits in the United States. However, others reported the greater valuation of male-associated traits (Hansson, O'Connor, Jones, & Mihelich, 1980; Eagly & Wood, 1982; Lii & Wang, 1982; Deaux & Kite, 1987). Some of these studies, such as that of Lii and Wang, were quite close in methodology to the current one and that of Rosenkrantz, *et al.* Williams and Best (1990), on the other hand, used a different instrument and a more complex analysis of social desirability, and this may account for some of the differences in conclusions. Other studies in the 1980s did not address social desirability, but showed in some cases the continued existence and strength of gender stereotypes (Ruble, 1983; Bergen & Williams, 1988) and in other cases a reduction in the number of stereotypes (Smith, 1980; Phillips & Gilroy, 1985; Poole & Tapley, 1988).

This paper reports a partial replication of the study by Rosenkrantz, *et al.* (1968) aimed at clarifying whether changes have occurred in the content of gender stereotypes and the relative perceived social desirability of traits associated with men and with women since 30 years ago.

METHOD

Participants

Two hundred and forty-eight students (83 men and 165 women) at San Diego area community colleges were given the Sex Role Stereotypes Questionnaire (SRSQ). The men's ages ranged from 20 to 70 years (M = 30.5 yr., SD = 11.9). The women's ages ranged from 18 to 57 years (M = 28.9, SD = 9.7). This age distribution is markedly different from that of the 74 men and 80 women who completed the questionnaire in the study of Rosenkrantz, *et al.* (1968). Those male respondents ranged in age from 18 to 25 years (M = 20.4, SD = 4.3), while female respondents' ages ranged from 17 to 25 years (M = 19.7, SD = 1.7). Therefore, to generate data more comparable to that of Rosenkrantz, *et al.* (1968), we divided our sample into two segments. Those participants less than 26 years of age are the Younger group, and those 30 years of age or older are the Older group. (We left the 26- to 29-yr.-old students out of the analysis to increase the differentiation of the two groups.) The cutoff at age 25 was chosen because it produced a Younger group with an age distribution similar to that of the participants in the study of Rosenkrantz, *et al.* In our Younger group, the mean age of the 44 male respondents was 21.5 yr. (range = 18–25, SD = 1.4), and the mean of the 87 female respondents was 21.6 yr. (range = 20–25, SD = 1.7). In our Older group, the mean age of the 32 male respondents was 43.4 yr. (range = 30–70, SD = 9.2) and that of the 60 female respondents was 39.9 yr. (range = 30–57, SD = 7.5). This division of our sample created four groups: Younger Men, Younger Women, Older Men, and Older Women.

Rosenkrantz, *et al.* (1968) administered the Social Desirability Questionnaire to a group of 121 students (73 men and 48 women) who had not filled out the other questionnaire. Likewise, we asked 103 students (60 men and 43 women), drawn from the same community college settings as participants who completed the Sex Role Stereotypes Questionnaire, to complete the Social Desirability Questionnaire. The mean age of males in this group was 22.5 yr. (range = 18–46, SD = 4.5), and that of females was 21.2 yr. (range = 18–36, SD = 2.9). Splitting this sample in the same way that we split the stereotype sample yielded a Younger group of 51 men aged 18 to 25 years (M = 21.0, SD = 1.7) and 41 women aged 18 to 23 years (M = 20.7, SD = 1.2). The Older group of this sample contained only four students and was not used for analysis.

Rosenkrantz, *et al.* (1968) did not report the ethnic composition of their sample, but it is likely to have been entirely or almost entirely Euro-American. The ethnic composition of our sample is probably more heterogeneous. Our Older participants were 66 (71.7%) Euro-American, 7 (7.6%) Hispanic, 14 (15.2%) African American, 2 (2.2%) Asian, and 2 (2.2%) mixed (1 person, or 1.1%, did not identify ethnicity). The participants in the Younger group reported they were 89 (67.9%) Euro-American, 12 (9.2%) Hispanic, 24 (18.3%) African American, 3 (2.3%) Asian, and 3 (2.3%) mixed.

Questionnaires

The Sex Role Stereotypes Questionnaire, a 122-item questionnaire developed by Rosenkrantz, *et al.* (1968) was administered to participants. The items are arranged in bipolar form, e.g., "not at all kind" vs "very kind," with the poles separated by a 60-point scale (10 to 70). Participants indicated their scores for each item by drawing a line through its scale at a particular point. Participants were given instructions to "Imagine that you are going to meet someone for the first time, and the only thing that you know in advance is that she (he) is an *adult female* (male)." When the participants finished marking the items following these instructions, they were asked to mark them again for a stranger of the other gender. Half the participants were given instructions to rate males first, and half to rate females first. Finally, the participants were asked to mark the items a third time, rating themselves. The imaginary "adult female" and "adult male" the participants in this study were asked to rate are hereafter referred to as the "Typical Man" and "Typical Woman."

The Social Desirability Questionnaire was created by altering the instructions so that the participants were directed to "place a mark through each of the scales provided at the point which indicates what you believe to be the most socially desirable way of being." This was a departure from the methodology of Rosenkrantz, *et al.* (1968) who asked their participants to choose one pole of each scale as more socially desirable, although they did a small study using the same method we employed and reported that the two methods yielded similar results (p. 290). After marking the scales at the point of maximum social desirability, the current participants were asked to mark the items again rating their own characteristics.

Data Analysis

Correlations and t tests for correlated samples were calculated using the SPSS 6.1 for Windows statistical software (SPSS, Inc., 1994). Significance of differences between correlation coefficients was calculated using a one-tailed test following z transformation (Edwards, 1984, pp. 72–73).

Results

Gender Stereotypes

Men and women rated the traits characteristic of the Typical Man and the Typical Woman as similarly now as they did 30 years ago. Rosenkrantz, *et al.* (1968) found a correlation of .96 between the scores assigned by men to the Typical Man and those assigned by women to the Typical Man and a .95 correlation between the scores assigned by men to the Typical Woman and those assigned by women to the Typical Woman. In our data (see Table 1), these correlations were similar to those observed by Rosenkrantz, *et al.*, ranging from .89 to .95, depending on whether the Older or Younger groups' scores were compared. Rosenkrantz, *et al.* found that men and women agreed about which end of the bipolar scale was more typical of the Typical Man than of the Typical Woman on 113 of the 122 items. Our Older male and Older female groups agreed on 106 of the 122 items, while the men and women in the Younger group agreed on 110 of the items.

The method chosen by Rosenkrantz, *et al.* (1968) to identify stereotypes among responses was to define "Stereotypic items" as those about which 75% or more of men and 75% or more of women agreed that the trait was more typical of one gender than the other, i.e., 75% of men and 75% of women rated the Typical Man higher than the Typical Woman (or the Typical Woman higher than the Typical Man) on a given trait. They found that 53 items met the criterion of 75% or more agreement for male respondents, that 50 items met this criterion for female respondents, and that 41 items met the criterion for both groups of respondents and thus qualified as stereotypes by their definition. Applying the same criterion (75% of men and 75% of women agree) to our data, we found that for our Younger group (comparable to the 1968 sample) only 19 items met the criterion of Rosenkrantz, *et al.* (1968) for Stereotypic items. In our Older group of participants, only 17 items met this criterion. (Twenty-nine items met the 75% agreement criterion among our female respondents and 31 items among our male respondents.) Table 2 shows these results. Only seven items met the criterion of

Table 1
Pearson Correlations Among Scores Assigned to the Typical Man and Typical Woman by Different Groups of Participants

Group Rating Trait	Rated Gender	r: 2	3	4	5	6	7	8
Older Group								
1. Women	Typical Woman	−.01	.93*	−.05	.96*	.09	.94*	.03
2. Women	Typical Man		−.003	.94*	−.03	.90*	.002	.89*
3. Men	Typical Woman			−.05	.91*	.08	.92*	.02
4. Men	Typical Man				−.07	.88*	−.06	.90*
Younger Group								
5. Women	Typical Woman					.09	.95*	.03
6. Women	Typical Man						.12	.91*
7. Men	Typical Woman							.05
8. Men	Typical Man							

*Significantly different from 0 at $p < .001$.

Table 2

Traits Meeting Criteria For Stereotypic Items (75% Agreement Among Male and Female Participants About Which Gender Scores Higher on the Trait) in Three Groups of Participants*

1968 Participants	1998 Younger Participants	1998 Older Participants
More aggressive	More aggressive	Less emotional
More independent	Less emotional	Hide emotions
Less emotional	Hide emotions	Less talkative
Hide emotions	Use harsh language	Less considerate
Use harsh language	Not honest in expressing emotion	Less tolerant
More objective	More dominant	More dominant
Less talkative	More reckless	More reckless
Less easily influenced	Less gentle	Less able to devote selves completely to others
More dominant	Less kind	Less gentle
Like math and science more	Feelings less easily hurt	More competitive
Less excitable in a minor crisis	Less aware of the feelings of others	Feelings less easily hurt
More active	Less mature	Less interested in own appearance
Less tactful	Cry less easily	More interested in sex
Less gentle	Louder	Cry less easily
More competitive	More careless	Less understanding of others
More logical	Prouder of sexual ability	Less cooperative
More worldly	Less understanding of others	Less able to express tender feelings
More skilled in business	Less warm in relationships	
More direct	Less able to express tender feelings	
Know the way of the world		
Feelings less easily hurt		
More adventurous		
Less aware of the feelings of others		
Less religious		
Less interested in own appearance		
Less difficulty making decisions		
Cry less easily		
Act as leaders		
Sloppier		
Louder		
More self-confident		
More comfortable about being aggressive		
Less need for security		
More ambitious		
More able to separate feelings from ideas		
Less dependent		
Enjoy art and literature less		
Less able to express tender feelings		
Less conceited about appearance		
Think men are superior		
Talk more freely about sex with men		

*Presented so that the Typical Man is characterized as rated.

Rosenkrantz, *et al.* for Sterotypic items in all three samples (those of Rosenkrantz, *et al.*, our Younger group, and our Older group): the Typical Woman is more emotional than the Typical Man, the Typical Man hides emotions more than the Typical Woman does, the Typical Man is more dominant than the Typical Woman, the Typical Woman is gentler than the Typical Man, the Typical Woman's feelings are hurt more easily than the Typical Man's are, the Typical Woman cries more easily than the Typical Man does, the Typical Man does not express tender feelings as easily as the Typical Woman does.

Rosenkrantz, *et al.* (1968) used the term "Differentiating items" to describe those questionnaire items which did not meet the criterion for Stereotypic items (75% of men and 75% of women agree) but on which the mean scores assigned to the Typical Man and Typical Woman were significantly different (in the same direction) for both the male and female samples at the 0.5 level according to a t test for correlated samples. "Nondifferentiating items" were those which met neither this criterion nor the criterion for Stereotypic items but on which male and female participants agreed as to which pole of the scale applied more to the Typical Man and which to the Typical Woman. Rosenkrantz, *et al.* found 48 Differentiating and 24 Nondifferentiating items in addition to their 41 Stereotypic items. This adds up to the 113 items about which men and women agreed as to which gender the trait typified. Rosenkrantz, *et al.* discarded the nine items about which men and women disagreed, although it might have been appropriate to include these among the Nondifferentiating items. The strategy employed by Rosenkrantz, *et al.* to distinguish Differentiating from Nondifferentiating items, namely, the presence or absence of a significant difference between mean ratings attributed to the Typical Woman and mean ratings attributed to the Typical Man, creates a problem in comparing our study with theirs because the significance of differences between means is sensitive to sample size. Often this problem can be solved by using a measure of effect size (Cohen, 1962), but in our case this would require knowing the difference in mean scores assigned to the Typical Man and to the Typical Woman and the variances of those scores for each survey item. While we have these data for the surveys completed by the current participants, they are not available for the study by Rosenkrantz, *et al.* In spite of this difficulty, we did use the criterion of significance of differences between mean scores assigned to the Typical Man and to the Typical Woman to classify non-Stereotypic items as Differentiating or Nondifferentiating, with the results shown in Table 3. The sample of Rosenkrantz, *et al.* is comparable in size to our younger group, so comparison of the numbers in Table 3 does indicate a decrease in the number of items perceived as different between the genders by our Younger group, as compared to that of Rosenkrantz, *et al.* The fact that our Older group is smaller than that of Rosenkrantz, *et al.* may account for part of the difference in number of Differentiating items between these two groups.

Another way to approach the question of which items represent stereotypes might be to ask on which questionnaire items the Typical Man and the Typical Woman were scored most differently by respondents. Table 4 lists the 10 items in which current participants rated the Typical Man and the Typical Woman most differently (of the 122 items in the survey, these 10 items yielded the largest absolute values of the differences between the mean score attributed to the Typical Man and the mean score attributed to the Typical Woman). Inspection of the table indicates that our participants, men and women in both Younger and Older groups, all perceived the most marked differences between the Typical Man and the Typical Woman to be in the area of emotional expressiveness. Furthermore, there is strong agreement among the groups of participants as to which items represent the most pronounced differences between the Typical Man and the Typical Woman. There is extensive overlap between the items listed in Table 4 as most different, and those listed in Table 2 as Stereotypic items.

Social Desirability

Rosenkrantz, *et al.* (1968, p. 290) found that men and women agreed about which pole of each of the 122 bipolar items represented the more socially desirable characteristics, with a correlation of .96 between the choices of men and those of women. Our data are similar, showing a correlation of .95 between the men's and women's ratings of the Social Desirability of traits. Table 5 shows the 10 traits

TABLE 3
Distribution of Questionnaire Items Over Three Categories

	Stereotypic	Differentiating	Nondifferentiating
Rosenkrantz, *et al.*	41	48	33*
Younger Group	19	55	48
Older Group	17	76	29

*We added the nine items on which males and females disagreed for accurate comparison.

TABLE 4
Ten Traits on Which the Typical Man (TM) and Typical Woman (TW) Were Rated Most Differently by Groups of Raters in Order of Decreasing Difference

Male Respondents	Female Respondents	Younger Respondents	Older Respondents
Cries easily (TW)	Cries easily (TW)	Cries easily (TW)	Cries easily (TW)
Express tender feelings easily (TW)	Emotional (TW)	Emotional (TW)	Hide emotions (TM)
Gentle (TW)	Hide emotions (TM)	Express tender feelings easily (TW)	Emotional (TW)
Hide emotions (TM)	Express tender feelings easily (TW)	Hide emotions (TM)	Express tender feelings easily (TW)
Emotional (TW)	Gentle (TW)	Gentle (TW)	Use harsh language (TM)
Use harsh language (TM)	Aware of feelings of others (TW)	Feelings are easily hurt (TW)	Gentle (TW)
Talk more freely about sex with men (TM)	Use harsh language (TM)	Dominant (TM)	Aware of feelings of others (TW)
Sloppy (TM)	Comfortable when others express emotion (TW)	Use harsh language (TM)	Dominant (TM)
Reckless (TM)	Feelings easily hurt (TW)	Reckless (TM)	Sloppy (TM)
Enjoy art and literature (TW)	Dominant (TM)	Enjoy art and literature (TW)	Understanding of others (TW)

TABLE 5
Ten Most Socially Desirable Traits According to Male and Female Raters in Decreasing Order of Desirability

Female Raters	Male Raters
Good sense of humor (62.7*)	Considerate (59.6)
Trustworthy (62.3)	Trustworthy (58.1)
Kind (61.8)	Intelligent (58.0)
Intelligent (61.6)	Friendly (57.5)
Considerate (61.5)	Interested in sex (56.9)
Protective (60.8)	Realistic (56.4)
Mature (60.3)	Adventurous (56.0)
Friendly (59.5)	Competent (55.6)
Honest in expressing emotions (59.4)	Kind (54.2)
Ambitious (57.9)	Good sense of humor (54.1)

*Mean social desirability score assigned to the item by male or female raters.

with the highest mean Social Desirability ratings as rated by the men and women in our sample.

Relationship Between Masculinity and Social Desirability

Rosenkrantz, *et al.* (1968) observed a significant tendency for traits associated with the Typical Man to be judged more socially desirable than traits associated with the Typical Woman. Thus, for example, in 29 or about 70% of their 41 Stereotypic items the pole judged to be higher on Social Desirability was the same as the pole judged to be more typical of the Typical Man.

In our data, over all 122 items, the scores assigned by both men and women to the traits of the Typical Woman are more strongly correlated with Social Desirability scores (see Table 6). The mean of the eight correlation coefficients in Table 6 which relate the ratings of the traits of the Typical Woman to Social Desirability is .74. The scores assigned by women and men raters to the traits of the Typical Man are less correlated with Social Desirability scores, the mean of the eight correlations being .34. The set of eight correlations relating to the traits of the Typical Woman is homogeneous ($p = .77$) according to a chi-squared test (Edwards, 1984, p. 75), meaning that there are

TABLE 6
Pearson Correlations Between Ratings Assigned to the Typical Man and the Typical Woman and Social Desirability Scores by Different Groups of Participants Over All Items

Social Desirability Rated by	Typical Woman				Typical Man			
	Female Raters		Male Raters		Female Raters		Male Raters	
	Older	Younger	Older	Younger	Older	Younger	Older	Younger
Women	.76†	.79†	.68†	.79†	.21*	.39†	.16	.33†
Men	.71†	.76†	.65†	.75†	.35†	.52†	.31†	.48†

*Significantly different from 0 at $p = .02$.
†Significantly different from 0 at $p < .001$.

no significant differences among these correlation coefficients. The set of eight correlations relating to the traits of the Typical Man is also homogeneous ($p = .40$) according to this criterion. However, the entire set of 16 correlations is inhomogeneous ($p < .01$). The higher correlations between Social Desirability ratings and the ratings of traits attributed to the Typical Woman exist whether Social Desirability is rated by men or by women, although the difference is more marked when Social Desirability is rated by women. All four classes of participants scored the traits attributed to the Typical Woman as having greater Social Desirability than the traits attributed to the Typical Man. In all eight of the paired correlations, e.g., the Older male group's ratings of the Typical Man vs Social Desirability rated by male participants, and the Older male group's ratings of the Typical Woman vs Social Desirability scored by male participants, the correlation between the ratings of traits attributed to the Typical Woman and Social Desirability is significantly greater than the correlation between the ratings of traits assigned to the Typical Man and Social Desirability.

The 19 items in our study which met the criterion of Rosenkrantz, *et al.* (1968) for being Stereotypic include only five in which the trait associated with the Typical Man is assigned a Social Desirability rating above the midpoint of our scale (40). The traits associated with the Typical Woman have Social Desirability scores above the midpoint in 13 cases, and in one case (cries easily) a trait associated with the Typical Woman was given a Social Desirability rating slightly above the midpoint by women raters, but a rating below the midpoint by male raters (see Table 7). Of the highest rated items on Social Desirability listed in Table 5, six (sense of humor, trustworthy, kind, intelligent, considerate, and friendly) appear on both the men's and women's lists. Both men and women participants rated the Typical Woman higher than the Typical Man on all six of these traits. The Typical Woman was also rated higher than the Typical Man by both male and female groups of participants on three of the unshared items (mature, honest in expressing emotions, and competent). The Typical Man was rated higher than the Typical Woman was by both male and female participants in three of the unshared items (protective, interested in sex, and adventurous). On the remaining two items (ambitious and realistic), women and men did not agree. Men rated the Typical Woman as more ambitious than the Typical Man, while women thought the Typical Man was more ambitious. Men rated the Typical Man as more realistic than the Typical Woman, while women rated the Typical Woman as more realistic.

Self-ratings

The ratings of self made by the participants in our study who completed the Sex Role Stereotypes Questionnaire were compared to the self-ratings of the participants who completed the same questionnaire in the 1968 study. Although we collected self-ratings from the participants who completed the Social Desirability Questionnaire, those ratings were not used other than to compare them to the self-ratings of our participants who completed the Sex Role Stereotypes Questionnaire. We found a correlation of .92 between the self-ratings of our two groups of participants.

Rosenkrantz, *et al.* (1968, p. 292) observed that the self-ratings of both male and female students differed from their ratings of the Typical Man and the Typical Woman, such that female students rated themselves as more "masculine" than the Typical Woman, and male students rated themselves as more "feminine" than the Typical Man. The participants' self-ratings in the current study showed this same pattern, as illustrated in Table 8. The self-ratings of both Older and Younger women were more highly correlated with their ratings of the Typical Man than their ratings of the Typical Woman. Similarly, the self-ratings of the Younger male group were more highly correlated with their ratings of the Typical Woman than their ratings of the Typical Man were correlated with their ratings of the Typical Woman. In the case of the Older male group, self-ratings were actually more highly correlated with their ratings of the Typical Woman than with their ratings of the

TABLE 7
Mean Social Desirability of Stereotypic Traits (Neutral Rating is 40)

Stereotypic Item (Present Study)	Stereotyped Gender	Social Desirability Rating	
		By Men	By Women
More aggressive	Typical Man	42.7	42.9
More emotional	Typical Woman	44.3	47.7
More often hide emotions	Typical Man	36.4	30.8
Use harsher language	Typical Man	36.0	24.8
More considerate	Typical Woman	59.6	61.5
More dominant	Typical Man	46.0	46.1
More reckless	Typical Man	37.8	33.1
More able to devote self completely to others	Typical Woman	51.2	50.3
Gentler	Typical Woman	47.6	50.9
More competitive	Typical Man	50.7	47.0
More aware of feelings of others	Typical Woman	51.0	59.2
More interested in own appearance	Typical Woman	50.5	48.0
More interested in sex	Typical Man	56.9	50.2
More mature	Typical Woman	54.3	60.3
Cry more easily	Typical Woman	36.5	40.5
More careless	Typical Man	29.9	26.8
More understanding of others	Typical Woman	55.3	58.1
Enjoy art and literature more	Typical Woman	48.2	54.8
Do not express tender feelings as easily	Typical Man	33.6	29.3

Typical Man. For both age groups, the self-ratings of male participants were significantly more highly correlated with their ratings of the Typical Woman than the self-ratings of female participants were correlated with their ratings of the Typical Man. Comparison of the correlation coefficients in Table 8 with those in Table 6 reveals that all groups of participants, except the Younger male group, rated themselves higher on the characteristics with higher mean Socially Desirability than they rated the Typical Man or Typical Woman. In the case of the Younger male group, the correlation of their self-ratings with Social Desirability ratings was not different from the correlation of their ratings of the Typical Woman with Social Desirability ratings.

There was somewhat more difference between the self-ratings of the Younger male and Younger female groups in this study (mean rating difference over 122 items = 4.6) than there was between the self-ratings of the Older male and Older female groups (mean difference = 3.6); however, this difference did not reach statistical significance. Interestingly, seven of the 10 items on which the Younger male and Younger female groups differed most in self-ratings were items that met the criteria for Stereotypic items in this group: women rated themselves higher than men rated themselves on the traits of having feelings easily hurt, crying easily, expressing tender feelings easily, being emotional, being aware of the feelings of others and being understanding of others, while men rated themselves higher than women rated themselves in being reckless. In addition, women rated themselves higher than men rated themselves in enjoying the company of men and making friends easily, while men rated themselves higher in being competitive. In the Older group only four of the 10 items on which the men and women rated themselves most differently met the criterion of Stereotypic items in this group: women rated themselves higher than men rated themselves on crying easily; men rated themselves higher than women rated themselves on hiding emotions, being interested in sex, and in being reckless. The Older female group's self-ratings were higher than those of the Older male group on being rational. The Older male group's self-ratings were higher than those of the Older female group on talking freely about sex with men, being conceited about their appearance, tending to see things in black and white terms, enjoying the company of women, and being proud of sexual ability.

Differences Between Responses of Men and the Responses of Women

Sherriffs and Jarrett (1953, p. 165) observed that men used a more restricted portion of their scale than women did in rating traits for Social Desirability. The same pattern exists in the data reported here. Thus, for 88 of the 122 traits

TABLE 8
Correlations Among Ratings of Self, Typical Man, Typical Woman, and Social Desirability for Four Groups of Participants

	Ratings by			
Ratings Compared	**Older Women**	**Younger Women**	**Older Men**	**Younger Men**
Typical Woman and Typical Man	−.01	.09	−.05†	.05†
Self and Typical Woman	**.85***	**.88**	**.58†**	**.56†**
Self and Typical Man	.11	**.33**	**.48**	**.68**
Self and Social Desirability Scored by Women	**.85**	**.86**	**.73**	**.76**
Self and Social Desirability Scored by Men	**.81**	**.83**	**.79**	**.84**

*Boldface correlations are significantly different from 0 ($p < .05$).
†Significant difference between correlation of Self and Typical Woman and correlation of Typical Man with Typical Woman.

TABLE 9
Ten Traits Which Men and Women Rated Most Differently on Social Desirability

	Social Desirability Score*		
Trait	**Women**	**Men**	***z* Score Difference**
Very interested in sex	50.2	56.9	0.91
Greatly enjoys the company of women	49.4	55.3	0.80
Uses very harsh language	24.8	36.0	0.75
Very protective	60.7	50.4	0.72
Greatly enjoys the company of men	53.5	45.4	0.66
Very adventurous	53.8	56.7	0.58
Very willing to accept change	55.2	47.6	0.56
Cries very easily	40.5	36.5	0.55
Very aware of feelings of others	59.2	51.0	0.52
Very competitive	47.0	50.7	0.49

*Neutral is 40.

which were rated by participants in our study, either both men and women rated Social Desirability of the trait below the midpoint of the scale (score less than 40) but women rated it lower than men did, or both men and women rated the trait above the midpoint of the scale, but women rated it higher than men did. Ratings by men ranged from 26.1 to 59.6, while those by women ranged from 20.2 to 62.7. In spite of the greater range of responses by female participants, the mean response over all items was the same for men ($M = 44.5$) and women ($M = 45.0$).

There were eight cases in which participants of one gender rated the trait below the midpoint of the Social Desirability scale, while those of the other gender rated it above the midpoint. Traits valued above the midpoint by men but below it by women were being stubborn, being strict, punishing often, being worldly, being religious, and always thinking about self. Traits valued above the midpoint by women but below it by men were crying very easily and always avoiding disagreements. These oppositely valued traits were not necessarily those given the most discrepant ratings by male and female participants.

Table 9 shows the 10 most discrepant traits. To correct for the tendency of males to use a restricted portion of the range in scoring Social Desirability, the male and female ratings were converted to z scores, based on the respective sample means and standard deviations for men and women.

DISCUSSION

It might be argued that the differences in number, types, and valuations of gender stereotypes between the Rosenkrantz, *et al.* (1968) study and this one are attributable to differences between the samples in the two studies rather than to real changes in gender stereotypes. Compared to the participants in the Rosenkrantz, *et al.* study, our participants were more ethnically heterogeneous, may have represented a lower average socioeconomic status, and were drawn from the southern west coast of the USA rather than the northern east coast. In addition, although women outnumbered men among the participants in the study by Rosenkrantz, *et al.,* our study had nearly twice as many women as men. Could these differences account for the discrepancies between the outcomes of the two studies? Since we analyzed the responses of men separately from those of women (as did Rosenkrantz, *et al.*), and since identification of an item as Stereotypic required agreement between the responses of women and men, the preponderance of women over men in our study cannot account for the apparent decline in the number of Stereotypic items that we observed.

The effect of the greater ethnic heterogeneity among participants in our study is more difficult to assess. If African-American and Hispanic participants held significantly fewer gender stereotypes than the Euro-American participants, their inclusion in our study might have contributed to our observing fewer Stereotypic items than did Rosenkrantz, *et al.* (1968). However, some evidence suggests that major ethnic groups within the United States do not exhibit pronounced differences in gender stereotyping and that the small differences which have been observed are such as would have produced more, rather than fewer, Stereotypic items in our study as compared to those of Rosenkrantz, *et al.* (Senour, 1977; Cromwell & Cromwell, 1978; Gonzales, 1982). Unfortunately, the numbers of participants in each of the non-Euro-American ethnic groups was too small for us to analyze them separately.

We found no evidence in the literature relevant to whether Boston area students would be expected to hold more or fewer gender stereotypes than Southern California students, although Williams and Best (1990, p. 272) did report a correlation between latitude and gender stereotyping in their large cross-national study. Both our sample and that of Rosenkrantz, *et al.* (1968) were drawn from urban or suburban areas. Although we have no relevant direct evidence, we suspect that our sample may reflect a lower average socioeconomic status than that of the sample of Rosenkrantz, *et al.,* as our sample was drawn from two-year colleges rather than the four-year college sampled by Rosenkrantz, *et al.* However, little relationship has been reported between socioeconomic status and gender stereotyping (Williams & Best, 1990, p. 272). Thus, it seems to us that none of the obvious differences between the participants in the study of Rosenkrantz, *et al.* and the participants in our study is likely to account for the observed differences in outcome between the two studies. Our plans are to pursue these questions by expanding our sample to include large numbers of participants from various ethnic and cultural groups and geographic settings.

Results of this study suggest that the contents of gender stereotypes have changed to some extent in the generation since the report by Rosenkrantz, *et al.* (1968). Twenty-six of the 41 traits which met the criterion for Stereotypic items in the original study did not meet that same criterion in this study. Inspection of Table 2 shows that the Sex Role Stereotypes Questionnaire items involving experiencing and expressing emotions continue to be seen as differentiating the Typical Man and the Typical Woman, but that the Typical Woman was not considered by the current groups of participants to be less logical, direct, or ambitious than the Typical Man or less able to separate feelings from ideas. Most of our participants also thought that the Typical Woman is not less objective than the Typical Man, does not have more difficulty in making decisions, and is not more dependent. These traits could be seen as representing a cluster of characteristics having to do with competence and capacity to be effective. The fact that the current participants did not identify these traits as parts of gender stereotypes may reflect the expected result of the greater integration of women into the work force, lessened sex-typing of many jobs and professions, and therefore greater exposure of men and women to women in responsible decision-making roles (Vogel, Broverman, Broverman, Clarkson, & Rosenkrantz, 1970). That increased exposure of people to women in a greatly expanded range of roles would produce changes in gender stereotypes is predicted by virtually all models of the process of stereotype change (Hilton & von Hippel, 1996, pp. 258–259).

The apparent fluidity of gender stereotypes, and our evidence suggesting a fairly dramatic change over a period of only one generation, leads to the question of how current social trends and changes in public policy may affect the gender stereotypes of the future. Governmental regulations such as the Civil Rights legislation of 1964, Affirmative Action, Title VII (prohibiting sexual harassment in the workplace), and Title IX (mandating the shared distribution of resources to women's athletic programs), have created altered work and school environments for many men and women. Men and women have gained familiarity with each other as persons outside family roles through affiliations in the workplace and associated formal and informal settings. This exposure to women in diversified roles would be expected to have created the experiences that led to stereotype change in both men and women.

Perhaps more significant than the changes in content of stereotypes have been apparent changes in the perceived social desirability of traits associated with the Typical Man and with the Typical Woman. Compared to the participants in the study of Rosenkrantz, *et al.* (1968), the groups of participants in our study indicated significantly less valuation of male-associated characteristics and greater valuation of female-associated characteristics. Assuming a strong relationship between gender stereotypes, differential valuation of gender-associated traits, and social stratification based on sex (Ridgeway, 1997), it will be interesting to see the extent to which fewer stereotypes and altered trait valuations are to be reflected in enhanced social status for women.

REFERENCES

Beckwith, J. B. (1993). Gender stereotypes and mental health revisited. *Social Behavior & Personality, 21,* 85–88.

Bergen, D. J., & Williams, J. E. (1988). Sex stereotypes in the United States revisited: 1972–1988. *Sex Roles, 24,* 413–423.

Broverman, I. K., Broverman, D. M., Clarkson, F. E., Rosenkrantz, P. S., & Vogel, S. R. (1970). Sex-role stereotypes and clinical judgments of mental health. *Journal of Consulting and Clinical Psychology, 34,* 1–7.

Broverman, I. K., Vogel, S. R., Broverman, D. M., Clarkson, F. E., & Rosenkrantz, P. S. (1972). Sex-role stereotypes: a current appraisal. *Journal of Social Issues, 28,* 59–78.

Cohen, J. (1962). The statistical power of abnormal-social psychological research: a review. *Journal of Abnormal and Social Psychology, 65,* 145–153.

Cromwell, V. L., & Cromwell, R. E. (1978). Perceived dominance in decision-making and conflict resolution among Anglo, Black, and Chicano couples. *Journal of Marriage and the Family, 40,* 749–759.

Deaux, K., & Kite, M. E. (1987). Gender stereotypes: some thoughts on the cognitive organization of gender-related information. Special issue: gender roles. *Academic Psychology Bulletin, 7,* 123–144.

de Lisi, R., & Soundranayagam, L. (1990). The conceptual structure of sex role stereotypes in college students. *Sex Roles, 23,* 593–611.

der Karabetian, A., & Smith, A. J. (1977). Sex-role stereotyping in the United States: is it changing? *Sex Roles, 3,* 193–198.

Eagly, A. H., & Wood, W. (1982). Inferred sex differences in status as a determinant of gender stereotypes about social influence, *Journal of Personality and Social Psychology, 43,* 915–928.

Edwards, A. L. (1984). *An introduction to linear regression and correlation.* (2nd ed.) New York: W. H. Freeman.

Fiebert, M. S., & Meyer, M. W. (1997). Gender stereotypes: a bias against men, *Journal of Psychology, 131,* 407–410.

Gonzales, A. (1982). Sex roles of the traditional Mexican family: a comparison of Chicano and Anglo students' attitudes. *Journal of Cross-Cultural Psychology, 13,* 330–339.

Hansson, R. O., O'Connor, M. E., Jones, W. H., & Mihelich, M. H. (1980). Role relevant sex typing and opportunity in agentic and communal domains. *Journal of Personality, 48,* 419–434.

Hilton, J. L., & von Hippel, W. (1996). Stereotypes. *Annual Review of Psychology, 47,* 237–271.

Lii, S-Y., & Wang, S-Y. (1982). A cross-cultural study on sex-role stereotypes and social desirability. *Sex Roles, 8,* 481–491.

McKee, J. P., & Sherriffs, A. C. (1957). The differential evaluation of males and females. *Journal of Personality, 25,* 356–371.

Phillips, R. D., & Gilroy, F. D. (1985). Sex-role stereotypes and clinical judgments of mental health: the Brovermans' findings reexamined. *Sex Roles, 12,* 179–193.

Poole, D. A., & Tapley, A. E. (1988). Sex roles, social roles, and clinical judgments of mental health. *Sex Roles, 19,* 265–272.

Reskin, B., & Roos, P. (1990). *Job queues, gender gueues: explaining women's inroads into male occupations,* Philadelphia, PA: Temple Univer. Press.

Ridgeway, C. L. (1997). Interaction and the conservation of gender inequality: considering employment. *American Sociological Review, 62,* 218–235.

Rosenkrantz, P. S., Vogel, S. R., Bee, H., Broverman, I. K., & Broverman, D. M. (1968). Sex role stereotypes and self-concepts in college students. *Journal of Consulting and Clinical Psychology, 32,* 287–295.

Ruble, T. L. (1983). Sex stereotypes: issues of change in the 1970s. *Sex Roles, 9,* 397–402.

Senour, M. N. (1977). Psychology of the Chicana. In J. L. Martinez (Ed.), *Chicano psychology.* New York: Academic Press. Pp. 329–342.

Sherriffs, A. C., & Jarrett, R. F. (1953). Sex differences in attitudes about sex differences. *Journal of Psychology, 35,* 161–168.

Sherriffs, A. C., & McKee, J. P. (1957). Qualitative aspects of beliefs about men and women. *Journal of Personality, 25,* 451–464.

Smith, M. L. (1980). Sex bias in counseling and psychotherapy. *Psychological Bulletin, 87,* 392–407.

SPSS, Inc. (1994). SPSS *6.1 for windows update.* Chicago, IL: SPSS, Inc.

Vogel, S. R., Broverman, I. K., Broverman, D. M., Clarkson, F. E., & Rosenkrantz, P. S. (1970). Maternal employment and perception of sex roles among college students. *Developmental Psychology, 3,* 384–391.

West, C., & Zimmerman, D. (1987). Doing gender. *Gender and Society, 1,* 125–151.

Williams, J. E., & Best, D. L. (1990). *Measuring sex stereotypes: a multinational study.* Newbury Park, CA: Sage.

Wolff, L., & Taylor, S. E. (1979). Sex, sex role identification, and awareness of sex-role stereotypes. *Journal of Personality, 47,* 177–184.

Accepted August 21, 2000.

RESPONSE SHEET

for Muriel N Nesbitt: Gender Stereotypes after Thirty Years

1. Nesbitt, et al., investigated whether gender stereotypes have changed in the last 30 years. What did they find?

2. Write one question regarding this article that can be used for class discussion.

3. Describe one application of the information in this article. It can be:
1) A next research step to take
2) An educational, clinical/counseling or rearing application
3) A personal application

Primitive Gender Roles

by Lynn Ourth

Thousands of years ago there were very clearly delineated and severely enforced gender roles assigned to females and males. Jean Auel, author of *The Clan of the Cave Bear,* observes that males were providers and protectors and females were homemakers, healthcaregivers and helpmeets. A good portion of the following discussion is based on her reporting.

There are three propositions that focus this discussion of gender roles. **One,** they were virtually universal, not just regional or associated with one or two language groups. **Two,** there is remarkable continuity over time to the present. **Three,** survival of the fittest was tied to gender roles. Males lost their lives if they got lost while on the hunt or got trampled, or were killed in combat. Females, rather than losing their lives, were not selected to give birth, if they were not effective in their roles, or misbehaved, genderwise. The key element in this proposition is that since the selection process over thousands of generations was tied to gender, there should be gender differentiation in the brain and in the body.

Propositions one and two are well established in the general literature. Proposition three will be considered here by first looking at the nature of the five gender roles identified above and next reviewing the current findings on brain differentiation.

Males

1. *Provider.* Most all of the males of the clan spent more time hunting big game than anything else. Each hunt was almost always in new, strange, territory, and far away from the camp base. Though they went out as a group, they engaged in individual excursions prior to the actual kill. The kill involved running, accurate throwing of a heavy spear, judging the prey's rate of movement (elapsed distance) and time of arrival. Following the kill, initial cutting of thick hides, moving very large body parts and guarding the meat were carried out.

   Look at how many of these activities call for spatial skills! Retracing requires recognizing differences in shapes that are very similar to each other. Also to be able to engage in mental rotation, which is the ability to turn an object mentally determine if it is the same. Being able to know what distance will be traversed by the speed of movement is a spatial calculation. As is the proper arc for a throw. They couldn't write these out on paper.

   Large muscle strength and coordination are the other common elements. They were hunks! In fact, enough so that they apparently would become muscle-bound and therefore inept in tasks calling for fine muscle applications—like threading a needle. You can see where this is going: another reason the females did these things.

   One other thing. Reading non-verbal signals, both those of colleagues and prey, was an essential ability. They were often too far from each other to hear. And they absolutely had to be able to read the intent of the behemoth prior to the actual behavior.
2. *Protector.* Most of the same skills needed for hunting are also involved in combat, save for fewer instances of being in distant strange territory and having to retrace. There is one element that is most emphasized in combat, though. To be successful, there must be heightened aggressive feelings, which inhibit fear, raise pain thresholds and sustain the desire to inflict injury and death upon the enemy. Females were absolutely forbidden to engage in combat or to hunt. If one was found even handling weapons, she would be severely punished.

Females

Central to an understanding of the nature of these female roles is that they are contingent upon the male's roles. The female had no independent existence; she served the male—and his children; he owned her and could discard her at will.

1. *Homemaker.* Most often, home meant a cave. When on the move, shelters made of hides were backup homes. The process of homemaking is quite similar today, except that they could not go and buy anything. They made finished foods, clothes and home furnishings and decorations from "scratch." This calls for an immense amount of eye-fine finger coordinated activity. If she were quite poor at these things, her mate could reject her and seek another. This rejection ordinarily influenced other males, and she could wind up not having any children.

2. *Healthcaregiver.* The primitive female has been characterized as a gatherer. She gathered edible plants, fish and small animals, wood and herbs. Gathering calls several abilities: some hand-eye coordination, memory for details, making fine discriminations among similar plants, and rapid scanning. Again, if she did quite poorly, she would not be sought as a mate, or would be beaten if she were chosen.
3. *Helpmeet.* A helpmeet understands, supports, anticipates, nurtures; this person's focus is upon mate and children, not self. To effectively engage in these interpersonal processes, the female had to be able to read verbal and non-verbal cues, understand others' feelings, listen and vocalize. All these activities had to be infused with positive feeling, especially supporting and nurturing. Females who were poor at these abilities, then as now, were much less likely to be chosen as durable companions. Linguistic and perceptual capabilities and proactive feelings are featured in all of these roles, and being good at them was close to essential to have the opportunity to give birth and transmit her genes to the next generation.

GENDER-RELATED BRAIN DIFFERENTIATION

As proposed above, gender roles were set up such that differential selection could directly occur with incumbents in these roles. It certainly appears that differentiation has taken place through hemispheric lateralization with the left being a repository for the female, and the right for the male. Finally, the differentiation should reflect those abilities that were differentially called upon by those early gender roles.

THE FEMALE BRAIN

1. *The left hemisphere.* There is additional gray matter on the rear portion of the lateral sulcus, which is in the upper portion of the temporal lobe (in the splanum temporale) and which is not present in the right temporal lobe. This increase is located exactly where the integration of linguistic inputs takes place (Warnicke's area)—that is, understanding. All linguistic processing takes place on the left side; and so do speaking abilities. It has been amply demonstrated that females are superior in all linguistic functions, from birth and throughout adulthood with equalizing in only a few functions in adulthood. There is one exception found, starting in middle childhood: solving analogies. This ability involves spatially based memory storage.
2. *Processing aspects.* There is a striking difference in how the female brain responds to most incoming stimuli, and especially social stimuli: a lot more of it "lights up." A key example of this is that eight times more of her brain responds to the presence of sadness in another than does the male brain. The single most important capability of a helpmeet is to be able to recognize and then be responsive to this condition in another. Taking linguistic and empathic skills together, there is little doubt that the female has evolved into a superior interpersonal being.
3. *The corpus callosum.* The female brain has about 20% more tissue in this neural bridge between the two hemispheres. This helps the greater whole brain response and it does another thing: it enables the female to engage in faster perceptual scanning, discrimination and memory.

The Male Brain

1. *The right hemisphere.* The lateral sulcus is extended substantially further than it is for the left hemisphere. This establishes greater spatial delineation and coordination, which are important bases for spatial discrimination and analysis. Males are more capable in both. They are also better in those mathematical forms that incorporate spatial analyses: geometry, analytical geometry and all "higher math." Also located in the right hemisphere are the proclivities for aggression (and other negative emotions) and non-verbal recognition.
2. *Large muscle density and strength.* What is obvious is also true. Males are stronger! A distinction must be made, though. They can engage in remarkable feats of strength for short periods of time, which is called kinetic strength. Female muscles have greater capability to sustain their level of functioning, or having endurance. It is probably fairly apparent that males' stints of strength relate more to engaging prey or an enemy, while females were engaged in more sustained activities such as carrying wood or babies and sewing garments.

CHAPTER

8

Gender Differences: Brain Lateralization

The concept gender lateralization refers to the now fairly reliable observation that the left side of the brain belongs to the female, the right side to the male. Which means that the specialized functions that are based on those sides "belong" to those genders. The five selections that are included in this section all address this possibility: What are those lateralized functions? Do they reflect the primitive roles that men and women started out with? What do men and women really do best? Read Hales, Kolata, Nadeau, Gorman and Phillips and discover the latest work on the questions just raised. And much more.

The Female Brain

by Dianne Hales

After twenty years of marriage, my husband still doesn't understand me. Why, he want to know, am I always doing three things at once? How is it that I am never at a loss for words? And how can I recall the names of the couple we met years ago in Hawaii when he can't?

Now I know what to tell him: It's my brain. Breakthrough research in neuroscience is revealing that the root of many puzzling gender differences may lie in our heads. This is not to say, as scientists once believed, that the female brain is in any way inferior. In fact, men's and women's brains have much in common, but they are definitely not the same—in size, structure or sensitivities.

Overall, a woman's brain, like her body, is on average 10 to 15 percent smaller than a man's, yet the regions dedicated to higher cognitive functions such as language are more densely packed with neurons. While we don't yet know the implications of all these findings, one thing is very clear: "Male and female brains do the same things, but they do them differently," says neuropsychiatrist Raquel Gur, M.D., Ph.D., of the University of Pennsylvania, in Philadelphia.

According to researchers, these are the ten most important ways women's brains differ from men's.

Research has finally proved what we've suspected all along: Women really do use more of their brains than men do. Here, the latest scientific findings about the way our minds work

1. Women Use More of Their Brains

"Whatever women do—even just wiggling their thumbs—their neuron activity is more greatly distributed throughout the brain," says Mark George, M.D., a psychiatrist and neurologist at the Medical University of South Carolina, in Charleston, and a pioneer in using sophisticated neuroimaging techniques, such as MRI (magnetic resonance imaging). As George explains it, when a male puts his mind to work, neurons turn on in highly specific areas. When a woman does, so many brain cells light up that the scans look like a night view of Las Vegas. Though researchers have not yet discovered the reason for this difference, one possible—though controversial—explanation is that the corpus callosum, the bridge of fibers running down the center of the brain, may be thicker in females, allowing more crosstalk between the emotional, intuitive right hemisphere and the rational, just-the-facts left.

Because the male brain is more compartmentalized, George notes, men may be better able to focus intensely. This may explain why husbands can immerse themselves in the sports pages while the baby cries, the phone rings and the dog barks.

"Traditionally, a male's main function was to defend territory, find food, find a female," says neuroanatomist Marian Diamond, Ph.D., of the University of California at Berkeley. "He had to be able to focus in order to survive. What the female needed as a mother was to be ready to go in all directions in order to protect her young."

A woman's whole-brain modus operandi is just as valuable for the way we live today. With so many things to do, no woman could possibly get by using half her brain.

2. The Female Brain Responds More Intensely to Emotion

Three years ago, when psychiatrist George scanned the brains of men and women as they recalled a range of emotional experiences, he wasn't expecting to find any major gender differences. "When I did, they were so huge that I hesitated to report them," he recalls. His research showed that the sexes clearly respond differently during emotions,

Boosting Your Brain Power

We've found that at every age, both genders can change brain structures and improve abilities," says neuroanatomist Marian Diamond. Here are some ways to go about it:

- SEEK OUT STIMULATION. "Newness is exceedingly important," says Diamond. "But no two human brains are the same, so each person will be stimulated by different things." For some, travel provides energizing novelty; for others, painting does.
- USE EMOTIONAL TAGS. If you want to remember the name of a restaurant, remember how you felt the last time you were there. Do the same when adding any new information to your memory banks.
- PRACTICE SKILLS THAT DON'T COME AUTOMATICALLY TO YOU. For instance, if you've never had a head for figures, strengthen your math skills by using your brain—rather than a calculator—to balance your checkbook.
- WATCH YOUR BLOOD PRESSURE. If untreated, hypertension can cause fuzzy thinking later in life and can increase the risk of stroke and age-related memory loss.
- DON'T NEGLECT SLEEP. "Women often underestimate the profound effect that fatigue has on memory and concentration," says psychologist Thomas Crook. "Variations in a normal sleep cycle can diminish performance by thirty percent." The impact of sleep loss gets even worse as we get older.
- EXERCISE YOUR BODY. "Strong data show that physical fitness is important to cognitive function," says Crook. Regular exercise—especially aerobic workouts—may enhance mental sharpness by improving circulation of blood and oxygen through the brain as well as the body.
- EAT SENSIBLY. "Protein is essential [to the brain], as are B vitamins," says Diamond. "You want to enrich your brain, so you need a balanced diet." —D.H.

especially sadness. In his experiments, melancholy feelings activated neurons in an area eight times larger in women than in men.

"The experiences that evoked sadness in our volunteers all involved family, friends and loved ones," says George. "They were rarely about work or achievement."

Neuroscience may be confirming what psychologists have been telling us for years: Relationships matter more to women. And our brains' intense reaction to their loss may, at least in theory, increase our vulnerability to depression, which is twice as common in women as in men.

The female brain also can detect others' emotions more accurately. Raquel Gur and her husband, Ruben Gur, Ph.D., a psychologist, did brain scans on volunteers who looked at photographs of actors depicting various emotions. Both sexes knew happiness when they saw it, but the men had a much harder time recognizing sadness, especially in women. "A woman's face had to be really sad for a man to see it," Ruben Gur says. "The subtle expressions went right by them, even though their brains were working harder to figure it out. When it comes to reading emotion, men just don't get it."

3. The Female Brain Is Wired for Expression, Not Aggression

When they studied women and men in a state of relaxation, the Gurs noticed differences in the limbic system, a ring of structures within the brain that process the entire spectrum of human emotion. Most male brains "idle" in an ancient region of this system sometimes called the *reptilian brain*—that gives rise to active expressions of emotion, such as aggression and violence. The resting gear of most female brains, in comparison, lies in a different ration—the *cingulate gyrus,* a more recently evolved part of the limbic system related to symbolic forms of expression, such as gestures and words.

> Are men emotionally more primitive than women? "The logical conclusion is yes," says one expert

Does this mean that men are emotionally more primitive than women? "The logical conclusion is yes," says Ruben Gur. "At the least, this difference may explain why men are prone to physical action, while women opt for verbal tactics. Beating somebody up comes from the old limbic brain. Saying 'I'm angry with you' comes from the new limbic. You could argue that women are one half step ahead of men in evolution in the sense that they use the newer part of the brain more in dealing with emotion."

4. The Female Brain Has a Way With Words

Girls generally speak sooner, learn to read faster and have fewer learning disorders. The reason, according to Yale University professors of neurology Sally Shaywitz, M.D., and Bennett Shaywitz, M.D., may be that they use neural regions on both sides of the brain when they read or engage in other verbal exercises. In contrast, males draw only on neural regions in the left hemisphere.

This bilateral approach may give women an advantage by allowing us to draw on the emotions and experiences of the right brain as well as the reasoning powers of the logical left brain. As adults, women tend to be more verbally adept than men: In timed tests, women think of more words that start with the same letter, list more synonyms and come up with names for colors or shapes more quickly than men. Women even memorize letters of the alphabet faster.

But the female brain's dual-hemisphere language processing provides a far more significant benefit: It helps women who suffer stroke or brain injury recover more easily. "Because women activate a larger number of neurons than men when they speak or read, they're less vulnerable if part of the brain is damaged," says George. "In medicine, we've observed that women who have strokes tend to regain more of their verbal abilities than men do, and their use of neurons in both hemispheres may be why."

5. Sexual Pleasure May Register in a Different Location in the Female Brain

According to a recent medical report, a Scottish woman developed a most unusual complaint: uncontrollable orgasms that interrupted her driving, conversations and daily routines. Since these "sexual seizures" began about the same time as intense headaches, her doctors suspected the problem might lie in her brain. Tests did indeed reveal an abnormality in the right temporal lobe—a highly developed part of the brain—that was probably caused by an undetected hemorrhage several years before. Treatment with antiseizure medication relieved the woman's symptoms—and led her doctors to speculate that female orgasms may originate in a different brain location than male climaxes. In a previous report on a man with a similar disorder, doctors had pinpointed the hypothalamus, a more primitive brain region, as the site of male sexual satisfaction.

6. Women Notice More Than Men and Navigate Differently

On the road, women pay more attention than men to what they see, particularly to landmarks like the coffee shop on the corner or the church across from the playground. When retracing a route or giving directions, women rely on such landmarks—unlike men, who think in terms of direction and distance (half a mile west, then north two miles).

An innate sense of space and distance may be part of a human male's biological legacy. "I suspect that males are born with some biological component that gives them an edge in spatial tasks," says Deborah Blum, a science writer and author of *Sex on the Brain* (Viking, 1997), who notes that males consistently score higher in exercises such as mentally rotating an object in three dimensions. Once this skill may have translated into better aim when hurling a spear at a woolly mammoth; today it may explain why my husband can park a minivan in a space the size of a postage stamp.

Women's spatial skills do improve with time and experience. By middle age, women's scores on spatial tests are about equal to men's; later in life, they surpass them.

7. A Woman's Vision Is More Acute and Her Hearing Is More Sensitive

Male and female brains perceive light and sound very differently, says neurologist Karl Pribram, M.D., director of the Center for Brain Research and Informational Sciences at Radford College, in Radford, Virginia. A woman's hearing tends to be so sensitive that she can often hear whispers that never even register to a man's ear. And her vision is so much more acute that she can tread her way along a slippery path by moonlight as he squints before taking a single step.

Sensory tests confirm that men are less tolerant of bright light but retain their ability to see well at all distances as they age. A woman's vision begins to decline between ages thirty-five and forty-four; a man's, between forty-five and fifty-four.

"At every age, women's memories outperform men's"

On the other hand, women hear a much broader range of sounds than men. Female hearing doesn't start to deteriorate until the late fifties; men start losing their ability to detect high tones in their late forties.

8. A Woman's Memory is Sharper

"At every age, women's memories outperform men's," reports psychologist Thomas Crook, Ph.D., president of Psychologix, a research organization based in Bethesda, Maryland, and Scottsdale, Arizona, that has tested the memories of more than 50,000 men and women. "Women have a greater ability to associate names with faces than men do, and they're also better at recalling lists of things, like groceries and details of personal experiences."

Both genders are prone to age-associated memory loss, which diminishes the ability to remember words and names by as much as 50 percent between ages twenty-five and sixty-five. However, says Crook, women's memories generally stay stronger. One reason may be that we have a unique way of filing information in our memory banks.

"The events people remember best are those that we tag with an emotion," Crook says. "Since women use more of their right brains, which process emotions, they may do this automatically."

9. The Female Brain Ages More Slowly Than the Male's

A new study reported in *The Archives of Neurology* earlier this year found that the male brain shrinks faster than the female brain.

In fact, according to Ruben Gur, who has done his own research on women and men at various ages, the male brain loses tissue at almost three times the rate the female brain does. Because of this gender difference, men's brains, which are larger and heavier than women's when both are young, shrink so much that their all-important frontal lobes are approximately the same size by the time both sexes reach their forties.

Other parts of men's brains also atrophy more rapidly. "If you look at men in the age range from eighteen to forty-five, you see a steady decline in abilities, and this decline is correlated with a decline in frontal-lobe volume," says Gur. "We don't see a trend in women the same age toward any deterioration of abilities or brain volume." Among the consequences of male brain shrinkage are poorer memory, less ability to pay attention—and greater irritability. "Yes, men do get grumpier with old age," says Gur. "You can blame it on their brains."

The reason that men's brains change size so drastically may have to do with fuel efficiency. The female brain seems able to reduce its metabolic rate—that is, its use of brain glucose—over time, whereas the brains of older men metabolize glucose at higher rates than when they were younger. Women, in other words, gear down to a more fuel-efficient cruising speed as they age, while male brains keep revving the engine—possibly because of testosterone's influence. "Even though women also lose some tissue as they age, they seem to be riding herd on what's left," says Gur. This difference, he speculates, may be part of the reason that females generally outlive males.

But while women's brains are more durable, they do have one greater vulnerability as they get older: a threefold increase in risk for Alzheimer's disease. Of the approximately four million Americans affected by this form of dementia, an estimated three quarters are women. Researchers believe this may be due to the declining levels of estrogen as women age. According to preliminary tests, estrogen replacement therapy may reduce the risk of Alzheimer's and delay the symptoms of the disease in women.

10. The Female Brain Is More Intuitive

Because of the constant crosstalk between the left brain's rationality and the right's emotionality, the female brain may make connections that might not occur to a man. Some call this skill a form of emotional intelligence; others think of it as woman's intuition.

"Intuition involves a network in the brain and the body," explains Mona Lisa Schulz, M.D., Ph.D., a psychiatrist in private practice in Portland, Maine, and author of *Awakening Intuition* (Crown, 1998). "We've learned that people use multiple areas of the brain when making decisions—intuitive or otherwise. And because women's brains are less lateralized, they may have better access to both sides of the brain. They usually don't see things as cut-and-dried, the way men do."

This can be a real advantage in every part of a woman's life—whether it's figuring out why a young child seems anxious or why office morale has slumped. "Because they're so good at seeing emotional nuances," notes Raquel Gur, "women can read what's happening quickly and ask themselves: What should I say now?"

Dianne Hales is a contributing editor of Ladies' Home Journal.

RESPONSE SHEET

for Dianne Hales: The Female Brain

1. This article identifies ten ways in which the female brain is more proficient than is the male's brain. BD three implications or so whats regarding this info.

2. Write one question regarding this article that can be used for class discussion.

3. Describe one application of the information in this article. It can be:
   1) A next research step to take
   2) An educational, clinical/counseling or rearing application
   3) A personal application

Man's World, Woman's World? Brain Studies Point to Differences

Gina Kolata

Dr. Ronald Munson, a philosopher of science at the University of Missouri, was elated when Good Housekeeping magazine considered publishing an excerpt from the latest of the novels he writes on the side. The magazine eventually decided not to publish the piece, but Dr. Munson was much consoled by a letter from an editor telling him that she liked the book, which is written from a woman's point of view, and could hardly believe a man had written it.

It is a popular notion: that men and women are so intrinsically different that they literally live in different worlds, unable to understand each other's perspectives fully. There is a male brain and a female brain, a male way of thinking and a female way. But only now are scientists in a position to address whether the notion is true.

The question of brain differences between the sexes is a sensitive and controversial field of inquiry. It has been smirched by unjustifiable interpretations of data, including claims that women are less intelligent because their brains are smaller than those of men. It has been sullied by over-interpretations of data, like the claims that women are genetically less able to do everyday mathematics because men, on average, are slightly better at mentally rotating three dimensional objects in space.

But over the years, with a large body of animal studies and studies of humans that include psychological tests, anatomical studies, and increasingly, brain scans, researchers are consistently finding that the brains of the two sexes are subtly but significantly different.

Now researchers have a new noninvasive method, functional magnetic resonance imaging, for studying the live human brain at work. With it, one group recently detected certain apparent differences in the way men's and women's brains function while they are thinking. While stressing extreme caution in drawing conclusions from the data, scientists say nonetheless that the groundwork was being laid for determining what the differences really mean.

New scanner finds more evidence of how the sexes differ in brain functions.

"What it means is that we finally have the tools at hand to begin answering these questions," said Dr. Sally Shaywitz, a behavioral scientist at the Yale University School of Medicine. But she cautioned: "We have to be very very careful. It behooves us to understand that we've just begun."

The most striking evidence that the brains of men and women function differently came from a recent study by Dr. Shaywitz and her husband, Dr. Bennett A. Shaywitz, a neurologist, who is also at the Yale medical school. The Shaywitzes and their colleagues used functional magnetic resonance imaging to watch brains in action as 19 men and 19 women read nonsense words and determined whether they rhymed.

In a paper, published in the Feb. 16 issue of Nature, the Shaywitzes reported that the subjects did equally well at the task, but the men and women used different areas of their brains. The men used just a small area on the left side of the brain, next to Broca's area, which is near the temple. Broca's area has long been thought to be associated with

Men have larger brains; women have more neurons.

From the *NewYork Times,* February 28, 1995, pp. c1, c7.

speech. The women used this area as well as an area on the right side of the brain. This was the first dear evidence that men and women can use their brains differently while they are thinking.

Another recent study by Dr. Ruben C. Gur, the director of the brain behavior laboratory at the University of Pennsylvania School of Medicine, and his colleagues, used magnetic resonance imaging to look at the metabolic activity of the brains of 37 young men and 24 young women when they were at rest, not consciously thinking of anything.

In the study published in the Jan. 27 issue of the journal Science, the investigators found that for the most part, the brains of men and women at rest were indistinguishable from each other. But there was one difference, found in a brain structure called the limbic system that regulates emotions. Men, on average, had higher brain activity in the more ancient and primitive regions of the limbic system, the parts that are more involved with action. Women, on average, had more activity in the newer and more complex parts of the limbic system, which are involved in symbolic actions.

Dr. Gur explained the distinction: "If a dog is angry and jumps and bites, that's an action. If he is angry and bares his fangs and growls, that's more symbolic."

Dr. Sandra Witelson, a neuroscientist at McMaster University in Hamilton, Ontario, has focused on brain anatomy, studying people with terminal cancers that do not involve the brain. The patients have agreed to participate in neurological and psychological tests and then to allow Dr. Witelson and her colleagues to examine their brains after they die, to look for relationships between brain structures and functions. So far she has studied 90 brains.

Several years ago, Dr. Witelson reported that women have a larger corpus callosum, the tangle of fibers that run down the center of the brain and enable the two hemispheres to communicate. In addition, she said, she found that a region in the right side of the brain that corresponds to the region women used in the reading study by the Shaywitzes was larger in women than in men.

Most recently Dr. Witelson discovered, by painstakingly counting brain cells, that although men have larger brains than women, women have about 11 percent more neurons. These extra nerve cells are densely packed in two of the six layers of the cerebral cortex, the outer shell of the brain, in areas at the level of the temple, behind the eye. These are regions used for understanding language and for recognizing melodies and the tones in speech. Although the sample was small, five men and four women, "the results are very very clear," Dr. Witelson said.

Going along with the studies of brain anatomy and activity are a large body of psychological studies showing that men and women have different mental abilities. Psychologists have consistently shown that men, on average, are slightly better than women at spatial tasks, like visualizing figures rotated in three dimensions, and women, on average, are slightly better at verbal tasks.

Dr. Gur and his colleagues recently looked at how well men and women can distinguish emotions on someone else's face. Both men and women were equally adept at noticing when someone else was happy, Dr. Gur found. And women had no trouble telling if a man or a woman was sad. But men were different. They were as sensitive as women in deciding if a man's face was sad—giving correct responses 90 percent of the time. But they were correct about 70 percent of the time in deciding if women were sad; the women were correct 90 percent of the time.

"A woman's face had to be really sad for men to see it," Dr. Gur said. "The subtle expressions went right by them."

Studies in laboratory animals also find differences between male and female brains. In rats, for example, male brains are three to seven times larger than female brains in a specific area, the preoptic nucleus, and this difference is controlled by sex hormones that bathe rats when they are fetuses.

"The potential existence of structural sex differences in human brains is almost predicted from the work in other animals," said Dr. Roger Gorski, a professor of anatomy and cell biology at the University of California in Los Angeles. "I think it's a really fundamental concept and I'm sure, without proof, that it applies to our brains."

But the question is, if there are these differences, what do they mean?

Dr. Gorski and others are wary about drawing conclusions. "What happens is that people overinterpret these things," Dr. Gorski said. "The brain is very complicated, and even in animals that we've studied for many years, we don't really know the function of many brain areas."

This is exemplified, Dr. Gorski said, in his own work on differences in rat brains. Fifteen years ago, he and his colleagues discovered that males have a comparatively huge preoptic nucleus and that the area in females is tiny. But Dr. Gorski added: "We've been studying this nucleus for 15 years, and we still don't know what it does. The most likely explanation is that it has to do with sexual behavior, but it is very very difficult to study. These regions are very small and they are interconnected with other things." Moreover, he said, "nothing like it has been shown in humans."

And, with the exception of the work by the Shaywitzes, all other findings of differences in the brains or mental abilities of men and women have also found that there is an amazing degree of overlap. "There is so much overlap that if you take any individual man and woman, they might show differences in the opposite direction" from the statistical findings, Dr. Gorski said.

Dr. Munson, the philosopher of science, said that with the findings so far, "we still can't tell whether the experiences are different" when men and women think. "All we can tell is that the brain processes are different," he said, adding that "there is no Archimedean point on which you can stand, outside of experience, and say the two are the same. It reminds me of the people who show what the world looks like through a multiplicity of lenses and say 'This is what the fly sees.' "But, Dr. Munson added, "We don't know what the fly sees." All we know he explained, is what we see looking through those lenses.

Some researchers, however, say that the science is at least showing the way to answering the ancient mind-body problem, as applied to the cognitive worlds of men and women.

Dr. Norman Krasnegor, who directs the human learning and behavior branch at the National Institute of Child Health and Human Development, said the difference that science made was that when philosophers talked about mind, they "always were saying, 'We've got this black box.' " But now he said, "we don't have a black box; now we are beginning to get to its operations."

Dr. Gur said science was the best hope for discovering whether men and women inhabited different worlds. It is not possible to answer that question simply by asking people to describe what they perceive, Dr. Gur said, because "when you talk and ask questions, you are talking to the very small portion of the brain that is capable of talking." If investigators ask people to tell them what they are thinking, "that may or may not be closely related to what was taking place" in the brain, Dr. Gur said.

On the other hand, he said, scientists have discovered that what primates perceived depends on how their brains function. Some neurons fire only in response to lines that are oriented at particular angles, while others seem to recognize faces. The world may well be what the philosopher Descartes said it was, an embodiment of the workings of the human mind, Dr. Gur said. "Descartes said that we are creating our world," he said. "But there is a world out there that we can't know."

Dr. Gur said that at this point he would hesitate to boldly proclaim that men and women inhabit different worlds. "I'd say that science might be leading us in that direction," he said, but before he commits himself he would like to see more definite differences in the way men's and women's brains function and to know more about what the differences mean.

Dr. Witelson cautioned that "at this point, it is a very big leap to go from any of the structural or organizational differences that were demonstrated to the cognitive differences that were demonstrated." She explained that "all you have is two sets of differences, and whether one is the basis of the other has not been shown." But she added, "One can speculate."

Dr. Witelson emphasized that in speculating she was "making a very big leap," but she noted that "we all live in our different worlds and our worlds depend on our brains.

"And," she said, "if these sex differences in the brain, with 'if' in big capital letters, do have cognitive consequences, and it would be hard to believe there would be none, then it is possible that there is a genuine difference in the kinds of things that men and women perceive and how these things are integrated. To that extent it may be possible that in some respects there is less of an easy cognitive or emotional communication between the sexes as a group because our brains may be wired differently."

The Shaywitzes said they were reluctant even to speculate from the data at hand. But, they said, they think that the deep philosophical questions about the perceptual worlds of men and women can eventually be resolved by science.

"It is a truism that men and women are different," Dr. Bennett Shaywitz said. "What I think we can do now is to take what is essentially folklore and place it in the context of science. There is a real scientific method available to answer some of these questions."

Dr. Sally Shaywitz added: "I think we've taken a qualitative leap forward in our ability to ask questions." But, she said, "the field is simply too young to have provided more than a very intriguing appetizer."

RESPONSE SHEET

for Gina Kolata: Man's World, Woman's World?

1. What does this article add to Dianne Hales' observations? Name five.

2. Write one question regarding this article that can be used for class discussion.

3. Describe one application of the information in this article. It can be:
1) A next research step to take
2) An educational, clinical/counseling or rearing application
3) A personal application

Brain Sex and the Language of Love

Robert L. Nadeau

If we can believe the experts, the standard for healthy intimacy in love relationships between men and women is female, and maleness is a disease in desperate need of a cure. Men, say social scientists, have a "trained incapacity to share" and have learned to overvalue independence and to fear emotional involvement. Female friendships, claim the intimacy experts, are based on emotional bonding and mutual support, and male friendships on competition, emotional inhibition, and aggression.[1] Social scientists have also pathologized maleness because men typically view love as action, or doing things for another, while women view love as talking and acknowledging feelings.

In fairness to the intimacy experts, what they say about differences in the behavior of men and women has been well documented. Numerous studies have shown that men feel close to other men when working or playing side by side, while women feel close to other women when talking face to face.[2] Male group behavior is characterized by an emphasis on space, privacy, and autonomy, and female group behavior by a need to feel included, connected, and attached.[3] Male conversation tends to center around activities (sports, politics, work), and personal matters are discussed in terms of strengths and achievements. Female conversation, in contrast, is more likely to center around feelings and relationships, and there is considerably less reluctance to reveal fears and weaknesses.

Men and women also appear to experience intimacy in disparate ways. In men's relationships with other men, the index of intimacy is the degree of comfort and relaxation felt when engaged in activities, such as helping a friend move furniture or repair cars. Even when men comfort one another in crisis situations, like the loss of a family member or a spouse, it is physical presence, rather than intimate talk, that tends to be most valued.[4]

The index for intimacy among women is the extent to which personal feelings can be shared in a climate of mutual support and trust. What tends to be most valued in these interactions is confirmation of feelings as opposed to constructive criticism and advice. When women are asked to describe the benefits of such conversations with other women, they typically mention relief from anxiety and stress, feeling better, and a more enhanced sense of self-worth. Although women also express intimacy by doing things for other women, the doing is typically viewed as an occasion for verbal intimacy.[5]

The response of males to depression also favors action, or a tendency to "run" when overcome with sadness, anxiety, or dread. And when men talk about their depression in therapy, they typically "rush through" an account of their emotions and describe depression with action metaphors, such as "running in place," "running wide open," and "pushing the edge."[6] When women are clinically depressed, they are more willing to talk about their feelings, to find opportunities to do so with other women, and to seek help in talk therapy. Women also typically disclose the sources of depression in detailed narratives that represent and analyze experience. And while men tend to respond to clinical depression by running or moving, women tend to respond with sedentary activities like uncontrollable crying, staying in bed, and compulsive eating.

The sex-specific patterns that lie beneath the diversity of these behaviors reduce to a male orientation toward action and a female orientation toward talking. Why is this

This article originally appeared in *The World & I*, November 1997, pp. 330-339. Reprinted by permission of *The World & I*, a publication of the Washington Times Corporation. © 1997.

[1]Mirra Komarovsky, *Blue-collar Marriage* (New York: Vintage, 1964).

[2]D. Goleman, "Two Views of Marriage Explored: His and Hers," *New York Times*, 1 Apr. 1989.

[3]C. Gilligan, *In a Different Voice* (Cambridge, Mass.: Harvard University Press, 1982).

[4]Scott Swain, "Covert Intimacy: Closeness in Men's Friendship," in B. J. Reisman and P. Schwartz, eds., *Gender in Intimate Relations* (Belmont, Calif.: Wadsworth, 1989).

[5]Robin Lakoff, *Talking Power: The Politics of Language* (New York: Basic Books, 1990).

[6]Catherine Riessman, *Divorce Talk: Women and Men Make Sense of Personal Relationships* (New Brunswick, N.J.: Rutgers University Press, 1990).

The human brain, like the human body, is sexed, and differences in the sex-specific human brain condition a wide range of behaviors that we typically associate with maleness or femaleness.

the case? According to the intimacy experts, it is entirely a product of learning and one of the primary sources of male pathology. As psychologist Carol Tavris puts it, "The doing-versus-talking distinction in the emotional styles of males and females begins in childhood, when boys begin to develop what psychologists call 'side by side' relationships, in which intimacy means sharing the same activity—sports, games, watching a movie or a sports event together." Girls, in contrast, "tend to prefer 'face to face' relationships, in which intimacy means revealing ideas and emotions in a heart-to-heart exchange."[7]

The problem is not, as a best-selling book would have us believe, that women are from Venus and men from Mars. It is that we have only recently come to realize something about the legacy of the evolution of our species on planet Earth. Throughout virtually all of our evolutionary history, men and women lived in small tribes of hunter-gatherers where the terms for survival were not the same. We have long recognized that the different terms for survival, along with mate selection, account for sexual differences in the human body. But only in the last few decades have we discovered that the legacy of our evolutionary past is also apparent in the human brain. The human brain, like the human body, is sexed, and differences in the sex-specific human brain condition a wide range of behaviors that we typically associate with maleness or femaleness.

The Legacy of the Hunter-Gatherers

The family album containing the record of our hunter-gatherer evolutionary past is DNA, and the legacy of that past begins to unfold following the union of sperm and ovum. Normal females have two long X chromosomes, contributed by each biological parent, that closely resemble one another. Normal males have a long X chromosome, contributed by the mother, and a short Y chromosome, contributed by the father. Although each sperm and ovum contributes half of the full complement of forty-six chromosomes, the ovum provides all of the cytoplasmic DNA.

A fetus will develop with a female brain unless a gene on the Y chromosome, known as SRY, is expressed about the sixth week of pregnancy and triggers the release of testosterone in the gonads. The testosterone transforms the developing fetus into a male by interacting with genes that regulate or are regulated by the expression of SRY. The result is a kind of chain reaction in which genes involved in the determination of maleness are activated in a large number of cells. But since the levels of hormones vary across individual brains, the response of brain regions to the presence of hormones is highly variable.

Many of the sex-specific differences in the human brain are located in more primitive brain regions, and they condition male and female copulatory behavior, sexual orientation, and cyclic biological processes like menstruation. Sex-specific differences also exist, however, in the more recently evolved neocortex or in the higher brain regions. The neocortex looks like a redundantly folded sheet and contains 70 percent of the neurons in the central nervous system. It is divided into two hemispheres that process different kinds of information fairly independently, and each communicates with the other via a 200-million-fiber network called the corpus callosum. While the symmetry is not exact, structures in one hemisphere are mirrored in the other. Thus we have two parietal lobes, two occipital lobes, and so on.

In people with normal hemispheric dominance, the left hemisphere has executive control. This hemisphere manages linguistic analysis and expression, as well as sequential motor responses or body movements. The right hemisphere is responsible for perception of spatial relationships, faces, emotional stimuli, and prosody (vocal intonations that modify the literal meaning of a word).[8] The two frontal lobes of each hemisphere, located behind the forehead, integrate inputs from other brain regions and are closely associated with conscious decision mak-

[7]Carol Tavris, *The Mismeasure of Women* (New York: Simon & Schuster, 1992), 251–52.

[8]S. F. Wietelson, "Neural Sexual Mosaicism: Sexual Differentiation of the Human Temporo-Parietal Region for Functional Asymmetry," *Psychoneuroendochrinology* 16:1–3 (1991): 131–55.

While males talk about their status in terms of simple descriptions of individual skills and achievements, Tannen says, females do so with complicated descriptions of overall character.

ing. This portion of our brain, which occupies 29 percent of the cortex, has undergone the most recent evolutionary expansion.

One piece of evidence that suggests why the brains of women and men tend to process information differently involves the corpus callosum, or the network of fibers connecting the two hemispheres. A subregion of this network, the splenium, is significantly larger in women than in men and more bulbous in shape.[9] More connections between the hemispheres in female brains could be a partial explanation for another significant discovery—both hemispheres are normally more active in the brains of females.

Computer-based imaging systems, such as positron emission tomography (PET) and magnetic resonance imaging (MRI), allow scientists to assess which areas of the brains of conscious subjects are active. All of these systems use advanced computers to construct three-dimensional images of brains as they process various kinds of information. Studies based on advanced imaging systems have revealed that cognitive tasks in the female brain tend to be localized in both hemispheres,[10] and that the same tasks in the male brain tend to be localized in one hemisphere.[11] Other recent studies using this technology have revealed sex-specific differences in the brain regions used to process language and sex-specific differences in feedback from more-primitive brain regions.[12] What this research suggests is that differences in the communication styles of men and women are not simply the product of learning.[13] They are also conditioned by differences in the sex-specific human brain.[14]

You Just Don't Understand Me

While none of the intimacy experts, to my knowledge, attribute differences in the conversation styles of men and women to the sex-specific human brain, there is a growing consensus that it is extremely difficult to eliminate these differences. In the best-seller *You Just Don't Understand: Women and Men in Conversation,* Deborah Tannen claims that while men use conversation "to preserve their independence and negotiate and maintain status in a hierarchical social order," women use conversation as "a way of establishing connections and negotiating relationships."[15] Based on this assumption, Tannen makes the case that there are some large differences in the languages of men and women.

Men, she says, are more comfortable with public speaking, or "report talk," and women are more comfortable with private or "rapport talk." Men use language that is abstract and categorical, or communicate in "messages," and women use language that conveys subtle nuances and hidden meanings, or communicate in "metamessages." Similarly, men respond to problems with concrete solutions and suggestions, and women respond with empathy and an emphasis on community.

Competitive males, claims Tannen, favor "commands," or statements that indicate what should be done without qualification, while consensus-building females favor "conditional propositions," or statements prefaced with words like "let's," "we could," and "maybe." And while males talk about their status in terms of simple descriptions of individual skills and achievements, Tannen says,

[9]Wietelson, "Neural Sexual Mosaicism," 137–38.

[10]I. Jibiki, H. Matsuda, et al., "Quantitative Assessment of Regional Blood Flow with 1231–IMP in Normal Adult Subjects," *Acta-Neurol-Napoli* 15:1 (1993): 7–15, and F. Okada, Y. Tokumitsu, et al., "Gender and Handedness-Related Differences of Forebrain Oxygenation and Hemodynamics," *Brain Research* 601:1–2 (1993): 337–47.

[11]S. P. Springer and G. Deutsch, *Left Brain, Right Brain* (San Francisco: W. H. Friedman Co., 1985).

[12]Ruben Gur, quoted in Gina Kolata, "Men's World, Women's World? Brain Studies Point to Differences," *New York Times,* 28 Feb. 1995, C1.

[13]Melissa Hines, "Gonadal Hormones and Human Cognitive Development," in Jacques Balthazart, ed., *Hormones, Brain and Behavior in Vertebrates* (Basel, Switz.: Karger, 1990), 51–63.

[14]Susan Phillips, Susan Steele, and Christine Tanz, eds., *Language, Gender and Sex in Comparative Perspective* (Cambridge, Eng.: Cambridge University Press, 1987); and David Martin and H. D. Hoover, "Sex Differences in Educational Achievement: A Longitudinal Study," *Journal of Early Adolescence* 7 (1987): 65–83.

[15]Deborah Tannen, *You Just Don't Understand: Women and Men in Conversation* (New York: Ballantine Books, 1990), 77.

females do so with complicated descriptions of overall character.

This sparse theoretical framework, however, does not account for the enormous popularity of Tannen's book. What most impresses readers are the conversations that Tannen uses to illustrate the distinctive character of the languages used by men and women. The following exchange occurs when a husband indicates that he did not get enough sleep:

He: I'm really tired. I didn't sleep well last night.
She: I didn't sleep well either. I never do.
He: Why are you trying to belittle me?
She: I'm not! I'm just trying to show you I understand!

"This woman," says Tannen, "was not only hurt by her husband's reaction; she was mystified by it. How could he think she was belittling him? By 'belittle me,' he meant 'belittle my experience.' He was filtering her attempts to establish connection through his concern with preserving independence and avoiding being put down."[16]

In a discussion of the differences between messages and metamessages, Tannen quotes from Anne Tyler's novel *The Accidental Tourist.* At this point in the narrative the character Macon has left his wife and moved in with a woman named Muriel. The conversation begins when Macon makes an observation about Muriel's son:

"I don't think Alexander's getting a proper education," he said to her one evening.
"Oh, he's okay."
"I asked him to figure what change they'd give back when we bought the milk today, and he didn't have the faintest idea. He didn't even know he'd have to subtract."
"Well, he's only in second grade," Muriel said.
"I think he ought to go to private school."
"Private schools cost money."
"So? I'll pay."
She stopped flipping the bacon and looked over at him. "What are you saying?" she said.
"Pardon?"
"What are you saying, Macon? Are you saying you're committed?"

Muriel then tells Macon that he must decide whether he wants to divorce his wife and marry her, and that she will not put her son in a new school when he could be forced to leave if Macon returns to his wife. Confused and frustrated by Muriel's attack, Macon responds, "But I just want him to learn to subtract." The problem, writes Tannen, is that "Macon is concerned with the message, the simple matter of Alexander's learning math. But Muriel is concerned with the metamessage. What would it say about the relationship if he began paying for her son's education?"[17]

Some reviewers of Tannen's book have rightly complained that these differences are made to appear too categorical. But they also concede, along with the majority of other reviewers, that Tannen has disclosed some actual disparities in the languages used by men and women. How, then, does Tannen account for these remarkable differences in the manner in which men and women linguistically construct reality? She claims that younger children "learn these languages from older children in single-sex groups on the playground.

Why Men Can't Always Talk Like Women

When we examine what Tannen says about differences in the languages used by men and women in the light of what we know about the sex-specific human brain, it seems clear the differences are not simply learned. Report talk and messages may reflect the orientation toward action associated with higher reliance on the primitive region of the limbic system in the male brain and with an orientation toward linear movement in abstract map space in the neocortex.

Although the usual biological explanation for the male tendency to give commands is higher levels of aggression, this linguistic habit also seems consistent with the manner in which reality tends to be constructed in the male brain. Commands may reflect the bias toward action and the organization of particulars in terms of movement between points in map space. All of which suggests that men may perceive commands, as opposed to requests, as more consistent with their sense of the real and as a more expedient way to solve problems.

The relationship between the two hemispheres in the female brain tends to be more symmetric, and there is a greater degree of interaction between these hemispheres. Since linguistic reality in the brains of women seems to invoke a wider range of right-brain cognitive functions, this may enhance awareness of emotionally relevant details, visual clues, verbal nuances, and hidden meanings. This suggests that the female brain tends to construct linguistic reality in terms of more extensive and interrelated cognitive and emotional contexts. If this is the case, all aspects of experience may appear more interdependent and interconnected, and this could contribute to the tendency to perceive people and events in a complex web of relation. Perhaps this is why the language of women tends to feature

[16] Tannen, *You Just Don't Understand,* 51.

[17] Quoted in Tannen, *You Just Don't Understand,* 175.

a more profound sense of identification with others, or why this language seems more "consensual."

Rapport talk may reflect this sense of identification and satisfy the need to feel interconnected. And metamessages, which allow analysis of single events to be extended through a complex web of relation, also seem consistent with the manner in which the female brain tends to construct reality. Since this reality seems more consensual, women may be more inclined to regard decision making as consensual and to prefer "us" instead of "I." Higher reliance in the female brain on the portion of the limbic system associated with symbolic action could also contribute to these tendencies.

Since the male brain tends to construct reality in terms of abstract solutions and sequential movements in map space, men probably perceive action as more commensurate with their sense of the real. If action in the reality of males seems more "actual" than talking, this could explain, in part at least, why men are more inclined to associate intimacy with shared activities, to respond to depression with action, and to describe feelings with action metaphors.

Neuroscience also suggests why women seem to believe that emotions are conveyed more through talking than action. If reality as it is constructed in the female brain features a more extended network of perceptions, memories, associations, and feelings, then the real could be more closely associated with language. This could also explain why women favor "rapport talk," or conversations about the personal and the private. If this talk is more commensurate with the actual character of reality in the female brain, women more than men might depend on conversation to reinforce their reality.

More emotional content in female constructions of reality could also explain why women are more inclined to equate talking with feeling, and to view caring actions that are not accompanied by verbal expressions of feeling as less than authentic. And if linguistic constructions of reality in the female brain feature a broader range of emotional experience, women may have less difficulty, on average, disclosing, describing, and contextualizing feelings.

A New View of the Language of Love

The use of qualifiers like "on average," "tends," "may," "probably," and "might" in the description of behavior associated with the sex-specific human brain is not a concession to political correctness. It is the only way to fairly characterize the differences. There is nothing in this research that argues for a direct causal connection between sex-specific brains and the behavior of men and women. Every human brain is unique and becomes more so as a result of learning, and there is more variation between same-sex brains than opposite-sex brains. What is most striking in virtually all of the research on the sex-specific human brain is not differences between the emotional and cognitive processes of men and women but the amazing degree of overlap, or sameness. And while nature may play a larger role in conditioning same-sex behavior than we previously realized, nurture, or learning, remains the most vital part of the equation.

Although many of the behaviors in the litany of male pathology are obviously learned and subject to change, the tendencies associated with the sex-specific male brain cannot be erased in the learning process. This means that the assumption that love is not love unless men must think, feel, and behave like women in love relationships is not, in the vast majority of instances, realistic. Consider, for example, the primary reason why women seek a divorce. When divorced women are asked to explain the failure of a marriage, the common refrain is "lack of communication," or the unwillingness of the ex-husband to talk about or share feelings.[18] In one recent study, over two-thirds of the women surveyed felt that men would never understand them, or that the men in their lives would remain forever clueless about the lives of women.[19] And yet numerous studies have also shown that women view men who deviate from the masculine norm by displaying or talking openly about emotions as "too feminine" and "poorly adjusted."[20]

Recognizing discrepancies in reality as it "tends" to be constructed in the brains of men and women does not frustrate the desire of men and women to communicate better with their partners. In fact, the opposite is true. Awareness of the discrepancies makes it much easier to negotiate differences and to communicate to our partners how they might better satisfy our expectations and desires without recourse to blame and anger. And this could lead to a greater willingness to embrace two additional assumptions about human reality that have been grandly reinforced by brain science—the total reality is that of both men and women, and the overlap or sameness of the realities of men and women is far greater than the differences.

Robert L. Nadeau is a professor at George Mason University. This article is based on his most recent book, S/he Brain: Science, Sexual Politics and the Feminist Movement *(Praeger, 1996).*

---

[18]Thomas Wills, Robert Weiss, and Gerald Patterson, "A Behavioral Analysis of the Determinants of Marital Separation," *Journal of Consulting and Clinical Psychology* 42 (1974): 802–11.
[19]Survey by Yankelovitch Partners, 1993.
[20]See, for example, John Robertson and Louise Fitzgerald, "The (Mis)treatment of Men: Effects of Client Gender Role and Lifestyle on Diagnosis and Attribution of Pathology," *Journal of Counseling Psychology* 37 (1990): 3–9.

RESPONSE SHEET

for Robert Nadeau: Brain Sex and the Language of Love

1. What does Nadeau add to both Hales and Kolata? (You must look at both again, to do this comparison.)

2. Write one question regarding this article that can be used for class discussion.

3. Describe one application of the information in this article. It can be:
1) A next research step to take
2) An educational, clinical/counseling or rearing application
3) A personal application

Sizing Up the Sexes

Scientists Are Discovering That Gender Differences Have as Much To Do with the Biology of the Brain As with the Way We Are Raised

Christine Gorman

What are little boys made of?
What are little boys made of?
Frogs and snails
And puppy dogs' tails,
That's what little boys are made of.

What are little girls made of?
What are little girls made of?
Sugar and spice
And all that's nice,
That's what little girls are made of.
—Anonymous

Many scientists rely on elaborately complex and costly equipment to probe the mysteries confronting humankind. Not Melissa Hines. The UCLA behavioral scientist is hoping to solve one of life's oldest riddles with a toybox full of police cars, Lincoln Logs and Barbie dolls. For the past two years, Hines and her colleagues have tried to determine the origins of gender differences by capturing on videotape the squeals of delight, furrows of concentration and myriad decisions that children from 2 1/2 to 8 make while playing. Although both sexes play with all the toys available in Hines' laboratory, her work confirms what most parents (and more than a few aunts, uncles and nursery-school teachers) already know. As a group, the boys favor sports cars, fire trucks and Lincoln Logs, while the girls are drawn more often to dolls and kitchen toys.

But one batch of girls defies expectations and consistently prefers the boy toys. These youngsters have a rare genetic abnormality that caused them to produce elevated levels of testosterone, among other hormones, during their embryonic development. On average, they play with the same toys as the boys in the same ways and just as often. Could it be that the high levels of testosterone present in their bodies before birth have left a permanent imprint on their brains, affecting their later behavior? Or did their parents, knowing of their disorder, somehow subtly influence their choices? If the first explanation is true and biology determines the choice, Hines wonders, "Why would you evolve to want to play with a truck?"

Not so long ago, any career-minded researcher would have hesitated to ask such questions. During the feminist revolution of the 1970s, talk of inborn differences in the behavior of men and women was distinctly unfashionable, even taboo. Men dominated fields like architecture and engineering, it was argued, because of social, not hormonal, pressures. Women did the vast majority of society's child rearing because few other options were available to them. Once sexism was abolished, so the argument ran, the world would become a perfectly equitable, androgynous place, aside from a few anatomical details.

But biology has a funny way of confounding expectations. Rather than disappear, the evidence for innate sexual differences only began to mount. In medicine, researchers documented that heart disease strikes men at a younger age than it does women and that women have a more moderate

From *Time,* January 20, 1992, pp. 42–48, 51.

Emotions

Female Intuition: There May Be Something to It

Do women really possess an ability to read other people's hidden motives and meanings? To some degree, they do. When shown pictures of actors portraying various feelings, women outscore men in identifying the correct emotion. They also surpass men in determining the emotional content of taped conversation in which the words have been garbled. This ability may result from society's emphasis on raising girls to be sensitive. But some researchers speculate that it has arisen to give women greater skill in interpreting the cues of toddlers before they are able to speak.

Male Insensitivity: It's a Cultural Relic

If men seem less adept at deciphering emotions, it is a "trained incompetence," says Harvard psychologist Ronald Levant. Young boys are told to ignore pain and not to cry. Some anthropologists argue that this psychic wound is inflicted to separate boys from their mothers and prepare them for warfare. Many men, says Levant, can recognize their emotions only as a physical buzz or tightness in the throat—a situation that can be reversed, he insists, with training.

physiological response to stress. Researchers found subtle neurological differences between the sexes both in the brain's structure and in its functioning. In addition, another generation of parents discovered that, despite their best efforts to give baseballs to their daughters and sewing kits to their sons, girls still flocked to dollhouses while boys clambered into tree forts. Perhaps nature is more important than nurture after all.

Even professional skeptics have been converted. "When I was younger, I believed that 100% of sex differences were due to the environment," says Jerre Levy, professor of psychology at the University of Chicago. Her own toddler toppled that utopian notion. "My daughter was 15 months old, and I had just dressed her in her teeny little nightie. Some guests arrived, and she came into the room, knowing full well that she looked adorable. She came in with this saucy little walk, cocking her head, blinking her eyes, especially at the men. You never saw such flirtation in your life." After 20 years spent studying the brain, Levy is convinced: "I'm sure there are biologically based differences in our behavior."

Now that it is O.K. to admit the possibility, the search for sexual differences has expanded into nearly every branch of the life sciences. Anthropologists have debunked Margaret Mead's work on the extreme variability of gender roles in New Guinea. Psychologists are untangling the complex interplay between hormones and aggression. But the most provocative, if as yet inconclusive, discoveries of all stem from the pioneering exploration of a tiny 3-lb. universe: the human brain. In fact, some researchers predict that the confirmation of innate differences in behavior could lead to an unprecedented understanding of the mind.

Some of the findings seem merely curious. For example, more men than women are lefthanded, reflecting the dominance of the brain's right hemisphere. By contrast, more women listen equally with both ears while men favor the right one.

Other revelations are bound to provoke more controversy. Psychology tests, for instance, consistently support the notion that men and women perceive the world in subtly different ways. Males excel at rotating three-dimensional objects in their head. Females prove better at reading emotions of people in photographs. A growing number of scientists believe the discrepancies reflect functional differences in the brains of men and women. If true, then some misunderstandings between the sexes may have more to do with crossed wiring than cross-purposes.

Most of the gender differences that have been uncovered so far are, statistically speaking, quite small. "Even the largest differences in cognitive function are not as large as the difference in male and female height," Hines notes. "You still see a lot of overlap." Otherwise, women could never read maps and men would always be lefthanded. That kind of flexibility within the sexes reveals just how complex a puzzle gender actually is, requiring pieces from biology, sociology and culture.

Ironically, researchers are not entirely sure how or even why humans produce two sexes in the first place. (Why not just one—or even three—as in some species?) What is clear is that the two sexes originate with two distinct chromosomes. Women bear a double dose of the large X chromosome, while men usually possess a single X and a short, stumpy Y chromosome. In 1990 British scientists reported they had identified a single gene on the Y chromosome that determines maleness. Like some kind of biomolecular Paul Revere, this master gene rouses a host of its compatriots to the complex task of turning a fetus into a boy. Without such a signal, all human embryos would develop into girls. "I have all the genes for being male except this one, and my husband has all the genes for being female," marvels evolutionary psychologist Leda Cosmides, of the University of California at Santa Barbara. "The only difference is which genes got turned on."

Yet even this snippet of DNA is not enough to ensure a masculine result. An elevated level of the hormone testosterone is also required during the pregnancy. Where does it come from? The fetus' own undescended testes. In those rare cases in which the tiny body does not respond to the hormone, a genetically male fetus develops sex organs that look like a clitoris and vagina rather than a penis. Such people look and act female. The majority marry and adopt children.

The influence of the sex hormones extends into the nervous system. Both males and females produce androgens, such as testosterone, and estrogens—although in different amounts. (Men and women who make no testosterone generally lack a libido.) Researchers suspect that an excess of testosterone before birth enables the right hemisphere to dominate the brain, resulting in lefthandedness. Since testosterone levels are higher in boys than in girls, that would explain why more boys are southpaws.

Subtle sex-linked preferences have been detected as early as 52 hours after birth. In studies of 72 newborns, University of Chicago psychologist Martha McClintock and her students found that a toe-fanning reflex was stronger in the left foot for 60% of the males, while all the females favored their right. However, apart from such reflexes in the hands, legs and feet, the team could find no other differences in the babies' responses.

One obvious place to look for gender differences is in the hypothalamus, a lusty little organ perched over the brain stem that, when sufficiently provoked, consumes a person with rage, thirst, hunger or desire. In animals, a region at the front of the organ controls sexual function and is somewhat larger in males than in females. But its size need not remain constant. Studies of tropical fish by Stanford University neurobiologist Russell Fernald reveal that certain cells in this tiny region of the brain swell markedly in an individual male whenever he comes to dominate a school. Unfortunately for the piscine pasha, the cells will also shrink if he loses control of his harem to another male.

Many researchers suspect that, in humans too, sexual preferences are controlled by the hypothalamus. Based on a study of 41 autopsied brains, Simon LeVay of the Salk Institute for Biological Studies announced last summer that he had found a region in the hypothalamus that was on average twice as large in heterosexual men as in either women or homosexual men. LeVay's findings support the idea that varying hormone levels before birth may immutably stamp the developing brain in one erotic direction or another.

These prenatal fluctuations may also steer boys toward more rambunctious behavior than girls. June Reinisch, director of the Kinsey Institute for Research in Sex, Gender and Reproduction at Indiana University, in a pioneering study of eight pairs of brothers and 17 pairs of sisters ages 6 to 18 uncovered a complex interplay between hormones and aggression. As a group, the young males gave more belligerent answers than did the females on a multiple-choice test in which they had to imagine their response to stressful situations. But siblings who had been exposed in utero to synthetic antimiscarriage hormones that mimic testosterone were the most combative of all. The affected boys proved significantly more aggressive than their unaffected brothers, and the drug-exposed girls were much more contentious than their unexposed sisters. Reinisch could not determine, however, whether this childhood aggression would translate into greater ambition or competitiveness in the adult world.

While most of the gender differences uncovered so far seem to fall under the purview of the hypothalamus, researchers have begun noting discrepancies in other parts of the brain as well. For the past nine years, neuroscientists have debated whether the corpus callosum, a thick bundle of nerves that allows the right half of the brain to communicate with the left, is larger in women than in men. If it is, and if size corresponds to function, then the greater crosstalk between the hemispheres might explain enigmatic phenomena like female intuition, which is supposed to accord women greater ability to read emotional clues.

These conjectures about the corpus callosum have been hard to prove because the structure's girth varies dramatically with both age and health. Studies of autopsied material are of little use because brain tissue undergoes such dramatic changes in the hours after death. Neuroanatomist Laura Allen and neuroendocrinologist Roger Gorski of UCLA decided to try to circumvent some of these problems by obtaining brain scans from live, apparently healthy people. In their investigation of 146 subjects, published in April, they confirmed that parts of the corpus callosum were up to 23% wider in women than in men. They also measured thicker connections between the two hemispheres in other parts of women's brains.

Encouraged by the discovery of such structural differences, many researchers have begun looking for dichotomies of function as well. At the Bowman Gray Medical School in Winston-Salem, N.C., Cecile Naylor has determined that men and women enlist widely varying parts of their brain when asked to spell words. By monitoring increases in blood flow, the neuropsychologist found that women use both sides of their head when spelling while men use primarily their left side. Because the area activated on the right side is used in understanding emotions, the women apparently tap a wider range of experience for their task. Intriguingly, the effect occurred only with spelling and not during a memory test.

Researchers speculate that the greater communication between the two sides of the brain could impair a woman's performance of certain highly specialized visual-spatial tasks. For example, the ability to tell directions on a map

Perception

He Can Read a Map Blindfolded, But Can He Find His Socks?

It's a classic scene of marital discord on the road. Husband: "Do I turn right?" Wife, madly rotating the map: "I'm not sure where we are." Whether men read maps better is unclear, but they do excel at thinking in three dimensions. This may be due to ancient evolutionary pressures related to hunting, which requires orienting oneself while pursuing prey.

If Lost in a Forest, Women Will Notice the Trees

Such prehistoric pursuits may have conferred a comparable advantage on women. In experiments in mock offices, women proved 70% better than men at remembering the location of items found on a desktop—perhaps reflecting evolutionary pressure on generations of women who foraged for their food. Foragers must recall complex patterns formed of apparently unconnected items.

Language

In Choosing Her Words, A Woman Really Uses Her Head

For both sexes, the principal language centers of the brain are usually concentrated in the left hemisphere. But preliminary neurological studies show that women make use of both sides of their brain during even the simplest verbal tasks, like spelling. As a result, a woman's appreciation of everyday speech appears to be enhanced by input from various cerebral regions, including those that control vision and feelings. This greater access to the brain's imagery and depth may help explain why girls often begin speaking earlier than boys, enunciate more clearly as tots and develop a larger vocabulary.

If Johnny Can't Read, is it Because He is a Boy?

Visit a typical remedial-reading class, and you'll find that the boys outnumber the girls 3 to 1. Stuttering affects four times as many boys as girls. Many researchers have used these and other lopsided ratios to support the argument that males, on average, are less verbally fluent than females. However, the discrepancy could also reflect less effort by teachers or parents to find reading-impaired girls. Whatever the case, boys often catch up with their female peers in high school. In the past few years, boys have even begun outscoring girls on the verbal portion of the Scholastic Aptitude Test.

without physically having to rotate it appears stronger in those individuals whose brains restrict the process to the right hemisphere. Any crosstalk between the two sides apparently distracts the brain from its job. Sure enough, several studies have shown that this mental-rotation skill is indeed more tightly focused in men's brains than in women's.

But how did it get to be that way? So far, none of the gender scientists have figured out whether nature or nurture is more important. "Nothing is ever equal, even in the beginning," observes Janice Juraska, a biopsychologist at the University of Illinois at Urbana-Champaign. She points out, for instance, that mother rats lick their male offspring more frequently than they do their daughters. However, Juraska has demonstrated that it is possible to reverse some inequities by manipulating environmental factors. Female rats have fewer nerve connections than males into the hippocampus, a brain region associated with spatial relations and memory. But when Juraska "enriched" the cages of the females with stimulating toys, the females developed more of these neuronal connections. "Hormones do affect things—it's crazy to deny that," says the researcher. "But there's no telling which way sex differences might go if we completely changed the environment." For humans, educational enrichment could perhaps enhance a woman's ability to work in three dimensions and a man's ability to interpret emotions. Says Juraska: "There's nothing about human brains that is so stuck that a different way of doing things couldn't change it enormously."

Nowhere is this complex interaction between nature and nurture more apparent than in the unique human abilities of speaking, reading and writing. No one is born knowing French, for example; it must be learned, changing the brain forever. Even so, language skills are linked to specific cerebral centers. In a remarkable series of experiments, neurosurgeon George Ojemann of the University of

Is Sex Really Necessary?

Birds do it. Bees do it. But dandelions don't. The prodigious spread of these winsome weeds underscores a little-appreciated biological fact. Contrary to human experience, sex is not essential to reproduction. "Quite the opposite," exclaims anthropologist John Tooby of the University of California at Santa Barbara. "From an engineer's standpoint, sexual reproduction is insane. It's like trying to build an automobile by randomly taking parts out of two older models and piecing them together to make a brand-new car." In the time that process takes, asexual organisms can often churn out multiple generations of clones, gaining a distinct edge in the evolutionary numbers game. And therein lies the puzzle: If sex is such an inefficient way to reproduce, why is it so widespread?

Sex almost certainly originated nearly 3.5 billion years ago as a mechanism for repairing the DNA of bacteria. Because ancient earth was such a violent place, the genes of these unicellular organisms would have been frequently damaged by intense heat and ultraviolet radiation. "Conjugation"—the intricate process in which one bacterium infuses genetic material into another—provided an ingenious, if cumbersome, solution to this problem, although bacteria continued to rely on asexual reproduction to increase their numbers.

Animal sex, however, is a more recent invention. Biologist Lynn Margulis of the University of Massachusetts at Amherst believes the evolutionary roots of egg and sperm cells can be traced back to a group of organisms known as protists that first appeared some 1.5 billion years ago. (Modern examples include protozoa, giant kelp and malaria parasites.) During periods of starvation, Margulis conjectures, one protist was driven to devour another. Sometimes this cannibalistic meal was incompletely digested, and the nuclei of prey and predator fused. By joining forces, the fused cells were better able to survive adversity, and because they survived, their penchant for union was passed on to their distant descendants.

From this vantage point, human sexuality seems little more than a wondrous accident, born of a kind of original sin among protozoa. Most population biologists, however, believe sex was maintained over evolutionary time because it somehow enhanced survival. The mixing and matching of parental genes, they argue, provide organisms with a novel mechanism for generating genetically different offspring, thereby increasing the odds that their progeny could exploit new niches in a changing environment and, by virtue of their diversity, have a better chance of surviving the assaults of bacteria and other tiny germs that rapidly evolve tricks for eluding their hosts' defenses.

However sex came about, it is clearly responsible for many of the most remarkable features of the world around us, from the curvaceousness of human females to the shimmering tails of peacocks to a lion's majestic mane. For the appearance of sex necessitated the evolution of a kaleidoscope of secondary characteristics that enabled males and females of each species to recognize one another and connect.

The influence of sex extends far beyond the realm of physical traits. For instance, the inescapable fact that women have eggs and men sperm has spurred the development of separate and often conflicting reproductive strategies. University of Michigan psychologist David Buss has found that men and women react very differently to questions about infidelity. Men tend to be far more upset by a lover's sexual infidelity than do women: just imagining their partner in bed with another man sends their heart rate soaring by almost five beats a minute. Says Buss: "That's the equivalent of drinking three cups of coffee at one time." Why is this so? Because, Buss explains, human egg fertilization occurs internally, and thus a man can never be certain that a child borne by his mate is really his. On the other hand, because women invest more time and energy in bearing and caring for children, they react more strongly to a threat of emotional infidelity. What women fear most is the loss of their mates' long-term commitment and support.

The celebrated war between the sexes, in other words, is not a figment of the imagination but derives from the evolutionary history of sex—from that magic moment long, long ago when our unicellular ancestors entwined in immortal embrace.

—By J. Madeleine Nash/Chicago

How Other Species do it

Humans think there's nothing more natural than males and females in mutual pursuit of the urge to be fruitful and multiply. But nature follows more than one script. Not every species has two sexes, for example. And even when it does, neither their behavior nor their origin necessarily conforms to human notions of propriety. Some of the more bizarre cases in point:

Turtles

Among most reptiles, males are literally made in the shade. The gender of a turtle hatchling, for instance, is determined not by sex chromosomes but by the temperature at which it was incubated. Eggs that develop in nests located in sunny areas, where it is warm and toasty, give rise to females. Eggs nestled in shady places, where it may be 5°C (10°F) cooler, will yield a crop of males.

Whiptail Lizards

For some varieties of these lizards there's no such thing as a battle of the sexes. All of them are female. In a process known as parthenogenesis, they produce eggs that hatch without ever being fertilized. Yet, because they evolved from lizards that come in two sexes, pairs of these single-minded creatures will take turns imitating males and mount each other. The act apparently stimulates greater egg production.

Jacana Birds

Females usually rule the roost on every shore, marsh and rice field where these long-legged "lily trotters" abound. They are generally larger than the males, which are saddled with the duties of building the nest, incubating the eggs and raising the chicks. In fact in some varieties, female Casanovas regularly jilt their domestic-minded mates and search for more sexually available males.

Cichlids

These fish come in three sexes: brightly hued macho males, paler females, and male wimps that look and act like females. There are only a few sexually active males in a school. But the minute a piscine Lothario dies, an ambitious wimp rises to the occasion. His brain unleashes sex hormones that bring color to his scales and make him feisty, but he can revert to pallid impotence if challenged by a more macho fish.

Washington has produced scores of detailed maps of people's individual language centers.

First, Ojemann tested his patients' verbal intelligence using a written exam. Then, during neurosurgery—which was performed under a local anesthetic—he asked them to name aloud a series of objects found in a steady stream of black-and-white photos. Periodically, he touched different parts of the brain with an electrode that temporarily blocked the activity of that region. (This does not hurt because the brain has no sense of pain.) By noting when his patients made mistakes, the surgeon was able to determine which sites were essential to naming.

Several complex sexual differences emerged. Men with lower verbal IQs were more likely to have their language skills located toward the back of the brain. In a number of women, regardless of IQ, the naming ability was restricted to the frontal lobe. This disparity could help explain why strokes that affect the rear of the brain seem to be more devastating to men than to women.

Intriguingly, the sexual differences are far less significant in people with higher verbal IQs. Their language skills developed in a more intermediate part of the brain. And yet, no two patterns were ever identical. "That to me is the most important finding," Ojemann says. "Instead of these sites being laid down more or less the same in everyone, they're laid down in subtly different places." Language is scattered randomly across these cerebral centers, he hypothesizes, because the skills evolved so recently.

What no one knows for sure is just how hardwired the brain is. How far and at what stage can the brain's extraordinary flexibility be pushed? Several studies suggest that the junior high years are key. Girls show the same aptitudes for math as boys until about the seventh grade, when more and more girls develop math phobia. Coincidentally, that is the age at which boys start to shine and catch up to girls in reading.

By one account, the gap between men and women for at least some mental skills has actually started to shrink. By looking at 25 years' worth of data from academic tests, Janet Hyde, professor of psychology and women's studies at the University of Wisconsin at Madison, discovered that overall gender differences for verbal and mathematical skills dramatically decreased after 1974. One possible explanation, Hyde notes, is that "Americans have changed their socialization and educational patterns over the past few decades. They are treating males and females with greater similarity."

Even so, women still have not caught up with men on the mental-rotation test. Fascinated by the persistence of that gap, psychologists Irwin Silverman and Marion Eals of York University in Ontario wondered if there were any spatial tasks at which women outperformed men. Looking at it from the point of view of human evolution, Silverman and Eals reasoned that while men may have developed strong spatial skills in response to evolutionary pressures to be successful hunters, women would have needed other types of visual skills to excel as gatherers and foragers of food.

The psychologists therefore designed a test focused on the ability to discern and later recall the location of objects in a complex, random pattern. In series of tests, student volunteers were given a minute to study a drawing that contained such unrelated objects as an elephant, a guitar and a cat. Then Silverman and Eals presented their subjects with a second drawing containing additional objects and told them to cross out those items that had been added and circle any that had moved. Sure enough, the women consistently surpassed the men in giving correct answers.

What made the psychologists really sit up and take notice, however, was the fact that the women scored much better on the mental-rotation test while they were menstruating. Specifically, they improved their scores by 50% to 100% whenever their estrogen levels were at their lowest. It is not clear why this should be. However, Silverman and Eals are trying to find out if women exhibit a similar hormonal effect for any other visual tasks.

Oddly enough, men may possess a similar hormonal response, according to new research reported in November by Doreen Kimura, a psychologist at the University of Western Ontario. In her study of 138 adults, Kimura found that males perform better on mental-rotation tests in the spring, when their testosterone levels are low, rather than in the fall, when they are higher. Men are also subject to a daily cycle, with testosterone levels lowest around 8 p.m. and peaking around 4 a.m. Thus, says June Reinisch of the Kinsey Institute: "When people say women can't be trusted because they cycle every month, my response is that men cycle every day, so they should only be allowed to negotiate peace treaties in the evening."

Far from strengthening stereotypes about who women and men truly are or how they should behave, research into innate sexual differences only underscores humanity's awesome adaptability. "Gender is really a complex business," says Reinisch. "There's no question that hormones have an effect. But what does that have to do with the fact that I like to wear pink ribbons and you like to wear baseball gloves? Probably something, but we don't know what."

Even the concept of what an innate difference represents is changing. The physical and chemical differences between the brains of the two sexes may be malleable and subject to change by experience: certainly an event or act of learning can directly affect the brain's biochemistry and physiology. And so, in the final analysis, it may be impossible to say where nature ends and nurture begins because the two are so intimately linked.

—Reported by J. Madeleine Nash/Los Angeles

RESPONSE SHEET

for Christine Gorman: Sizing up the Sexes

1. This is still another pathway to the gendered brain. Identify (ID) five contributions that Gorman makes that are either new, or build, or modify, or challenge the approaches you have already encountered (Hales, Kolata, Nadeau).

2. ID the finding, application or implication among the four that you found most stimulating, challenging or meaningful. Consider that you may be invited to bring it up in class.

3. Now, try to capture as fully as possible why your choice has the impact on you that it does.

Why Can't a Man Be More Like a Woman . . . and Vice Versa

Male and Female Brains Aren't the Same. Does This Mean That Sexual Differences Are Biologically Determined?

Kathryn Phillips

For a year Marie-Christine De Lacoste waited for phone calls from the Southwestern Medical Center Forensics Institute telling her that one more undamaged brain was available after autopsy. With each call she would hurry to the morgue and collect another brain. Eventually the Columbia University graduate student had a cache of 14, nine from men and five from women, most of them shooting victims. De Lacoste's study in the early Eighties would change her life. It would also alter the way scientists thought about sex differences in the brain. De Lacoste took each new brain to her lab at the University of Texas Southwestern Medical Center, where she was a research assistant. There, using a combination of cameras, old-fashioned metric rulers, and computers, she measured each brain's corpus callosum. This thick, boomerang-shaped band of fibers connects the brain's hemispheres and is the massive midline conduit for processing and relaying information between the two cerebral halves. De Lacoste suspected she would find a significant difference in callosum size between the men and women. And she did. Her research was the first study of the human corpus callosum showing a possible anatomical basis for sexual differences in intellect, skills, and behavior.

The publication of her paper caused an uproar, and De Lacoste became a "branded" woman. Overnight the popular press trumpeted that science had determined that one sex's brainpower was superior to the other's (although there was considerable confusion about which sex that was). "I'd say the paper really hurt my career as opposed to enhancing it," comments De Lacoste, now at Yale Medical School. At meetings she was known before she was introduced, based solely on that paper, and not always favorably. "It generated quite a stir and I was very young. It made me an 'infamous' neuroscientist."

De Lacoste had not merely entered a field of research but strode into a mine field of contentious debate. "That stuff is hokey," says Anne Fausto-Sterling, a Brown University biologist and prominent critic of the brain research. "The evidence that there are differences is so fragmentary and so weak, it ought to stop there." Critics fear that simply by publishing their data, these neuroscientists may have handed society a means to justify sexual discrimination.

"I was giving a seminar at an Eastern university," recalls De Lacoste, "and this man stood up and said, 'How dare you do work in this area when the politics are such?'" Yet each time the debate seemed nearly suppressed, another study would appear indicating that differences may not stop at the neck but reach into the brain itself, affecting how the average man and woman think. Brain differences, in fact, may explain some—not all—of the differences featured in the disputations about which sex is better at what.

Current theory—and battleground—propounds that boys seem to excel in math and computational skills, whereas girls are superior in language, spoken and written. Motor coordination tests give women the edge in executing fine finger and hand movements, and in overall agility. But men tend to have faster reaction times. Male supremacy appears greatest in tasks involving spatial visualization—the ability to see, manipulate, and compute the position of a real or abstract figure in the mind's eye.

Although the typical cognitive profile of women may be different from that of men, there is a huge overlap. Many women do better than men on some spatial tests, and vice versa. "In large groups, if you look at the mean score or the

---

Reprinted by permission from *Omni,* October 1990, pp. 42–44, 46, 48, 68.

tendency, that's where you see the difference," says Sandra Witelson, professor of psychiatry at McMaster University in Hamilton, Ontario. "But this doesn't mean that you know the cognitive skills of an individual." That is, you can't predict sexwise who will do better on real-life tasks such as running a company or an experiment. Still, when men and women perform equally on a test in a lab environment, there are indications that their brains go about it in different ways.

In the last decade neurobiologists have reported structural differences in at least two regions of the human brian. One is the corpus callosum, the mind's big "telephone" cable, connecting as it does hundreds of millions of neurons between the two hemispheres. The other is the hypothalamus, the master controller for the integration of many basic behavioral patterns—from temperature regulation and appetite to sex drives—involving brain and endocrine functions. Neuroendocrine research also strongly indicates that nervous system differences begin as sex hormones bathe the developing fetus in the womb. Hormonal differences continuing throughout childhood—and perhaps even through adult life—affect brain activity and guide performance. Other studies suggest that men and women may process the same information differently and yet come to the same or similar conclusions. Nonetheless with every significant new findings comes the researcher's caveat: "No one knows for sure what this means in terms of behavior, but I think. . . ."

Corpus Callosum: Left Brain, Right Brain

In her pioneering research De Lacoste studied the splenium. Shaped like a light bulb, the splenium, which composes the back fifth of the corpus callosum, is a pathway connecting the visual areas of both hemispheres as well as associational areas that serve complex cognitive functions. She discovered that the splenium's surface area and width were greater in women than men, relative to brain weight. She speculated that the larger splenium probably meant women and men have different interhemispheric connections.

De Lacoste's findings are in line with a prominent theory that goes back at least to the famous "split-brain" work of Nobel laureate Roger Sperry and still dominates thinking on brain differences. Male brains with fewer connections across the corpus callosum are more lateralized than those of females. This increased lateralization, so the theory goes, allows for greater right-brain performance—visuospatial skills. Women, with their theoretically increased *bi* lateralization, excel at verbal skills because, with more cross-communication, they have decreased focus on the right hemisphere.

Even before De Lacoste stated gathering brains from the Dallas morgue, Witelson patiently collected data for a ten-year study correlating people's hand preference—right- or left-handed—with anatomical measurements in their brains. Hand preference is a behavioral index of, or "window" into, the wiring of the brain. Witelson figured she would find a structural difference between left- and right-handers, since they have differing patterns of brain lateralization. Among right-handers, the left side of the brain controls language ad motor skills, and the right side controls spatial perception. Among left-handers, there is more bilateral representation of these functions. Also, in psychological tests left-handers appear to have more bilateral function. Since the corpus callosum is the great communicator between hemispheres, Witelson thought she might see the differences there.

Running into the usual problem—how to do behavioral anatomy in living humans—she devised an unusual solution. Cancer patients who were seriously ill and wanted to make a contribution to science were asked to participate in a study. They were given psych tests, and they agreed to donate their brains to her lab when they died. With the psychological tests, Witelson determined whether each patient was consistently right-, left-, or mixed-handed. By the end of ten years, she had collected test data and brains from 50 people—35 women and 15 men.

> 'Differences in language processing in women suggest something more global—that women recruit areas of the brain that enable them to use more strategies than men.'

What she found after analyzing the brains surprised her. She discovered that among men, the isthmus, a segment linking the mid-portions of the two cortices, was larger in the left- or mixed-handed men than in the right-handed men. She had anticipated this. However, she found there was no difference among women in isthmus size based on handedness. Furthermore the isthmus was larger in women across the board. "I did not suspect—there would be no reason to predict—this difference between men and women," Witelson says. "The idea was that the callosum might be bigger for left- than right-handers, not specifically for men but for everyone."

The significance of a larger isthmus? "One possibility is a greater total number of fibers," Witelson says, "or the fibers could be thicker. It will take closer studies to find the answers." A greater number of or thicker fibers could be an anatomical basis for more communication between the hemispheres. "Remember a headline when our report was published?" she muses. "SUBTLE SEX DIFFERENCES FOUND?" It is 'subtle' in the sense that it is complex but not subtle in the sense that it's more elusive, harder to find, or smaller."

Witelson found the variation in isthmus size to be strongly related to hand preference—but only in her male subjects. There was almost no correlation with the handedness measure in women. "The variation in women is not associated with handedness, and it is in men. That means the neurobiological substrate of handedness in women, which obviously must exist, must be mediated by different brain structures than it is in men. That's a big sex difference," says Witelson.

Although men and women do a lot of things similarly, if not identically, they may be doing them with different parts of the brain. This could relate to differences in verbal and spatial skills, she thinks, because they are controlled by the temporal and parietal lobes of the cortex, and these regions send their fibers through the isthmus. "If one part of a package is different, there could be a domino effect. There must be other parts that are different as well." Do Witelson's findings mean one sex is better able to process information than the other? "The key: Different is different. It's so easy to fall into the words *better* or *worse*. What's better, an apple or an orange?"

The Language Maker

Cecile Naylor, a neuropsychologist at The Bowman Gray School of Medicine in Winston-Salem, North Carolina, stumbled upon dramatic sex differences almost accidentally as she was studying people with learning disabilities. As part of her study she recruited a control group of 30 men and 30 women "unhindered" by neurological problems. She gave them an oral spelling test that required them to identify whether a word was exactly four letters long. To take the test, each person lay flat on a table, wearing what Naylor describes as "basically a revised motorcycle helmet." The helmet contained devices that measured blood flow through the cortex.

She found no essential difference in how well the men and women scored on the spelling test. An analysis of blood flow, however, showed sex differences in brain activity during the test. In men the patterns of blood flow showed that the most intense brain activity seemed to occur "in a tight linkage" between two areas known to be involved in language and verbal communication: Wernicke's area in the left temporal lobe and Broca's area in the left frontal lobe adjacent to the motor cortex region controlling muscles of the face, jaw, tongue, and throat. The two areas are connected by a thick band of fibers. The standard model for language holds that language making and comprehension arise in Wernicke's area and then travel via the pathway to Broca's, where they call up the program that causes the phrases to be spoken.

In women, though, she found no such intense coupling between the two areas. Instead Wernicke's was actively en-

> 'Some of these early behaviors, such as playing with Lincoln Logs, may lead to changes in cognitive function—you might develop better visual-spatial skills.'

gaged with two other areas, one behind it in the left temporal lobe. Wernicke's was also linked to its "mirror" area in the *right* temporal lobe. Without further research, Naylor is loath to say what these startling differences mean, but she will speculate a little. "The area behind Wernicke's lies between the primary visual and auditory regions," she says, "so one might ague that women have an additional imaging function" during the language process. The area opposite Wernicke's in the right hemisphere is involved in the emotional comprehension and expression aspect of language. If this region is engaged in women, than it is not farfetched to think that during language processes a typical woman brings a richer, more expanded emotional component into play than most men do.

In men, as language impulses move toward speech, only Broca's area is engaged. In women, Naylor found, "almost every area of the cortex, left and right hemisphere, has some unique relationship with Broca's during the task, as if there were many independent things going on between Broca's and lots of different regions." Is it almost as if a woman's brain is "ablaze" during language processing? "Well," Naylor responds carefully, "it suggest something more global—that women are recruiting areas of the brain that enable them to use more strategies than men."

The male arrangement follows the classical model of language function "as a unit independent from the rest of the brain," she says, adding that most language-area studies have been made with men. The classical model may be classic for only about 50 percent of the human population. Naylor's work may also explain why, according to some studies, women recover faster than men from certain types of strokes attacking the core language regions.

The Master Controller

Sex differences have also been located deep within the hypothalamus, the small structure that orchestrates many vital functions. In 1978 UCLA's Roger Gorski discovered what became known as the sexually dimorphic nucleus (SDN) in the preoptic area of the male rate. This area, located in the front part of the hypothalamus and believed to help direct sexual behavior, was five times larger in males. Investigators began hunting for a similar area in humans.

In 1985 Dick Swaab, a Dutch neuroscientist, reported that he had found two areas in the human hypothalamus that showed sex differences. One was the superchiasmatic nucleus (SCN), a group of neurons that acts as a built-in clock, controlling circadian rhythms and, in women, ovulation. Swaab saw that in women the SCN has a more elongated shape. "Because there's a difference in shape, the nucleus can make different contacts, and that way it might have a different function," he says. "But we haven't got a clue about the difference in function at this point."

Swaab also looked at the preoptic area, pinpointing a cell group he believes is similar to the one Gorski investigated in rats. Swaab found it was twice as large in men and had about twice as many neurons as the women's cell group. And last year a team led by Gorski reported a sex difference in two regions of the human preoptic area. The UCLA scientists stopped short of describing the cell groups as analogous to those of the rat. "We don't know if either of these [Swaab's or UCLA's] is the same cell group as the rodent SDN, but they would be candidates for it," says Melissa Hines, a neuroscientist then on Gorski's team. Hines speculates that hormone regulation might be a function of the cell groups. They might also be involved in male sexual behavior, although just how, too, is still unknown.

Swaab noted in one rat study that the size of the SDN appears to be related to the male rat's "libido." "For instance, there's a correlation between the number of mounts and the size of the SDN." The bigger the nucleus, the more the mounts. Implications for men? Again unknown. Scientists in this field exercise caution in making rat-to-man leaps. In their sexual behavior humans have overcome, to a greater degree than rats at least, the tyranny of their hormones. Yet Swaab's and Gorski's research has encouraged animal investigators by providing "evidence that the human brain has sex differences very much like those seen in rats and lower animals," says Bruce McEwen, a leading Rockefeller University neuroscientist.

Sea of Love

Based on animal models scientists are increasingly convinced, furthermore, that prenatal hormone exposure in humans may govern some brain anatomy and behavioral differences between the sexes. For the last several years, Hines has conducted human studies to test this idea. In 1975 she began her graduate work on physical aggression and its causes. But her interest soon turned from the problem of aggression to the question of hormonal influence on behavioral development.

Now on the UCLA faculty, Hines has studied two special groups: women whose mothers took diethylstilbestrol (DES), an estrogen, or "female" hormone, during pregnancy; and girls who had congenital adrenal hyperplasia (CAH), a genetic disorder resulting in excessive production of androgens, or "male" hormones. In animal studies DES had been shown to masculinize female reproductive systems and behavior. "We think of estrogen as a female hormone. But during development, at least in the rat, testosterone is converted into estradiol [an estrogen] before it masculinizes certain brain cells. By giving DES, you're mimicking what would occur with testosterone," Hines says. "So that's why DES masculinizes."

Hines wanted to know if DES might masculinize human female brains. So she gave dichotic listening tests to DES women and their sisters who had not been exposed to DES. In the tests, different words are presented simultaneously to each ear. Because of the brain's circuitry, the word going in the right ear is recorded by the left hemisphere, and the word going into the left ear recorded by the right hemisphere.

"Because their left hemisphere is dominant in language, most people have what is called a right-ear advantage," Hines explains. "They're better at recognizing the syllables from the right ear." And there's a sex difference: Men typically are more right eared than women, because as the theory goes, women tend to be more bilateral. Hines found that in the 25 DES women she studied, there was a bigger right-ear advantage than in their unexposed sisters. The women performed more like men, suggesting a subtle masculinizing from the early hormone exposure.

More recently Hines and psychologist Sheri Berenbaum studied CAH girls, ages two and a half to eight, to see if their prenatal exposure to excess androgens had masculinized their behavior. The scientists created a playroom with toys classified as female-type toys, male-type toys, and neutral toys. Then one by one the children—including CAH girls, their unaffected female cousins and sisters, and unaffected boys—were placed in the room and observed. "We found that more often than the other girls and about as often as the control boys, the androgenized girls played with cars, trucks, Lincoln Logs, and other male-type toys, and less with dolls," Hines says.

"I was quite surprised," she admits, "because you don't think of there being a brain region governing toy preferences." The result suggests that prenatal exposure to androgens helped create a brain that thinks more like a typical male than a typical female brain. But Hines says the research is still incomplete. "There may be other steps in the pathway between the hormone and the preference for the truck over the doll. I'm looking at that now. And of course these could be early behaviors, such as playing with Lincoln Logs, that subsequently lead to changes in cognitive function—you might develop better visual-spatial skills."

Barbara Lippe, chief of pediatric endocrinology at UCLA Medical School, is skeptical of suggestions, based on studies of hormonally abnormal people, that prenatal hormonal exposure has masculinized or feminized brain function or behavior. "The problem is that 'abnormal' experiences in the womb are more often than not coupled with abnormal hormonal levels postnatally, and it's difficult to separate them out," she says. CAH girls may also have unusual genitalia that affect the way the child is treated. "So it's a difficult model to use."

Sexual Orientation

If early hormonal exposure can shape your brain and behavior, can it also explain sexual orientation—who turns you on? Could it answer the riddle of why some people are homosexual and others heterosexual? Witelson believes this may be a factor. In testing this, she and her colleagues found that in a group of lesbians there were nearly twice as many left-handers as in the general population. A group of gay men, too, showed a trend toward greater-than-average left-handedness.

"We don't think the increased left-handedness can be explained by learned or socially induced factors," she says. "In contrast, because left-handedness is well documented to be related to a typical pattern of brain organization, we feel there must be a neurobiological factor to homosexuality."

Witelson suspects that in women "higher levels of masculinizing hormones in utero lead to the increased left-handedness and the homosexual orientation." In men, the process may work a little differently. "We'd guess fewer androgens in utero leads to increased left-handedness and homosexual orientation." It doesn't mean, though, that "every left-handed person is homosexual or every homosexual left-handed, but as a group there's an atypical pattern of cerebral dominance [right brain] compared to the general population." It does suggest, however, that sexual orientation may develop differently in men and women.

Shelton E. Hendricks, a University of Nebraska psychologist who studies sexual orientation, says Witelson's research, while interesting, is weakened by her choice of populations to compare with the homosexual groups. She used a general population collected by another scientist in 1970 in Britain to compare with an Eighties homosexual population in Canada. "The rate of left-handedness varies with the population," Hendrick says, and factors such as time, place, age, ethnicity, and cultural pressures can affect that rate.

Witelson has also found evidence of differences in thinking patterns between homosexual and heterosexual populations, suggesting that the differences between the two groups—on average—may extend beyond the issue of what turns them on. Last year Witelson's group reported that in spatial tests, gay men performed somewhat less well than heterosexual men and better than heterosexual women—who typically do less well on spatial tests than heterosexual men. In verbal tests, the gay men again fell between the heterosexual men and women. This month at the Society for Neuroscience's meeting, Witelson and Cheryl McCormick will report how lesbians fared on the same spatial and verbal tests.

"The difference in the pattern of skills suggests something different in the organ of thought, the brain," she says. She predicts that difference may be found in the anatomy of the corpus callosum. "Unfortunately, we don't have MRIs of the brains of people we tested. This might provide further evidence of a neurobiological basis to sexual orientation and might be convincing to those strongly biased to a solely environmental theory."

Witelson hopes such findings could improve the way homosexuals are understood by society. "Our results suggest that homosexual orientation is not unnatural for homosexuals," she says. "It's as natural for them as heterosexual orientation is for heterosexuals. The way the brain develops anatomically then functionally, has a large early hormonal component. One of the things the brain develops is sexual orientation. This is one of many variations within each genetic sex."

Hormonal changes throughout life may affect thinking as well. Canadian psychologists Doreen Kimura and Eliza-

'The way the brain develops anatomically, then functionally, has a large hormonal component. One thing it develops is sexual orientation. It's one of many variations within each genetic sex.'

'Scientists are going to discover that sex hormones have a pervasive influence not only on the development of the brain but on aging and on various stages of life.'

beth Hampson found that during different stages of their menstrual cycle 150 women performed differently on various tests. The difference appeared to be controlled by shifts in estrogen levels. When estrogen levels were high, just before ovulation, women performed as much as 10 percent better on such items as tongue twisters, a test of motor and verbal dexterity—or, as Kimura puts it, "the articulatory, complex manual, verbal fluency, and some perceptual speed tests, on which women are often superior to men." Tests of spatial ability showed the reverse effect "in that they were depressed for women in the high-estrogen phase." In the low-estrogen phase marking the beginning of the cycle, though, the women performed better than usual on spatial perception tests, such as picking a shape out of a complex pattern. They might complete 40 spatial tasks in three minutes on low estrogen days and only 35 on high-estrogen days.

"I'm not at all surprised by Kimura's findings," says Gorski. "They fit with everything we've seen. If anything, her work is an updating of [American pioneer endocrinologist] Charles Sawyer's. More than thirty years ago he showed that female sex hormones altered the level of excitability in the brain stem in rabbits. This leads to changes in firing rates elsewhere, higher in the brain. The speed and quality of how we think, move, and speak could well be affected by hormones."

Men, too, experience daily fluctuations in their sex steroids. Testosterone is higher in the morning than in the evening. How these changes affect thinking skills is unknown. But recent reports indicate testosterone levels correlate surprisingly well with certain behavioral traits, such as dominance and power seeking. Testosterone levels in individuals are also influenced by environment and can vary with changing personal environmental situations.

There is also growing evidence that steroids alter connectivity between various parts of the brain throughout life. Neurons can remodel their synapses—develop new or retract old ones. It's conceivable that women make new neuronal connections when estrogen is rising and, in the postovulatory phase at the end of the cycle, lose them. "I'm in the obstetrics and gynecology department at Yale," says De Lacoste, "because the department has a longstanding interest in the role of estrogen in synaptic remodeling. This is an ideal environment to find out in what ways steroids influence how neurons live or die by synaptic remodeling. I think scientists are going to find that sex hormones have a pervasive influence not only on brain development but on aging and various stages throughout life. They aren't at all there just for your preovulatory surge or stuff like that."

Even with mounting data on sex differences, the controversy goes on. "On average, women and men perform differently. But when it comes to trying to assign causes or reasons, that's where [the scientists] get into trouble," says Ruth Hubbard, a retired Harvard biologist who has written extensively about women and biology. "In most societies men and women live very different lives, and so we develop very different capabilities. We don't know how to translate anatomical sex differences into behavioral difference."

Hines thinks much of the criticism is based on faulty logic. "The thought is that if women are demonstrated to be different from men, and it is linked to biological factors, then it will be used to justify social inequities. It's assumed that if women are different, they'll be devalued for it. Unfortunately, this has been true historically, but it doesn't have to be true." Still, she is concerned that neurobiology may be twisted to justify discrimination. "I've seen research, not mine but others', misused—you know, quoted as justifying why men are more likely to be engineers. That's a giant leap from actual knowledge. It's a big step from seeing relatively subtle hormonal contributions to behavior to seeing the average woman make substantially less money than the average man, or seeing the vast majority of heads of state and CEOs being male."

Yet while critics worry that women may become objects of increased oppression because of sex differences in the brain, most of the prominent researchers in the field are women. Hines suspects there is just a natural interest in the field among women because women are most often the victims of sex stereotypes. Witelson says, "The sexes are different and it does no good to assume they're not. We're not going to help equal opportunity and equal recognition when we assume both are equally good in all aspects, when it may well be that there are certain things each sex is somewhat better at." And many women biologists say the findings will have a positive impact.

Indeed, sex research is uncovering variations in the way brain cells are programmed to respond to chemical signals such as neurotransmitters and circulating hormones. In animal studies investigators have found that male as well as female neurons have receptors for estrogens. "Those receptors in the male and female brain are pretty similar; both have the same number and distribution," says McEwen. "But if you then look at what estrogens and progesterones, another female hormone group, *do* to male and female brains, you'll find that the male is not always responding in the same way as the female brain. It's at that level you can begin to see how the program of the cell has become different."

This is basic chemical information scientists will obtain only after identifying sex differences in the brain. The knowledge could lead to drugs targeted more accurately to each sex. "If we're going to give women the equivalent medical treatment as men," says Jean Hamilton, a psychiatrist at the University of Texas Southwestern Medical School, "we'd better find out about sex differences where they exist. Someday men and women may be treated differently for conditions such as Alzheimer's disease and epilepsy, and the treatments will be more effective because they are different."

Finally, the value of the research is not just for understanding why men and women differ, says Hines, "but also for understanding basic processes of brain and behavioral development." Yet the added bonus would be that the ancient question about the sexes could be permanently replaced by a simple declaration: Vive la différence.

RESPONSE SHEET

for Kathryn Phillips: Why Can't a Man Be More Like a Woman . . .

1. Now comes the task that each of you have been yearning to do: compile a complete list of all the gendered brain characteristics that are contained in the Hales, Kolata, Nadeau, Gorman and Phillips articles. If in doubt as to whether a particular characteristic is sufficiently different, list it. If there seem to be two in one, separate them and list both. Do not include implications in this list; only characteristics. Here are steps in compiling:

1) Draft a list of your own, on your own.
2) Bring this list in to use in a small group that will be dedicated to comparing these lists and compiling them. The group activity will be to set up a master list that captures all the additions of the individual lists.
3) A person in each group will volunteer/be volunteered (this will earn that person the full 5 points extra credit possible) to publish this list and bring it in, let's say, two class sessions later.
4) The lists from all the small groups will then be compiled and published. Whoever does this will earn the full 5 EC points, also.
5) This list will constitute the basis for 2/3 of the next exam, thus it is a review sheet also.

CHAPTER 9

Gender Differences: Early Differences and Gendered Rearing

Behavioral gender differences start showing up in the newborn period (0–10 days of life). Newborn girls like to be covered up more than boys; they cry and whimper less. They are born with their hands open; boys' are usually clenched. Boys frown and grimace more, and are more bodily active. In the first thirty days, girls are smiling, cooing and reaching for mother more. In another thirty days, girls are vocalizing more and responding more to their mothers' voices.

These little girls' appealing expressive behaviors evoke being picked up, cuddled, patted and stroked more. Mothers talk to them more and do not let them cry as long.

The above differences are primarily unlearned. However, the prevailing American culture builds on them in such a way that gender differences are increased and solidified. As Hoffman points out in her discussion of gender segregation, the peer culture is organized around peer gender differences, not similarities. And the next major socialization agent—schools—continues gender differentiation, at the expense of the girls. This AAUW report emphasizes that schools have not changed in this respect as much as many think.

There is rather overwhelming evidence that American gender differentiation has been at females' expense. Enough so that this orientation to females has to be regarded as prejudicial; in fact, it has to be regarded as the deepest prejudice in our culture. Racial prejudice is second and all the rest are tertiary.

Gender Segregation in Childhood: A Test of the Interaction Style Theory

Melissa L. Hoffmann
Division of Child and Adolescent Psychiatry
University of Tennessee, Memphis

Kimberly K. Powlishta
Department of Psychology
Washington University

ABSTRACT. The authors investigated the play/interaction-style theory of gender segregation with a sample of 39 children aged 2 to 5 years (primarily Caucasian). According to this theory, children prefer playmates with styles of play or interaction that are similar to their own. Because such styles are sex differentiated, same-sex playmate preference (i.e., gender segregation) results. The authors observed children during free play to determine preferred playmates and gender segregation level, and they used teacher ratings to derive play/interaction-style scores. The authors used a multiple regression approach to path analysis to analyze effects of sex of participant, participants' play/interaction-style scores, playmates' play/interaction-style scores, and degree of gender segregation to determine their effects on one another. The authors observed significant levels of gender segregation, with highly aggressive or active children displaying less segregation than their peers did. However, gender segregation was not associated with a preference for playmates with similar play or interaction styles.

Key words: gender, gender segregation, play

Beginning around age three, children show a preference for same-sex playmates, a preference that increases over time, at least through middle childhood (Hayden-Thomson, Rubin, & Hymel, 1987; La Freniere, Strayer, & Gauthier, 1984; Maccoby, 1998; Maccoby & Jacklin, 1987; Powlishta, 1995a; Powlishta, Sen, Serbin, Poulin-Dubois, & Eichstedt, 2001; Ruble & Martin, 1998). Children's tendency to engage in *gender segregation* is a widespread and well-documented phenomenon. For example, in a review of studies in which the sex composition of playmate groups and pairs has been reported, Maccoby (1988) found a clear tendency toward same-sex groupings whenever children had a choice of playmates in their age range. Not only has gender segregation been demonstrated in interactions among children, but it is also evident in the voicing of same-sex preferences on sociometric measures (e.g., Hayden-Thomson et al.; Powlishta, 1995a; Powlishta et al., 2001; Powlishta, Serbin, & Moller, 1993; Ruble & Martin; Serbin, Powlishta, & Gulko, 1993). Gender segregation is a robust phenomenon, with children playing with same-sex peers as much as 11 times more often than with other-sex peers (Maccoby & Jacklin, 1987). Segregation also appears to be very resistant to long-term change (Serbin, Tonick, & Sternglanz, 1977).

The authors thank M. Christine Lovejoy and William O'Donohue for their helpful comments on an earlier version of this article, and Kim Smith and Greg Stevens for their assistance in collecting and coding data.

Address correspondence to Melissa L. Hoffmann, University of Tennessee, Memphis. Division of Child and Adolescent Psychiatry, 711 Jefferson Avenue, Memphis, TN 38105; mhoffmann@utmeml.utmem.edu (e-mail).

The phenomenon of gender segregation may have important implications. Because boys and girls grow up in distinctive cultures, sex differences may be amplified (Maccoby, 1988, 1998). In addition, because boys and girls have relatively little experience with each other, they may not be adequately prepared for the adult world, which is not nearly as gender segregated as the child world (Maccoby, 1990, 1998; Powlishta, 1995a). Thus, sex-differentiated styles of interaction may be perpetuated by childhood gender segregation and may continue into adulthood in the form of communication problems between men and women and gender segregation in the workplace (Lockheed & Klein, 1985; Maccoby, 1998).

Play/Interaction-Style Theory

Despite this potential significance, the causes of gender segregation are still not fully understood. In the present study, we investigated one potential explanation that has been proposed but never adequately tested: namely, that segregation is related to sex-differentiated play or interaction styles (Maccoby, 1988; Moller & Serbin, 1996; Serbin, Moller, Gulko, Powlishta, & Colburne, 1994). According to this play/interaction-style theory, children prefer to play with other children who have styles of play or interpersonal interaction that are similar to their own. For example, roughhousers choose to play with other roughhousers, and cooperative children prefer to be around other cooperative children. Because there are socially, cognitively, and biologically based sex differences in children's typical play or interaction styles (e.g., Hines & Kaufman, 1994; Powlishta et al., 2001; Ruble & Martin, 1998), children with similar styles are likely to be of the same sex, thereby leading to gender segregation.

One assumption of the play/interaction-style theory is that boys and girls have different play or interaction styles. Indeed, research has shown that boys' and girls' groups differ in a number of characteristics (Maccoby, 1986, 1998). Boys tend to play in larger groups, and girls often cluster in twos and threes (Eder & Hallinan, 1978). Boys tend to play in more public places, and with less proximity to, surveillance by, and structuring from, adults (e.g., Carpenter & Huston-Stein, 1980; Powlishta et al., 1993; Thorne, 1986). Boys' play is rougher than girls' and involves more body contact (DiPietro, 1981; Moller, Hymel, & Rubin, 1992). Verbal and physical fights are also more frequent in boys' groups than in girls' groups. In addition, boys have been shown to be more active than girls Eaton & Enns, 1986). Boys' social interactions tend to be focused on dominance and having a specific leader, whereas girls have a stronger convention for turn-taking, with all group members participating in decision making (DiPietro). Boys make a greater number of attempts to influence peers, mostly by using direct forms of social influence (e.g., demanding, commanding), and girls tend to use indirect forms (e.g., speaking politely, hinting rather than directly requesting; Serbin, Sprafkin, Elman, & Doyle, 1982). Boys and girls differ in their ability to influence and dominate others as well. Even 33-month-old girls have difficulty influencing boys (Jacklin & Maccoby, 1978). Serbin et al. reported that although girls remain relatively compliant, boys become increasingly resistant to influence attempts with age. As a result, boys often win in conflicts over resources (Charlesworth & La Freniere, 1983; Powlishta & Maccoby, 1990). Overall, boys and girls appear to have different ideals, to use different techniques, and to have different levels of success regarding dominance (Charlesworth & Dzur, 1987; Charlesworth & La Freniere; Knight & Chao, 1989; Powlishta & Maccoby). Boys and girls also differ in their reactions to conflict situations, in that girls are more likely than boys to engage in behaviors that defuse or mitigate the conflict (e.g., proposing compromise, changing the topic), whereas boys are more likely to engage in heavy-handed behavior (e.g., threatening, using physical force; Miller, Danaher, & Forbes, 1986).

Thus, sex differences in play or interaction styles seem to be wide reaching. Such differences may prompt children to interact primarily with peers of their own sex. Some indirect support has been generated for this hypothesis. First, children do seem to choose playmates on the basis of their play or interaction style. For example, Alexander and Hines (1994) found that 4- to 8-year-old boys selected playmates (depicted by simple line drawings) on the basis of play styles, choosing female targets with masculine activities over male targets with feminine activities. Older (6- to 8-year-old) girls performed similarly by choosing feminine male targets over masculine female targets. However, the task used to measure playmate choice was somewhat artificial, and it is unclear whether children were choosing playmates on the basis of style or on the basis of the particular toys and activities with which the target was depicted.

Greater support for the importance of play style has been found using actual observations and ratings of children's play. For example, when comparing the observed play behaviors of "best friends," Serbin et al. (1994) found that friends showed similar levels of "watching others" and "adult-oriented play." Furthermore, teacher ratings of the children's behavior revealed that "socially sensitive" and "popular" children had best friends who also received high social sensitivity ratings, whereas "disruptive" children had best friends who received low popularity ratings. Thus, children both plays with compatible peers and avoided incompatible ones.

Similar results were obtained by Rubin, Lynch, Coplan, Rose-Krasnor, and Booth (1994), who brought together groups of 4 unacquainted, same-sex 7-year-olds. They found that "discriminating" children (i.e., those who expressed a clear preference for one of their playmates over the others) were more behaviorally similar to preferred playmates than to nonpreferred playmates in the areas of social participation (solitary, parallel, and group play) and cognitive play (functional, constructive, and dramatic play as well as exploratory activity).

Another aspect of the play/interaction-style hypothesis that has been supported is the link between play or interaction style and gender segregation. Moller and Serbin (1996) found no sex differences in their teacher-rated social sensitivity play style among children who were not yet segregating. However, among children who had begun to show gender segregation, girls displayed higher levels of social sensitivity than did boys. Social sensitivity was also one of the styles on which best friends tended to be similar, regardless of sex (Serbin et al., 1994).

These findings are consistent with the play/interaction-style theory of gender segregation. However, to provide more conclusive support, researchers must show not only that children seek out playmates with play or interaction styles that are similar to their own and that there are sex differences in the play or interaction styles of segregating children, but also that this similar playmate preference is related directly to gender segregation. We designed the present study to examine this missing link: specifically, we observed preschoolers during free play to determine the identity of their preferred playmates as well as their overall level of gender segregation. Teachers provided ratings of each child on numerous characteristics so that the play or interaction styles of the children and their playmate could be identified. Following the play/interaction-style theory, we hypothesize that (a) there would be sex differences for at least some of the play or interactive styles identified; (b) a child's play or interaction style would predict the style of his or her playmates, even after controlling for the sex of the child; (c) a child's own play or interaction style would be related to the degree of gender segregation. Specifically, *masculine-typed* styles would predict high gender segregation for boys and low gender segregation for girls, and *feminine-typed* styles would predict high gender segregation for girls and low gender segregation for boys; and (d) the relationship between a child's own play or interaction style and his or her degree of gender segregation would be mediated by the child's preference for playmates with similar styles. Specifically, we predicted that when the style of the child's average playmate was controlled for, the relationship between the child's style and level of gender segregation would be nonsignificant. However, we expected the average playmates' style to remain a significant predictor of gender segregation, even after controlling for the child's own style. That is, boys who preferred masculine playmates and girls who preferred feminine playmates would know the highest levels of gender segregation. Thus, we expected the preference for playmates with similar styles to have the most direct effect on gender segregation. These hypothesized pathways, which would provide strong support for one play/interaction-style theory of gender segregation, are depicted in Figure 1.

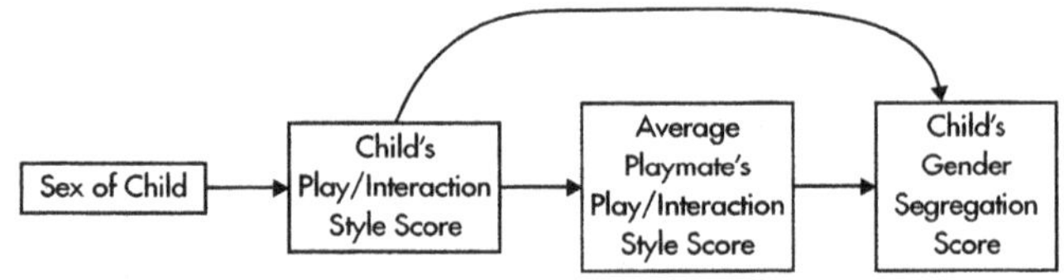

FIGURE 1
Path analytic model depicting the hypothesized direct (straight lines) and indirect (curved line) predictors of gender segregation.

METHOD

Participants

Thirty-nine children (20 male, 19 female; 85% Caucasian, 8% African American, 8% Asian American) from primarily middle-class families were the main participants in this study. They ranged in age from 28 to 67 months at the beginning of data collection (M = 47.5 months; boys' M = 50.0 months, SD = 7.0; girls' M = 44.9 months, SD = 10.1). We recruited the children from two daycare centers on the campus of a midwestern university, with the cooperation of the preschool teachers and directors. We observed three separate classrooms. Class 1 consisted of 3 boys and 8 girls, with a mean age of 49.6 months (range 43–59 months). Class 2 consisted of 7 boys and 4 girls, with a mean age of 52.9 months range 42–67 months). Class 3 consisted of 10 boys and 7 girls, with a mean age of 42.7 months (range 28–53 months). Only children with parental consent were asked to participate. We obtained 100% participation in all three classes.

PROCEDURE

Teacher Rating Questionnaire. We asked the head teacher and 1 to 5 assistant teachers (all female) in each of the participating classes to fill out a questionnaire designed to determine the play or interaction style of each child in the class. The questionnaire lists 48 behaviors that a preschool child might engage in, most of which were obtained from the Teacher Rating Questionnaire developed by Moller, 1991; Moller & Serbin, 1996; Serbin et al., 1994). These items were designed to assess various play styles that have been shown to differentiate boys and girls or to be correlated with gender segregation (e.g., activity level, rough-and-tumble play, cooperation, aggregation, social sensitivity, adult proximity, influence style, dominance, conflict resolution). We instructed the teachers to rate each child on a scale of 1 *(rarely happens)* to 5 *(happens a lot)* for each item, and to complete the item for every child in the class before moving on to the next item.

In addition to the teachers of the 39 main participants in the study, teachers from six additional preschools in the same middle-class community were asked to fill out the questionnaires regarding their students, providing ratings for are additional 214 children (49% girls and 51% boys, representing the same age range as the main participants). We did not know the identities of the children not considered main participants in the study. These additional ratings were performed to ensure an accurate cluster analysis of the questionnaire.

Videotaping. We videotaped each main participant engaged in free play, after receiving permission to do so from each child individually. The children had 3 days to acclimate to the presence of the researcher and video camera in the classroom. During this time we practiced using the video camera and collected pilot data to be used for training coders. After the initial period of acclimation, each child was videotaped in random order for 5 min at a time, once or twice a day, over a period of several weeks. With the exception of 1 child, each child was videotaped for a total of 20–30 min (M = 25.37 min, SD = 3.53 min).[1] Individual children were not told when they were being videotaped, in order not to disrupt their normal behavior. We recorded the number of boys and girls present in the class each day.

Videotape coding. At each 10-s interval, the primary researcher and one of two assistants recorded the identities of the target child's playmates. These assistants had undergone training, using pilot data, until 80% agreement with the primary researcher had been achieved. Once training was completed, the primary researcher coded all observation sessions, and we used these data in all analyses. The two assistants coded half of the participant videos, randomly chosen from each classroom (10 boys, 9 girls), to establish reliability. We assessed interrater reliability by calculating for each participant the correlation between the two raters' scores for the total frequency of play with each classmate. These correlation coefficients were then averaged across participants to obtain an overall index of interrater reliability, which was .94.

Results

Play/Interaction-Style Scores

We analyzed the data from the teacher questionnaires with an oblique principal component cluster analysis (SAS Institute, 1989). This procedure is resigned to cluster variables into nonfuzzy, disjoint clusters. We chose a five-cluster solution, which explain 46% of the variance. This solution yielded clusters that were interpretable, with eigenvalues greater than 1. We labeled the five clusters *aggressive/immature* (e.g., grabs toys, has temper outbursts; α = .91), *social sensitive* (e.g., expresses concern for others, takes turns; α = .87), *popular* (e.g., appears accepted by peers, meets new situations easily; α = .82), *active* (e.g., enjoys wrestling with others, likes to roughhouse; α = .92), and *timid* (e.g., gives up easily, accepts bossing from same-sex peers and opposite-sex peers; α = .11). These clusters are similar to factors reported by other researchers (i.e., Howes, 1988; Moller, 1991; Moller & Serbin, 1996; Pekarik, Prinz, Liebert, Weintraub, & Neale, 1967; Serbin et al., 1994). Given the poor alpha coefficient for the timid cluster, we eliminated it from further analyses. The complete set of items in each cluster is listed in Table 1.

We calculated four play/interaction-style scores for each child by averaging the child's ratings on each of the items that contributed to each cluster. Items that negatively loaded on a cluster (indicated by the word "not" in Table 1, e.g., "is not cooperative") were first reverse scored. We then standardized scores on each play/interaction style within each class to control for any possible teacher differences in scale use. We evaluated interrater reliability for each style by correlating the head teachers' scores on each style with the average scores from assistant teachers in the same class. Interrater reliability was .89 for aggressive/immature, .79 for socially sensitive, .69 for popular, and .77 for active. Because the head teacher was present in the classroom every day and knew the children better than did the assistant teachers, and because the number of assistant teachers varied from class to class, only the head teachers' ratings were used in subsequent analyses.

Finally, we computed the average style of each child's playmates for each style as follows: the number of intervals that the child played with each playmate was multiplied by that playmate's style score; the products were summed and then divided by the child's total number of play contacts.

Correlational analyses revealed that the four play styles were not fully independent. In particular, the aggressive/immature and active styles were highly related (r = .76, p = .0001). However, they were not redundant. Aggression/immaturity was correlated negatively with social sensitivity ($r = -.48, p = .0002$) but not at all with popularity ($r = -.01, p = .97$), whereas activity was correlated positively with popularity (r = .44, p = .005) but not with social sensitivity (r = $-.01$, p = .96). The aggressive/immature style appeared to capture behaviors that were more negative, whereas the behaviors representing the active style were more playful. Similarly, the social sensitivity and popular styles were highly related (r = .77, p = .0001), but, as noted previously, they were differen-

[1]One of the children was available to be videotaped only for a total of 15 min. Although this time differs from that of the other participants, the results of analyses run without this participant were largely identical to the results of analyses with the child included. Thus, the participant was not removed from the sample.

TABLE 1
Cluster Analysis Solution for Teacher Rating Questionnaire

Aggressive/Immature	Socially Sensitive	Popular	Active
Has temper outbursts	Expresses concern	Accepted by peers	Likes to rough-house
Grabs toys	Shares toys	Gets along with opposite sex	Playful physical assaults
Is restless	Helps others	Gets along with same sex	Is excitable
Is not cooperative	Takes turns	Expresses ideas	Is physically active
Is stubborn/defiant	Prefers structured activities	Interacts with the teacher	Playfully chases others
Disrupts others	Tends to stay near teacher	Good verbal skills	Constantly seeks attention
Is bossy	Compromises in conflict	Appears happy and content	Kicks, hits, or bites
Is not shy	Uses hints in conflict	Meets new situations easily	Uses commands and demands in conflict
More active in a group	Asks politely in conflict	Goes to teacher for help in conflict	Avoids conflict
Asserts rights in conflict	Attempts to convince in conflict		Gives in when in conflict
Threatens in conflict	Appeals to the rules in conflict		Makes fun of others when in conflict
Uses force in conflict			

tially related to the aggressive/immature and active styles. The social sensitivity style appeared to capture characteristics that reflect a consideration of others, whereas the behaviors representing the popular style were more outgoing in nature.

Gender Segregation Scores

Because unequal numbers of boys and girls were present in each class, we calculated gender segregation scores based on each child's frequency of playing with boys and girls, relative to chance expectations (Powlishta et al., 1993). Specifically, we subtracted the proportion of all classmates who were of a child's own sex from the proportion of classmates with whom the child actually played who were of the child's own sex, collapsed it across all observations, and divided it by the appropriate standard deviation. A resulting score greater than 1.96 indicates that the child displayed a significant amount of gender segregation (see Powlishta et al., for more detail).

Overall, 59% (23 of 39) of the children displayed significant gender segregation, with 70% (14 of 20) of the boys and 47% (9 of 19) of the girls showing a significant preference for same-sex playmates. Chi-squared analyses revealed that this apparent difference between boys and girls was not significant, $\chi^2(1, N = 39) = 2.07$, $p > .05$. The gender segregation score can also be retained in its continuous form to indicate the degree of segregation. A one-sample t test indicated an overall amount of gender segregation significantly greater than zero ($M = 2.52$, $SD = 4.85$); $t(38) = 3.25$, $p = .002$. Once again, boys ($M = 3.53$, $SD = 4.53$) and girls ($M = 1.46$, $SD = 5.06$) did not differ in their level of segregation, $t(37) = 1.34$, $p = .19$.

Links Among Sex, Play Style, and Gender Segregation

Preliminary analyses indicated that the child's age was not correlated significantly with any other variables. We therefore excluded age from subsequent analyses. We analyzed the three scores described earlier (child's play/interaction style, average playmate's play/interaction style, and continuous gender segregation score) for their potential causal effects on one another using a series of multiple regression equations, or a path analysis, separately for each of the four play/interaction styles. Zero-order correlations among the variables used in the path analysis are shown in Table 2.

To examine the first prediction that some play/interaction styles would show gender differentiation, we conducted a regression equation for each style, with the child's style score as the dependent variable and sex (1 = boys, 2 = girls) as the independent variable. Contrary to expectations, there were no sex differences on any of the play interaction styles (unstandardized regression coefficients [*B*s] were .19 for the aggressive/immature style. −.04 for socially sensitive, −.09 for popular, and −.13 for active; all *p*s > .46).

To evaluate the second prediction, that children would prefer playmates with play/interaction styles similar to their own, we conducted a second set of regression equations in which average playmate's style scores were regressed on sex and the corresponding child's style scores. We did not find the expected results. Although girls had playmates who were more popular and more active than did boys (*B*s = .21 and .18, respectively, *p*s < .05), there were no sex differences in playmates' aggression or social sensitivity (*B*s = .16 and .09, respectively; *p*s > .11). Fur-

TABLE 2
Correlations Among Path Analysis Variables

Variable	1	2	3	4	5	6
1. Sex	—					
2. Child, aggressive/immature	.12	—				
3. Child, socially sensitive	−.03	−.48**	—			
4. Child, popular	−.06	.01	.77***	—		
5. Child, active	−.09	.76***	−.01	.44**	—	
6. Gender segregation	−.22	−.34*	.02	−.17	−.29	—
7. Playmates, aggressive/immature	.26	−.03	.15	.16	−.01	−.13
8. Playmates, socially sensitive	.19	.04	−.14	−.06	−.05	.09
9. Playmates, popular	.38*	−.02	−.01	−.01	−.07	.02
10. Playmates, active	.33*	−.05	.17	.21	−.09	−.17

Note. Sex is coded as 1 = boys, 2 = girls.
*$p < .05$, **$p < .005$, ***$p < .0001$.

TABLE 3
Summary of Unstandardized Regression Coefficients, Dependent Variable: Gender Segregation

	Regression Equation			
Independent Variable	Aggressive/Immature	Socially Sensitive	Popular	Active
Sex	−1.70	−2.06	−2.18	−2.33
Child's Style	−1.95*	0.13	−1.28	−2.02*
Sex × Child's Style	−0.39	−1.61	−0.59	−0.50

Note: Sex is coded as 1 = boys, 2 = girls.
*$p < .05$. All other *ps* > .12.

thermore, children's scores were nonsignificant predictors of their average playmates' scores for all four play/interaction styles ($B = -.02$ for aggressive/immature, −.05 for socially sensitive, .01 for popular, and −.02 for active; *ps* > .41).

To evaluate the third prediction, that children's play styles would predict their level of segregation, we conducted a third set of regression equations. For each play/interaction style, gender segregation scores were regressed on sex and child's style. The sex by child's style interaction term was added to the equation in a second hierarchical step. Because we expected play styles to predict segregation differently for boys and girls (with masculine boys and feminine girls showing the most segregation), we anticipated significant interaction terms. None were found, however. Instead, regardless of sex, children who were highly aggressive or active showed relatively low levels of gender segregation (see Table 3).

Finally, to evaluate the fourth prediction, that the style of a child's average playmate would significantly predict segregation, even after controlling for the child's own style, we repeated the previous set of regressions, adding playmate style and the sex-by-playmate-style interaction terms to the equations (with interaction terms entered in a second hierarchical step). The tendency for aggressive and active children to have low segregation scores was again apparent. In addition, the playmate-style-by-sex interaction for the popular style also reached significance (see Table 4). We conducted follow-up regressions separately for boys and girls. The results indicated that, for boys, having popular playmates positively predicted segregation, whereas the reverse pattern was seen for girls (*B*s = 5.9 and −8.94, respectively, *ps* < .10).

DISCUSSION

In the present study, we explored one possible source of gender segregation in the preschool years. We hypothesized that such segregation is due to a preference for peers

Table 4
Summary of Unstandardized Regression Coefficients, Dependent Variable: Gender Segregation

	Regression Equation			
Variable	Aggressive/Immature	Socially Sensitive	Popular	Active
Sex	−1.45	−2.32	−2.62	−2.70
Child's Style	−1.98*	0.27	−1.30	−1.99
Playmates' Style	−1.56	2.77	2.11	1.80
Sex × Child's Style	−0.13	−2.16	−0.71	−0.15
Sex × Playmates' Style	6.40	−11.32	−15.76*	−1.89

Note. Sex is coded as 1 = boys, 2 = girls.
†$p < .10$, *$p < .05$. All other *ps* > .10.

with similar play or interaction styles. Because these styles tend to be differentiated by sex, the outcome is gender segregation. The results did not support the play/interaction-style theory, however. Consistent with previous research, when observed during free-play periods, the children spent significantly more time with same-sex peers than would be expected by chance. However, such segregation did not seem to be a function of same-sex play style compatibility: We did not detect any sex differences in play styles, nor did we observe children seeking out playmates with similar play/interaction styles.

One interpretation of these findings is that the teacher rating questionnaire failed to detect important aspects of play/interaction styles. However, the style obtained from these ratings (i.e., aggressive/immature, socially sensitive, popular, active, and timid) were remarkably consistent with those found in previous observational and rating-based research. For example, Pekarik et al. (1967) identified three styles: aggression, liability, and withdrawal. Similarly, Howes (1988) identified difficult, sociable, and hesitant styles, and Moller (1991; Serbin et al., 1994) found disruptive/active, socially sensitive, popular, and adult dependent styles. Furthermore, in the present study, all but the timid style (which was dropped from subsequent analyses) had excellent internal consistency, with alpha coefficients ranging from .82 to .92. By having assistant teachers as well as hear teachers evaluate each child independently, we also calculated interrater reliability, a rather unique feature in a study using teacher ratings. This index of reliability also was very good, ranging from .69 to .89. Thus, the questionnaire appear to have done a good job in identifying consistently important and reliable aspects of preschoolers' play/interaction styles and in differentiating individual children.

Why, then, were no sex differences found in these play or interaction styles? Characteristics of the participating child-care centers may help to explain the non-traditional play patterns. First, all three classes were located on a university campus. Being in an academic setting, they may have consciously avoided sex-differentiated treatment of their students. Consistent with this interpretation, previous studies have found that children in "progressive" schools tend to behave less stereotypically than do those in "traditional" schools (Zammuner, 1993). Second, the children's parents were predominantly students and faculty members. The tendency for gender-role attitudes and behaviors to be less traditional among children of higher socioeconomic status (e.g., Lackey, 1989) may account for the absence of sex-differentiated play styles. Finally, children tended to be closely monitored in two of the three classrooms—a context that has been shown to reduce sex differences in children's play (Oettingen, 1985).

Despite having similar play styles, boys and girls nevertheless preferred same-sex playmates. We did detect meaningful individual differences in degree of gender segregation; however, those differences were not accounted for by sex-differentiated play styles. Instead, children who were highly aggressive or active displayed less segregation than their peers, regardless of sex. Several interpretations of these unexpected findings are plausible. Perhaps highly active and aggressive children tended to be rejected by peers of both sexes (Dodge, 1983), yielding low segregation scores. However, correlations between a child's aggressive or active style scores and his or her total number of peer contacts were nonsignificant (*rs* = −.07 and .00, respectively, *ps* > .05), arguing against this interpretation. A second possibility is that lower levels of aggression/activity and higher levels of segregation both indicate an individual who is more developmentally advanced than his or her peers. Although plausible, this interpretation is called into question by the absence of significant correlations between age and either play style or gender segregation. A third possibility is that being in single-sex groups encourages more mature behavior (Gulko, 1991; Urberg & Kaplan, 1989), so that children who spend a great deal of time in such groups display lower levels of activity and aggression.

Given that we found neither sex-differentiated play styles nor preferences for similar playmates, it is not surprising that the play styles of children's typical playmates were largely unrelated to gender segregation. Only playmate popularity predicted level of segregation, positively for boys and negatively for girls. Perhaps having popular playmates and having same-sex playmates co-occur for boys (but not girls) because both reflect an attraction to high-status peers. Although the finding requires replication, and its interpretation is speculative, it is consistent with previous work demonstrating that gender functions as a diffuse status characteristic among children (Lockheed & Klein, 1985). Recent research indicates that even some preschoolers are aware of such status differences (Ward, 1995).

But the most striking finding of this study is that the children displayed significant levels of gender segregation, even in the absence of sex-differentiates play/interaction styles. This finding indicates that the play/interaction-style theory cannot fully account for the emergence of gender segregation in childhood. Although sex differences in play or interaction styles may sometimes lead to gender segregation (Moller & Serbin, 1996; Serbin et al., 1994), such differences do not seem to be necessary to produce segregation. What factors, then, may have led to the segregation that we observed in the present study? Although any such discussion is necessarily speculative, perhaps cognitive factors were involved. For example, children may have evaluated positively and been drawn toward other children whom they had classified as "like me," with similarity judged not on the basis of compatible play styles, but instead on male and female group membership (Powlishta, 1995a, 1995b). Children also may have chosen their playmates based on their stereotypical expectations regarding the play styles of boys and girls, regardless of the actual behaviors exhibited (Martin, 1994). Finally, children's beliefs about social approval or social norms may have influenced their playmate choices (Martin, 1994).

Gender segregation has been documented across a wide range of studies using various methodologies (e.g., observation, sociometric measures), within variety of settings (e.g., schools, homes), and in many different cultures. In fact in a review of studies, Maccoby (1988) reported a clear tendency toward segregation whenever children have a choice of playmates near their own age. Give the extensive nature of this phenomenon, it seems unlikely that a single underlying factor can account for segregation across such varied circumstances. Future research may need to examine multiple causes of gender segregation, including cognitive as well as behavioral factors.

REFERENCES

Alexander, G. M., & Hines, M. (1994). Gender labels and play styles: Their relative contribution to children's selection of playmates. *Child Development, 65,* 869–879.

Carpenter, C. J., & Huston-Stein, A. (1980). Activity structure and sex-typed behavior in preschool children. *Child Development, 51,* 862–872.

Charlesworth, W. R., & Dzur, C. (1987). Gender comparisons of preschoolers' behavior and resource utilization in group problem-solving. *Child Development, 58,* 191–200.

Charlesworth, W. R. & La Freniere, P. (1983). Dominance, friendship, and resource utilization in preschool children's groups. *Ethology and Sociobiology, 4,* 15–26.

DiPietro, J. A. (1981). Rough and tumble play: A function of gender. *Developmental Psychology, 17,* 50–58.

Dodge, K. A. (1983). Behavioral antecedents of peer social status. *Child Development, 54,* 1386–1399.

Eaton, W. O., & Enns, L. R. (1986). Sex differences in human motor activity level. *Psychological Bulletin, 100,* 19–28.

Eder, D., & Hallinan, M. (1978). Sex differences in children's friendships. *American Sociological Review, 43,* 237–250.

Gulko, J. (1991). *Same-sex compatibility: Comparing social relations in same- and mixed-gender groupings of young preschoolers (gender segregation).* Unpublished doctoral dissertation. Concordia University, Montreal, Quebec, Canada.

Hayden-Thomson, L., Rubin, K. H., & Hymel, S. (1987). Sex preferences in sociometric choices. *Developmental Psychology, 23,* 558–562.

Hines, M., & Kaufman, F. R. (1994). Androgen and the development of human sex-typical behavior: Rough-and-tumble play and sex of preferred playmates in children with congenital adrenal hyperplasia (CAH). *Child Development, 65,* 1042–1053.

Howes, C. (1988). Peer interaction of young children. *Monographs of the Society for Research in Child Development, 53.*

Jacklin, C. N., & Maccoby, E. E. (1978). Social behavior at thirty-three months in same-sex and mixed-sex dyads. *Child Development, 49,* 557–569.

Knight, G. P., & Chao, C. (1989). Gender differences in the cooperative, competitive, and individualistic social values of children. *Motivation and Emotion, 13,* 125–141.

La Freniere, P., Strayer, F. F., & Gauthier, R. (1984). The emergence of same-sex affiliative preferences among preschool peers: A developmental/ethological perspective. *Child Development, 55,* 1958–1965.

Lackey, P. N. (1989). Adults' attitudes about assignments of household chores to male and female children. *Sex Roles, 20,* 271–281.

Lockheed, M. E., & Klein, S. S. (1985). Sex equity in classroom organization and climate. In S. Klein (Ed.), *Handbook for achieving sex equity through education* (pp. 617–628). Baltimore, MD: Johns Hopkins University Press.

Maccoby, E. E. (1986). Social groupings in childhood: Their relationship to prosocial and antisocial behavior in boys and girls. In D. Olweus, J. Block, & M. Radke-Yarrow (Eds.). *Development of antisocial and prosocial behavior: Research, theories, and issues* (pp. 263–284). Orlando, FL: Academic Press.

Maccoby, E. E. (1988). Gender as a social category. *Developmental Psychology, 24,* 755–765.

Maccoby, E. E. (1990). Gender and relationships: A developmental account. *American Psychologist, 45,* 513–520.

Maccoby, E. E. (1998). *The two sexes: Growing up apart, coming together.* Cambridge, MA: Harvard University Press.

Maccoby, E. E., & Jacklin, C. N. (1987). Gender segregation in childhood. In H. Reese (Ed.), *Advances in child development and behavior* (Vol. 20, pp. 239–288). New York: Academic Press.

Martin, C. L. (1994). Cognitive influences on the development and maintenance of gender segregation. In W. Damon (Series Ed.) & C. Leaper (Vol. Ed.), *New directions for child development: No. 65. Childhood gender segregation: Causes and consequences* (pp. 35–51). San Francisco: Jossey-Bass.

Miller, P. M., Danaher, D. L., & Forbes, D. (1986). Sex-related strategies for coping with interpersonal conflict in children aged five and seven. *Developmental Psychology, 22,* 543–548.

Moller, L. C. (1991). *Toddler peer preferences: The role of gender awareness, sex-typed toy preferences and compatible play styles.* Unpublished doctoral dissertation, Concordia University, Montreal, Quebec, Canada.

Moller, L. C., Hymel, S., & Rubin, K. H. (1992). Sex typing in play and popularity in middle childhood. *Sex Roles, 26,* 331–353.

Moller, L. C., & Serbin, L. A. (1996). Antecedents of toddler gender segregation: Cognitive consonance, gender-typed toy preferences and behavioral compatibility. *Sex Roles, 35,* 445–460.

Oettingen, G. (1985). The influence of the kindergarten teacher on sex differences in behavior. *International Journal of Behavioral Development, 8,* 3–13.

Pekarik, E. G., Prinz, R. J., Liebert, D. E., Weintraub, S., & Neale, J. M. (1967). The pup evaluation inventory: A sociometric technique for assessing children's social behavior. *Journal of Abnormal Child Psychology, 4,* 83–96.

Powlishta, K. K. (1995a). Gender segregation among children: Understanding the "Cooting Phenomenon," *Young Children, 50,* 61–69.

Powlishta, K. K. (1995b). Intergroup processes in childhood: Social categorization an sex-role development. *Developmental Psychology, 31,* 781–788.

Powlishta, K. K., & Maccoby, E. E. (1990). Resource utilization in mixed-sex dyads: The influence of adult presence and task type. *Sex Roles, 23,* 223–240.

Powlishta, K. K., Sen, M. G., Serbin, L. A., Poulin-Dubois, D., & Eichstedt, J. A. (2001). From infancy through middle childhood: The role of cognitive and social factors is becoming gendered. In R. Unger (Ed.), *Handbook of the psychology of women and gender* (pp. 116–132). New York: Wiley.

Powlishta, K. K., Serbin, L. A., & Moller, L. C. (1993). The stability of individual differences in gender typing: Implications for understanding gender segregation. *Sex Role, 29,* 723–737.

Rubin, K. H., Lynch, D., Coplan, R., Rose-Krasnor, L., & Booth, C. L. (1994). "Birds of a feather. . .": Behavioral concordances and preferential personal attraction in children. *Child Development, 65,* 1778–1785.

Ruble, D. N., & Martin, C. L. (1998). Gender development. In W. Damon (Series Ed.) & N. Eisenberg (Vol. Ed.), *Handbook of child psychology: Vol. 3. Social, emotional, and personality development* (5th ed., pp. 933–1016). New York: Wiley.

SAS Institute, Inc. (1989). *SAS/STAT user's guide, version 6* (4th ed., Vol. 2). Cary, NC, SAS Institute.

Serbin, L. A., Moller, L. C., Gulko, J., Powlishta, K. K., & Colburne, K. A. (1994). The emergence of gender segregation in toddler playgroups. In W. Damon (Series Ed.) & C. Leaper (Vol. Ed.), *New directions for child development: No. 65. Childhood gender segregation: Causes and consequences* (pp. 7–17). San Francisco: Jossey-Bass.

Serbin, L. A., Powlishta, K. K., & Gulko, J. (1993). The development of sex-typing in middle childhood. *Monographs of the Society for Research in Child Development, 58*(Serial No. 232).

Serbin, L. A., Sprafkin, C., Elman, M., & Doyle, A. (1982). The early development of sex differentiated patterns of social influence. *Canadian Journal of Behavioral Science, 14,* 350–368.

Serbin, L. A., Tonick, I. J., & Sternglanz, S. H. (1977). Shaping cooperative cross-sex play. *Child Development, 48,* 924–929.

Thorne, B. (1986). Girls and boys together. . . but mostly apart: Gender arrangements in elementary schools. In W. W. Hartup & Z. Rubin (Eds.), *Relationships and development* (pp. 167–184). Hillsdale, NJ: Erlbaum.

Urberg, K., & Kaplan, M. (1989). An observational study of race-, age-, and sex-heterogeneous interactions in preschoolers. *Journal of Applied Developmental Psychology, 10,* 299–311.

Ward, L. M. (1995, March). *Does knowing that males have higher status than female affect preschoolers?* Poster session presented at the Biennial Meeting of the Society for Research in Child Development, Indianapolis, IN.

Zammuner, V. L. (1993). Perception of male and female personality attributes and behaviors by Dutch children. *Bulletin of the Psychonomic Society, 31,* 87–90.

RESPONSE SHEET

for Melissa Hoffman: Gender Segregation in Childhood

1. Report three possible causes of childhood gender segregation as discussed by Hoffman.

2. Write two questions regarding this article that can be used for class discussion.

The AAUW Report: How Schools Shortchange Girls —Overview—

Why a Report on Girls?

The invisibility of girls in the current education debate suggests that girls and boys have identical educational experiences in school. Nothing could be further from the truth. Whether one looks at achievement scores, curriculum design, or teacher-student interaction, it is clear that sex and gender make a difference in the nation's public elementary and secondary schools.

The educational system is not meeting girls' needs. Girls and boys enter school roughly equal in measured ability. Twelve years later, girls have fallen behind their male classmates in key areas such as higher-level mathematics and measures of self-esteem. Yet gender equity is still not a part of the national debate on educational reform.

Neither the *National Education Goals* issued by the National Governors Association in 1990 nor *America 2000,* the 1991 plan of the President and the U.S. Department of Education to "move every community in America toward these goals" makes any mention of providing girls equitable opportunities in the nation's public schools. Girls continue to be left out of the debate—despite the fact that for more than two decades researchers have identified gender bias as a major problem at all levels of schooling.

Schools must prepare both girls and boys for full and active roles in the family, the community, and the work force. Whether we look at the issues from an economic, political, or social perspective, girls are one-half of our future. We must move them from the sidelines to the center of the education-reform debate.

A critical step in correcting educational inequities is identifying them publicly. The *AAUW Report: How Schools Short-change Girls* provides a comprehensive assessment of the status of girls in public education today. It exposes myths about girls and learning, and it supports the work of the many teachers who have struggled to define and combat gender bias in their schools. The report challenges us all—policymakers, educators, administrators, parents, and citizens—to rethink old assumptions and act now to stop schools from shortchanging girls.

Our public education system is plagued by numerous failings that affect boys as negatively as girls. But in many respects girls are put at a disadvantage simply because they are girls. *The AAUW Report* documents this in hundreds of cited studies.

When our schools become more gender-fair, education will improve for all our students—boys as well as girls—

Research shows that policies developed to foster the equitable treatment of students and the creation of gender-equitable educational environments can make a difference. They can make a difference, that is, if they are strongly worded and vigorously enforced.

V. Lee, H. Marks and T. Knowles, "Sexism in Single-Sex and Coeducational Secondary School Classrooms," paper presented at the American Sociological Association annual meeting, Cincinnati, OH, August 1991; S. Bailey and R. Smith, *Policies for the Future,* Council of Chief State School Officers, Washington, DC, 1982.

because excellence in education cannot be achieved without equity in education. By studying what happens to girls in school, we can gain valuable insights about what has to change in order for each student, every girl and every boy, to do as well as she or he can.

What Do We Teach Our Students?

- The contributions and experiences of girls and women are still marginalized or ignored in many of the textbooks used in our nation's schools.
- Schools, for the most part, provide inadequate education on sexuality and healthy development despite national concern about teen pregnancy, the AIDS crisis, and the increase of sexually transmitted diseases among adolescents.
- Incest, rape, and other physical violence severely compromise the lives of girls and women all across the country. These realities are rarely, if ever, discussed in schools.

Curriculum delivers the central messages of education. It can strengthen or decrease student motivation for engagement, effort, growth, and development through the images it gives to students about themselves and the world. When the curriculum does not reflect the diversity of students' lives and cultures, it delivers an incomplete message.

Studies have shown that multicultural readings produced markedly more favorable attitudes toward nondominant groups than did the traditional reading lists, that academic achievement for all students was linked to use of nonsexist and multicultural materials, and that sex-role stereotyping was reduced in students whose curriculum portrayed males and females in non-stereotypical roles. Yet during the 1980s, federal support for reform regarding sex and race equity dropped, and a 1989 study showed that of the ten books most frequently assigned in public high school English courses only one was written by a woman and none by members of minority groups.

The "evaded" curriculum is a term coined in this report to refer to matters central to the lives of students that are touched on only briefly, if at all, in most schools. The United States has the highest rate of teenage childbearing in the Western industrialized world. Syphilis rates are now equal for girls and boys, and more teenage girls than boys contract gonorrhea. Although in the adult population AIDS is nine times more prevalent in men than in women, the same is not true for young people. In a District of Columbia study, the rate of HIV infection for girls was almost three times that for boys. Despite all of this, adequate sex and health education is the exception rather than the rule.

Adolescence is a difficult period for all young people, but it is particularly difficult for girls, who are far more likely to develop eating disorders and experience depression. Adolescent girls attempt suicide four to five times as often as boys (although boys, who choose more lethal methods, are more likely to be successful in their attempts).

Perhaps the most evaded of all topics in schools is the issue of gender and power. As girls mature they confront a culture that both idealizes and exploits the sexuality of young women while assigning them roles that are clearly less valued than male roles. If we do not begin to discuss more openly the ways in which ascribed power—whether on the basis of race, sex, class, sexual orientation, or religion—affects individual lives, we cannot truly prepare our students for responsible citizenship.

These issues are discussed in detail and the research fully annotated in Part 4/Chapters 1 and 3 of The AAUW Report.

> Despite medical studies indicating that roughly equal proportions of girls and boys suffer from learning disabilities, more than twice as many boys are identified by school personnel as in need of special-education services for learning-disabled students.
>
> U.S. Department of Education, Office for Civil Rights, 1988.

How Do Race/Ethnicity and Socioeconomic Status Affect Achievement in School?

- Girls from low-income families face particularly severe obstacles. Socioeconomic status, more than any other variable, affects access to school resources and educational outcomes.
- Test scores of low-socioeconomic-status girls are somewhat better than for boys from the same background in the lower grades, but by high school these differences disappear. Among high-socioeconomic-status students, boys generally outperform girls regardless of race/ethnicity.
- Girls and boys with the same Math SAT scores do not do equally well in college—girls do better.

In most cases tests reflect rather than cause inequities in American education. The fact that groups score differently on a test does not necessarily mean that the test is biased. If, however, the score differences are related to the validity of the test—for example, if girls and boys know about the same amount of math but boys' test scores are consistently and significantly higher—then the test is biased.

A number of aspects of a test—beyond that which is being tested—can affect the score. For example, girls tend to score better than boys on essay tests, boys better than girls on multiple-choice items. Even today many girls and boys come to a testing situation with different interests and experiences. Thus a reading-comprehension passage that focuses on baseball scores will tend to favor boys, while a question testing the same skills that focuses on child care will tend to favor girls.

These issues are discussed in detail and the research fully annotated in Part 3 of The AAUW Report.

Why Do Girls Drop Out and What Are the Consequences?

- Pregnancy is not the only reason girls drop out of school. In fact, less than half the girls who leave school give pregnancy as the reason.
- Dropout rates for Hispanic girls vary considerably by national origin: Puerto Rican and Cuban American girls are more likely to drop out than are boys from the same cultures or other Hispanic girls.
- Childhood poverty is almost inescapable in single-parent families headed by women without a high school diploma: 77 percent for whites and 87 percent for African Americans.

In a recent study, 37 percent of the female drop-outs compared to only 5 percent of the male drop-outs cited "family-related problems" as the reason they left high school. Traditional gender roles place greater family responsibilities on adolescent girls than on their brothers. Girls are often expected to "help out" with caretaking responsibilities; boys rarely encounter this expectation.

However, girls as well as boys also drop out of school simply because they do not consider school pleasant or worthwhile. Asked what a worthwhile school experience would be, a group of teenage girls responded, "School would be fun. Our teachers would be excited and lively, not bored. They would act caring and take time to understand how students feel. . . . Boys would treat us with respect. If they run by and grab your tits, they would get into trouble."*

Women and children are the most impoverished members of our society. Inadequate education not only limits opportunities for women but jeopardizes their children's—and the nation's—future.

These issues are discussed in detail and the research fully annotated in Part 2/Chapters 4 and 6 of The AAUW Report.

The research reviewed in this report challenges traditional assumptions about the egalitarian nature of American schools. Young women in the United States today are still not participating equally in our educational system. Research documents that girls do not receive equitable amounts of teacher attention, that they are less apt than boys to see themselves reflected in the materials they study, and that they often are not expected or encouraged to pursue higher level mathematics and science courses. The implications are clear; the system must change.

> There has been little change in sex-segregated enrollment patterns in vocational education: girls are enrolled primarily in office and business-training programs, boys in programs leading to higher-paying jobs in the trades.
>
> U.S. Department of Education, 1989.

We now have a window of opportunity that must not be missed. Efforts to improve public education are under way around the nation. We must move girls from the sidelines to the center of educational planning. The nation can no longer afford to ignore the potential of girls and young women. Whether one looks at the issues from an economic, political, or social perspective, girls are one-half of our future.

Significant improvements in the educational opportunities available to girls have occurred in the past two decades. However, twenty years after the passage of Title IX, the achievement of sex- and gender-equitable education remains an elusive dream. The time to turn dreams to reality is now. The current education-reform movement cannot succeed if it continues to ignore half of its constituents. The issues are urgent; our actions must be swift and effective.

---

*As quoted in *In Their Own Voices: Young Women Talk About Dropping Out,* Project on Equal Education Rights (New York, National Organization for Women Legal Defense and Education Fund, 1988), p. 12.

The Recommendations

Strengthened Reinforcement of Title IX Is Essential

1. Require school districts to assess and report on a regular basis to the Office for Civil Rights in the U.S. Department of Education on their own Title IX compliance measures.
2. Fund the Office for Civil Rights at a level that permits increased compliance reviews and full and prompt investigation of Title IX complaints.
3. In assessing the status of Title IX compliance, school districts must include a review of the treatment of pregnant teens and teen parents. Evidence indicates that these students are still the victims of discriminatory treatment in many schools.

Teachers, Administrators and Counselors Must Be Prepared and Encouraged to Bring Gender Equity and Awareness to Every Aspect of Schooling

4. State certification standards for teachers and administrators should require course work on gender issues, including new research on women, bias in classroom-interaction patterns, and the ways in which schools can develop and implement gender-fair multicultural curricula.
5. If a national teacher examination is developed, it should include items on methods for achieving gender equity in the classroom and in curricula.
6. Teachers, administrators, and counselors should be evaluated on the degree to which they promote and encourage gender-equitable and multicultural education.
7. Support and released time must be provided by school districts for teacher-initiated research on curricula and classroom variables that affect student learning. Gender equity should be a focus of this research and a criterion for awarding funds.
8. School-improvement efforts must include a focus on the ongoing professional development of teachers and administrators, including those working in specialized areas such as bilingual, compensatory, special, and vocational education.
9. Teacher-training courses must not perpetuate assumptions about the superiority of traits and activities traditionally ascribed to males in our society. Assertive and affiliative skills as well as verbal and mathematical skills must be fostered in both girls and boys.
10. Teachers must help girls develop positive views of themselves and their futures, as well as an understanding of the obstacles women must overcome in a society where their options and opportunities are still limited by gender stereotypes and assumptions.

The Formal School Curriculum Must Include the Experiences of Women and Men From All Walks of Life. Girls and Boys Must See Women and Girls Reflected and Valued in the Materials They Study.

11. Federal and state funding must be used to support research, development, and follow-up study of gender-fair multicultural curricular models.
12. The Women's Educational Equity Act Program (WEEAP) in the U.S. Department of Education must receive increased funding in order to continue the development of curricular materials and models, and to assist school districts in Title IX compliance.
13. School curricula should deal directly with issues of power, gender politics, and violence against women. Better informed girls are better equipped to make decisions about their futures. Girls and young women who have a strong sense of themselves are better able to confront violence and abuse in their lives.
14. Educational organizations must support, via conferences, meetings, budget deliberations, and policy decisions, the development of gender-fair multicultural curricula in all areas of instruction.
15. Curricula for young children must not perpetuate gender stereotypes and should reflect sensitivity to different learning styles.

Girls Must Be Educated and Encouraged to Understand That Mathematics and the Sciences Are Important and Relevant to Their Lives. Girls Must Be Actively Supported in Pursuing Education and Employment in These Areas.

16. Existing equity guidelines should be effectively implemented in all programs supported by local, state, and federal governments. Specific attention must be directed toward including women on planning committees and focusing on girls and women in the goals, instructional strategies, teacher training, and research components of these programs.
17. The federal government must fund and encourage research on the effect on girls and boys of new curricula in the sciences and mathematics. Research is needed particularly in science areas where boys appear to be improving their performance while girls are not.
18. Educational institutions, professional organizations, and the business community must work together to dispel myths about math and science as "inappropriate" fields for women.
19. Local schools and communities must encourage and support girls studying science and mathematics by showcasing women role models in scientific and technological fields, disseminating career information, and

offering "hands-on" experiences and work groups in science and math classes.

20. Local schools should seek strong links with youth-serving organizations that have developed successful out-of-school programs for girls in mathematics and science and with those girls' schools that have developed effective programs in these areas.

Continued Attention to Gender Equity in Vocational Education Programs Must Be a High Priority at Every Level of Educational Governance and Administration.

21. Linkages must be developed with the private sector to help ensure that girls with training in nontraditional areas find appropriate employment.
22. The use of a discretionary process for awarding vocational-education funds should be encouraged to prompt innovative efforts.
23. All states should be required to make support services (such as child care and transportation) available to both vocational and prevocational students.
24. There must be continuing research on the effectiveness of vocational education for girls and the extent to which the 1990 Vocational Education Amendments benefit girls.

Testing and Assessment Must Serve as Stepping Stones Not Stop Signs. New Tests and Testing Techniques Must Accurately Reflect the Abilities of Both Girls and Boys.

25. Test scores should not be the only factor considered in admissions or the awarding of scholarships.
26. General aptitude and achievement tests should balance sex differences in item types and contexts. Tests should favor neither females nor males.
27. Tests that relate to "real life situations" should reflect the experiences of both girls and boys.

Girls and Women Must Play a Central Role in Educational Reform. The Experiences, Strengths, and Needs of Girls From Every Race and Social Class Must Be Considered in Order to Provide Excellence and Equity for All Our Nation's Students.

28. National, state, and local governing bodies should ensure that women of diverse backgrounds are equitably represented on committees and commissions on educational reform.
29. Receipt of government funding for in-service and professional development programs should be conditioned upon evidence of efforts to increase the number of women in positions in which they are underrepresented. All levels of government have a role to play in increasing the numbers of women, especially women of color, in education-management and policy positions.
30. The U.S. Department of Education's Office of Educational Research and Improvement (OERI) should establish an advisory panel of gender-equity experts to work with OERI to develop a research and dissemination agenda to foster gender-equitable education in the nation's classrooms.
31. Federal and state agencies must collect, analyze, and report data broken down by race/ethnicity, sex, and some measure of socioeconomic status, such as parental income or education. National standards for use by all school districts should be developed so that data are comparable across district and state lines.
32. National standards for computing dropout rates should be developed for use by all school districts.
33. Professional organizations should ensure that women serve on education-focused committees. Organizations should utilize the expertise of their female membership when developing educational initiatives.
34. Local schools must call on the expertise of teachers, a majority of whom are women, in their restructuring efforts.
35. Women teachers must be encouraged and supported to seek administrative positions and elected office, where they can bring the insights gained in the classroom to the formulation of education policies.

A Critical Goal of Education Reform Must Be to Enable Students to Deal Effectively with the Realities of Their Lives, Particularly in Areas Such as Sexuality and Health.

36. Strong policies against sexual harassment must be developed. All school personnel must take responsibility for enforcing these policies.
37. Federal and state funding should be used to promote partnerships between schools and community groups, including social service agencies, youth-serving organizations, medical facilities, and local businesses. The needs of students, particularly as highlighted by pregnant teens and teen mothers, require a multi-institutional response.
38. Comprehensive school-based health- and sex-education programs must begin in the early grades and continue sequentially through twelfth grade. These courses must address the topics of reproduction and reproductive health, sexual abuse, drug and alcohol use, and general mental and physical health issues. There must be a special focus on the prevention of AIDS.

39. State and local school board policies should enable and encourage young mothers to complete school, without compromising the quality of education these students receive.
40. Child care for the children of teen mothers must be an integral part of all programs designed to encourage young women to pursue or complete educational programs.

RESPONSE SHEET

for AAUW: Shortchanging Girls in Schools

1. Identify five ways that girls are shortchanged in school.

2. Write one question/observation for class discussion.

3. Describe one application for use in school systems.

CHAPTER 10

Gender Differences: Contemporary Roles

We have been drawing on the expertise of a wide number of specialists so far in this edited series. Now, we want to draw on those who have the best expertise regarding the status of current gender roles. And the best experts are you. There is simply no one who is as aware of where things stand gender-wise as you. We are going to use the small groups that have been set up in the course to carefully review what changed and what has stayed the same. The baseline typically used is your grandparents (for the furthest back in time). Then parents are brought into it; these two sets have been your primary socialization agents regarding gender. You can't cover the entire gender array, so its helpful to get an up front consensus about the aspects you want to talk about. As has been the case in your earlier group sessions, you will want someone to be the recorder. Shoot for about three 'stayed the same' and three 'changed', as far as reporting purposes in the next class session.

CHAPTER

11

Gender Differences: In Gender Relationships

It is quite likely that the context that brings out gender differences more fully than any other is a romantic relationship that is becoming intimate. It would appear that every percept, assumption, prejudice if you will, regarding the opposite sex will be activated. We are going to look at this in two ways: What *is* intimacy, which Barry F Moss pursues. How it develops is addressed through the five stage model discussed in the last chapters of this text.

Marriage and Romantic Relationships

Defining Intimacy in Romantic Relationships*

Although the ongoing sharing of romantic intimacy is recognized as being health promoting and as a sought-after goal, there has been no consensus in the literature on a definition of the construct. The present paper proposes a multidimensional definition of romantic intimacy that was developed following a review and analysis of published definitions of intimacy. The differences between the constructs of love and intimacy are also discussed, as well as how the present definition may have value to family practitioners.

BARRY F. MOSS AND ANDREW I. SCHWEBEL

Barry F. Moss is a Post-doctoral Fellow in Psychology at the University of Washington, Seattle, WA 98105. Andrew I. Schwebel is Professor of Psychology, Ohio State University, 1885 Neil Avenue Mall, Columbus, OH 43210.

The level of intimacy that individuals experience within relationships exerts a profound influence on their social development, personal adjustment, and physical health. Specifically, intimacy plays an integral role in individuals' successful passage through developmental stages, solidification of friendships, attainment of marital happiness, and success in psychotherapeutic encounters (Erikson, 1963; Fisher & Stricker, 1982; Schaefer & Olson, 1981; Sullivan, 1953). Further, individuals in intimate relationships are more resistant to a number of diseases and physically disabling conditions, have a lower rate of mental illness, and are involved in fewer automobile fatalities than others in the general population (Brown, Harris & Copeland, 1977; Lynch, 1977; Traupmann, Eckels, & Hatfield, 1982).

Failure to obtain satisfactory levels of intimacy in a romantic relationship has been identified as the largest category of problem behavior which motivates people to obtain outpatient psychotherapy (Horowitz, 1979) and as the most frequent reason given by couples for their divorce (Waring, 1988). People in intimacy-deficient committed relationships, compared to those in intimacy-providing relationships and those who are single or divorced, experience greater vulnerability to stress-related psychophysiological disorders, depression, and other nonpsychotic emotional illnesses (Medalie & Goldbourt, 1976; Patton & Waring, 1984; Waring, Patton, Neron, & Linker, 1986).

Although individuals could experience intimacy in many kinds of interpersonal relations, in present-day Western societies, intimacy is particularly sought in romantic relationships. In fact, people typically evaluate their romantic relationship in terms of its level of intimacy and, if they find it deficient, may choose to attend relationship enrichment programs designed to help couples reach their intimacy potential (Frankel, 1982; Greenberg & Johnson, 1986).

Although intimacy is of central importance in enduring romantic relationships, practitioners and researchers interested in this topic have to contend with a slow-developing literature (Sexton & Sexton, 1982). In fact, many authors have stressed the need for more perspicacious definitional and investigative efforts (Hinde, 1978; Oden, 1974; Schaefer & Olson, 1981; Tolstedt & Stokes, 1983; Waring, 1988; Wynne & Wynne, 1986).

TYPES OF DEFINITIONS

The focus of the present paper is on the development of a parsimonious, widely applicable definition of intimacy in romantic relationships by analyzing, integrating, and build-

From *Family Relations,* Vol. 42, No. 1, January 1993, pp. 31–37.

*Preparation of this manuscript was supported in part by an Ohio State Graduate Student Research Alumni Award and by a Sigma Xi Grant-in-Aid Research Award.

Key Words: definition, intimacy, love, relationships, romantic.

ing upon the definitions of intimacy found in the literature. Such a definition can stimulate research by specifying the nature of intimacy as it manifests itself in romantic relationships, and by identifying the elements that comprise it. It also will have indirect and direct benefits for practitioners. Specifically, practitioners will be able to use it to help clients better understand the concept of intimacy, intimacy-related problems they are experiencing, and steps they can take to attain the level of intimacy they seek.

The present authors conducted an extensive, computer-assisted search of scholarly publications and books for definitions of intimacy and, through this process, found 61 unique definitions. Three types were identified: general, multidimensional, and operational definitions. Respectively, these types described intimacy in global terminology, as a composite of discrete subcomponents, and with behavioral measurement criteria. Each type offered a unique perspective on the construct of intimacy.

General Definitions

General definitions were usually based on their authors' personal interpretation of the meaning of intimacy (Billow & Mendelsohn, 1982; Hinde, 1978) or were part of a larger theoretical model (Berne, 1964; Erikson, 1963; Sullivan, 1953). Hinde illustrates the former case, defining intimacy as "the number of different facets of the personality which are revealed to the partner and to what depth" (1978, p. 378). Berne (1964) illustrates the latter case, drawing his definition from Transactional Analysis, "The spontaneous game-free candidness of an aware person" (p. 180).

Most general definitions are vague and lack operational clarity and empirical validation. For example, Eshleman and Clarke (1978) propose that "intimacy . . . refers to any close association or friendship that involves informal warmth, openness, and sharing" (p. 127). Similarly, Nowinski (1988) suggests, "Intimacy means getting close. It means opening up, which means being vulnerable" (p. 49). Although the general definitions are essentially veridical in content and capture the nuances and complexities of the intimacy construct, their global nature leaves open a large array of interpretive and operational possibilities.

Multidimensional Definitions

Multidimensional definitions, although also subjectively derived, are typically based in part on an empirical foundation. Investigators analyzed subjects' statements about the meaning of intimacy and then compiled them into reliably scaled items in accordance with an a priori multidimensional theory (McAdams, 1988; Oden, 1974; Schaefer & Olson, 1981; Waring, McElrath, Lefcoe, & Weisz, 1981).

For example, Oden asked individuals to visually recall a time of fulfilling intimacy and to write down their experiences as clearly and descriptively as possible. Oden analyzed the data generated for common themes and used them to formulate a 12-component definition of intimacy (duration, ecstasy, account-ability, negotiability, empathy, congruence, emotive warmth, conflict capability, self-disclosure, letting-be, finitude, and transcendence). Others who derived multidimensional definitions through data collection also developed definitions with a large number of components had a broad conceptual field (McAdams, 1988; Waring, 1988).

Authors also built multidimensional definitions by drawing from existing research findings relevant to the construct of intimacy (Dahms, 1972; Hatfield, 1982; White, Speisman, Jackson, Bartis, & Costos, 1986). For example, Dahms and Hatfield included a physical expressiveness component, citing work (Patterson, 1984) showing the necessity of physical touch for adequate psychological development and the tendency for those involved in close relationships to initiate more physical contact with each other than they would with other individuals. Because of their empirical derivation and the fact that their authors tended to focus on committed couples, the multidimensional definitions are particularly germane to specifying the nature of intimacy in enduring romantic relationships.

Operational Definitions

The operational definitions, which were chiefly derived from pragmatic concerns for behavioral indices of intimacy, can be grouped into three subtypes: behavioral manifestations, self-report measures, and relationship status indicators of intimacy. Examples of measures of these subtypes are: an assessment of the amount of pleasurable stimulation given to another's thighs and buttocks (Davis & Martin, 1978), Jourard Self-Disclosure Questionnaire scores (Carpenter & Freese, 1979), and indices of marital status (Stone, 1973).

Most operational definitions were not developed to be inclusive. One criticism of them is that they view intimacy as being synonymous with other constructs or a limited number of circumscribed behaviors. For example, Carpenter and Freese (1979) and Buhrmester and Furman (1987) equate intimacy with self-disclosure. However, certain disclosures, such as the "no-holding-back" type that often occur prior to divorce, may function as "attacks" that hurt self-esteem and serve to reduce intimacy (Gilbert, 1976). Other operational definitions measure intimacy in terms of cohesion, marital satisfaction, or amount of direct physical contact (Chelune, Waring, Vosk, Sultan, & Ogden, 1984; Heslin & Boss, 1980).

Identification of Predominant Intimacy Themes

Of the 61 unique definitions of intimacy found in the literature, 31, 10, and 20 were general, multidimensional, and operational definitions, respectively. These definitions, plus three general definitions from the *American Heritage Dictionary* (1992), *Webster's Encyclopedic Unabridged Dictionary* (1989), and *Webster's New World Dictionary*

(1989) were evaluated by the authors and the main theme(s) in each recorded. Rather than limiting themes to mutually exclusive categories, all possible themes were recorded. Next, all definitions were reexamined to determine how many times each of the themes had occurred. When this process was completed, the identified themes and the tabulations were reviewed by three judges with family science interests. These individuals, Ph.D.-trained scientist/practitioners in the health and social science fields, agreed that the decisions made in the analysis were sound.

Finally, the authors identified those themes that occurred in at least 50% of any of the three types of definitions (general, multidimensional, operational). Seven such themes were found and are presented in Table 1 and discussed below:

1. An exchange or mutual interaction (characterizing intimacy as a process that occurs between individuals).
2. In-depth affective awareness-expressiveness (the reception or expression of affect from and to another).
3. In-depth cognitive awareness-expressiveness (the reception or expression of cognitive material from and to another).
4. In-depth physical awareness-expressiveness (the reception or expression of physical acts from or towards another, ranging from interpersonal distance to sexuality).
5. A shared commitment and feeling of cohesion.
6. Communication or self-disclosure (disclosing or communicating information from any content domain to another).
7. A generalized sense of closeness to another.

Examination of Table 1 reveals that the themes of mutuality and of cognitive awareness and expressiveness were included in more than half the definitions of each type. More than half the general and multidimensional definitions also included the themes of affective awareness/expressiveness and communication/self-disclosure. Further, the multidimensional definitions, which focused on committed romantic relationships, also placed emphasis on the themes of physical awareness/expressiveness and commitment/cohesion, both factors which distinguish intimacy in romantic relationships from intimacy in other types of relationships (e.g., friendships, therapist-client relations, etc.).

A Formal Definition

Based on the literature and the material summarized in Table 1, the following definition is proposed:

> Intimacy in enduring romantic relationships is determined by the level of commitment and positive affective, cognitive, and physical closeness one expe-

Table 1
Themes Found in at Least 50% of the General (GEN), Multidimensional (MLT), or Operational (OPR) Definitions of Intimacy*

GEN Intimacy Theme	GEN #	GEN %
Mutual Interaction/Exchange	27/34	79%
Depth of Affective Awareness/Expressiveness	20/34	59%
Depth of Cognitive Awareness/Expressiveness	18/34	53%
Communication/Self-Disclosure in general	17/34	50%
MLT Intimacy Theme	**MLT #**	**MLT %**
Mutual Interaction/Exchange	10/10	100%
Depth of Affective Awareness/Expressiveness	10/10	100%
Depth of Cognitive Awareness/Expressiveness	9/10	90%
Depth of Physical Awareness/Expressiveness	9/10	90%
Communication/Self-Disclosure in general	8/10	80%
Commitment/Cohesion	6/10	60%
Closeness in general	5/10	50%
OPR Intimacy Theme	**OPR #**	**OPR %**
Mutual Interaction/Exchange	15/20	75%
Depth of Physical Awareness/Expressiveness	12/20	60%
Depth of Cognitive Awareness/Expressiveness	10/20	50%

*GEN refers to 34 general definitions; MLT refers to the 10 multidimensional definitions; OPR to the 20 operational definitions of intimacy.

riences with a partner in a reciprocal (although not necessarily symmetrical) relationship.

The definition specifies five components of intimacy: a) Commitment; b) Affective Intimacy; c) Cognitive Intimacy; d) Physical Intimacy; and e) Mutuality. Thus, it includes all seven major intimacy themes occurring in the reviewed definitions with the exception of the themes of Closeness, which was thought to be inherent in the themes of Cognitive, Affective, and Physical Intimacy, and Communication/Self-disclosure.

Although the theme of communication or self-disclosure is found in many definitions, there are several reasons for conceptualizing this theme as a facilitator rather than as a component of intimacy. First, self-disclosure occurs in committed romantic relationships devoid of intimacy (Cuber & Harroff, 1965; Gilbert, 1976; Wynne & Wynne, 1986). Second, separating self-disclosure from intimacy facilitates operational clarity (Chelune et al., 1984; Davis, 1973; Gilbert, 1976; Hatfield, 1988). Researchers have found moderate to strong correlations between measures of intimacy and interpersonal communication (Chelune et al., 1984; Schaefer & Olson, 1981) suggesting these two constructs are related yet distinct. Third, marital therapists often conceptualize mutual disclosure exercises as a vehicle to promote intimacy in couples (Gottman, Notarius, Gonso, & Markman, 1976; Greenberg & Johnson, 1986; Guerney, 1977; Waring, 1988).

By restricting the definition to these five themes, an attempt was made to define romantic intimacy parsimoniously, without being too narrow or so general that its operational and empirical testability and its utility in practice would be compromised. In this definition, "level" indicates the amount of intimacy individuals experience in an enduring relationship while "commitment" refers to their desire to permanently remain with the partner. Commitment is viewed as the foundation that provides opportunities for the other intimacy dimensions to develop.

The word "positive" signifies valence (rather than pleasantness). More specifically, "positive" refers to those thoughts, feelings, and physical encounters that attract (as opposed to repel) individuals to the partner. While "affective closeness" refers to the depth of awareness individuals have about their partner's emotional world and the exchanges of emotions they share, (e.g., feelings of caring and compassion), "cognitive closeness" refers to the depth of awareness individuals have of their partner's cognitive world and the exchanges of cognitions they share (e.g., values, goals, and other information). Physical closeness refers to the extent of shared physical encounters (ranging from proximity to sexuality) as well as to the physiological arousal state experienced toward the partner at each level of physical encounter.

The term "reciprocal" refers to the mutual interaction/exchange theme of intimacy, whereas the statement regarding symmetry indicates that partners may differ in the energy they invest in maintaining intimacy and in the value they place on the intimacy achieved. This definition assumes that to experience genuine intimacy, partners must be able to accurately process information about their partner's cognitive, affective, and physical levels.

Although the present definition partitions romantic intimacy into five components to provide descriptive clarity, in actuality, the components are highly interrelated. For example, cognitive factors influence the perception, interpretation, and encoding of emotional experiences in relationships and vice versa. Likewise, emotional and cognitive experiences are linked to neurochemical and autonomic nervous system activity (Hatfield, 1988).

Evaluation

To evaluate the efficacy of the proposed definition for practice and research, it was examined from three perspectives: 1) How do the levels of the five romantic intimacy components (Commitment, Affective Intimacy, Cognitive Intimacy, Physical Intimacy, and Mutuality) differ in romantic relationships compared to nonintimate relationships and intimate relationships that are not romantic? 2) Do empirical findings support the proposed definition? 3) How does the proposed definition of romantic intimacy differ from definitions of romantic love?

The Levels of Intimacy Themes in Various Relationships

Romantic relationships compared with nonintimate relationships. Davis (1973) categorized relationships in terms of the presence or absence of intimacy. He suggests that strangers, role relations, acquaintances, and enemies comprise a set of basically nonintimate relationships. Davis provided the following definitions: Strangers are those individuals with whom we engage in few reciprocal behaviors; role relations are individuals with whom we engage in only a few narrowly prescribed reciprocal behaviors (such as the behavioral transactions between a bank teller and a customer); acquaintances are individuals we have met and with whom we continue to interact, using only a limited number of prescribed behaviors; and enemies are individuals to whom we obsessively harbor destructive intentions.

Romantic partners, strangers, role relations, acquaintances, and enemies can be differentiated in terms of the level of the five components of romantic intimacy in each relationship. Whereas romantic relationships involve high levels of all five intimacy components, the stranger relationship typically involves a low level of one or two of the components. For example, as strangers pass on the street, their eyes may fleetingly meet and they may both feel attracted (Mutuality, with a positive valence). Role relations and acquaintances, in contrast, are characterized as having some level of Mutuality, Affective Intimacy, and Cognitive Intimacy, but rarely any Physical Intimacy or Commitment. The Mutuality, Affective, and Cognitive Intimacy components can have a positive valence, meaning that people feel attracted and want to share some thoughts or feelings as they interact, or a negative valence, meaning they feel a pull away as they interact and have no desire to transact more than the business at hand.

Finally, enemy relationships, which encompass all five romantic intimacy components, are distinguished from romantic relationships by the valence of the themes. An enemy may readily interact with a partner (Mutuality), know and feel a great deal about a partner (Cognitive and Affective Intimacy), and be committed (Commitment) to continuing the relationship until the opportunity for doing physical harm arises (Physical Intimacy). Although this description may fit some couples, especially some involved in the divorce process (Vaughan, 1986), its primary purpose is to highlight that the essential difference between romantic intimates and enemies is in the valence of the components and not in their presence or absence.

Romantic intimacy compared with other intimate relationships. Intimacy in romantic relationships will be compared with intimacy in three other types of relationships: a) unfamiliar-other, b) therapist-client, and c) friends. Unfamiliar-others are persons who are not well known at the time when intimacy is shared. Further, both parties intend the relationship to be short-term. Examples of such relationships range from a discussion with a passenger occupying an adjacent seat on an airplane to a one-night affair with a person met in a bar. Although the former relationship involves significantly less Physical Intimacy than the latter, both are characterized as having very low levels of Commitment. Although these relationships involve intense but brief sharing along one or more intimacy dimension(s), the low level of Commitment involved limits the levels of Cognitive and Affective Intimacy and makes unfamiliar-other relationships differ sharply from romantic relationships. Further, the Mutuality component of intimacy may also not be well-balanced. Figure 1 shows that, compared to a romantic relationship, the unfamiliar-others relationship has low levels of Mutuality and Commitment and moderately low levels of Cognitive, Affective, and Physical Intimacy.

The therapist-client relationship has been characterized as exceptionally intimate (Fisher & Stricker, 1982). However, in comparison to romantic intimacy, it is limited in terms of Physical Intimacy, Commitment, and the balance of reciprocity (Mutuality) (Billow & Mendelsohn, 1982). Figure 1 represents this relationship, assigning the lowest level of intimacy to Physical Intimacy followed by Mutuality and Commitment and then Cognitive and Affective Intimacy. As also shown in Figure 1, the intimacy exchanged between friends differs from romantic intimacy, primarily in the depth of Physical Intimacy and possibly Commitment experienced between partners, as well as in the capacity to tolerate shifts in Mutuality (Derlega & Winstead, 1986).

Empirical Foundation of Proposed Definition of Romantic Intimacy

Research findings bearing on four aspects of the present definition will be examined next: 1) mutual, positive cognitive closeness; 2) mutual, positive affective closeness; 3) mutual, positive physical closeness; and, 4) commitment.

Mutual, positive cognitive closeness. A considerable body of research suggests that friends, dating partners, and spouses involved in intimate relationships develop deep cognitive understandings of one another, sharing a range of personal information including their values, strengths, weaknesses, hopes, fears, and idiosyncrasies (Altman & Taylor, 1973; Huesmann & Levinger, 1976). The amount of personal information individuals disclose is positively related to how intimate they consider their relationship (Altman & Taylor, 1973; Miller, 1976) and to marital satisfaction (Miller, Corrales, & Wackman, 1975; Hendrick, 1981). Moreover, Waring (1988; Waring & Russell, 1980) demonstrated that increasing the amount of cognitively based information spouses exchanged increased the level of intimacy they experienced.

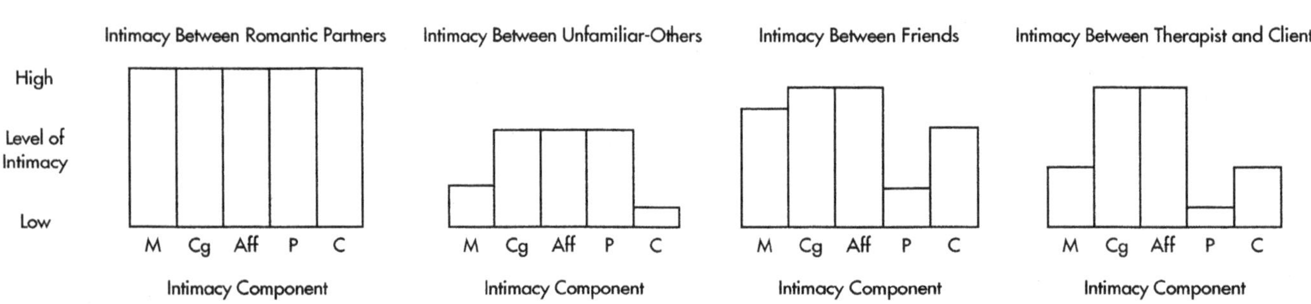

FIGURE 1
Level of Romantic Intimacy Components in Four Types of Intimate Relationships

The valence of the information partners exchange may be more crucial to intimacy than the amount or depth of cognitive disclosure alone (Gilbert, 1976; Tolstedt & Stokes, 1983). While sharing positive information may enhance the level of intimacy, disclosing other information (criticisms, attacks) may reduce the level of intimacy within a marriage or relationship (Strong, 1975).

One enriching aspect of the cognitive exchange process is becoming aware that a partner shares similar attitudes, values, and beliefs. Byrne and Clore (1968) suggest that this discovery is intrinsically rewarding because the mutual consensus validates each partner's ability to correctly interpret the stimulus world. Married couples, in particular, exhibit greater similarities in beliefs, attitudes, and values than random pairs of spouses and randomly assigned stranger dyads (Byrne & Murnen, 1988). Further, couples exhibiting high levels of belief, attitude, value, and personality similarity have greater levels of relationship satisfaction than couples with less cognitive similarity (Cattell & Nesselroade, 1967; Murstein, 1976).

Finally, several empirically derived scales that measure romantic intimacy found the cognitive aspect of intimacy strongly associated with scales measuring other intimacy components. For example, researchers who have used the Personal Assessment of Intimacy in Relationships Inventory (PAIR; Schaefer & Olson, 1981) and the Waring Intimacy Questionnaire (WIQ; Waring, 1984) found high intercorrelations between intellectual intimacy scales and scales measuring emotional, physical, and commitment aspects of relationships.

Mutual, positive affective closeness. Emotions of a positive valence such as love, a deep sense of caring, and a generalized sense of positive attraction or likability toward the intimate partner have been commonly identified Levinger and Senn (1967) found that couples reporting high levels of marital satisfaction, in contrast to those reporting lower levels, tended to discuss positive feelings more often than negative feelings. Further, again in contrast to their counterparts, when the more maritally satisfied couples discussed negative feelings, they tended to be more directed toward external events than toward each other.

The Affect Model of Mutual Attraction (Clore & Byrne, 1974) provides one theoretical explanation for the Levinger and Senn (1967) findings. This model asserts that overall attraction to another is based on the proportion of positive and negative feelings aroused by the other. A number of studies have found support for the operation of the Affect Model in intimate relationships such as friendship, serious dating partnerships, and marriage (e.g., Gold, Ryckman, & Mosley, 1984).

Mutual, positive physical closeness. Individuals in romantic relationships are comfortable in close physical proximity (e.g., Allgeier & Byrne, 1973), exhibit extended periods of mutual gaze (e.g., Exline, 1972), and engage in deeper stages of tactile involvement (e.g., Rosenfeld, Kartus, & Ray, 1976). While physiological changes in autonomic nervous system and neurochemical transmitters have been associated with attraction toward an intimate partner (Zillman, 1984), disclosing information considered highly intimate to another can result in physiological changes associated with increased blood pressure, heart rate, and palmar sweating (e.g., Ashworth, Furman, Chaikin, & Derlega, 1976).

Sexual aspects of romantic intimacy have also been studied. Findings indicated that the sexuality subscales of the Intimacy Mutuality Scale (IMS; White et al., 1986), PAIR, and WIQ are significantly correlated with scales assessing cognitive and affective aspects of intimacy, and that the PAIR and IMS sexuality scales are positively correlated with measures of marital adjustment and satisfaction.

Commitment. The more commitment a person feels toward another, the more likely he or she is to focus affective and cognitive attention toward that other individual (Beach & Tesser, 1988). To illustrate, subjects led to believe they would have to date a person assigned to them exclusively for a five-week period exhibited greater attentiveness to a taped presentation of this partner than counterparts who believed they would have only one date (Berscheid, Graziano, Monson, & Dermer, 1976). Increased attention, in turn, can foster polarized feelings regarding that person (Tesser & Leone, 1977). For example, Tesser and Paulhus (1978) found that the amount of time a subject spent thinking about someone he/she had dated was positively related to higher scores on the Rubin Love Scale (1970). Research on cognitive dissonance theory also suggests that once an individual commits to the decision to remain with another, mental processes are activated which can polarize thoughts and feelings about that individual in a positive direction (Brehm & Cohen, 1962).

Commitment is also related to other dimensions of romantic intimacy. The WIQ Cohesion (marital commitment) Subscale and the IMS Commitment Scale correlate significantly with measures of affective, cognitive, and physical aspects of intimacy. Further, studies have found measures of commitment positively associated with scales of marital adjustment and satisfaction (Murstein & MacDonald, 1983; Tolstedt & Stokes, 1983).

Distinguishing Romantic Intimacy from Romantic Love

The construct of love, like intimacy, has been theoretically and operationally defined in varied ways, ranging from the extent of positive reinforcement given to a partner to self-actualization (Brehm, 1985; Foa & Foa, 1980; Maslow, 1954). Many definitions suggest that love is a subset of intimacy or, more precisely, that individuals assess their level of love by subjectively evaluating the extent to which they experience one or more of the five presently described intimacy components.

Several theories of love are multidimensional (Sternberg & Barnes, 1988), including Sternberg's (1986) triangular theory of love, which most closely approximates the presently proposed intimacy paradigm. Sternberg suggests that love is composed of three components: intimacy, passion, and decision/commitment. He defines intimacy in loving relationships as feelings of bondedness, closeness, connectedness; passion as the drives and motivations that lead to arousal in loving relationships; and the decision/commitment component as the decision that one loves another and the subsequent decision of whether to commit to maintaining that love over time.

Although not identical, there is an overlap between Sternberg's three components of love and the five components of intimacy in the present definition. Cognitive and Affective Intimacy approximate Sternberg's intimacy, Physical Intimacy approximates passion, and Commitment and Mutuality approximate the decision/commitment component. However, romantic intimacy as presently defined is a broader concept than love, as defined in Sternberg's theory. A key difference between the two resides in the decision/commitment component. The experience of romantic intimacy with another does not necessarily contribute to an individual's decision that he or she loves another. Instead, the individual continually monitors and evaluates his or her level of intimacy with another and experiences love when he or she decides that the assessed level of the intimate experience matches expectations of what an individual in love experiences. In other words, it is presently argued that love is experienced after an individual makes a subjective assessment of the level of intimacy experienced with another.

Another major difference is that love does not have the same emphasis on mutuality as does intimacy. An individual can feel unrequited love, but there can be no "unrequited intimacy." Although one partner may behave in more intimate ways than the other, there must be an active mutual sharing (Mutuality) on the component dimensions of Cognitive, Affective, and Physical Intimacy, and Commitment for intimacy to exist. To illustrate, after a divorce, one ex-spouse may still love the other, despite the absence of romantic intimacy.

IMPLICATIONS

The proposed definition, which delineates the components of romantic intimacy, may have utility for family practitioners, regardless of the theoretical perspective that guides their work. Practitioners often encounter clients who have only a vague notion of why they are not achieving the intimacy they want in their relationships. These clients may express their problem with statements or questions like: "I just don't know where our relationship went wrong," "My relationship just seems to be boring. Why did we lose our romantic feelings?" or "We just don't seem to care about one another the same way anymore."

Providing clients with a clear definition of intimacy in romantic relationships and an explanation of its components may be an important first step in helping them manage their problems or solve them. Clients with such understandings are empowered in problem-solving in many ways. First, this information provides partners with a common definition of intimacy which, in turn, gives them the potential to communicate more effectively. Second, the definition structures partners' efforts in examining their problems and the relative health of their relationship, leading them to explore the reciprocity in their relationship and how they relate along cognitive, affective, physical, and commitment domains of intimacy. Through this process clients often develop a more profound awareness of both the strengths and weaknesses of their romantic relationship.

In addition to helping practitioners and clients identify areas of difficulty in a relationship's intimacy, the present definition also suggests avenues for effective therapeutic interventions. Specifically, the present definition states that romantic intimacy is strongest when all five components of intimacy (Mutuality, Commitment, and Cognitive, Affective, and Physical Intimacy) are thriving. Therefore, treatment strategies designed to address all five domains are expected to be most efficacious.

A number of strategies have been developed that can be used to foster intimacy and curtail its loss in each of the domains. For example, Frijda (1988) proposed that repeatedly bringing into consciousness pleasant aspects of one's relationship and how it could be (or was) otherwise permits positive cognitive and emotional associations toward a partner to be perpetually reinstated through imagination and recollection. This may minimize general habituation to the partner and strengthen commitment. Byrne and Murnen (1988) suggested that emotional habituation to the partner may be curtailed by using strategies such as continually finding pleasurable intellectual and physical activities to share and by introducing novelty into the relationship.

Finally, besides thinking carefully about the definition of intimacy, pinpointing the nature of their intimacy problems, and engaging in interventions like those described above, clients may be able to benefit from a series of cognitive-behavioral techniques aimed at enhancing their intimacy in all domains. In this connection, Schwebel and Fine (1992) suggest that practitioners, in work with couples and families, can apply behavioral rehearsal, communication enhancement, in vivo assignments, modeling, problem-solving training, role playing, and other interventions from individual cognitive behavioral therapy approaches, along with interventions from behavioral marital therapy (Jacobson & Gurman, 1986) and cognitive-behavioral therapy for families (Epstein, Schlesinger, & Dryden, 1988).

Specifically, Schwebel and Fine (1992) suggest that practitioners can use such interventions both to help clients make health-promoting changes and to guide them in discovering the links between their intimacy-related cognitions and the thoughts, feelings, and behaviors they experience in their relationship. For example, consider spouses who seek assistance because they feel their relationship has became more distant, rather than closer as they had expected, since the birth of their baby. Practitioners can offer these spouses a series of cognitive-behavioral interventions that will enable them to identify the cognitions they hold regarding what family life should be like after a baby is born, to evaluate how realistic their expectations are, and to help them identify discrepancies between these and recognize the impact such discrepancies may have. Following this, practitioners might also assist the spouses in working toward the development of new behaviors and associated cognitions that will provide them with healthy ways to share intimacy as a couple and as a three-person family. In sum, then, practitioners could use cognitive-behavioral interventions to help the spouses come to better understand what was unfolded between them since the baby was born and to take steps to try to build their level of intimacy to a level that suits them at this point in their family's development.

CONCLUSION

Most individuals seek and work to achieve intimacy in their lives. Experiencing intimacy, in turn, has been identified as a factor that helps individuals maintain their physical and mental health. Given its importance in human well-being, intimacy has been relatively understudied. Perhaps this has been caused, at least in part, by the construct's complexity and the difficulties it poses to researchers who wish to quantity it. Because the definition of romantic intimacy developed in this paper is comprehensive, yet parsimonious, it may be of value to researchers as well as to practitioners, who can use it as a tool in assisting clients with problems involving intimacy.

REFERENCES

Allgeier, A. R., & Byrne, D. (1973). Attraction toward the opposite sex as a determinant of physical proximity. *Journal of Social Psychology,* **90,** 213–219.

Altman, I., & Taylor, D. A. (1973). *Social penetration: The development of interpersonal relationships.* New York: Holt.

American heritage dictionary of the English language (third edition). (1992). Boston: Houghton Mifflin.

Ashworth, C., Furman, G., Chaikin, A., & Derlega, V. (1976). Physiological responses to self-disclosure. *Journal of Humanistic Psychology,* **16**(2), 17–80.

Beach, S. H., & Tesser, A. (1988). Love in marriage: A cognitive account. In R. J. Sternberg & M. L. Barnes (Eds.), *The psychology of love* (pp. 330–355). New York: Vali-Ballou Press.

Berne, E. (1964). *Games people play.* New York: Grove Press.

Berscheid, E., Graziano, W., Monson, T., & Dermer, M. (1976). Outcome dependency: Attention, attribution, and attraction. *Journal of Personality and Social Psychology,* **34,** 978–989.

Billow, R. M., & Mendelsohn, R. (1982). Intimacy in the initial interview. In M. Fisher & G. Stricker (Eds.), *Intimacy* (pp. 383–401). New York: Plenum Press.

Brehm, J. W., & Cohen, A. R. (1962). *Explorations in cognitive dissonance.* New York: John Wiley & Sons, Inc.

Brehm, S. S. (1985). *Intimate relationships.* New York: Random House.

Brown, G. W., Harris, T., & Copeland, J. R. (1977). Depression and loss. *British Journal of Psychiatry,* **30,** 1–18.

Buhrmester, D., & Furman, W. (1987). The development of companionship and intimacy. *Child Development,* **58,** 1101–1113.

Byrne, D., & Clore, G. (1968). *A reinforcement model of evaluative responses.* Unpublished manuscript, Purdue University.

Byrne, D., & Mumen, S. K. (1988). Maintaining loving relationships. In R. J. Sternberg & M. L. Barnes (Eds.), *The psychology of love* (pp. 293–310). New York: Vali-Ballou Press.

Carpenter, J., & Freese, J. (1979). Three aspects of self-disclosure as they relate to quality of adjustment. *Journal of Personality Assessment,* **43,** 78–85.

Cattell, R. B., & Nesselroade, J. R. (1967). Likeness and completeness theories examined by Sixteen Personality Factor measures on stably and unstably married couples. *Journal of Personality and Social Psychology,* **7,** 351–361.

Chelune, G. J., Waring, E. M., Vosk, B. N., Sultan, F. E., & Ogden, J. K. (1984). Self-disclosure and its relationship to marital intimacy. *Journal of Clinical Psychology,* **40,** 216–219.

Clore, G. L., & Byrne, D. (1974). A reinforcement-affect model of attraction. In T. L. Huston (Ed.), *Foundations of interpersonal attraction* (pp. 143–170). New York: Academic Press.

Cuber, J. F., & Harroff, P. B. (1965). *Sex and the significant Americans: A study of sexual behavior among the affluent.* Baltimore: Penguin Books.

Dahms, A. M. (1972). *Emotional intimacy: Overlooked requirement for survival.* Boulder, Colorado: Pruett Publishing Co.

Davis, D., & Martin, H. (1978). When pleasure begets pleasure: Recipient responsiveness as a determinant of physical pleasuring between heterosexual dating couples and strangers. *Journal of Personality and Social Psychology,* **36,** 767–777.

Davis, M. (1973). *Intimate relations.* New York: The Free Press.

Derlega, V. J., & Winstead, B. A. (1986). *Friendship and social interaction.* New York: Springer-Verlag, Inc.

Epstein, N., Schlesinger, S., & Dryden, W. (1988). *Cognitive-behavioral therapy with families.* New York: Brunner/Mazel.

Erikson, E. H. (1963). *Childhood and society.* New York: W. W. Norton.

Eshleman, J. R., & Clarke, J. N. (1978). Intimacy in relating: Love and cohabitation. In J. R. Eshleman & J. N. Clarke (Eds.), *Intimacy, commitments, and marriage: Development of relationships* (p. 127). Boston, MA: Allyn and Bacon, Inc.

Exline, R. (1972). Visual interaction: The glances of power and preference. In J. Cole (Ed.), *Nebraska symposium on motivation, 1971* (pp. 163–206). Lincoln: University of Nebraska Press.

Fisher, M., & Stricker, G. (1982). *Intimacy.* New York: Plenum Press.

Foa, E. B., & Foa, U. G. (1980). Resource theory: Interpersonal behavior as exchange. In K. J. Gergen, M. S. Greenberg, & R. H. Willis (Eds.), *Social exchange: Advances in theory and research* (pp. 77–94). New York: Plenum Press.

Frankel, B. (1982). Intimacy and conjoint marital therapy. In M. Fisher & G. Stricker (Eds.), *Intimacy* (pp. 247–266). New York: Plenum Press.

Frijda, N. H. (1988). The laws of emotion. *American Psychologist,* **45**(5), 349–358.

Gilbert, S. J. (1976). Self-disclosure, intimacy, and communication in family. *Family Coordinator,* **25,** 221–231.

Gold, J. A., Ryckman, R. M., & Mosley, N. R. (1984). Romantic mood induction and attraction to a dissimilar other: Is love blind? *Personality and Social Psychology Bulletin,* **10,** 358–368.

Gottman, J., Notarius, C., Gonso, J., & Markman, H. (1976). *A couple's guide to communication.* Illinois: Research Press Co.

Greenberg, L. F., & Johnson, S. M. (1986). Affect in marital therapy. *Journal of Marital and Family Therapy,* **12,** 1–10.

Guerney, B. G. (1977). *Relationship enhancement.* San Francisco, CA: Jossey-Bass, Inc.

Hatfield, E. (1982). Passionate love, companionate love, and intimacy. In M. Fisher & G. Stricker (Eds.), *Intimacy,* (pp. 267–292). New York: Plenum Press.

Hatfield, E. (1988). Passionate and companionate love. In R. J. Sternberg & M. L. Barnes (Eds.), *The psychology of love* (pp. 191–217). New York: Vali-Ballou Press.

Hendrick, S. S. (1981). Self-disclosure and marital satisfaction. *Journal of Personality and Social Psychology,* **40,** 1150–1159.

Heslin, R., & Boss, D. (1980). Nonverbal intimacy in airport arrival and departure. *Personality and Social Psychology Bulletin,* **6,** 248–252.

Hinde, R. A. (1978). Interpersonal relationships—In quest of a science. *Psychological Medicine,* **8,** 373–396.

Horowitz, M. J. (1979). *States of mind: Analysis of change in psychotherapy.* New York: Plenum Publishing.

Huesmann, L. R., & Levinger, G. (1976). Incremental exchange theory: A formal model for progression in dyadic social interaction. In L. Berkowitz & E. Walster (Eds.), *Advances in experimental social psychology,* (pp. 192–229). New York: Academic Press.

Jacobson, N. S., & Gurman, A. S. (1986). *Clinical handbook of marital therapy.* New York: Guilford.

Levinger, G., & Senn, D. J. (1967). Disclosure of feelings in marriage. *Merrill-Palmer Quarterly,* **13,** 237–249.

Lynch, J. (1977). *The broken heart.* New York: Basic Books.

Maslow, A. H. (1954). *Motivation and personality.* New York: Harper and Row, Publishers.

McAdams, D. P. (1988). *Power, intimacy, and the life story.* New York: The Guilford Press.

Medalie, J. H., & Goldbourt, U. (1976). Angina pectoris among 10,000 men. *American Journal of Medicine,* **60,** 910–921.

Miller, B. (1976). A multivariate developmental model of marital satisfaction. *Journal of Marriage and the Family,* **38,** 643–657.

Miller, S., Corrales, R., & Wackman, D. B. (1975). Recent progress in understanding and facilitating marital communication. *Family Coordinator,* **24,** 143–152.

Murstein, B. I. (1976). *Who will marry whom?* New York: Springer Publishing Co., Inc.

Murstein, B. I., & MacDonald, M. G. (1983). The relationship of "exchange-orientation" and "commitment" scales to marriage adjustment. *International Journal of Psychology,* **18,** 297–311.

Nowinski, J. (1988). *A lifelong love affair: Keeping sexual desire alive in your relationship.* New York: Dodd, Mead & Company, Inc.

Oden, T. C. (1974). *Game free: A guide to the meaning of intimacy.* New York: Harper & Row.

Patterson, M. L. (1984). Intimacy, social control, and nonverbal involvement: A functional approach. In V. J. Derlega (Ed.), *Communication, intimacy, and close relationships* (pp. 105–132). Orlando, FL: Academic Press, Inc.

Patton, D. P., & Waring, E. M. (1984). The quality and quantity of marital intimacy in the marriages of psychiatric patients. *Journal of Sex and Marital Therapy,* **10,** 201–206.

Rosenfeld, L. B., Kartus, S., & Ray, C. (1976). Body accessibility revisited. *Journal of Communication,* **26,** 27–30.

Rubin, Z. (1970). Measurement of romantic love. *Journal of Personality and Social Psychology,* **16,** 267–273.

Schaefer, M. T., & Olson, D. H. (1981). Assessing intimacy: The PAIR inventory. *Journal of Marital and Family Therapy,* **7,** 47–60.

Schwebel, A. I., & Fine, M. A., (1992). Cognitive-behavioral family therapy. *Journal of Family Psychotherapy,* **3,** 73–91.

Sexton, R. E., & Sexton, V. S. (1982). Intimacy: A historical perspective. In M. Fisher & G. Stricker (Eds.), *Intimacy,* (pp. 1–20). New York: Plenum Press.

Sternberg, R. J. (1986). A triangular theory of love. *Psychological Review,* **93,** 119–135.

Sternberg, R. J., & Barnes, M. L. (1988). *The psychology of love.* New Haven and London: Yale University Press.

Stone, W. F. (1973). Patterns of conformity in couples varying in intimacy. *Journal of Personality and Social Psychology,* **27**(3), 413–418.

Strong, J. R. (1975). A marital conflict resolution model: Redefining conflict to achieve intimacy. *Journal of Marriage and Family Counseling,* **55,** 269–276.

Sullivan, H. S. (1953). *The interpersonal theory of psychiatry.* New York: W. W. Norton.

Tesser, A., & Leone, C. (1977). Cognitive schemas and thought as determinants of attitude change. *Journal of Experimental Social Psychology,* **13,** 340–356.

Tesser, A., & Paulhus, D. L. (1978). Toward a causal model of love. *Journal of Personality and Social Psychology,* **34,** 1095–1105.

Tolstedt, B. E., & Stokes, J. P. (1983). Relation of verbal, affective, and physical intimacy to marital satisfaction. *Journal of Counseling Psychology,* **30,** 573–580.

Traupmann, J., Eckels, E., & Hatfield, E. (1982). Intimacy in older women's lives. *The Gerontologist,* **22,** 493–498.

Vaughan, D. (1986). *Uncoupling: Turning point in intimate relationships.* New York: Oxford University Press.

Waring, E. M. (1984). The measurement of marital intimacy. *Journal of Marital and Family Therapy,* **10,** 185–192.

Waring, E. M. (1988). *Enhancing marital intimacy through facilitating cognitive self-disclosure.* New York: Brunner/Mazel.

Waring, E. M., McElrath, D., Lefcoe, D., & Weisz, G. (1981). Dimensions of intimacy in marriage. *Psychiatry,* **44,** 169–175.

Waring, E. M., Patton, D., Neron, C. A., & Linker, W. (1986). Types of marital intimacy and prevalence of emotional illness. *Canadian Journal of Psychiatry,* **31,** 720–726.

Waring, E. M., Russell, L. (1980). Family structure, marital adjustment, and intimacy in patients referred to a consultation-liaison service. *General Hospital Psychiatry,* **3,** 198–203.

Webster's encyclopedic unabridged dictionary of the English language. (1989). Avenel, NJ: Gramercy Books.

Webster's new world dictionary (third college edition). (1989). New York: Simon and Schuster.

White, K. M., Speisman, J. C., Jackson, D., Bartis, S., & Costos, D. (1986). Intimacy maturity and its correlates in young married couples. *Journal of Personality and Social Psychology,* **50**(1), 152–162.

Wynne, L. C., & Wynne, A. R. (1986). The quest for intimacy. *Journal of Marital and Family Therapy,* **12,** 383–394.

Zillman, D. (1984). *Connections between sex and aggression.* Hillsdale, NJ: Lawrence Erlbaum.

RESPONSE SHEET

for Barry Moss: Defining Intimacy in Romantic Relationships

1. What is their definition of romantic intimacy? What do you think of it? Are there any modifications that you would make?

2. Write a question for class discussion.

3. Describe a research, or practice or personal application

The Five Stage Model of Dyadic Intimacy Development

Lynn Ourth

Introduction. There are two routes to adult dyadic intimacy: mutual attraction and friendship. In our culture, the vast majority of adult pairs grope their way towards an intimate relationship via the mutual attraction route. Some, however, traverse the friendship route. Many more of the latter achieve an effective intimate relationship. These two routes are each designated by their first stages; the way they start makes all the difference in how they unfold. The mutual attraction start-up is powerful and ever so narrow in its focus. Thus, there has to be some fancy cultural footwork to make it go beyond its thinly veiled biological intentions. The friendship start-up positions the pair for stage III; and they have already worked on some of the core ingredients of this stage. But, cross-sex friendships are still relatively infrequent, and are still somewhat suspect in a number of quarters, e.g., parents. And, they face the dilemma of whether to move into a romantic relationship or keep it a platonic friendship. The friendship route has four stages; stage two is unnecessary; and, the mutual attraction involves interests and values.

The five stages of Intimacy Development are briefly outlined below.

Stage I Mutual Attraction

1. This is essentially biologically based with a thin cultural veneer. It is powerfully driven, and the attraction is greatly enhanced when it is mutual. In fact, it causes people to become downright goofy, and the feeling is oh, so great. The root "cause" is the most primitive: to reproduce. A very strong part of the attraction is tied to reproduction characteristics, many physical, a few psychological.
2. The challenge is to "make this last." The attempt to do so is where our culture come in. It has generated some interesting myths and other inventions. A major set of these constitutes Stage II.
3. A non-traditional context needs to be created for sexual involvement in this stage.

Stage II Mutual Deception

1. Dating, American style. Best foot forward. Never let them see you sweat. Plenty of time later to change him; first, though . . . If he(she) finds out who I really am, won't like, won't stay. We really are very much alike: we both like pizza and the same movies. See *Grease.*
2. A core element of this stage is to deny, downplay, discount our differences. A second is to exalt attractiveness: If I am only attractive enough, the person will stay with me. Thus, the beauty/handsomeness cult is extended beyond initial attraction, in order to have staying power.
3. Exploration of interests is allowed; so is looking at beliefs. But the search is for similarities; the dimensions for which there are differences are devalued.

Stage III The Paradox of Intimacy

1. The thesis of this stage is that precisely because the pair is moving into an intimate experience, becoming closer, a series of issues, past interpersonal baggage, and related, "suddenly" become crucially important. Whereas before they didn't make a difference, now they make all the difference. Often this is experienced as an emergence of distrust, and it is bewildering, as the anticipation of mutual trust has been growing. "The closer we get, the further apart we become."

   To be able to communicate now becomes crucial, and any indication of what seems an unwillingness to do so (usually the man) creates an impasse.
2. There are three kinds of baggage that we carry into a prospective intimate relationship: Developmental, peer experience and previous romantic experience. Males have one unique developmental component. All self-

esteem vulnerabilities, and virtually all trust issues, are pulled out of both persons' psychological woodwork. This process is why some never let themselves get very far into this stage, and physically or psychologically flee once they are there. Including from the alter.

Central, of course, is becoming able to discover trust within the intimacy version of the relationship.

There is one other set of differences that is pulled to center stage: real personality differences. This is the focus of the Stage IV.

Stage IV The Personality Saga

1. There is no such thing as two people being similar for all aspects of personality. Hopefully, you discover something of this in PRP#3, with the Myers-Briggs differences that show up between yourself and a significant other.
2. Ordinarily, we take the differences we have personally. The other person is willfully engaging in those (different) behaviors, and doesn't really have to. And, if I love him/her enough, he/she will be willing to change. On top of that, most are taught to deny that they argue, since arguing has been seen as an indicator that there is something terribly wrong, and this denial slows down realistic dealing with these natural differences.
3. What has to be accomplished in this stage? Change? This is the least likely outcome, though a possible one. Learning how to discuss such things. Mutual understanding. Starting the process of acceptance. Sometimes, painfully enough, discovering that the specific kinds of differences are such priority issues that the two can't live with them. Tolerating them? Will prolong, but not "solve."

Stage V Durable Intimacy

1. Passionate friendship. We have come full circle. If this process doesn't start out with friendship, it must reach that point, if the relationship is going to be an effective one.
2. There are a number of defining characteristics of an effective intimate relationship.
3. Durable intimacy is possible to achieve, but our prevailing culture is of little help.

CHAPTER

12

Intimacy Development: Stage #1—Mutual Attraction

A true romantic relationship starts with a powerful mutual attraction. In fact, the potency comes from the mutuality. When each discovers that the other is smitten, it unleashes positive feelings that continue to reciprocally grow in a dizzying swirl. This generates an altered state in which bonding seems limitless, in which possibilities seem limitless and in which there is a surety that the relationship will go on forever. Sexual attraction is intense and it seems that only through sexual involvement can these unbelievable feelings of affection and oneness be adequately expressed. The most important of these, for our understanding, is the unshakeable belief that the relationship is for eternity. This makes everything OK. It is safe to trust the other one without reserve. It is safe to tell the other about one's secret dreams, hopes, desires. It is quite OK to start thinking about building a nest somewhere out in the west and let the rest of the world go by.

This is a singularly remarkable occurrence, each time it happens. It brings forth feelings and thoughts from people who insist that they would never have such feelings and thoughts. No, not them. It directly affects attitudes, reflected in the time-honored reference to rose-tinted glasses. It turns the cynic into an optimist, who starts blithering about 'his cup runneth over'.

How on earth does something like this happen? We have several who are very interested in responding to this question (so to speak). Geoffrey Cowley posits that we are genetically wired to become interested, turned on to certain cues in each other. These cues have considerable arousal capabilities. Cowley points out that Nature intends make sure that couples get together and procreate, almost no matter what the circumstances. Martin K. Whyte joins in by showing that the American dating culture is to facilitate the romantic approach. Joann Ellison Rodgers and Deborah Lott specify how this romantic approach unfolds.

The Biology of Beauty

By Geoffrey Cowley

Looking good is a universal human obsession. How do we perceive physical beauty, and why do we place so much stock in it? Scientists are now taking those questions seriously, and gaining surprising insights.

When it comes to choosing a mate, a female penguin knows better than to fall for the first creep who pulls up and honks. She holds out for the fittest suitor available—which in Antarctica means one chubby enough to spend several weeks sitting on newly hatched eggs without starving to death. The Asian jungle bird *Gallus gallus* is just as choosy. Males in that species sport gaily colored head combs and feathers, which lose their luster if the bird is invaded by parasites. By favoring males with bright ornaments, a hen improves her odds of securing a mate (and bearing offspring) with strong resistance to disease. For female scorpion flies, beauty is less about size or color than about symmetry. Females favor suitors who have well-matched wings—and with good reason. Studies show they're the most adept at killing prey and at defending their catch from competitors. There's no reason to think that any of these creatures understands its motivations, but there's a clear pattern to their preferences. "Throughout the animal world," says University of New Mexico ecologist Randy Thornhill, "attractiveness certifies biological quality."

Is our corner of the animal world different? That looks count in human affairs is beyond dispute. Studies have shown that people considered attractive fare better with parents and teachers, make more friends and more money, and have better sex with more (and more beautiful) partners. Every year, 400,000 Americans, including 48,000 men, flock to cosmetic surgeons. In other lands, people bedeck themselves with scars, lip plugs or bright feathers. "Every culture is a 'beauty culture'," says Nancy Etcoff, a neuroscientist who is studying human attraction at the MIT Media Lab and writing a book on the subject. "I defy anyone to point to a society, any time in history or any place in the world, that wasn't preoccupied with beauty." The high-minded may dismiss our preening and ogling as distractions from things that matter, but the stakes can be enormous. "Judging beauty involves looking at another person," says University of Texas psychologist Devendra Singh, "and figuring out whether you want your children to carry that person's genes."

It's widely assumed that ideals of beauty vary from era to era and from culture to culture. But a harvest of new research is confounding that idea. Studies have established that people everywhere—regardless of race, class or age—share a sense of what's attractive. And though no one knows just how our minds translate the sight of a face or a body into rapture, new studies suggest that we judge each other by rules we're not even aware of. We may consciously admire Kate Moss's legs or Arnold's biceps, but we're also viscerally attuned to small variations in the size and symmetry of facial bones and the placement of weight on the body.

This isn't to say that our preferences are purely innate—or that beauty is all that matters in life. Most of us manage to find jobs, attract mates and bear offspring despite our physical imperfections. Nor should anyone assume that the new beauty research justifies the biases it illuminates. Our beautylust is often better suited to the Stone Age than to the Information Age; the qualities we find alluring may be powerful emblems of health, fertility and resistance to

From *Newsweek,* June 3, 1996, pp. 61–66.

disease, but they say nothing about people's moral worth. The human weakness for what Thornhill calls "biological quality" causes no end of pain and injustice. Unfortunately, that doesn't make it any less real.

No one suggests that points of attraction never vary. Rolls of fat can signal high status in a poor society or low status in a rich one, and lip plugs go over better in the Kalahari than they do in Kansas. But local fashions seem to rest on a bedrock of shared preferences. You don't have to be Italian to find Michelangelo's David better looking than, say, Alfonse D'Amato. When British researchers asked women from England, China and India to rate pictures of Greek men, the women responded as if working from the same crib sheet. And when researchers at the University of Louisville showed a diverse collection of faces to whites, Asians and Latinos from 13 countries, the subjects' ethnic background scarcely affected their preferences.

To a skeptic, those findings suggest only that Western movies and magazines have overrun the world. But scientists have found at least one group that hasn't been exposed to this bias. In a series of groundbreaking experiments, psychologist Judith Langlois of the University of Texas, Austin, has shown that even infants share a sense of what's attractive. In the late '80s, Langlois started placing 3- and 6-month-old babies in front of a screen and showing them pairs of facial photographs. Each pair included one considered attractive by adult judges and one considered unattractive. In the first study, she found that the infants gazed significantly longer at "attractive" white female faces than at "unattractive" ones. Since then, she has repeated the drill using white male faces, black female faces, even the faces of other babies, and the same pattern always emerges. "These kids don't read Vogue or watch TV," Langlois says. "They haven't been touched by the media. Yet they make the same judgments as adults."

What, then, is beauty made of? What are the innate rules we follow in sizing each other up? We're obviously wired to find robust health a prettier sight than infirmity. "All animals are attracted to other animals that are healthy, that are clean by their standards and that show signs of competence," says Rutgers University anthropologist Helen Fisher. As far as anyone knows, there isn't a village on earth where skin lesions, head lice and rotting teeth count as beauty aids. But the rules get subtler than that. Like scorpion flies, we love symmetry. And though we generally favor average features over unusual ones, the people we find extremely beautiful share certain exceptional qualities.

When Randy Thornhill started measuring the wings of Japanese scorpion flies six years ago, he wasn't much concerned with the orgasms and infidelities of college students. But sometimes one thing leads to another. Biologists have long used bilateral symmetry—the extent to which a creature's right and left sides match—to gauge what's known as developmental stability. Given ideal growing conditions, paired features such as wings, ears, eyes and feet would come out matching perfectly. But pollution, disease and other hazards can disrupt development. As a result, the least resilient individuals tend to be the most lopsided. In chronicling the scorpion flies' daily struggles, Thornhill found that the bugs with the most symmetrical wings fared best in the competition for food and mates. To his amazement, females preferred symmetrical males even when they were hidden from view; evidently, their smells are more attractive. And when researchers started noting similar trends in other species, Thornhill turned his attention to our own.

Working with psychologist Steven Gangestad, he set about measuring the body symmetry of hundreds of college-age men and women. By adding up right-left disparities in seven measurements—the breadth of the feet, ankles, hands, wrists, and elbows, as well as the breadth and length of the ears—the researchers scored each subject's overall body asymmetry. Then they had the person fill out a confidential questionnaire covering everything from temperament to sexual behavior, and set about looking for connections. They weren't disappointed. In a 1994 study, they found that the most symmetrical males had started having sex three to four years earlier than their most lopsided brethren. For both men and women, greater symmetry predicted a larger number of past sex partners.

That was just the beginning. From what they knew about other species, Thornhill and Gangestad predicted

---

Beauty isn't all that matters in life; most of us manage to attract mates and bear offspring despite our physical imperfections. And the qualities we find alluring say nothing about people's moral worth. Our weakness for 'biological quality' is the cause of endless pain and injustice.

---

that women would be more sexually responsive to symmetrical men, and that men would exploit that advantage. To date, their findings support both suspicions. Last year they surveyed 86 couples and found that women with highly symmetrical partners were more than twice as likely to climax during intercourse (an event that may foster conception by ushering sperm into the uterus) than those with low-symmetry partners. And in separate surveys, Gangestad and Thornhill have found that, compared with regular Joes, extremely symmetrical men are less attentive to their partners and more likely to cheat on them. Women showed no such tendency.

It's hard to imagine that we even notice the differences between people's elbows, let alone stake our love lives on them. No one carries calipers into a singles bar. So why do these measurements predict so much? Because, says Thornhill, people with symmetrical elbows tend to have "a whole suite of attractive features." His findings suggest that besides having attractive (and symmetrical) faces, men with symmetrical bodies are typically larger, more muscular and more athletic than their peers, and more dominant in personality. In a forthcoming study, researchers at the University of Michigan find evidence that facial symmetry is also associated with health. In analyzing diaries kept by 100 students over a two-month period, they found that the last symmetrical had the most physical complaints, from insomnia to nasal congestion, and reported more anger, jealousy and withdrawal. In light of all Thornhill and Gangestad's findings, you can hardly blame them.

If we did go courting with calipers, symmetry isn't all we would measure. As we study each other in the street, the office or the gym, our beauty radars pick up a range of signals. Oddly enough, one of the qualities shared by attractive people is their averageness. Researchers discovered more than a century ago that if they superimposed photographs of several faces, the resulting composite was usually better looking than any of the images that went into it. Scientists can now average faces digitally, and it's still one of the surest ways to make them more attractive. From an evolutionary perspective, a preference for extreme normality makes sense. As Langlois has written, "Individuals with average population characteristics should be less likely to carry harmful genetic mutations."

So far, so good. But here's the catch: while we may find average faces attractive, the faces we find most beautiful are not average. As New Mexico State University psychologist Victor Johnston has shown, they're extreme. To track people's preferences, Johnston uses a computer program called FacePrints. Turn it on, and it generates 30 facial images, all male or all female, which you rate on a 1–9 beauty scale. The program then "breeds" the top-rated face with one of the others to create two digital offspring, which replace the lowest-rated faces in the pool. By rating round after round of new faces, you create an ever more beautiful population. The game ends when you award some visage a perfect 10. (If you have access to the World Wide Web, you can take part in a collective face-breeding experiment by visiting http://www-psych.nmsu.edu/~vic/faceprints/.)

For Johnston, the real fun starts after the judging is finished. By collecting people's ideal faces and comparing them to average faces, he can measure the distance between fantasy and reality. As a rule, he finds that an ideal female has a higher forehead than an average one, as well as fuller lips, a shorter jaw and a smaller chin and nose. Indeed, the ideal 25-year-old woman, as configured by participants in a 1993 study, had a 14-year-old's abundant lips and an 11-year-old's delicate jaw. Because her lower face was so small, she also had relatively prominent eyes and cheekbones.

The participants in that study were all college kids from New Mexico, but researchers have since shown that British and Japanese students express the same bias. And if there are lingering doubts about the depth of that bias, Johnston's latest findings should dispel them. In a forthcoming study, he reports that male volunteers not only consciously prefer women with small lower faces but show marked rises in brain activity when looking at pictures of them. And though Johnston has yet to publish specs on the ideal male, his unpublished findings suggest that a big jaw, a strong chin and an imposing brow are as prized in a man's face as their opposites are in a woman's.

Few of us ever develop the heart-melting proportions of a FacePrints fantasy. And if it's any consolation, beauty is not an all-or-nothing proposition. Madonna became a sex symbol despite her strong nose, and Melanie Griffith's strong jaw hasn't kept her out of the movies. Still, special things have a way of happening to people who approximate the ideal. We pay them huge fees to stand on windblown bluffs and stare into the distance. And past studies have found that square-jawed males not only start having sex earlier than their peers but attain higher rank in the military.

None of this surprises evolutionary psychologists. They note that the facial features we obsess over are precisely the ones that diverge in males and females during puberty, as floods of sex hormones wash us into adulthood. And they reason that hormonal abundance would have been a good clue to mate value in the hunter-gatherer world where our preferences evolved. The tiny jaw that men favor in women is essentially a monument to estrogen—and, obliquely, to fertility. No one claims that jaws reveal a woman's odds of getting pregnant. But like breasts, they imply that she could.

Likewise, the heavy lower face that women favor in men is a visible record of the surge in androgens (testosterone and other male sex hormones) that turns small boys into 200-pound spear-throwers. An oversized jaw is biologically expensive, for the androgens required to produce it tend to compromise the immune system. But from a female's perspective, that should make jaw size all the more revealing. Evolutionists think of androgen-based features as "honest advertisements" of disease resistance. If a male can afford them without falling sick, the thinking goes, he must have a superior immune system in the first place.

No one has tracked the immune responses of men with different jawlines to see if these predictions bear out (Thornhill has proposed a study that would involve comparing volunteers' responses to a vaccine). Nor is it clear whether penis size figures into these equations. Despite what everyone thinks he knows on the subject, scientists haven't determined that women have consistent preferences one way or the other.

Our faces are signatures, but when it comes to raw sex appeal, a nice chin is no match for a perfectly sculpted torso—especially from a man's perspective. Studies from around the world have found that while both sexes value appearance, men place more stock in it than women. And if there are social reasons for that imbalance, there are also biological ones. Just about any male over 14 can produce sperm, but a woman's ability to bear children depends on her age and hormone levels. Female fertility declines by two thirds between the ages of 20 and 44, and it's spent by 54. So while the both sexes may eyeball potential partners, says Donald Symons, an anthropologist at the University of California in Santa Barbara, "a larger proportion of a woman's mate value can be detected from visual cues." Mounting evidence suggests there is no better cue than the relative contours of her waist and hips.

Before puberty and after menopause, females have essentially the same waistlines as males. But during puberty, while boys are amassing the bone and muscle of paleolithic hunters, a typical girl gains nearly 35 pounds of so-called reproductive fat around the hips and thighs. Those pounds contain roughly the 80,000 calories needed to sustain a pregnancy, and the curves they create provide a gauge of reproductive potential. "You have to get very close to see the details of a woman's face," says Devendra Singh, the University of Texas psychologist. "But you can see the shape of her body from 500 feet, and it says more about mate value."

Almost anything that interferes with fertility—obesity, malnutrition, pregnancy, menopause—changes a woman's shape. Healthy, fertile women typically have waist-hip ratios of .6 to .8, meaning their waists are 60 to 80 percent the size of their hips, whatever their actual weight. To take one familiar example, a 36-25-36 figure would have a WHR of .7. Many women outside this range are healthy and capable of having children, of course. But as researchers in the Netherlands discovered in a 1993 study, even a slight increase in waist size relative to hip size can signal reproductive problems. Among 500 women who were attempting in vitro fertilization, the odds of conceiving during any given cycle declined by 30 percent with every 10 percent increase in WHR. In other words, a woman with a WHR of .9 was nearly a third less likely to get pregnant than one with a WHR of .8, regardless of her age or weight. From an evolutionary perspective, it's hard to imagine men not responding to such a revealing signal. And as Singh has shown repeatedly, they do.

Defining a universal standard of body beauty once seemed a fool's dream; common sense said that if spindly Twiggy and Rubens's girthy Three Graces could all excite admiration, then nearly anyone could. But if our ideals of size change from one time and place to the next, our taste in shapes is amazingly stable. A low waist-hip ratio is one of the few features that a long, lean Barbie doll shares with a plump, primitive fertility icon. And Singh's findings suggest the fashion won't change any time soon. In one study, he compiled the measurements of Playboy centerfolds and Miss America winners from 1923 to 1990. Their bodies got measurably leaner over the decades, yet their waist-hip ratios stayed within the narrow range of .68 to .72. (Even Twiggy was no tube; at the peak of her fame in the 1960s, the British model had a WHR of .73.)

The same pattern holds when Singh generates line drawings of different female figures and asks male volunteers to rank them for attractiveness, sexiness, health and fertility. He has surveyed men of various backgrounds, nationalities and ages. And whether the judges are 8-year-olds or 85-year-olds, their runaway favorite is a figure of average weight with a .7 WHR. Small wonder that when women were liberated from corsets and bustles, they took up girdles, wide belts and other waist-reducing contraptions. Last year alone, American women's outlays for shape-enhancing garments topped a half-billion dollars.

Even infants spend more time gazing at pictures of 'attractive' faces than at 'unattractive' ones. 'These kids don't read Vogue or watch TV, yet they make the same judgments as adults', says psychologist Judith Langlois.

To some critics, the search for a biology of beauty looks like a thinly veiled political program. "It's the fantasy life of American men being translated into genetics," says poet and social critic Katha Pollitt. "You can look at any feature of modern life and make up a story about why it's genetic." In truth, says Northwestern University anthropologist Micaela di Leonardo, attraction is a complicated social phenomenon, not just a hard-wired response. If attraction were governed by the dictates of baby-making, she says, the men of ancient Greece wouldn't have found young boys so alluring, and gay couples wouldn't crowd modern sidewalks. "People make decisions about sexual and marital partners inside complex networks of friends and relatives," she says. "Human beings cannot be reduced to DNA packets."

Homosexuality is hard to explain as a biological adaptation. So is stamp collecting. But no one claims that human beings are mindless automatons, blindly striving to replicate our genes. We pursue countless passions that have no direct bearing on survival. If we're sometimes attracted to people who can't help us reproduce, that doesn't mean human preferences lack any coherent design. A radio used as a doorstop is still a radio. The beauty mavens' mission—and that of evolutionary psychology in general—is not to explain everything people do but to unmask our biases and make sense of them. "Our minds have evolved to generate pleasurable experiences in response to some things while ignoring other things," says Johnston. "That's why sugar tastes sweet, and that's why we find some people more attractive than others."

The new beauty research does have troubling implications. First, it suggests that we're designed to care about looks, even though looks aren't earned and reveal nothing about character. As writer Ken Siman observes in his new book, "The Beauty Trip," "the kind [of beauty] that inspires awe, lust, and increased jeans sales cannot be evenly distributed. In a society where everything is supposed to be within reach, this is painful to face." From acne to birth defects, we wear our imperfections as thorns, for we know the world sees them and takes note.

A second implication is that sexual stereotypes are not strictly artificial. At some level, it seems, women are designed to favor dominant males over meek ones, and men are designed to value women for youthful qualities that time quickly steals. Given the slow pace of evolutionary change, our innate preferences aren't likely to fade in the foreseeable future. And if they exist for what were once good biological reasons, that doesn't make them any less nettlesome. "Men often forgo their health, their safety, their spare time and their family life in order to get rank," says Helen Fisher, the Rutgers anthropologist, "because unconsciously, they know that rank wins women." And all too often, those who can trade cynically on their rank do.

But do we have to indulge every appetite that natural selection has preserved in us? Of course not. "I don't know any scientist who seriously thinks you can look to nature for moral guidance," says Thornhill. Even the fashion magazines would provide a better compass.

With Karen Springen

RESPONSE SHEET

for Geoffrey Cowley: The Biology of Beauty

1. Choose five features (any combination of male/female) that are high in attractiveness, and state what biological/survival value each has. (8 pts)

2. Write a question for class discussion.

Choosing Mates—The American Way

Martin King Whyte

Martin King Whyte is professor of sociology and faculty associate in the Center for Chinese Studies at the University of Michigan. He has published numerous works on family sociology and contemporary Chinese social organization. His is currently involved in a comparative study of mate choice and marital relations in China and the United States. His latest book is Dating, Mating, and Marriage.

As America's divorce rate has been soaring, popular anxieties about marriage have multiplied. Is it still possible to "live happily ever after," and if so, how can this be accomplished? How can you tell whether a partner who leaves you breathless with yearning will, as your spouse, drive you to distraction? Does "living together" prior to marriage provide a realistic assessment of how compatible you and your partner might be as husband and wife? Questions such as these suggest a need to examine our American way of mate choice. How do we go about selecting the person we marry, and is there something wrong with the entire process?

For most twentieth-century Americans choosing a mate is the culmination of a process of dating. Examination of how we go about selecting mates thus requires us to consider the American dating culture. Dating is a curious institution. By definition it is an activity that is supposed to be separate from selecting a spouse. Yet, dating is expected to provide valuable experience that will help in making a "wise" choice of a marital partner. Does this combination work?

How well dating "works" may be considered in a number of senses of this term. Is it easy or difficult to find somebody to go out with? Do dates mostly lead to enjoyable or painful evenings? However, these are not the aspects of dating I wish to consider. The issue here is whether dating works in the sense of providing useful experience that helps pave the way for a successful marriage.

Dating is a relatively new institution. The term, and the various practices associated with it, first emerged around the turn of the century. By the 1920s dating had more or less completely displaced earlier patterns of relations among unmarried Americans. Contrary to popular assumptions, even in colonial times marriages were not arranged in America. Parents were expected to give their approval to their children's nuptial plans, a practice captured in our image of a suitor asking his beloved's father for her hand in marriage. Parental approval, especially among merchants and other prosperous classes, put some constraint on the marriages of the young. For example, through the eighteenth century, children in such families tended to marry in birth order and marriage to cousins was not uncommon. (Both practices had declined sharply by the nineteenth century.) However, parents rarely directly arranged the marriages of their children. America has always exhibited "youth-driven" patterns of courtship. Eligible males and females took the initiative to get to know each other, and the decision to marry was made by them, even if that decision was to some degree contingent on parental approval. (Of course, substantial proportions of later immigrant groups from Southern and Eastern Europe, Asia, and elsewhere brought with them arranged marriage traditions, and contention for control over marriage decisions was often a great source of tension in such families.)

How did young people get to know one another well enough to decide to marry in the era before dating? A set of customs, dominant for the two centuries, preceded the rise of the dating culture. These activities came to be referred to as "calling" and "keeping company." Young people might meet in a variety of ways—through community and church socials, informally in shops or on the street, on boat and train trips, or through introductions from friends or relatives. (America never developed a system of chaperoning young women in public, and foreign observers often commented on the freedom unmarried women had to travel and mix socially on their own.) Usually young people would go to church fairs, local dances, and other such activities with family, siblings, or friends, rather than paired off with a partner. Most activities would involve a substantial degree of adult and community supervision. Nonetheless, these gatherings did encourage some pairing off and led to hand holding, moonlit walks home, and other romantic exploration.

As relationships developed beyond the platonic level, the suitor would pay visits to the home of the young

From *Society,* Vol. 29, No. 3, March/April 1992, pp. 71–77.

By late nineteenth century, a formal pattern of "calling" developed among the upper and middle classes.

woman. By the latter part of the nineteenth century, particularly among the middle and upper classes, this activity assumed a formal pattern referred to as "calling." Males would be invited to call on the female at her home, and they were expected to do so only if invited. (A bold male could, however, request an invitation to call.) Invitations might be extended by the mother of a very young woman, but eventually they would come from the young woman herself. Often a woman would designate certain days on which she would receive callers. She might have several suitors at one time, and thus a number of men might be paying such calls. A man might be told that the woman was not at home to receive him, and he would then be expected to leave his calling card. If this happened repeatedly, he was expected to get the message that his visits were no longer welcome.

Initiative and control in regard to calling were in the hands of women (the eligible female and her mother). Although some variety in suitors was possible, even in initial stages the role of calling in examining potential marriage partners was very clear to all involved. The relatively constrained and supervised nature of calling make it certain that enjoyment cannot have been a primary goal of this activity. (During the initial visits the mother was expected to remain present; in later visits she often hovered in an adjacent room.) If dating is defined as recreational and romantic pairing off between a man and a woman, away from parental supervision and without immediate consideration of marriage, then calling was definitely not dating.

The supervised and controlled nature of calling should not, however, lead us to suppose that propriety and chastity were always maintained until marriage. If the relationship had deepened sufficiently, the couple might progress from calling to "keeping company," a precursor of the twentieth-century custom of "going steady." At this stage, the primary activity would still consist of visits by the suitor to the woman's home. However, now she would only welcome calls from one man, and he would visit her home on a regular basis. Visits late into the evening would increasingly replace afternoon calls. As the relationship became more serious, parents would often leave the couple alone. Nineteenth-century accounts mention parents going off to bed and leaving the young couple on the couch or by the fireplace, there to wrestle with, and not infrequently give in to, sexual temptation.

Even though some women who headed to the altar toward the end of the nineteenth century had lost their virginity prior to marriage, premarital intimacy was less common than during the dating era. (The double standard of the Victorian era made it possible for many more grooms to be non-virgins at marriage than brides. Perhaps 50 percent or more of men had lost their virginity prior to marriage, as opposed to 15 to 20 percent of women, with prostitutes and "fallen women" helping to explain the differential.) What is less often realized is that the formalization of the calling pattern toward the end of the nineteenth century contributed to a decline in premarital sexual intimacy compared to earlier times. America experienced not one but two sexual revolutions—one toward the end of the eighteenth century, at the time of the American Revolution, and the other in the latter part of the twentieth century.

The causes of the first sexual revolution are subject to some debate. An influx of settlers to America who did not share the evangelical puritanism of many early colonists, the expansion of the population into the unsettled (and "unchurched") frontier, the growth of towns, and the individualistic and freedom-loving spirit of the American revolution may have contributed to a retreat from the fairly strict emphasis on premarital chastity of the early colonial period. Historians debate the extent to which the archetypal custom of this first sexual revolution, bundling, (which allowed an unmarried couple to sleep together, although theoretically fully clothed and separated by a "bundling board") was widespread or largely mythical. Whatever the case, other evidence is found in studies of communities, such as those by Daniel Scott Smith and Michael Hindus, which found that the percentage of married couples whose first births were conceived premaritally increased from about 11 percent before 1700 to over 33 percent in the last decades of the eighteenth century.

This first sexual revolution was reversed in the nineteenth century. The reasons for its demise are also not clear. The closing of the frontier, the rise of the middle class, the defensive reactions of that new middle class to new waves of immigrants, the growth of Christian revivalism and reform movements, and the spread of models of propriety from Victorian England (which were in turn influenced by fear of the chaos of the French Revolution)—all these have been suggested as having contributed to a new sexual puritanism in the nineteenth century. According to Smith and Hindus, premarital conceptions decreased once again to about 15 percent of first births between 1841 and 1880.

It was in the latter time period that the customs of calling and keeping company reached their most formal elaboration—calling, in less ritualized forms, can be traced back to the earliest colonial period. Not long after reaching the formal patterns described, calling largely disappeared. In little more than a generation, dating replaced calling as the dominant custom.

Dating involved pairing off of couples in activities not supervised by parents, with pleasure rather than marriage as the primary goal. The rules governing dating were defined by peers rather than by adults. The initiative, and much of the control, shifted from the female to the male. The man asked the woman out, rather than waiting for her invitation to call. The finances and transportation for the date were also his responsibility. The woman was expected to provide, in turn, the pleasure of her company and perhaps some degree of romantic and physical intimacy. By giving or withholding her affection and access to her body, she exercised considerable control over the man and the date as an event. Nonetheless, the absence of parental oversight and the pressure to respond to a man's initiatives placed a woman in a weaker position than she was in the era of calling.

> Rules governing dating were defined by peers rather than adults.

The man might pick up the woman at her home, but parents who tried to dictate whom their daughters dated and what they did on dates generally found such efforts rejected and evaded. Parents of a son might not even know where junior was going or whom he was dating. Dates were conducted mostly in the public arena, and in some cases—such as at sporting events or school dances—adults might be present. But dates often involved activities and venues where no adults were present or where young people predominated—as at private parties or at local dance halls. Or in other cases the presence of adults would have little inhibiting effect, as in the darkened balconies of movie theaters. American youths also developed substantial ingenuity in finding secluded "lovers' lanes" where they could escape the supervision of even peers. (Localities varied in the places used for this purpose and how they were referred to. In locales near bodies of water young people spoke of "watching submarine races;" in the rural area of upstate New York where I grew up the phrase was "exploring tractor roads.") Community dances and gatherings for all generations and ages practically disappeared in the dating era.

Greater privacy and autonomy of youths promoted romantic and physical experimentation. Not only kissing but petting was increasingly accepted and widespread. Going beyond petting to sexual intercourse, however, involved substantial risks, especially for the female. This was not simply the risk of pregnancy in the pre-pill era. Dating perpetuated the sexual double standard. Men were expected to be the sexual aggressors and to try to achieve as much intimacy as their dates would allow. But women who "went too far" risked harming their reputations and their ability to keep desirable men interested in them for long. Women were expected to set the limits, and they had to walk a careful line between being too unfriendly (and not having males wanting to date them at all) and being too friendly (and being dated for the "wrong reasons").

During the initial decades of the dating era, premarital intimacy increased in comparison with the age of calling, but still a majority of women entered marriage as virgins. In a survey in the greater Detroit metropolitan area, I found that of the oldest women interviewed (those who dated and married prior to 1945), about one in four had lost her virginity prior to marriage. (By the 1980s, according to my survey, the figure was closer to 90 percent.) Escape from parental supervision provided by dating weakened, but did not immediately destroy, the restraints on premarital intimacy.

When Americans began dating, they were primarily concerned with enjoyment, rather than with choosing a spouse. Indeed, "playing the field" was the ideal pursued by many. Dates were not suitors or prospects. Seeing different people on successive nights in a hectic round of dating activity earned one popularity among peers. One of the early students and critics of the dating culture, Willard Waller, coined the term "rating and dating complex" to refer to this pattern. After observing dating among students at Pennsylvania State University in the 1930s, Waller charged that concern for impressing friends and gaining status on campus led to superficial thrill-seeking and competition for popularity, and eliminated genuine romance or sincere communication. However, Waller has been accused of both stereotyping and exaggerating the influence of this pattern. Dating was not always so exploitative and superficial as he charged.

Dating was never viewed as an endless stage or an alternative to courtship. Even if dates were initially seen as quite separate from mate selection, they were always viewed as only the first step in a progression that would lead to marriage. By the 1930s, the stage of "going steady" was clearly recognized, entailing a commitment by both partners to date each other exclusively, if only for the moment. A variety of ritual markers emerged to symbolize the increased commitment of this stage and of further steps toward engagement and marriage, such as wearing the partner's high school ring, being lavaliered, and getting pinned.

> Growing affluence fueled new industries designed to entertain and fill leisure time.

Going steady was a way-station between casual dating and engagement. Steadies pledged not to date others, and they were likely to become more deeply involved romantically and physically than casual daters. They were not expected explicitly to contemplate marriage, and the majority of women in our Detroit survey had several steady boyfriends before the relationships that led to their marriages. If a couple was of a "suitable age," though, and if the steady relationship lasted more than a few months, the likelihood increased of explicit talk about marriage. Couples would then symbolize their escalated commitment by getting engaged. Dating arose first among middle and upper middle class students in urban areas, and roughly simultaneously at the college and high school levels. The practice then spread to other groups—rural young people, working class youths, to the upper class, and to employed young people. But what triggered the rapid demise of calling and the rise of dating?

One important trend was prolonged school attendance, particularly in public, co-educational high schools and colleges. Schools provided an arena in which females and males could get to know one another informally over many years. Schools also organized athletic, social, and other activities in which adult supervision was minimal. College campuses generally allowed a more total escape from parental supervision than high schools.

Another important influence was growing affluence in America. More and more young people were freed from a need to contribute to the family economy and had more leisure time in which to date. Fewer young people worked under parental supervision, and more and more fathers worked far from home, leaving mothers as the primary monitors of their children's daily activities. These trends also coincided with a rise in part-time and after-school employment for students, employment that provided pocket money that did not have to be turned over to parents and could be spent on clothing, makeup, movie tickets, and other requirements of the dating culture. Rising affluence also fueled the growth of entire new industries designed to entertain and fill leisure time—movies, popular music recording, ice cream parlors, amusement parks, and so on. Increasingly, young people who wanted to escape from supervision of their parents found a range of venues, many of them catering primarily to youth and to dating activities.

Technology also played a role, and some analysts suggest that one particular invention, the automobile, deserves a lion's share of the credit. Automobiles were not only a means to escape the home and reach a wider range of recreation spots. They also provided a semi-private space with abundant romantic and sexual possibilities. New institutions, such as the drive-in movie theater, arose to take advantage of those possibilities. As decades passed and affluence increased, the borrowed family car was more and more replaced by cars owned by young people, advancing youth autonomy still further.

All this was part of a larger trend: the transformation of America into a mass consumption society. As this happened, people shifted their attention partially from thinking about how to work and earn to pondering how to spend and consume. Marketplace thinking became more and more influential. The image of the individual as *homo economicus* and of modern life typified by the rational application of scientific knowledge to all decisions became pervasive. The new ideological framework undermined previous customs and moral standards and extended to the dating culture.

Dating had several goals. Most obviously and explicitly, dates were expected to lead to pleasure and possibly to romance. It was also important, as Waller and others have observed, in competition for popularity. But a central purpose of dating was to gain valuable learning experience that would be useful later in selecting a spouse. Through dating young people would learn how to relate to the opposite sex. Dating would increase awareness of one's own feelings and understanding of which type of partner was appealling and which not. Through crushes and disappointments, one would learn to judge the character of people. And by dating a variety of partners and by increasingly intimate involvement with some of them, one would learn what sort of person one would be happy with as a marital partner. When it came time to marry one would be in a good position to select "Mr. Right" or "Miss Right." Calling, which limited the possibilities of romantic experimentation, often to only one partner, did not provide an adequate basis for such an informed choice.

What emerged was a "marketplace learning viewpoint." Selecting a spouse is not quite the same as buying a car or breakfast cereal, but the process was seen as analogous. The assumptions involved in shopping around and test driving various cars or buying and tasting Wheaties, Cheerios, and Fruit Loops were transferred to popular thinking about how to select a spouse.

According to this marketplace learning viewpoint, getting married very young and without having acquired much dating experience was risky, in terms of marital happiness. Similarly, marrying your first and only sweetheart was not a good idea. Neither was meeting someone, falling head over heels in love, and marrying, all within the course of a month. While Americans recognized that in some cases such beginnings could lead to good marriages, the rationale of our dating culture was that having had a variety of dating partners and then getting to know one or more serious prospects over a longer period time and on fairly intimate terms were experiences more likely to lead to marital success.

Eventually, this marketplace psychology helped to undermine America's premarital puritanism, and with it the sexual double standard. The way was paved for acceptance of new customs, and particularly for premarital cohabitation. Parents and other moral guardians found it increasingly difficult to argue against the premise that, if sexual enjoyment and compatibility were central to marital happiness, it was important to test that compatibility before marrying. Similarly, if marriage involved not just hearts and flowers, but also dirty laundry and keeping a budget, did it not make sense for a couple to live together prior to marriage to see how they got along on a day-to-day basis? Such arguments on behalf of premarital sex and cohabitation have swept into popular consciousness in the United States, and it is obvious that they are logical corollaries of the marketplace learning viewpoint.

Our dating culture thus is based upon the premise that dating provides valuable experience that will help individuals select mates and achieve happy marriages. But is this premise correct? Does dating really work? What evidence shows that individuals with longer dating experience, dates with more partners, or longer and more intimate acquaintances with the individuals they intend to marry end up with happier marriages? Surprisingly, social scientists have never systematically addressed this question. Perhaps this is one of those cherished beliefs people would prefer not to examine too closely. When I could find little evidence on the connection between dating and other premarital experiences and marital success in previous studies, I decided to conduct my own inquiry.

My desire to know whether dating experiences affected marriages was the basis for my 1984 survey in the Detroit area. A representative sample of 459 women was interviewed in three counties in the Detroit metropolitan area (a diverse, multi-racial and multi-ethnic area of city and suburbs containing about 4 million people in 1980). The women ranged in ages from 18 to 75, and all had been married at least once. (I was unable to interview their husbands, so unfortunately marriages in this study are viewed only through the eyes of women.) The interviewees had first married over a sixty year span of time, between 1925 and 1984. They were asked to recall a variety of things about their dating and premarital experiences. They were also asked a range of questions about their marital histories and (if currently married) about the positive and negative features of their relations with their husbands. The questionnaire enabled us to test whether premarital experiences of various types were related to marital success, a concept which in turn was measured in several different ways. (Measures of divorce and of both positive and negative qualities in intact marriages were used.)

> Dating was to give valuable experience to help in future mate selection.

The conclusions were a surprise. It appears that dating does not work and that the "marketplace learning viewpoint" is misguided. Marrying very young tended to produce unsuccessful marriages. Premarital pregnancy was associated with problems in marriage. However, once the age of marriage is taken into account, none of the other measures—dating variety, length of dating, length of courtship or engagement, or degree of premarital intimacy with the future husband or others—was clearly related to measures of marital success. A few weak tendencies in the results were contrary to predictions drawn from the marketplace learning viewpoint. Women who had dated more partners or who had engaged in premarital sex or cohabited were slightly less likely to have successful marriages. This might be seen as evidence of quite a different logic.

> Individuals who had been living together were less likely to have successful marriages.

Perhaps there is a "grass is greener" effect. Women who have been led less sheltered and conventional lives prior to marriage may not be as easily satisfied afterward. Several other researchers have found a similar pattern with regard to premarital cohabitation. Individuals who had been living together prior to marriage were significantly less likely to have successful marriages than those who did not.

In the Detroit survey, these "grass is greener" patterns were not consistent or statistically significant. It was not that women with more dating experience and greater premarital intimacy had less successful marriages; rather, the amount and type of dating experience did not make a clear difference one way or the other.

Women who had married their first sweethearts were just as likely to have enduring and satisfying marriages as women who had married only after considering many alternatives. Similarly, women who had married after only a brief acquaintance were no more (nor less) likely to have a successful marriage than those who knew their husbands-to-be for years. And there was no clear difference between the marriages of women who were virgins at marriage and those who had had a variety of sexual partners and who had lived together with their husbands before the wedding.

Dating obviously does not provide useful learning that promotes marital success. Although our dating culture is based upon an analogy with consumer purchases in the marketplace, it is clear that in real life selecting a spouse is quite different from buying a car or a breakfast cereal. You cannot actively consider several prospects at the same time without getting your neck broken and being deserted by all of them. Even if you find Ms. Right or Mr. Right, you may be told to drop dead. By the time you are ready to marry, this special someone you were involved with earlier may no longer be available, and you may not see anyone on the horizon who comes close to being as desirable. In addition, someone who is well suited at marriage may grow apart from you or find someone else to be with later. Dating experience might facilitate marital success if deciding whom to marry was like deciding what to eat for breakfast (although even in the latter regard tastes change, and toast and black coffee may replace bacon and eggs). But these realms are quite different, and mate selection looks more like a crap-shoot than a rational choice.

Is there a better way? Traditionalists in some societies would argue that arranged marriages are preferable. However, in addition to the improbability that America's young people will leave this decision to their parents, there is the problem of evidence. The few studies of this topic, including one I have been collaborating on in China, indicate that women who had arranged marriages were less satisfied than women who made the choice themselves. So having Mom and Dad take charge is not the answer. Turning the matter over to computerized matchmaking also does not seem advisable. Despite the growing sophistication of computers, real intelligence seems preferable to artificial intelligence. As the Tin Woodman in *The Wizard of Oz* discovered, to have a brain but no heart is to be missing something important.

Perhaps dating is evolving into new patterns in which premarital experience will contribute to marital success. Critics from Waller onward have claimed that dating promotes artificiality, rather than realistic assessment of compatibility. Some observers suggest that the sort of superficial dating Waller and others wrote about has become less common of late. Dating certainly has changed significantly since the pre-Second World War era. Many of the rigid rules of dating have broken down. The male no longer always takes the initiative; neither does he always pay. The sexual double standard has also weakened substantially, so that increasingly Americans feel that whatever a man can do a woman should be able to do. Some writers even suggest that dating is going out of style, replaced by informal pairing off in larger groups, often without the prearrangements of "asking someone out." Certainly the terminology is changing, with "seeing" and "being with" increasingly preferred to "dating" and "going steady." To many young people the latter terms have the old fashioned ring that "courting" and "suitor" had when I was young.

My daughter and other young adults argue that current styles are more natural and healthier than the dating experienced by my generation and the generation of my parents. Implicit in this argument is the view that, with formal rules and the "rating and dating" complex in decline, it should be possible to use dating (or whatever you call it) to realistically assess compatibility and romantic chemistry. These arguments may seem plausible, but I see no evidence that bears them out. The youngest women we interviewed in the Detroit survey should have experienced these more informal styles of romantic exploration. However, for them dating and premarital intimacy were, if anything, less closely related to marital success than was the case for the older women. The changes in premarital relations do not seem to make experience a better teacher.

While these conclusions are for the most part quite negative, my study leads to two more positive observations. First, marital success is not totally unpredictable. A wide range of features of how couples structure their day-to-day marital relations promote success—sharing in power and decision-making, pooling incomes, enjoying similar leisure time activities, having similar values, having mutual friends and an active social life, and other related qualities. Couples are not "doomed" by their past histories, including their dating histories, and they can increase their mutual happiness through the way they structure their marriages.

Second, there is something else about premarital experience besides dating history that may promote marital success. We have in America not one, but two widely shared, but quite contradictory, theories about how individuals should select a spouse: one based on the marketplace learning viewpoint and another based on love. One viewpoint sees selecting a spouse as a rational process, perhaps even with lists of criteria by which various prospects can be judged. The other, as song writers tell us, is based on the view that love conquers all and that "all you need is love." Love is a matter of the heart (perhaps with some help from the hormonal system) and not the head, and love may blossom unpredictably, on short notice or more gradually. Might it not be the case, then, that those couples who are most deeply in love at the time of their weddings will have the most successful marriages? We have centuries of poetry and novels, as well as love songs, that tell us that this is the case.

In the Detroit study, we did, in fact, ask women how much they had been in love when they first married. And we did find that those who recalled being "head over heels in love" then, had more successful marriages. However, there is a major problem with this finding. Since we were asking our interviewees to recall their feelings prior to their weddings—in many cases weddings that took place years or even decades earlier—it is quite possible and even likely that their answers are biased. Perhaps whether or not their marriage worked out influenced these "love reports" from earlier times, rather than having the level of romantic love then explain marital success later. Without either a time machine or funds to interview couples prior to marriage and then follow them up years later, it is impossible to be sure that more intense feelings of love lead to more successful marriages. Still, the evidence available does not question the wisdom of poets and songwriters when it comes to love. Mate selection may not be a total crap-shoot after all, and even if dating does not work, love perhaps does.

READINGS SUGGESTED BY THE AUTHOR:

Bailey, Beth. *From Front Porch to Back Seat.* Baltimore: Johns Hopkins University Press, 1988.

Burgess, Ernest W. and Paul Wallin. *Engagement and Marriage.* Chicago: Lippincott, 1953.

Modell, John. "Dating Becomes the Way of American Youth," in *Essays on the Family and Historical Change,* Leslie P. Moch and Gary Stark (eds.). College Station, Tex.: Texas A&M University Press, 1983.

Rothman, Ellen K. *Hands and Hearts: A History of Courtship.* New York: Basic Books, 1984.

Smith, Daniel S. and Michael Hindus. "Premarital Pregnancy in America, 1640–1971: An Overview and Interpretation," *Journal of Interdisciplinary History,* 4 (1975), 537–570.

Waller, Willard, "Rating and Dating Complex," *American Sociological Review,* (1937), 2:737–739.

Whyte, Martin King. *Dating, Mating, and Marriage.* New York: Aldine de Gruyter, 1990.

RESPONSE SHEET

for Martin K. Whyte: Choosing Mates—the American Way

1. What is Whyte's definition of dating (given later in the article)? Any additions/deletions that you'd make?

2. Write a question for class discussion

3. ID three things you have experienced that he has described.

"Flirting Fascination"

By Joann Ellison Rodgers

It's been trivialized, even demonized, but the coquettish behavior indulged in by men and women alike is actually a vital silent language exchanging critical—and startling—information about our general health and reproductive fitness.

"She was," he proclaimed, "so extraordinarily beautiful that I nearly laughed out loud. She . . . [was] famine, fire, destruction and plague . . . the only true begetter. Her breasts were apocalyptic, they would topple empires before they withered . . . her body was a miracle of construction . . . She was unquestionably gorgeous. She was lavish. She was a dark, unyielding largesse. She was, in short, too bloody much . . . Those huge violet blue eyes . . . had an odd glint . . . Aeons passed, civilizations came and went while these cosmic headlights examined by flawed personality. Every pockmark on my face became a crater of the moon."

So Richard Burton described his first sight of a 19-year-old Elizabeth Taylor. He didn't record what happened next, but a growing cadre of scientists would bet their lab coats and research budgets that sometime after that breath-catching, gut-gripping moment of instant mutual awareness, Liz tossed her hair, swayed her hips, arched her feet, giggled, gazed wide-eyed, flicked her tongue over her lips and extended that apocalyptic chest, and that Dick, for his part, arched his back, stretched his pecs, imperceptibly swayed his pelvis in a tame Elvis performance, swaggered, laughed loudly, tugged his tie and clasped the back of his neck, which had the thoroughly engaging effect of stiffening his stance and puffing his chest.

What eventually got these two strangers from across the fabled crowded room to each other's side was what does it for all of us—in a word, flirtation, the capacity to automatically turn our actions into sexual semaphores signaling interest in the opposite sex as predictably and instinctively as peacocks fan their tails, codfish thrust their pelvic fins or mice twitch their noses and tilt their backs to draw in the object of their attention.

Long trivialized and even demonized, flirtation is gaining new respectability thanks to a spate of provocative studies of animal and human behavior in many parts of the world. The capacity of men and women to flirt and to be receptive to flirting turns out to be a remarkable set of behaviors embedded deep in our psyches. Every come-hither look sent and every side-long glance received are mutually understood signals of such transcendent history and beguiling sophistication that only now are they beginning to yield clues to the psychological and biological wisdom they encode.

WE SIGNAL our interest in the OPPOSITE SEX as instinctively as PEACOCKS flare their TAILS or FISH their FINS.

SCIENCE has calculated just how CURVY a woman has to be to GARNER male appreciation.

This much is clear so far: flirting is nature's solution to the problem every creature faces in a world full of potential mates—how to choose the right one. We all need a partner who is not merely fertile but genetically different as well as healthy enough to promise viable offspring, provide some kind of help in the hard job of parenting and offer some social compatibility.

Our animal and human ancestors needed a means of quickly and safely judging the value of potential mates without "going all the way" and risking pregnancy with every possible candidate they encountered. Flirting achieved that end, offering a relatively risk-free set of signals with which to sample the field, try out sexual wares and exchange vital information about candidates' general health and reproductive fitness.

Flirting is a negotiation process that takes place after there has been some initial attraction," observes Steven W. Gangestad, Ph.D., an evolutionary psychologist at the University of New Mexico in Albuquerque who is currently studying how people choose their mates. "Two people have to share with each other the information that they are attracted, and then test each other" on an array of attributes. Simply announcing, 'I'm attracted to you, are you attracted to me?" doesn't work so well. "It works much better to reveal this and have it revealed to you in smaller doses," explains Gangestad. "The flirting then becomes something that enhances the attraction."

It is an axiom of science that traits and behaviors crucial to survival—such as anything to do with attraction and sex—require, and get, a lot of an animal's resources. All mammals and most animals (including birds, fish, even fruit flies) engage in complicated and energy-intensive plots and plans for attracting others to the business of sex. That is, they flirt.

From nature's standpoint, the goal of life is the survival of our DNA. Sex is the way most animals gain the flexibility to healthfully sort and mix their genes. Getting sex, in turn, is wholly dependent on attracting attention and being attracted. And flirting is the way a person focuses the attention of a specific member of the opposite sex. If our ancestors hadn't done it well enough, we wouldn't be around to discuss it now.

A silent language of elaborate visual and other gestures, flirting is "spoken" by intellect-driven people as well as instinct-driven animals. The very universality of flirting, preserved through evolutionary history from insects to man, suggests that a flirting plan is wired into us, and that it has been embedded in our genes and in our brain's operating system the same way and for the same reasons that every other sexual trait has been—by trial and error, with conservation of what works best.

Like any other language, flirting may be deployed in ways subtle or coarse, adolescent or suave. Nevertheless, it has evolved just like pheasant spurs and lion manes: to advertise ourselves to the opposite sex.

Flirtation first emerged as a subject of serious scrutiny a scant 30 years ago. Irenäus Eibl-Eibesfeldt, now honorary director of the Ludwig-Boltzmann Institute for Urban Ethology in Vienna, was already familiar with the widespread dances and prances of mate-seeking animals. Then he discovered that people in dozens of cultures, from the South Sea islands to the Far East, Western Europe, Africa and South America, similarly engage in a fairly fixed repertoire of gestures to test sexual availability and interest.

FLIRTING is self PROMOTION—but nature DEMANDS a certain amount of TRUTH in advertising.

Having devised a special camera that allowed him to point the lens in one direction while actually photographing in another, he "caught" couples on film during their flirtations, and discovered, for one thing, that women, from primitives who have no written language to those who read *Cosmo* and *Marie Claire,* use nonverbal signals that are startlingly alike. On Eibl-Eibesfeldt's screen flickered identical flirtation messages: a female smiling at a male, then arching her brows to make her eyes wide, quickly lowering her lids and, tucking her chin slightly down and coyly to the side, averting her gaze, followed within seconds, almost on cue, by putting her hands on or near her mouth and giggling.

Regardless of language, socioeconomic status or religious upbringing, couples who continued flirting placed a palm up on the table or knees, reassuring the prospective partner of harmlessness. They shrugged their shoulders, signifying helplessness. Women exaggeratedly extended their neck, a sign of vulnerability and submissiveness.

For Eibl-Eibesfeldt, these gestures represented primal behaviors driven by the old parts of our brain's evolutionary memory. A woman presenting her extended neck to a man she wants is not much different, his work suggested, than a gray female wolf's submissiveness to a dominant male she's after.

Since then, researchers have turned up the intensity, looking, for example, at compressed bouts of flirting and courtship in their natural habitat—hotel bars and cocktail lounges. From observations at a Hyatt hotel cocktail lounge, researchers documented a set of signals that whisks a just-met man and woman from barroom to bedroom. Her giggles and soft laughs were followed by hair twirling and head-tossing; he countered with body arching, leaning back in the chair and placing his arms behind head, not unlike a pigeon puffing his chest.

If all went well, a couple would invariably progress from touching themselves to touching each other. The first tentative contacts could be termed "lint-picking." She would lift an imaginary mote from his lapel; he would brush a real or imaginary crumb from her lips. Their heads moved closer, their hands pressed out in front of them on the table, their fingers inches from each other's, playing with salt shakers or utensils. Whoops! An "accidental" finger touch, then perhaps some digital "dirty dancing," more touching and leaning in cheek to cheek. By body language alone, the investigators could predict which pairs would ride up the elevators together.

Social psychologist Timothy Perper, Ph.D., an independent scholar and writer based in Philadelphia, and anthropologist David Givens, Ph.D., spent months in dimly lit lounges documenting these flirtation rituals. Like the ear wiggles, nose flicks and back arches that signal "come hither" in rodents, the women smiled, gazed, swayed, giggled, licked their lips, and aided and abetted by the wearing of high heels, they swayed their backs, forcing their buttocks to tilt out and up and their chests to thrust forward.

The men arched, stretched, swiveled, and made grand gestures of whipping out lighters and lighting up cigarettes. They'd point their chins in the air with a cigarette dangling in their mouth, then loop their arms in a wide arc to put the lighter away. Their swaggers, bursts of laughter and grandiose gestures were an urban pantomime of the prancing and preening indulged in by male baboons and gorillas in the wild. Man or monkey, the signals all said, "Look at me, trust me, I'm powerful, but I won't hurt you." And "I don't want anything much . . . yet."

All the silent swaying, leaning, smiling, bobbing and gazing eventually brought a pair into full frontal alignment. Face to face, they indulged in simultaneous touching of everything from eyeglasses to fingertips to crossed legs. Says Perper, "This kind of sequence—attention, recognition, dancing, synchronization—is fundamental to courtship. From the *Song of Songs* until today, the sequence is the same: look, talk, touch, kiss, do the deed."

The fact that flirting is a largely non-explicit drama doesn't mean that important information isn't being delivered in those silent signals. By swaying her hips, or emphasizing them in a form-fitting dress, a flirtatious woman is riveting attention on her pelvis, suggesting its ample capacity for bearing a child. By arching her brows and exaggerating her gaze, her eyes appear large in her face, the way a child's eyes do, advertising, along with giggles, her youth and "submissiveness." By drawing her tongue along her lips, she compels attention to what many biologists believe are facial echoes of vaginal lips, transmitting sexual maturity and her interest in sex. By coyly averting her gaze and playing "hard to get," she communicates her unwillingness to give sex to just anyone or to someone who will love her and leave her.

For his part, by extended a strong chin and jaw, expanding and showing off pectoral muscles and a hair chest, flashing money, laughing loudly or resonantly, smiling, and doing all these things without accosting a woman, a man signals his ability to protect offspring, his resources and the testosterone-driven vitality of his sperm as well as the tamer side of him that is willing to stick around, after the sex, for fatherhood. It's the behavioral equivalent of "I'll respect you in the morning."

> The sequence FLIRTATION takes is ALWAYS the same: LOOK, talk, touch, kiss, do the DEED.

I can't tell you why I was attracted to her the instant she walked into my office," recalls a 32-year-old screenwriter. "It was chemistry. We both flirted and we both knew it would lead nowhere. I'm happily married." The statement is almost stupefyingly commonplace, but also instructive. Each of us "turns on" not to mankind or womankind but to a particular member of the opposite sex. Certain stances, personal styles, gestures, intimations of emotional compatibility, perhaps even odors, automatically arouse our interest because they not only instantly advertise genetic fitness but they match the template of Desired Mate we all carry in our mind's eye.

As with Dick and Liz, or any couple, the rational, thinking part of their brains got them to the place where girl met boy; they had the event on their calendars, planned what they would wear, arranged for transportation. But in that first meeting, their capacity to react with their instinct and hearts, not their heads, overrode their cognitive brains. Otherwise, they might not have had the nerve to look at each other.

The rational brain is always on the lookout for dangers, for complexities, for reasons to act or not act. If every time man and woman met they immediately considered all the possible risks and vulnerabilities they might face if they mated or had children, they'd run screaming from the room.

It's no secret that the brain's emotionally loaded limbic system sometimes operates independently of the more rational neocortex, such as in the face of danger, when the fight-or-flight response is activated. Similarly, when the matter is sex—another situation on which survival depends—we also react without even a neural nod to the neocortex. Instead, the flirtational operating system appears to kick in without conscious consent. If, at the moment they had met, Dick and Liz had stopped to consider all the possible outcomes of a relationship, they both would have been old before they got close enough to speak.

The moment of attraction, in fact, mimics a kind of brain damage. At the University of Iowa, where he is professor and head of neurology, Antonio Damasio, M.D., has found that people with damage to the connection between their limbic structures and the higher brain are smart and rational—but unable to make decisions. They bring commitment phobia to a whole new level. In attraction, we don't stop and think, we react, operating on a "gut" feeling, with butterflies, giddiness, sweaty palms and flushed faces brought on by the reactivity of the emotional brain. We suspend intellect at least long enough to propel us to the next step in the mating game—flirtation.

Somewhere beyond flirtation, as a relationship progresses, courtship gets under way, and with it, intellectual processes resume. Two adults can then evaluate potential mates more rationally, think things over and decide whether to love, honor and cherish. But at the moment of attraction and flirtation, bodies, minds and sense are temporarily hostage to the more ancient parts of the brain, the impulsive parts that humans share with animals.

> The instant of ATTRACTION in fact MIMICS a kind of BRAIN DAMAGE.

If flirting is a form of self promotion, nature demands a certain amount of truth in advertising. "For a signaling system to convey something meaningful about a desirable attribute, there has to be some honesty," explains Gangestad, "so that if you don't have the attribute you can't fake it." Just as the extravagant colors of birds that figure so prominently in their flirting rituals proclaim the health of animals so plumed, humans have some signals that can't be faked.

Waist-hip ratio is likely one of them. It's no secret that men snap to attention and even go dry at the mouth at the sight of a shapely woman. Science has now calculated just how curvy a woman has to be to garner such appreciation: the waist must measure no more than 60 to 70% of her hip circumference. It is a visual signal that not only figures powerfully in attraction, but is a moving force in flirtation. And unless steel-boned corsets stage a comeback, it is an attribute that just can't be put into play unless it is real.

In simplest terms, says Gangestad, waist-hip ratio is an honest indicator of health. Studies have shown that hourglass-shaped women are less likely than other women to get diabetes and cardiac disease. They are also most likely to bear children, as hips take their shape at puberty from the feminizing hormone estrogen.

"The literature shows that women with a 0.7 waist-hip ratio have a sex-typical hormone profile in the relationship of estrogen to testosterone, and that women with a straighter torso, meaning a waist-hip ratio closer to 1:1, indeed have lower fertility," Gangestad reports. "It appears that males have evolved to pay attention to this cue that ancestrally was related to fertility."

The virtually visceral responsiveness to physical features in flirtation may also be as good a guarantee as one can get that a potential partner shapes up on a hidden but crucial aspect of health: immunity to disease. Scientists know that the testosterone that gives men jutting jaws, prominent noses and big brows, and, to a lesser extent, the estrogen that gives women soft features and curving hips, also suppresses the ability to fight disease. But looks have their own logic, and bodies and faces that are exemplars of their gender signal that their bearer has biological power to spare; after all, he or she has survived despite the hormonal "handicap."

Take the case of such elaborate male ornamentation as peacock tails and stag antlers. In the 1980s, evolutionary biologists William Hamilton and Marlena Zuk linked such features to inborn resistance to disease parasites. Antlers and tail feathers are known to be attractive to females of their species and are major machinery of flirtation. But developing and maintaining such extravagant equipment is costly, taking huge nutritional resources and even slowing the animals down, making them more vulnerable to predators.

The only animals that can afford such ornamentation are those with tiptop constitutions. So, like big bones, big horns, big tails and big spurs in animals, jutting jaws are honest markers for a healthy immune system. Scientists point out that such features are in fact respected by other men as well as attractive to women. Studies show that tall, square-jawed men achieve higher ranks in the military than do those with weak chins, and that taller men are over-represented in boardrooms as well as bedrooms.

Whatever specific physical features men and women are primed to respond to, they all have a quality in common—symmetry. That is, attributes deemed attractive have an outward appearance of evenness and right-left balance. Unlike the color and condition of tail feathers, symmetry serves not so much as an honest marker of current health status, but as a signal of a general capacity to be healthy. Symmetry, says Gangestad, is "a footprint left by your whole developmental history." It alone explains why Elizabeth Taylor, Denzel Washington and Queen Nefertiti are universally recognized as beautiful—and full of sex appeal.

"Bilateral symmetry is a hot topic these days," beams Albert Thornhill, a biologist at the University of New Mexico and a pioneer in the study of symmetry in attraction and flirtation. He and Gagestad believe it is a marker of "developmental precision," the extent to which a genetic blueprint is realized in the flesh despite all the environmental and other perturbations that tend to throw development off course.

Recent studies conducted by the two demonstrate not only what women prefer symmetrical men, they prefer them at a very specific time—when they are most fertile. "We found that female preferences change across the menstrual cycle," Gangestad reports. "We think the finding says something about the way female mate preferences are designed. Because the preference for male symmetry is specific to the time of ovulation, when women are most likely to conceive, we think women are choosing a mate who is going to provide better genes for healthy babies. It's an indirect benefit, rather than a direct or material benefit to the female herself."

In their study, 52 women rated the attractiveness of 42 men—by their smell. Each of the men slept in one T-shirt for two nights, after which the women were given a whiff of it. Prior to the smell test, all the men had undergone careful calipered measurement of 10 features, from ear width to finger length. Those whose body features were the most symmetrical were the ones whose smells were most preferred, but only among women who were in the ovulatory phase of their menstrual cycle. At other times in their cycle, women had no preference either for symmetrical or asymmetrical males.

The preference for symmetry is not limited to humans. Thornhill first stumbled upon symmetry two decades ago, during experiments with scorpion flies in Australia, Japan and Europe. He noticed that females chose particular male flies on the basis of the level and quality of "nuptial gifts," nutrients passed to the female during courtship and mating.

"That was the first inkling I had that insects were very sophisticated about their mating strategies," Thornhill recalls. But the more time he spent recording the sexual lives of scorpion flies, the more he realized that the females were selecting partners long before they sampled any gifts, and they were reckoning by the symmetry of the males' wings. "I discovered that males and females with the most symmetrical wings had the most mating success and that by using wing symmetry, I—and presumably the fly—could predict reproductive fitness better than scent or any other factor."

Symmetrical men give women more orgasms, but they also are more likely to be unfaithful to their partners.

Since then, Thornhill and colleagues around the world have conducted more than 20 separate tests of symmetry of everything from eyes, ears and nostrils to limbs, wrists and fingers. Even if they never speak a word or get closer than a photograph, women view symmetrical men as more dominant, powerful, richer and better sex and marriage material. And symmetrical men view themselves the same way! Men, for their part, rate symmetrical women as more fertile, more attractive, healthier and better sex and marriage material, too—just as such women see themselves as having a competitive edge in the mating sweepstakes.

Flirtation, it turns out, is most successful among the most symmetrical. Men's bodily symmetry matches up with the number of lifetime sex partners they report having. Symmetrical men also engage in more infidelity in their romantic relationships—"extra-pair copulations" in the language of the lab. And they get to sex more quickly after meeting a romantic partner compared to asymmetrical men. They lose their virginity earlier in life, too.

When women flirt with symmetrical men, what their instincts are reading might once have been banned in Boston. Male symmetry is also shorthand for female sexual satisfaction. Gangestad and Thornhill surveyed 86 couples in 1995 and found that symmetrical men "fire off more female copulatory orgasms than asymmetrical men." Women with symmetrical partners were more than twice as likely to climax during intercourse. Thrills are only a short-term payoff, however; female orgasm is really a shill for fertilization, pulling sperm from the vagina into the cervix.

Successful as symmetrical men are at flirtation, it's only their presumably better genes that women really want. Women definitely do not prefer symmetrical men for long-term relationships. There's a definite downside to getting someone with really good DNA. Symmetry, Gangestad explains, affords those men who possess it to take a dastardly mating strategy. His studies show that symmetrical men invest less in any one romantic relationship—less time, less attention, less money. And less fidelity. They're too busy spreading around their symmetry. "They also tend to sexualize other women more," Gangestad reports. "It may be that males who can have the most access without giving a lot of investment take advantage of that."

A guy who will stick around and help out with parenting is on most women's wish list of qualities in a mate, Gangestad concedes. "I wouldn't exclude the possibility that men have been doing some direct parental care for some time, and so a preference for that might also have an evolutionary basis." But also on a woman's wish list from an evolutionary standpoint would be someone who is going to provide good genes for healthy babies. Unfortunately, says the Albuquerque researcher, "what can and does happen in a mating market is that those things don't all come in the same package."

Although the signals and semaphores of flirting are largely devoid of explicit content, the style with which one flirts can be downright revelatory. "*How* a person flirts honestly reveals some important qualities about an individual," says Gangestad. Symmetry isn't everything; there are signals of more subtle skills.

In some species, the females watch the males fight each other and then choose the one who can hold the central territory. But we humans are more differently evolved creatures with more complex lives in which our higher faculties presumably contribute something to success, whether it's surviving in primitive equatorial caves or sophisticated urban ones.

Enter creativity, humor and intelligence. Deployed in flirting, they disclose more about an individual person than all the antlers do about leching animals. "They are likely saying something important about our very viability," says Gangestad. "When we can engage in humor and creativity, they act as an honest signal that we've got a reasonably well put together nervous system. They may indicate there's some developmental integrity underneath our brain." And a certain ability to withstand whatever challenges life throws a person's way.

What's more, our basic social ability to "read" another's facial gestures and emotional expressions acts as a fact-checking system in flirtation. It enables us to glimpse the tone of a prospective mate's inner life and to check for the presence or absence of psychological weakness. And in fact, women are pretty good at doping out information about such important attributes—even when they get very little time to make a judgment.

In a recent set of studies, Gangestad and a colleague extracted one-minute segments from more extensive videotaped interviews with men not in committed relationships. The brief segments were then shown to women who were asked to rate the men on a variety of characteristics, including how attractive they'd be in a pair relationship. The women were able to make judgments about each man's intelligence, ability to be caring and how nice he seemed. They also paid attention to another set of characteristics—how effective a man was likely to be with other males, how socially influential he was.

The men who were rated most attractive for long-term relationships scored high on both sets of characteristics. But what may be most notable about the study was that women's observations, from a mere snippet of videotape, were remarkably accurate. They correlated closely with the men's ratings of their own personality.

After two people share the information that they are attracted, then, through the way they flirt, they may unwittingly let on more about themselves. "It becomes a testing ground as well as an information-revealing process," says Gangestad.

Thus, while we appear to be preprogrammed with an urge to wile or wiggle our way onto another's mental radar screen, we also seem psychologically constituted to pay rapt attention to looks and actions intended to be sexually appealing. Otherwise, neither Liz and Dick nor any two contenders would have a reliable, safe or peaceful means of communicating attraction and getting to the more durable business of courtship, mating and commitment to the offspring that will carry our DNA into the next generation.

The New Flirting Game

It may be an ages-old, biologically-driven activity, but today it's also played with artful self-awareness and even conscious calculation.

By Deborah A. Lott

To hear the evolutionary determinists tell it, we human beings flirt to propagate our genes and to display our genetic worth. Men are constitutionally predisposed to flirt with the healthiest, most fertile women, recognizable by their biologically correct waist-hip ratios. Women favor the guys with dominant demeanors, throbbing muscles and the most resources to invest in them and their offspring.

Looked at up close, human psychology is more diverse and preserve than the evolutionary determinists would have it. We flirt as thinking individuals in a particular culture at a particular time. Yes, we may express a repertoire of hardwired non-verbal expressions and behaviors—staring eyes, flashing brows, opened palms—that resemble those of other animals, but unlike other animals, we also flirt with conscious calculation. We have been know to practice our techniques in front of the mirror. In other words, flirting among human beings is culturally modulated as well as biologically driven, as much art as instinct.

In our culture today, it's clear that we do not always choose as the object of our desire those people the evolutionists might deem the most biologically desirable. After all, many young women today find the pale, androgynous, scarcely muscled yet emotionally expressive Leonardo DiCaprio more appealing than the burly Tarzans (Arnold Schwartzenegger, Bruce Willis, etc.) of action movies. Woody Allen may look nerdy but he's had no trouble winning women—and that's not just because he has material resources, but because he has material resources, but because humor is also a precious cultural commodity. Though she has no breasts or hips to speak of, Ally McBeal still attracts because there's ample evidence of a quick and quirky mind.

In short, we flirt with the intent of assessing potential lifetime partners, we flirt to have easy, no-strings-attached sex, and we flirt when we are not looking to either. We flirt because, most simply, flirtation can be a liberating form of play, a game with suspense and ambiguities that brings joys of its own. As Philadelphia-based social psychologist Tim Perper says, "Some flirters appear to want to prolong the interaction because it's pleasurable and erotic in its own right, regardless of where it might lead."

Here are some of the ways the game is currently played.

Taking the Lead

When it comes to flirting today, women aren't waiting around for men to make the advances. They're taking the lead. Psychologist Monica Moore, Ph.D. of Webster University in St. Louis, Missouri, has spent more than 2000 hours observing women's flirting maneuvers in restaurants, singles bars and at parties. According to her findings, women give non-verbal cues that get a flirtation rolling fully two-thirds of the time. A man may think he's making the first move because he is the one to literally move from wherever he is to the woman's side, but usually he has been summoned.

Who determined that baring the neck is a sign of female submissiveness? It may have a lot more to do with the neck being on erogenous zone.

By the standards set out by evolutionary psychologists, the women who attract the most men would most likely be those with the most symmetrical features or the best hip-to-waist ratios. Not so, says Moore. In her studies, the woman who draw the most response are the ones who send the most signals. "Those who performed more than 35 displays per hour elicited greater than four approaches per hour," she notes, "and the more variety the woman used in her techniques, the more likely she was to be successful."

Sexual Semaphores

Moore tallied a total of 52 different nonverbal courtship behaviors used by women, including glancing, gazing (short and sustained), primping, preening, smiling, lip licking, pouting, giggling, laughing and nodding, as if to nonverbally indicate, "Yes! yes!" A woman would often begin with a room-encompassing glance, in actuality a casing-the-joint scan to seek out prospects. When she'd zeroed in on a target she'd exhibit the short darting glance—looking at a man, quickly looking away, looking back and then away again. There was something shy and indirect in this initial eye contact.

But women countered their shy moves with other, more aggressive and overt tactics. Those who liked to live dangerously took a round robin approach, alternately flirting with several different men at once until one responded in an unequivocal fashion. A few women hiked their skirts up to bring more leg into a particular man's field of vision. When they inadvertently drew the attention of other admirers, they quickly pulled their skirts down. If a man failed to get the message, a woman might parade, walking across the room towards him, hips swaying, breasts pushed out, head held high.

Who's Submissive?

Moore observed some of the same nonverbal behaviors that Eibl-Eibesfeldt and other ethologists had deemed universal among women: the eyebrow flash (an exaggerated raising of the eyebrows of both eyes, followed by a rapid lowering), the coy smile (a tilting of the head downward, with partial averting of the eyes and, at the end, covering of the mouth), and the exposed neck (turning the head so that the side of the neck is bared).

But while many ethologists interpret these signs as conveying female submissiveness, Moore has an altogether different take. "If these behaviors serve to orchestrate courtship, which they do, then how can they be anything but powerful?" she observes. "Who determined that to cover your mouth is a submissive gesture? Baring the neck may have a lot more to do with the neck being an erogenous zone than its being a submissive posture." Though women in Moore's sample used the coy smile, they also maintained direct eye contact for long periods and smiled fully and unabashedly.

Like Moore, Perper believes that ethologists have overemphasized certain behaviors and misinterpreted them as signifying either dominance or submission. For instance, says Perper, among flirting American heterosexual men and women as well as homosexual men, the coy smile is less frequent than direct eye contact and sustained smiling. He suggests that some cultures may use the coy smile more than others, and that it is not always a sign of deference.

In watching a flirtatious couple, Perper finds that a male will perform gestures and movements that an ethologist might consider dominant, such as sticking out his chest and strutting around, but he'll also give signs that could be read as submissive, such as bowing his head lower than the woman's. The woman may also do both. "She may drop her head, turn slightly, bare her neck, but then she'll lift her eyes and lean forward with her breasts held out, and that doesn't look submissive at all," Perper notes.

Men involved in these encounters, says Perper, don't describe themselves as "feeling powerful." In fact, he and Moore agree, neither party wholly dominates in a flirtation. Instead, there is a subtle, rhythmical and playful back and forth that culminates in a kind of physical synchronization between two people. She turns, he turns; she picks up her drink, he picks up his drink.

Still, by escalating and de-escalating the flirtation's progression, the woman controls the pace. To slow down a flirtation, a woman might orient her body away slightly or cross her arms across her chest, or avoid meeting the man's eyes. To stop the dance in its tracks, she can yawn, frown, sneer, shake her head from side to side as if to say "No," pocket her hands, hold her trunk rigidly, avoid the man's gaze, stare over his head, or resume flirting with other men.

Men are able to recite in enormous detail what they do once they are in bed with a woman, but it is women who remember each and every step in the flirtation game that got them there.

If a man is really dense, she might hold a strand of hair up to her eyes as if to examine her split ends or even pick her teeth.

Planning It Out

Do women make these moves consciously? You bet. "I do these things *incidentally* but not *accidentally,*" one adept female flirter told Perper. She wanted her movements and gestures to look fluid and spontaneous but they were at least partly planned. In general, says Perper, women are more aware than are men of exactly what they do, why they do it and the effect it has. A man might simply say that he saw a women he was attracted to and struck up a conversation; a woman would remember all the steps in the flirtation dance. "Men can tell you in enormous detail what they do once they are in bed with a woman," declares Perper. But it is the women who know how they got there.

Learning the Steps

If flirting today is often a conscious activity, it is also a learned one. Women pick up the moves early. In observations of 100 girls between the ages of 13 and 16 at shopping malls, ice skating rinks and other places adolescents congregate, Moore found the teens exhibiting 31 of the 52 courtship signals deployed by adult women. (The only signals missing were those at the more overt end of the spectrum, such as actual caressing.) Overall, the teens' gestures looked less natural than ones made by mature females: they laughed more boisterously and preened more obviously, and their moves were broader and rougher.

The girls' clearly modeled their behavior on the leader of the pack. When the alpha female stroked her hair or swayed her hips, her companions copied quickly. "You never see this in adult women," says Moore. "Indeed, women go to great lengths to stand out from their female companions."

Compared with adults, the teens signaled less frequently—7.6 signs per hour per girl, as opposed to 44.6 per woman—but their maneuvers, though clumsy, were equally effective at attracting the objects of their desire, in this case, teen boys.

Beyond the Straight and Narrow

Flirting's basic purpose may be to lure males and females into procreating, but it's also an activity indulged in by gays as well as straights. How do flirting rituals compare?

Marny Hall, a San Francisco-area psychologist who's been an observer and participants in lesbian courtship, recalls that in the 1950s, gay women adhered to rigid gender-role models. Butches did what men were supposed to do: held their bodies tight, lit cigarettes with a dominating flourish, bought drinks, opened doors and otherwise demonstrated strength and gallantry. "Butches would swagger and wear chinos and stand around with one hip cocked and be hold in their gazes," she observes. "Femmes would sashay and wiggle their hips and use indirect feminine wiles."

Beginning in the late 1960s, such fixed role-playing began to dissolve. Lesbians meeting in consciousness-raising groups rejected gender assumptions. It was considered sexually attractive, says Hall, to "put yourself out without artifice, without deception." In the 90s, however, the butch-femme distinction has returned.

But with a difference. Today's lesbians have a sense of irony and wit about the whole charade that would do Mae West proud. "A butch today might flirt by saying to a femme, 'Can I borrow your lipstick? I'm trying to liberate the woman within,'" she says with a laugh. "The gender roles are more scrambled, with 'dominant femmes' and 'soft butches.' There's more plurality and less polarization."

Male homosexuals also exhibit a wide range of flirting behaviors. In his studies, Perper has observed two gay men locked in a stalemate of sustained eye contact for 45 minutes before either made the next move. At the other end of the spectrum, he's seen gay dyads go through the entire flirtation cycle—"gaze, approach, talk, turn, touch, synchronize"—and be out the door on the way to one or the other's abode within two minutes.

The advent of AIDS and the greater societal acceptance of long-term gay attachments are changing flirtation rituals in the gay community. A sign of the times may be a courtship and dating course currently offered at Harvey Milk Institute in San Francisco. It instructs gay men in the repertoire of gestures long used by straight women seeking partners—ways of slowing down the flirtation, forestalling physical contact and assessing the other's suitability as a long-term mate. In short, it teaches homosexuals how to employ what the ethologists call a "long-term strategy."

Flirting Bi-Ways

"When you're a crossdresser, all possibilities are open to you," says a male heterosexual who goes by the name Stephanie Montana when in female garb. In feminine persona, says Montana, "I can be more vulnerable, more animated and use more intermittent eye contact."

On one occasion Montana discovered what women seem to learn early on. A man was flirting with her, and, giddy with the attention, Montana sustained eye contact for a bit too long, gave too many overt sexual signals. In response, the man started acting in a proprietary fashion, frightening Montana with "those voracious male stars." Montana had learned the courtship signals but not the rejection repertoire. She didn't yet know how to put on the brakes.

Bisexuals have access to the entire panoply of male and female gestures. Loree Thomas of Seattle, who refers to herself as a bisexual non-op transsexual (born male, she is taking female hormones and living as a woman, but will not have a sex-change operation), has flirted *four* ways: dressed as a man interacting with men or with women, and dressed as a woman in encounters with women or men.

In San Francisco, gay men are learning the flirting repertoire long used by straight women.

As a man flirting with a woman, Thomas found it most effective to maintain eye contact, smile, lean close, talk in a low voice and offer sincere compliments about the woman's best features. Man to man, says Thomas, the progression to direct physical contact accelerates. As a woman with a woman, Thomas' flirting has been "more shy, less direct than a man would be." As a woman with a man, she's played the stereotypical female role, "asking the man questions about himself, and listening as if totally fascinated." In all cases, eye contact and smiling are universal flirtation currency.

What the experience of cross-dressers reinforces is the degree to which all flirtation is a game, a careful charade that involves some degree of deception and role-playing. Evolutionists talk about this deception in terms of men's tendency to exaggerate their wealth, success and access to resources, and women's strategic use of cosmetics and clothing to enhance their physical allure.

Some of the exhilaration of flirting, of course, lies in what is hidden, the tension between what is felt and what is revealed. Flirting pairs volley back and forth, putting out ambiguous signals, neither willing to disclose more than the other, neither wanting to appear more desirous to the other.

To observers like Moore and Perper, flirtation often seems to most resemble the antics of children on the playground or even perhaps the ritual peek-a-boo that babies play with their caregivers. Flirters jostle, tease and tickle, even sometimes stick out a tongue at their partner or reach around from behind to cover up their eyes. As Daniel Stern, researcher, psychiatrist, and author of *The Interpersonal World of the Infant* (Karnac, 1998), has pointed out, the two groups in our culture that engage in the most sustained eye contact are mothers and infants, and lovers.

And thus in a way, the cycle of flirting takes us full circle. If flirting sets us off on the road to producing babies, it also whisks us back to the pleasures of infancy.

RESPONSE SHEET

for Joann E. Rodgers: Flirting Fascination

And

Deborah A. Lott: The New Flirting Game

Note: Please read both of these first. Then do the following:

From these two articles, identify ten different flirting behaviors. Say what each is, what effect(s) each has, and if is predominantly used by males or females. Please number each. (20 pts.)

CHAPTER

13

Intimacy Development: Stage #2—Mutual Deception

In many respects, mutual deception is the reciprocal of mutual attraction. The power of mutual attraction is consuming and creates a reality of its own. Its going to go on forever; it is invincible. So even a little crack in the blissful cocoon has to be dealt with; when interpersonal realities begin to surface, major maintenance may be called for. The American dating culture calls for putting one's best foot forward from the outset; the other partner is to accept this presenting behavior as an honest representation. Its these kinds of collusions that are mutual deceptions. There is a don't ask, don't tell mindset involved. To a significant extent, we are to sell ourself, not be ourself. So, its not unusual for two to date for sometime before they find out that one is a Lutheran and the other is a Roman Catholic. It is not unusual to hear: "A spouse should only be told certain things; its better to keep the rest to oneself". This starts a pattern that builds to the point of capping a relationship such that it does not reach true intimacy. It directly contributes to such things as child abuse continuing because the non-abusing partner knows but doesn't know. It is involved almost always when one partner is having an affair, and the other one first discovers it and then denies those meanings to any originally suspect cues.

It is important to understand that some degree of deception is inevitable, when the start-up is in a romantic mode. An alternative? Start with a friendship first.

Kimberly K. McClanahan's study is a compelling demonstration of how we will distort in order to maintain a first positive impression.

Infatuation and Attraction to a Dissimilar Other: Why Is Love Blind?

Kimberly K. McClanahan
Department of Psychiatry, Baylor Medical School

Joel A. Gold, Ellen Lenney, Richard M. Ryckman, and Gordon E. Kulberg
Department of Psychology, University of Maine

ABSTRACT. The present experiment attempted to increase understanding of the "love is blind" phenomenon. White male American undergraduates exposed to an infatuation induction with an attitudinally dissimilar female confederate showed greater attraction to her than unexposed control subjects. The use of a misattribution-of-arousal manipulation eliminated this difference in attraction between the infatuation induction and control groups, thereby providing support for the role of positive emotional arousal in creating attraction toward the dissimilar other in the infatuation condition. Evidence was also found that suggested that attraction toward the dissimilar other was based not on a distortion by the subjects of her dissimilar attitudes, but rather on a more favorable evaluation of these attitudes.

Dissimilar others are disliked: This finding is one of the most reliable in the literature on interpersonal attraction. People have been shown to respond negatively to attitudinally dissimilar others not only in experimental laboratory situations (Bryne, 1961, 1971; Bryne & Nelson, 1965) but also in naturalistic field settings (Newcomb, 1961). Even investigators who debate the exact role of attitude similarity in interpersonal attraction (Rosenbaum, 1986; Smeaton, Byrne, & Murnen, 1989) agree that dissimilarity elicits strong disliking.

We speculated, however, that infatuation may create an exception to this positive association between dissimilarity and disliking. Infatuation or infatuated love is the intense state of passion experienced in the absence of intimacy and commitment (Sternberg, 1986). This state, which Tennov (1979) termed limerence and Hatfield and Walster (1981) referred to as romantic love, often begins very quickly and is quite intense, but it may also diminish in intensity quite rapidly. We contend that infatuation is the type of love referred to in the adage "love is blind." If the adage is true, it implies that those who are in a state of infatuation are blind either to the imperfections of the object of their infatuation or, more important for our focus, to the differences in attitudes between themselves and the adored other.

Byrne and Murnen (1988) summarized both field and laboratory studies in the United States showing that infatuation does bypass a usual criterion for friendship: namely, that the other's attitudes be perceived as similar to one's own. But is the adage true in the sense that infatuated individuals will be attracted to others whose attitudes are actually dissimilar from their own? Research by Gold, Ryckman, and Mosley (1984) suggested that it is. In two experiments, these investigators found that male subjects who underwent an infatuation induction, or what the authors termed a "romance induction," with an attractive female confederate scored higher on measures of love and liking toward her than those who did not, even though her attitudes were made to appear strongly dissimilar from those of all subjects.

If love is blind, as this research indicated, then it is important to understand why it is blind, that is, to determine the process underlying this unusual phenomenon. One possibility, that infatuated individuals may distort their dissimilar lovers' attitudes by misperceiving or misremembering them as similar to their own, is challenged by

Requests for reprints should be sent to Joel A. Gold, Department of Psychology, University of Maine, Orono, ME 04469.

results from Gold et al. (1984). Specifically, when subjects recalled the confederate's attitudes, there were no differences in their accuracy scores. Thus, both the infatuated and noninfatuated subjects knew that the confederate was dissimilar from themselves, but the infatuated subjects exhibited elevated love scores in spite of this difference.

A second possibility is that infatuated individuals may evaluate their lovers' known-to-be-dissimilar attitudes more favorably than they would if evaluating these same attitudes in a stranger or an acquaintance. In a similar argument, Tennov (1979) maintained that negative features of the limerence object are seen but emotionally ignored. Of the 2,000 couples she studied, two thirds of the men and three fourths of the women were able to indicate defects of their partners even though they were in a state of limerence. She argued that the infatuated individual sees the deficiencies of the limerence object but responds positively to them. Clark and Isen (1982) also suggested that people in positive mood states typically view the world through "rose-colored glasses." Indeed, a number of investigators have shown evidence for the relationship between affective states and evaluations of stimuli in the surrounding environment (Clark & Teasdale, 1982; Clark & Waddell, 1983; Milberg & Clark, 1988). Consequently, we speculated that the positive mood state produced by infatuation would lead to relatively favorable evaluations of dissimilar attitudes associated with the object of infatuation. The present investigation directly tested this explanation by having subjects recall the attitudes of an attitudinally dissimilar, attractive female confederate and then evaluate them. We predicted that both infatuated and noninfatuated subjects would accurately recall her dissimilar attitudes but only infatuated subjects would evaluate them positively.

If infatuated individuals do evaluate the dissimilarities of the adored other more positively than do noninfatuated individuals, it is likely that the positive emotional arousal that may be an integral component of infatuation is responsible. Whereas Gold et al. (1984) simply assumed that positive emotional arousal was present in their infatuation condition, the present study employed a standard misattribution-of-arousal manipulation (Zanna & Cooper, 1974) to determine more directly whether emotional arousal played a crucial role in attraction to a dissimilar confederate. It was reasoned that the behavior of the confederate produced positive arousal and that attribution of that arousal to its correct source was necessary for the induction of infatuation. If this reasoning is valid, failure to make the attribution to the dissimilar confederate would result in relatively low infatuation with her. Thus, we predicted that subjects in an infatuation-induction condition who were led to believe that their feelings of positive arousal were caused by something other than the dissimilar confederate would show significantly less attraction to her than those who attributed their arousal to her. Consistent with this expectation, it was also predicted that subjects who misattributed their arousal would show a relatively negative evaluation of the confederate's accurately recalled, dissimilar attitudes.

METHOD

Overview

White male American undergraduates were randomly assigned to conditions in this 2 × 2 (Misattribution-No Misattribution × Infatuation Induction-No Infatuation Induction) fully factorial design. All subjects first completed an attitude survey and then examined a bogus survey, allegedly completed by an attractive female subject, that indicated that her attitudes were dissimilar from their own. The misattribution or no misattribution manipulation was then introduced: After reading the bogus survey, subjects were given a placebo "vitamin mixture" that was described as having or not having arousing side effects. They then interacted with the attractive female confederate (in the infatuation induction conditions) or did not (in the no infatuation induction conditions). Finally, all subjects completed measures of love and liking, recalled and evaluated the confederate's attitudes, and were given a measure of their behavioral intent for future interaction with the confederate.

Subjects and Procedure

Thirty-two White male American undergraduates at the University of Maine participated in this study as a partial fulfillment of course requirements. They were randomly assigned to each of the cells of the experimental design with an equal number of subjects in all cells.

Each subject was tested individually by an experimental team of a female and a male experimenter and a female confederate. The student was brought into a room by the female experimenter, who asked him to read and sign a general consent form and to complete a 15-item attitude survey, identical to that employed by Gold et al. (1984). The first five items dealt with various interest areas: sports, music, films, books, and seasons of the year. Subjects simply indicated their preference from the alternatives listed for each interest. The last 10 items assessed attitudes toward such topics as money, drinking on campus, student needs, and drug laws and were presented in the format employed in previous bogus attitude research (Byrne & Clore, 1967). This format consists of a topic followed by six statements, three that indicate varying degrees of favorability and three that indicate varying degrees of unfavorability; the subjects marked the statement with which they agreed.

As the subject began to fill out the survey, the experimenter left and then returned accompanied by the female confederate, who posed as another subject. The confederate and subject were introduced and told that they might be working together later in the experiment. Thus, all subjects saw the attractive confederate and heard a rationale for seeing her attitude survey later in the experiment.

The experimenter then left with the confederate and returned alone to collect the completed attitude measure. At this point, subjects engaged in one of two tasks in order to give the experimenter time to portray the confederate's attitudes as dissimilar from those of the subjects. Subjects assigned to the infatuation induction condition ranked Rokeach's (1968) instrumental values; subjects in the no infatuation induction condition completed the following questionnaire:

How many psychology experiments have you participated in before today?
Have you been able to participate in as many as you wished?
Did you have trouble finding the location of this study?
Have you heard from any previous psychology students about the experiments?
Are you planning to major in psychology?
If you are not planning to major in psychology, what are you planning to major in? Why?
Are you a freshman this year: Yes___ No___. If not, what year of college are you in?
What classes are you taking this year?
How have you liked your experience as a college student at UMO?
What would you like to be when you finish college? Why?
Do you have relatives who went to UMO? Yes___ No___. Where is your hometown?

Whereas the value rankings acted merely as a filler task, the questionnaire served the additional function of equating subjects' information about the confederate across conditions.

While the subject engaged in one of the above filler tasks, the experimenter left the room and completed a blank survey to portray the confederate's attitudes as dissimilar from the subject's own. For four of the first five items, which concerned interests, different alternatives from those chosen by the subject were marked. For 7 of the 10 attitude items, disagreement with the subject was indicated by marking the bogus attitude on the opposite side of the six-position scale from the subject's attitude, with the specific position being randomly determined. Thus, the confederate appeared to have only 1 of the 5 interests in common with the subject and to fall on the same side of an opinion issue on only 3 of the 10 attitudes.

After completing the bogus attitude survey, the experimenter returned and collected the filler task. She then reminded the subject that he might be working with the confederate later in the experiment on a task that would be explained at that time, and that it would be helpful if he knew something about her. She then gave the subject the bogus attitudes to peruse, left the room, and returned after a few minutes to collect the bogus survey.

At that point, all subjects were told that the focus of the study was on the effect of a high potency vitamin on memory. They were then asked to sign a special release form, because they had been unaware that they would be asked to take a vitamin when they volunteered for the study. The release form, which the subject was asked to read carefully, contained the misattribution-no misattribution manipulation.

Misattribution/no misattribution conditions. For subjects in the misattribution conditions, the release form indicated that the vitamin would have very pleasant side effects lasting only a few minutes. It informed them that they might feel excited, aroused, and a little flushed. For those not in the misattribution conditions, the release form explicitly stated that there were no side effects from the vitamin. In all cases, the experimenter orally paraphrased the contents of the release form in order to buttress the manipulation. The subject then signed the release form, and the experimenter witnessed it. All subjects agreed to take the vitamin. To support the deception, the subjects were weighed; the experimenter then looked at a weight chart on the wall and measured out the proper dose of the vitamin mixture, which was actually a combination of brewer's yeast and flour. The subjects then took the mixture in their choice of juice or water.

After the mixture was taken, all subjects were told that there would be a delay before the next phase of the study. Each subject was taken to a waiting room where the confederate (who was blind to the misattribution-no misattribution manipulation) was already seated, and the two were reintroduced.

Infatuation induction/no infatuation induction conditions. In the infatuation induction conditions, the experimenter left the waiting room and the subject and confederate conversed for approximately 5 minutes. The conversation was initiated by the confederate, who had been trained to appear interested in the subject by engaging in appropriate amounts of eye contact, smiling, and leaning toward the subject. She was told to discuss only certain topics, unrelated to the content of the attitude survey. If a subject brought up an issue that differed from the targeted topics, the confederate answered it briefly and then returned to the prearranged topics. This procedure was designed to ensure that no attitudinal information would be discussed.

In the no infatuation induction conditions, the experimenter told the subject that she wanted exchange of more information between him and the confederate. The experimenter then handed the subject a questionnaire, supposedly completed by the confederate, that was identical to the one he had filled out as the filler task during the bogus survey preparation; she also handed the subject's questionnaire to the confederate. The two were asked to peruse the questionnaires silently.

For half of the no infatuation induction subjects, the experimenter then left, and the confederate and the subject remained in the room. To ensure that the subject would not initiate conversation with her while they were alone, the confederate read the subject's questionnaire and then completed another measure. No interaction occurred between any subject and the confederate. For the other half of the no infatuation induction subjects, the experimenter took the confederate out of the room with her as soon as the questionnaires were exchanged, on the pretext of needing more information from her. This variation in procedure was included to allow a check on effects of the simple presence or absence of the confederate. Because interaction per se was assumed to be the romance-inducing factor and no interaction occurred in either of the categories of the no infatuation induction conditions, responses in the two categories were not expected to differ. Indeed, preliminary analyses on the control-group data showed no effects of the two categories on any dependent variable; accordingly, the categories were combined in all analyses.

The topics covered on the questionnaire were the same topics discussed by the confederate in the infatuation induction conditions, because the purpose of the questionnaire was to equate the information available to the subjects across conditions. Thus, even though subjects in the no infatuation induction conditions did not interact with the confederate, they obtained the same information about her as those who did.

After approximately 5 minutes of interaction in the infatuation induction conditions and of silent reading in the no infatuation induction conditions, the male experimenter took the subject from the room to complete the dependent measures.

Dependent Measures

Attraction. The subject was told that although the researchers were interested in memory, they would first like him to fill out a questionnaire concerning his impressions of the confederate. This measure consisted of Rubin's (1973) 13-item Liking Scale and 13-item Love Scale, in which the love and liking scale items were randomly interspersed and presented in an 18-point format ranging from *strongly agree* (18) to *strongly disagree* (1). Examples of liking scale items are: "In my opinion, ____ is an exceptionally mature person" and "I think that ____ is unusually well adjusted." Because the encounter with the female confederate was very brief, we felt that it would be difficult for subjects to respond to many of the items on the love scale, which is designed for partners in an ongoing relationship. Therefore, the love scale items were modified by wording them in the subjunctive mood. Examples of modified items are: "I would feel very possessive toward ____" and "If I could never be with ____, I would feel miserable."

To supplement the love and liking scales, the subject was asked to give an indication of behavioral intent toward the confederate. He was told that the experimenters needed help in coding data, although they could offer no credit or other inducement. The experimenter then said the confederate also had been asked to help and that she had agreed to work 2 hours for each of the next 3 weeks. The subject was told that if he chose to help, he and the confederate would be given a room in another building where they would work together. The subject was asked how many of those 6 hours he would be willing to work with the confederate.

Recall and evaluation of attitudes. The subject was presented with a blank attitude survey, on which the 5 interest and 10 attitude items were presented in a new order, and was asked to recall the confederate's responses by reconstructing them. After the reconstruction, the subject was asked to evaluate each of the 10 reconstructed attitudes on six 6-point bipolar adjective scales (*good–bad, rational–irrational, wise–foolish, meaningful–meaningless, complex–simple, mature–immature*) selected from Osgood, Suci, and Tannenbaum (1957).

Debriefing

After each subject completed all dependent measures, the male experimenter questioned him to ascertain whether he had discovered the purpose of the experiment. No subject was able to state the true purpose, nor did any indicate disbelief of the experimental manipulations. Finally, in a complete and lengthy debriefing, all subject were informed that (a) the other subject was actually a confederate whose attitudes had been manipulated to appear dissimilar from their own, (b) the high-potency vitamin mixture was actually brewer's yeast and flour, and (c) they would not be coding data with the confederate. Further, subjects in the infatuation induction conditions were told that the experimenters were interested in how people react to an attractive female when she shows interest in them. Subjects in the no infatuation induction conditions were told that they were in a control group and that the experimenters were interested in how attracted they would be to the confederate when they did not interact with her but had information about her. All subjects were thoroughly questioned concerning their reactions to the study and to its deceptions. No subject appeared upset by any aspect of the procedure. Finally, the experimenter apologized for the deceptions, explained their necessity, and thanked the subject.

Results

Scoring and Data Reduction

Love and liking scales. Because one of the liking scale items dealt with the perceived global similarity of the confederate, it was of interest in its own right. Further, this item was treated separately by Gold et al. (1984). Therefore, it was also treated separately in the present analyses. Internal consistency reliabilities (coefficient alpha) computed for the love scale and the liking scale with the perceived similarity item removed were .88 and .93, respectively. The 13 love scale items and 12 liking scale items were averaged separately to produce reliable measures of love and liking.

Reconstruction of dissimilar attitude items. Because it was possible to derive a measure of reconstruction that reflected both magnitude and direction of distortion only for the seven dissimilar attitude items, only these items were analyzed. The reconstruction measure was derived as follows. First, the items were recoded so that the subject always scored on the high side and the confederate (bogus survey) on the low side. Specifically, if the subject responded favorably to a topic, the favorable categories were given the high scores (6, 5, 4) and the unfavorable categories were given the low scores (3, 2, 1). If the subject was opposed to the topic, the unfavorable categories received the high scores (6, 5, 4) and the favorable categories the low scores (3, 2, 1). Scores on the bogus scale were then subtracted from the corresponding scores on the reconstructed scale and were averaged to yield a measure reflecting both magnitude and direction of distortion. A positive score indicated a distortion toward the subject's attitude, a negative score a distortion away from the subject's attitude, and a zero score an accurate reconstruction.

Evaluation of dissimilar items. Each of the attitude items had been evaluated on six bipolar dimensions. For each dissimilar item, scores on these dimensions were summed and item-total score correlations were computed. For all 10 attitude items, the dimension *complex-simple* showed low item-total score correlations and was dropped from further analyses. Internal consistency reliabilities were then computed on the five remaining dimensions for each of the seven dissimilar attitudes; they ranged from .84 to .95. To produce a single measure of evaluation, the 35 scores (consisting of five dimensions for each of seven attitudes, overall alpha = .93) were averaged.

Analyses

The six dependent measures (love, liking, perceived similarity, number of hours volunteered, reconstruction, and evaluation) were entered into a 2 × 2 (Misattribution–No Misattribution × Infatuation Induction–No Infatuation Induction) multivariate analysis of variance. There was a significant multivariate interaction, $F(6, 23) = 2.68, p = .04$. As predicted, significant univariate interactions occurred

TABLE 1
Mean Attraction, Reconstruction, and Evaluation Scores

Condition	Love	Perceived Similarity	Number of Hours Volunteered	Evaluation	Liking	Reconstruction
Misattribution (M)						
Infatuation induction (I)						
M	6.40	7.13	1.13	3.11	11.15	.02
SD	2.33	4.67	1.36	.62	3.83	.38
No infatuation induction (NI)						
M	8.26	7.00	1.75	3.71	10.81	.04
SD	2.63	3.21	1.39	.79	1.92	.29
No misattribution (NM)						
Infatuation induction						
M	9.13	9.88	2.38	3.91	13.47	−.13
SD	1.86	3.00	2.07	.59	1.95	.38
No infatuation induction						
M	6.62	4.13	.38	3.06	9.96	.05
SD	2.22	2.30	.74	1.00	2.14	.64
I vs. NI under M						
	2.66	1.00	1.00	2.39	*F*(1, 28)	
I vs. NI under NM						
	4.89*	11.40**	7.45**	4.96*	*F*(1, 28)	

$^*p < .05$. $^{**}p < .01$.

for love, $F(1, 28) = 7.38, p = 0.1$, number of hours volunteered, $F(1, 28) = 6.42, p = .02$, and the evaluation measure, $F(1, 28) = 7.12, p = .01$. Interestingly, the perceived global similarity item also showed a significant univariate interaction, $F(1, 28) = 5.46, p = .03$. The means for all the dependent measures, as well as simple main effects tests of infatuation induction under conditions of misattribution and no misattribution are presented in Table 1. The pattern of the simple main effects was consistent with predictions and was the same for each of the dependent measures.

The infatuation induction and no infatuation induction conditions did not differ when misattribution had occurred but did differ when misattribution did not take place. Specifically, in the no misattribution conditions, infatuation induction subjects scored higher on love, perceived the confederate as more similar to themselves on the single perceived similarity item, and volunteered to work more hours with her than the no infatuation induction subjects.

Finally, the infatuation induction subjects also evaluated her dissimilar attitudes more favorably than their no infatuation induction counterparts. It should be noted that, even for liking, the univariate interaction approached significance, $F(1, 28) = 3.02, p = .09$, and showed the same pattern as the other measures. Only the reconstruction measure showed no effect $F(1, 28), < 1.00$, a finding in line with reasoning discussed earlier and consistent with the results of Gold et al. (1984). The multivariate infatuation induction and misattribution main effects were both nonsignificant.

Discussion

The results of this experiment provide evidence for the processes proposed to account for the love-is-blind phenomenon. First, the results support the concept that infatuation is indeed an aroused state and that this arousal is a causal agent in the infatuated person's failure to follow the traditional rules of interpersonal attraction by rejecting those who differ attitudinally. Specifically, among subjects in the no misattribution conditions, those given the infatuation induction were more strongly attracted to the confederate than those who were not, both in terms of their love scale scores and their commitment to work with her without compensation. On the other hand, subjects in the infatuation induction condition who were provided with an opportunity to attribute their arousal to the side effects of the vitamin were no more attracted to the confederate than were subjects not given an infatuation induction. These results support the contention that the infatuation induction produced an aroused state in the subjects and that this arousal, attributed to the confederate, was a critical element in their attraction to her in spite of her dissimilar attitudes.

Second, this unusual attraction was accompanied by a more positive (or, technically, a less negative) evaluation of dissimilar positions when they were held by the object of infatuation. It is important to note that, as in the Gold et al. (1984) studies, distortion of the dissimilar confederate's attitudes did not occur. Instead, all subjects recalled her attitudes with equal accuracy. Infatuated subjects were thus not blind in the sense of lacking accurate knowledge about the other; however, they were more blindly accepting of her very dissimilar viewpoints, seeing them, for example, as less irrational, foolish, and immature. Specifically, the pattern of findings for evaluation of the reconstructed attitudes was identical to that for the attraction measures: Subjects in the infatuation induction conditions evaluated the confederate's dissimilar attitudes more favorably than their no infatuation induction condition counterparts, but only when there was no misattribution.

Future research should investigate two potential limitations to the present findings. First, our view that subjects accepted the dissimilar attitudes of the object of their infatuation rests upon the assumption that their own attitudes did not change. If they instead altered their viewpoints to coincide more closely with those of the confederate, they could perhaps be more accurately described as influenced than as accepting. It is true that, in both the Gold et al. (1984) research and the present study, infatuated subjects did perceive the confederate as more similar to themselves than did noninfatuated subjects on a single global judgment of perceived similarity, and it is conceivable that this perception arose as a result of changes in their attitudes. However, this item did not specifically refer to attitudes, and it seems more likely to us that subjects were simply reporting a rather undifferentiated impression of general similarity.

Second, subjects in both the Gold et al. (1984) research and the present study were shown the confederate's bogus attitude survey before the infatuation induction manipulation and consequent arousal occurred. It may be that the attitudes were stored and retrieved accurately precisely because of this sequence of events. The pattern of findings might have been quite different if subjects had interacted with the confederate before being presented with her dissimilar attitudes. Distortion in the latter circumstance might occur as a function of either the state of arousal experienced by the subject or the commitment to the confederate prior to learning about her attitudes.

The present results contain hints of certain possible adverse effects of an aroused emotional state. Even a brief encounter with the attractive confederate produced elevated feelings of attraction toward a woman who was actually quite dissimilar from the subject.

It attitude similarity is a central aspect of friendship, and friendship is a quality of more enduring relationships, then infatuation, which produces either blindness or indifference to attitudinal dissimilarity, could be detrimental to the establishment of more enduring relationships.

REFERENCES

Byrne, D. (1961). Interpersonal attraction and attitude similarity. *Journal of Abnormal and Social Psychology, 62,* 713–715.

Byrne, D. (1971). *The attraction paradigm.* New York: Plenum.

Byrne, D., & Clore, G. L. (1967). Effectance arousal and attraction. *Journal of Personality and Social Psychology Monographs, 6* (Whole No. 638).

Byrne, D., & Murnen, S. K. (1988). Maintaining loving relationships. In R. J. Sternberg & M. L. Barnes (Eds.), *The psychology of love* (pp. 293–310). New Haven: Yale University Press.

Byrne, D., & Nelson, D. (1965). Attraction as a linear function of proportion of positive reinforcements. *Journal of Personality and Social Psychology, 1,* 659–663.

Clark, D. M., & Teasdale, J. D. (1982). Diurnal variation in clinical depression and accessibility of memories of positive and negative experiences. *Journal of Abnormal Psychology, 91,* 87–95.

Clark, M. S., & Isen, A. M. (1982). Toward understanding the relationship between feeling states and social behavior. In A. H. Hastorf & A. M. Isen (Eds.), *Cognitive social psychology* (pp. 73–108). New York: Elsevier/North-Holland.

Clark, M. S., & Waddell, B. A. (1983). Effects of moods on thoughts about helping, attraction, and information acquisition. *Social Psychology Quarterly, 46,* 31–35.

Gold, J. A., Ryckman, R. M., & Mosley, N. R. (1984). Romantic mood induction and attraction to a dissimilar other: Is love blind? *Personality and Social Psychological Bulletin, 10,* 358–368.

Hatfield, E., & Walster, G. W. (1981). *A new look at love.* Reading, MA: Addison-Wesley.

Milberg, S., & Clark, M. S. (1988). Moods and compliance. *British Journal of Social Psychology, 27,* 79–90.

Newcomb, T. M. (1961). *The acquaintance process.* New York: Holt, Rinehart, & Winston.

Osgood, C. E., Suci, G. J., & Tannenbaum, P. H. (1957). *The measurement of meaning.* Chicago: University of Illinois Press.

Rokeach, M. (1968). *Beliefs, attitudes, and values.* San Francisco: Jossey-Bass.

Rosenbaum, M. E. (1986). The repulsion hypothesis: On the nondevelopment of relationships. *Journal of Personality and Social Psychology, 51,* 1156–1166.

Rubin, Z. (1973). *Liking and loving: An invitation to social psychology.* New York: Holt, Rinehart, & Winston.

Smeaton, G., Byrne, D., & Murnen, S. K. (1989). The repulsion hypothesis revisited: Similarity irrelevance or dissimilarity bias? *Journal of Personality and Social Psychology, 56,* 54–59.

Sternberg, R. J. (1986). A triangular theory of love. *Psychological Review, 93,* 119–135.

Tennov, D. (1979). *Love and limerence: The experience of being in love.* New York: Stein & Day.

Zanna, M. P., & Cooper, J. (1974). Dissonance and the pill: An attribution approach to studying the arousal properties of dissonance. *Journal of Personality and Social Psychology, 29,* 703–709.

RESPONSE SHEET

for Kimberley McClanahan: Infatuation and Attraction to a Dissimilar Other

The sole question for this study: What is the significance of this study? (10 pts).

CHAPTER

14

Intimacy Development: Stage #3— The Paradox of Intimacy

At the core of this stage is a paradox that confounds conventional cultural wisdom. The relationship state that should bring the highest levels of trust, comfort, openness and effortless communication instead unleashes the highest levels of distrust in the relationship to date. Unexplainable discomfort, guardedness, and avoidance are experienced. A number of romantic pairs break up at this point. The mutual deception is not working sufficiently. For those who do move into this stage, there is at least a moderate level of commitment and/or the determination not to be quitters. The tasks the pair must work through are discussed in Chapter 12.

Cary Barber identifies an array of more detailed types of psychological baggage that are drug out of the psychological woodwork by the advent of intimacy.

Finding Real Love

by Cary Barbor

Human beings crave intimacy, to love and be loved. Why then do people feel isolated in their intimate relationships? Four researchers and clinicians, Ayala Malach Pines, Shirley Glass, Lisa Firestone and Joyce Catlett, discuss the alienation that affects so many people and how to overcome it.

We need to be close to other people as surely as we need food and water. But while it's relatively easy to get ourselves a good meal, it is difficult for many of us to create and maintain intimacy with others, particularly with a romantic partner. There are many variables that affect the quality of our relationships with others; it's difficult to pin it on one thing or another. But in this article, based on a symposium recently held at the annual American Psychological Association convention in Washington, D.C., four mental health professionals discuss their ideas about how we sabotage our intimate relationships—and what we can do to fix them.

Choose to Lose?

Many factors influence the level of intimacy we enjoy in our relationships. The various decisions we make, and our behavior toward one another, are what foster closeness or drives us apart. These decisions are all under our control, although we are influenced by old patterns that we must work to change.

The first decision we make about a relationship is the partner we choose. Whom we fall in love with determines the level of intimacy in our relationships, according to Ayala Malach Pines, Ph.D., who heads the behavioral sciences in management program at Ben-Gurion University in Israel. We often choose partners who remind us of significant people from our childhood—often our parents—and we set out to recreate the patterns of our childhood. Let's look at an example:

Tara met Abe at a party. She was instantly attracted to the tall, lean man with a faraway look in his eyes. Abe, who had been standing alone, was delighted when Tara approached him with her open smile and outstretched hand. She was not only beautiful, but she struck him as warm and nurturing as well. The conversation between them flowed instantly. It felt comfortable and easy. Eventually, they fell in love, and after a year, they were married.

At first things were wonderful. They had the kind of closeness Tara had always dreamed about with her father. Though she was sure he loved her, she never felt she had her father completely to herself. Even when he held her on his lap, he had a faraway look. But with Abe things were different. He was there with her completely.

> The first decision we make about a relationship is the partner we choose.

The intimacy between them also felt terrific to Abe. It was not the kind of suffocating closeness he always dreaded—the kind of intrusive closeness he experienced as a child with his mother, who used to enter his room uninvited and arrange his personal belongings with no regard to his privacy. But Tara was different. She did not intrude.

But occasionally, Abe would come home from work tired and annoyed. All he wanted was a drink and to sit with the paper until he could calm down and relax. Seeing him that way, Tara would become concerned. "What is going on?" she would ask anxiously. "Nothing," he would answer. Sure that there was something very wrong, and assuming that it must be something about her or their marriage, Tara would insist that he tell her. She reminded him of his mother, and he responded the way he did with his mother: by withdrawing. To Tara, this felt similar to the way her father behaved. She responded in the same way she did when her father withdrew: by clinging. The struggle between them continued and became more and more intense over time, with Tara demanding more intimacy and Abe demanding more space.

Recreating the Family

Like Abe and Tara, people choose partners who help them recreate their childhood struggles. Tara fell in love with a man with "a faraway look in his eyes," and subsequently had to struggle for greater intimacy. Abe fell in love with a woman who was "warm and nurturing," then spent a lot of energy struggling for more space.

Tara's unresolved intimacy issues complement Abe's. For example, one partner (often the woman) will fight to break down defenses and create more intimacy while the other (often the man) will withdraw and create distance. So the "dance of intimacy" follows: If the woman gets to close, the man pulls back. If he moves too far away, she pursues, and so on.

To achieve greater intimacy, the partners must overcome the anxiety that compels them to take their respective parts in that dance. In the example, Tara needs to control her abandonment anxiety and not pursue Abe when he withdraws, and Abe needs to control his engulfment anxiety when Tara pursues him and not withdraw. Working to overcome these anxieties is an opportunity to resolve childhood issues and can be a major healing experience for both partners.

Infidelity: The Road Back

If a couple can't overcome their anxieties and achieve a balance, however, fear and an inability to achieve intimacy will linger. This can create a vulnerability to affairs, says Shirley P. Glass, Ph.D., a clinical psychologist in private practice in Baltimore. Either partner may feel burned out from trying to get his or her emotional intimacy needs met in the relationship. A pursuing woman, who wonders if her needs will ever be met, may withdraw out of hopelessness. Yet her partner may think that the relationship has improved because the complaining has stopped. Meanwhile, she could be supplementing her unmet intimacy needs through an extramarital relationship that could ultimately lead to separation or divorce.

Once an affair has occurred, it only serves to erode intimacy further. Intimacy requires honesty, openness and self-disclosure. The deception that accompanies an affair makes this impossible. In addition, if the affair partner becomes the confidante for problems in the marriage, it can be threatening to the marriage because it creates a bond of friendship between the affair partners that goes beyond sexuality.

For trust to be rebuilt and intimacy reestablished, the walls of deception created by the affair need to be broken down. The spouse needs to be back on the "inside" of the partnership and the extramarital partner on the "outside." The involved spouse must stop all personal exchanges with the affair partner and disclose to the marital partner any unavoidable encounters with the affair partner, without prompting. Unfaithful partners can only regain credibility by being completely honest. People report that they recover from their partner having a sexual relationship with another person before they recover from being deceived.

But if both partners can be totally honest, and if communication in the partnership improves, there is a good chance that the marriage can survive the infidelity and the relationship can become strong again.

Overcoming Fear of Intimacy

It is our fear of intimacy that inspires these ingenious ways of avoiding it. This raises the question: How can we overcome our fear of intimacy? We can start by breaking down our defenses.

We all bring defenses to relationships, and, unfortunately, it is often these defenses that spell trouble. We develop our defenses and negative beliefs in childhood. They are what we utilized to protect ourselves against emotional pain and, later, against anxiety about death.

A core defense that often leads to the downfall of a partnership is "the fantasy bond," according to Lisa Firestone, Ph.D., adjunct faculty at the University of California Santa Barbara Graduate School of Education, and Joyce Catlett, M.A., co-author of *Fear of Intimacy,* published recently by the American Psychological Association. The fantasy bond is an illusion of a connection to another person. It develops first with the mother or primary parent figure, and people often try to recreate it in their adult relationships.

People use various techniques to reestablish this primary relationship. They may first select a partner who fits their model, someone they can relate to in the way they related to their parent or other family member. They can distort their partner and perceive them as being more like this significant person than they are. Third, if all else fails, they tend to provoke their partner into the behavior they seek. All of these mechanisms curtail their ability to relate and

Many factors influence the level of intimacy we enjoy in our relationships. The various decisions we make, and our behavior toward one another, is what fosters closeness or drives us apart.

The View

People have conflicting views and beliefs about relationships. Here are a few common ones:

1. Relationships are important and central in affecting a person's life.
2. Relationships are generally unstable. Young people marrying for the first time face a 40% to 50% chance of divorce.
3. There is a good deal of dishonesty in relationships. People are duplicitous in many ways: sexually, emotionally, etc.
4. Relationships are often based on emotional hunger and desperation. People mistake longing and desperation for love.
5. Few long-term relationships are based on high-level choices. Often people "take what they can get."
6. Choices can be made for negative as well as positive reasons. For example, people have a tendency to select mates who are similar to a parent, which can be good or bad.
7. People confuse sex with love. During the early phase of a relationship, attraction and pleasure in sex are often mistaken for love.
8. People feel they are failures unless they succeed in finding mates.

(Source: *Fear of Intimacy,* 1999)

make it less likely that people will be successful in achieving true intimacy in their relationships.

A secondary defense that helps preserve the fantasy bond is, according to Firestone and Catlett, "the voice." All people tend to carry on some form of internal dialogue within themselves as though another person were talking to them: reprimanding them, denouncing them, divulging negative information about others, and so on.

In intimate relationships, both individuals may be listening to the dictates of their respective voices. Unfortunately, these only create more defensiveness. Both partners may use rationalizations promoted by "the voice" to ward off loving responses from the other and justify their distancing behavior.

Speak Up, Therapeutically

A technique developed by Robert Firestone, Ph.D., and used to reverse this process and allow greater intimacy is voice therapy. Voice therapy brings these internalized negative thoughts to consciousness. The goal of voice therapy with couples is to help each individual identify the "voice attacks" that are creating conflict and distance in the relationship. In identifying specific self-criticisms as well as judgmental, hostile thoughts about the other, each partner is able to relate more openly.

Here is an example of someone using voice therapy. Sheryl is in a four-year relationship and was starting to have problems. She and her partner Mark came to therapy for help, and they progressed through these four steps of voice therapy over the course of treatment. Following is a glimpse into Sheryl's process.

Formulate the problem each individual perceives is limiting his or her satisfaction within the relationship.

Sheryl: The feeling I have is that I've always liked Mark, but lately I feel like I can't stand it when he's nice to me. I feel like I have a mean streak.

Therapist: In response to his liking you.

Sheryl: Yes.

Verbalize self-critical thoughts and negative perceptions of the other in the form of the voice, and let go of the feelings associated with them.

Therapist: What are you telling yourself about the relationship?

Sheryl: It's like, 'Don't show him anything, don't show him you like him.' I tell myself, 'Just don't show it, you're such a sucker if you show it.' When he's vulnerable I just want to squash him. And it's for no reason except for he's being sweet.

Develop insight into the origins of the voice and make connections between past experience and present conflicts.

Sheryl: I've seen myself be like my mother millions of times. In previous relationships I've acted so much like her, I didn't even know it. I saw her as being a really critical person, she was very critical of my father. And she would be mean to him. Sometimes I act like that myself.

Alter behaviors and communications in a direction that counteracts the dictates of the voice.

Therapist: So the hope is for you to hang in there and to tolerate the anxiety of giving up these defenses and the fantasized connection you have with your mother. If you do sweat it out then you'll be able to have more in your life. It takes a lot of courage to go through that process but it's really worth it.

Sheryl: I feel like it would make me sad, too, because I would feel a lot. When I have that other point of view, I feel big and mean. And when I just let things be, and don't act in ways to push Mark away, I feel like a soft, sweet person.

After trying voice therapy, Sheryl reported that she felt closer to Mark. She noticed a shift in her feelings, both in accepting his caring about her and genuinely caring about him.

The Ideal and Not So Ideal

Interactions in an ideal and healthy relationship:

1. Nondefensiveness and openness
2. Honesty and integrity
3. Respect for the other's boundaries, priorities and goals, separate from self
4. Physical affection and responsive sexuality
5. Understanding—lack of distortion of the other
6. Noncontrolling, nonmanipulative and nonthreatening behavior

(Source: *Fear of Intimacy,* 1999)

Interactions in an unhealthy relationship:

1. Angry and negative reactions to feedback; being closed to new experiences
2. Deception and duplicity
3. Overstepping boundaries Other seen only in relation to self
4. Lack of affection, inadequate or impersonal, routine sexuality
5. Misunderstanding—distortion of the other
6. Manipulations of dominance and submission

(Source: *Fear of Intimacy,* 1999: The Glendon Association)

In therapy sessions, both partners reveal negative thoughts and attitudes toward himself or herself and each other. In this way, they share each other's individual psychotherapy. In tracing back the source of their self-attacks and cynical views to early family interactions, they gain perspective on each other's problems and feel more compassion for their mates as well as themselves. Changing old patterns often brings up anxiety, so part of the treatment is to learn to tolerate the anxiety and work through it, so the partners can maintain the behavioral changes and ultimately increase intimacy.

Homework

For couples who are not in therapy, there are many ways to change destructive patterns that prevent intimacy. Partners could become aware of the times when they attack themselves or think negatively about their partner. They could record their self-critical thoughts and hostile attitudes in a journal; they could reveal the contents of their destructive thoughts to a trusted friend or to their mate. They could assess how close to reality these thoughts are (usually not very). Each could set goals for what he or she wants out of the relationship and then keep track of how closely his or her actions match these goals.

> We all bring defenses to relationships, and, unfortunately, it is often these defenses that spell trouble.

Another good idea for couples is to make an active effort to move away from isolated couple interaction and toward an extended circle of family and friends. This often affords a better perspective and provides a potential background for understanding and breaking destructive, habitual patterns of relating. Partners need to admit to themselves and their partner if they have become distant, and that their actions are no longer loving or respectful. By reawakening their feeling for one another, they can achieve a higher level of intimacy.

We always have choices to make about intimacy—from the partners we choose to the way we interact with them each day. Recognizing our patterns, tolerating our anxieties, and working together on our relationships will help us overcome our fear of intimacy. Learning how best to communicate with each other and treat one another will help us enjoy loving, lasting relationships.

Read More About It

Fear of Intimacy, Robert Firestone and Joyce Catlett (American Psychological Association Books, 1999)

The Trauma of Infidelity: Research and Treatment, Shirley Glass (Norton Professional Books, 2001)

Falling in Love: Why We Choose the Lovers We Choose, Ayala Malach Pines (Routledge, 1999)

Combating Destructive Thought Processes: Voice Therapy and Separation Theory, Robert Firestone (Sage Publications, 1997)

Romantic Jealousy: Causes, Symptoms and Cures, Ayala Malach Pines (Routledge, 1998)

Cary Barbor is a freelance writer based in New York. Her work has appeared on CBS Healthwatch and in Walking *and* Women's Sports and Fitness, *among other publications.*

RESPONSE SHEET

for Cary Barbor: Finding Real Love

1. How does the experience of intimacy itself bring about some of the most difficult problems? Find three that Barbor offers. (7 pts)

2. Write a question for class discussion. (3 pts)

CHAPTER

15

Intimacy Development: Stage #4—Working on Personality Differences

All romantic pairs have personality differences. They are downplayed in the first three stages of intimacy development. They surface in the fourth stage, and become a dominating presence in the relationship until they are managed. There are several management options that can be used singly or in combination. The first step, though, is to have valid information about what those differences are. This can be facilitated through assessment workshops.

In this course, you are going be invited to engage in such information gathering with your partner. You will be using the Myers-Briggs Type Indicator to establish the differences between you and your partner. You will then engage in two or more discussions regarding the utility of this information and any other related data.

CHAPTER 16

Intimacy Development: Stage #5—A Durable Intimacy

It is possible. Many people, once they learn what constitutes intimacy, feel that it cannot be achieved. If it is achieved, it won't last. Beth Livermore discusses what it takes to get there and stay there, including the learning we should be doing from our relationship experience. Intimacy is the highest form of personal relationship, and one of two of the most important things that can happen in our lives. The other is deeply satisfying, intrinsically rewarding work. When Sigmund Freud was asked what the two most important adult experiences were, he said "arbeiten und lieben". May each of you make these the two the abiding personal objectives in your life.

The Lessons of Love

Yes, we've learned a few things. We now know that it is the insecure rather than the confident who fall in love most readily. And men fall faster than women. And who ever said sex had anything to do with it?

Beth Livermore

As winter thaws, so too do icicles on cold hearts. For with spring, the sap rises—and resistance to love wanes. And though the flame will burn more of us than it warms, we will return to the fire—over and over again.

Indeed, love holds central in everybody's everyday. We spend years, sometimes lifetimes pursuing it, preparing for it, longing for it. Some of us even die for love. Still, only poets and songwriters, philosophers and playwrights have traditionally been granted license to sift this hallowed preserve. Until recently. Over the last decade and a half, scientists have finally taken on this most elusive entity. They have begun to parse out the intangibles, the *je ne sais quoi* of love. The word so far is—little we were sure of is proving to be true.

Out of the Lab, Into the Fire

True early greats, like Sigmund Freud and Carl Rogers, acknowledged love as important to the human experience. But not till the 1970s did anyone attempt to define it—and only now is it considered a respectable topic of study.

One reason for this hesitation has been public resistance. "Some people are afraid that if they look too close they will lose the mask," says Arthur Aron, Ph.D., professor of psychology at the University of California, Santa Cruz. "Others believe we know all that we need to know." But mostly, to systematically study love has been thought impossible, and therefore a waste of time and money.

No one did more to propagate this false notion than former United States Senator William Proxmire of Wisconsin, who in 1974 launched a very public campaign against the study of love. As a member of the Senate Finance Committee, he took it upon himself to ferret out waste in government spending. One of the first places he looked was the National Science Foundation, a federal body that both funds research and promotes scientific progress.

Upon inspection, Proxmire found that Ellen Berscheid, Ph.D., a psychologist at the University of Minnesota who had already broken new ground scrutinizing the social power of physical attractiveness, had secured an $84,000 federal grant to study relationships. The proposal mentioned romantic love. Proxmire loudly denounced such work as frivolous—tax dollars ill spent.

The publicity that was given Proxmire's pronouncements not only cast a pall over all behavioral science research, it set off an international firestorm around Berscheid that lasted the next two years. Colleagues were fired. Her office was swamped with hate mail. She even received death threats. But in the long run, the strategy backfired, much to Proxmire's chagrin. It generated increased scientific interest in the study of love, propelling it forward, and identified Berscheid as the keeper of the flame. Scholars and individuals from Alaska to then-darkest Cold War Albania sent her requests for information, along with letters of support.

Berscheid jettisoned her plans for very early retirement, buttoned up the country house, and, as she says, "became a clearinghouse" for North American love research. "It became eminently clear that there were people who really did want to learn more about love. And I had tenure."

Reprinted with permission from *Psychology Today,* March/April 1993, pp. 30–34, 36–39, 80.

PUTTING THE SOCIAL INTO PSYCHOLOGY

This incident was perfectly timed. For during the early 1970s, the field of social psychology was undergoing a revolution of sorts—a revolution that made the study of love newly possible.

For decades behaviorism, the school of psychology founded by John B. Watson, dominated the field. Watson argued that only overt actions capable of direct observation and measurement were worthy of study. However, by the early seventies, dissenters were openly calling this approach far too narrow. It excluded unobservable mental events such as ideas and emotions. Thus rose cognitive science, the study of the mind, or perception, thought, and memory.

Now psychologists were encouraged to ask human subjects what they thought and how they felt about things. Self-report questionnaires emerged as a legitimate research tool. Psychologists were encouraged to escape laboratory confines—to study real people in the real world. Once out there, they discovered that there was plenty of mine.

Throughout the seventies, soaring divorce rates, loneliness, and isolation began to dominate the emotional landscape of America. By the end of that decade, love had become a pathology. No longer was the question "What is love?" thought to be trivial. "People in our culture dissolve unions when love disappears, which has a lasting effect on society," says Berscheid. Besides, "we already understood the mating habits of the stickleback fish." It was time to turn to a new species.

Today there are hundreds of research papers on love. Topics range from romantic ideals to attachment styles of the young and unmarried. "There were maybe a half dozen when I wrote my dissertation on romantic attraction in 1969," reports Aron. These days, a national association and an international society bring "close relationship" researchers close together annually. Together or apart they are busy producing and sharing new theories, new questionnaires to use as research instruments, and new findings. Their unabashed aim: to improve the human condition by helping us to understand, to repair, and to perfect our love relationships.

SO WHAT *IS* LOVE?

"If there is anything that we have learned about love it is its variegated nature," says Clyde Hendrick, Ph.D., of Texas Tech University in Lubbock. "No one volume or theory or research program can capture love and transform it into a controlled bit of knowledge."

Instead, scholars are tackling specific questions about love in the hopes of nailing down a few facets at a time. The expectation is that every finding will be a building block in the base of knowledge, elevating understanding.

Elaine Hatfield, Ph.D., now of the University of Hawaii, has carved out the territory of passionate love. Along with Berscheid, Hatfield was at the University of Minnesota in 1964 when Stanley Schacter, formerly a professor there and still a great presence, proposed a new theory of emotion. It said that any emotional state requires two conditions: both physiological arousal and relevant situational cues. Already studying close relationships, Hatfield and Berscheid were intrigued. Could the theory help to explain the turbulent, all-consuming experience of passionate love?

Hatfield has spent a good chunk of her professional life examining passionate love, "a state of intense longing for union with another." In 1986, along with sociologist Susan Sprecher, she devised the Passionate Love Scale (PLS), a questionnaire that measures thoughts and feelings she previously identified as distinctive of this "emotional" state.

Lovers rate the applicability of a variety of descriptive statements. To be passionately in love is to be preoccupied with thoughts of your partner much of the time. Also, you likely idealize your partner. So those of you who are passionately in love would, for example, give "I yearn to know all about—" a score somewhere between "moderately true" and "definitely true" on the PLS.

> True erotic love is intense and involves taking risks. It seems to demand a strong sense of self.

The quiz also asks subjects if they find themselves trying to determine the other's feelings, trying to please their lover, or making up excuses to be close to him or her—all hallmarks of passionate, erotic love. It canvasses for both positive and negative feelings. "Passionate lovers," explains Hatfield, "experience a roller coaster of feelings: euphoria, happiness, calm, tranquility, vulnerability, anxiety, panic, despair."

> For a full 10 percent of lovers, previous romantic relationships proved so painful that they hope they will never love again.

Passionate love, she maintains, is kindled by "a sprinkle of hope and a large dollop of loneliness, mourning, jealousy, and terror." It is, in other words, fueled by a juxtaposition of pain and pleasure. According to psychologist Dorothy Tennov, who interviewed some 500 lovers, most of them expect their romantic experiences to be bittersweet. For a full 10 percent of them, previous romantic relationships proved so painful that they hope never to love again.

Contrary to myths that hold women responsible for romance, Hatfield finds that both males and females love with equal passion. But men fall in love faster. They are, thus, more romantic. Women are more apt to mix pragmatic concerns with their passion.

And people of all ages, even four-year-old children, are capable of "falling passionately in love." So are people of any ethnic group and socioeconomic stratum capable of passionate love.

Hatfield's most recent study, of love in three very different cultures, shows that romantic love is not simply a product of the Western mind. It exists among diverse cultures worldwide.

Taken together, Hatfield's findings support the idea that passionate love is an evolutionary adaptation. In this scheme, passionate love works as a bonding mechanism, a necessary kind of interpersonal glue that has existed since the start of the human race. It assures that procreation will take place, that the human species will be perpetuated.

Up From the Swamp

Recent anthropological work also supports this notion. In 1991, William Jankowiak, Ph.D., of the University of Nevada in Las Vegas, and Edward Fischer, Ph.D., of Tulane University published the first study systematically comparing romantic love across 166 cultures.

They looked at folklore, indigenous advice about love, tales about lovers, love potion recipes—anything related. They found "clear evidence" that romantic love is known in 147, or 89 percent, of cultures. Further, Jankowiak suspects that the lack of proof in the remaining 19 cultures is due more to field workers' oversights than to the absence of romance.

Unless prompted, few anthropologists recognize romantic love in the populations that they study, explains Jankowiak. Mostly because romance takes different shapes in different cultures, they do not know what to look for. They tend to recognize romance only in the form it takes in American culture—a progressive phenomenon leading from flirtation to marriage. Elsewhere, it may be a more fleeting fancy. Still, reports Jankowiak, "when I ask them specific questions about behavior, like 'Did couples run away from camp together?', almost all of them have a positive response."

For all that, there is a sizable claque of scholars who insist that romantic love is a cultural invention of the last 200 years or so. They point out that few cultures outside the West embrace romantic love with the vigor that we do. Fewer still build marriage, traditionally a social and economic institution, on the individualistic pillar of romance.

Romantic love, this thinking holds, consists of a learned set of behaviors; the phenomenon is culturally transmitted from one generation to the next by example, stories, imitation, and direct instruction. Therefore, it did not rise from the swamps with us, but rather evolved with culture.

The Anxious are Its Prey

Regardless whether passionate, romantic love is universal or unique to us, there is considerable evidence that what renders people particularly vulnerable to it is anxiety. It

Love Me Tender

How to Make Love to a Man (what men like, in order of importance)	**How to Make Love to a Woman** (what women like, in order of importance)
taking walks together	taking walks together
kissing	flowers
candle-lit dinners	kissing
cuddling	candle-lit dinners
hugging	cuddling
flowers	declaring "I love you"
holding hands	love letters
making love	slow dancing
love letters	hugging
sitting by the fireplace	giving surprise gifts

whips up the wherewithal to love. An anxiety is not alone; in fact, there are a number of predictable precursors to love.

To test the idea that emotions such as fear, which produces anxiety, can amplify attraction, Santa Cruz's Arthur Aron recorded the responses of two sets of men to an attractive woman. But one group first had to cross a narrow 450-foot-long bridge that swayed in the wind over a 230-foot drop—a pure prescription for anxiety. The other group tromped confidently across a seemingly safe bridge. Both groups encountered Miss Lovely, a decoy, as they stepped back into terra firm.

Love depends as much on the perception of being liked as on the presence of a desirable partner. Love isn't possible without it.

Aron's attractive confederate stopped each young man to explain that she was doing a class project and asked if he would complete a questionnaire. Once he finished, she handed him her telephone number, saying that she would be happy to explain her project in greater detail.

Who called? Nine of the 33 men on the suspension bridge telephoned, while only two of the men on the safe bridge called. It is not impossible that the callers simply wanted details on the project, but Aron suspects instead that a combustible mix of excitement and anxiety prompted the men to become interested in their attractive interviewee.

Along similar if less treacherous lines, Aron has most recently looked at eleven possible precursors to love. He compiled the list by conducting a comprehensive literature search for candidate items. If you have a lot in common with or live and work close to someone you find attractive, your chances of falling in love are good, the literature suggests.

Other general factors proposed at one time or another as good predictors include being liked by the other, a partner's positive social status, a partner's ability to fill your needs, your readiness for entering a relationship, your isolation from others, mystery, and exciting surroundings or circumstances. Then there are specific cues, like hair color, eye expression, and face shape.

To test the viability and relative importance of these eleven putative factors, Aron asked three different groups of people to give real-life accounts of falling in love. Predictably, desirable characteristics, such as good looks and personality, made the top of the list. But proximity, readiness to develop a relationship, and exciting surroundings and circumstances ranked close behind.

The big surprise: reciprocity. Love is at heart a two-way event. The perception of being liked ranked just as high as the presence of desirable characteristics in the partner. "The combination of the two appears to be very important," says Aron. In fact, love just may not be possible without it.

Sprecher and his colleagues got much the same results in a very recent cross-cultural survey. They and their colleagues interviewed 1,667 men and women in the U.S., Russia, and Japan. They asked the people to think about the last time they had fallen in love or been infatuated. Then they asked about the circumstance that surrounded the love experience.

Surprisingly, the rank ordering of the factors was quite similar in all three cultures. In all three, men and women consider reciprocal liking, personality, and physical appearance to be especially important. A partner's social status and the approval of family and friends are way down the list. The cross-cultural validation of predisposing influences suggests that reciprocal liking, desirable personality and physical features may be universal elements of love, among the *sine qua non* of love, part of its heart and soul.

FRIENDSHIP OVER PASSION

Another tack to the intangible of love is the "prototype" approach. This is the study of our conceptions of love, what we "think" love is.

In 1988, Beverly Fehr, Ph.D., of the University of Winnipeg in Canada conducted a series of six studies designed to determine what "love" and "commitment" have in common. Assorted theories suggested they could be anything from mutually inclusive to completely separate. Fehr asked subjects to list characteristics of love and to list features of commitment. Then she asked them to determine which qualities were central and which more peripheral to each.

People's concepts of the two were to some degree overlapping. Such elements as trust, caring, respect, honesty, devotion, sacrifice, and contentment were deemed attributes of both love and commitment. But such other factors as intimacy, happiness, and a desire to be with the other proved unique to love (while commitment alone demanded perseverance, mutual agreement, obligation, and even a feeling of being trapped).

The findings of Fehr's set of studies, as well as others', defy many expectations. Most subjects said they consider caring, trust, respect, and honesty central to love—while passion-related events like touching, sexual passion, and physical attraction are only peripheral. "They are not very central to our concept of love," Fehr shrugs.

Both men and women deem romance and passion far less important than support and warm fuzzies . . .

Recently, Fehr explored gender differences in views of love—and found remarkably few. Both men and women put forth friendship as primary to love. Only in a second study, which asked subjects to match their personal ideal of love to various descriptions, did any differences show up. More so than women, men tended to rate erotic, romantic love closer to their personal conception of love.

Still, Fehr is fair. On the whole, she says, "the essence, the core meaning of love differs little." Both genders deem romance and passion far less important than support and warm fuzzies. As even Nadine Crenshaw, creator of steamy romance novels, has remarked, "love gets you to the bathroom when you're sick."

Love Me Tender

Since the intangible essence of love cannot be measured directly, many researchers settle for its reflection in what people do. They examine the behavior of lovers.

Clifford Swensen, Ph.D., professor of psychology at Purdue University, pioneered this approach by developing a scale with which to measure lovers' behavior. He produced it from statements people made when asked what they did for, said to, or felt about people they loved . . . and how these people behaved towards them.

Being supportive and providing encouragement are important behaviors to all love relationships—whether with a friend or mate, Swensen and colleagues found. Subjects also gave high ratings to self-disclosure, or talking about personal matters, and a sense of agreement on important topics.

But two categories of behaviors stood out as unique to romantic relationships. Lovers said that they expressed feelings of love verbally; they talked about how they enjoyed being together, how they missed one another when apart, and other such murmurings. They also showed their affection through physical acts like hugging and kissing.

Elaborating on the verbal and physical demonstrations of love, psychologist Raymond Tucker, Ph.D., of Bowling Green State University in Ohio probed 149 women and 48 men to determine "What constitutes a romantic act?" He asked subjects, average age of 21, to name common examples. There was little disagreement between the genders.

Both men and women most often cited "taking walks" together. For women, "sending or receiving flowers" and "kissing" followed close on its heels, then "candle-lit dinners" and "cuddling." Outright declarations of "I love you" came in a distant sixth. (Advisory to men: The florists were right all along. Say it with flowers instead.)

. . . as one romance novelist confides, "love gets you to the bathroom when you're sick."

For men, kissing and "candle-lit dinners" came in second and third. If women preferred demonstrations of love to outright declarations of it, men did even more so; "hearing and saying 'I love you didn't even show up among their top ten preferences.'" Nor did "slow dancing or giving or receiving surprise gifts," although all three were on the women's top-ten list. Men likewise listed three kinds of activity women didn't even mention: "holding hands," "making love"—and "sitting by the fireplace." For both sexes, love is more tender than most of us imagined.

All in all, says Tucker, lovers consistently engage in a specific array of actions. "I see these items show up over and over and over again." They may very well be the bedrock behaviors of romantic love.

Six Colors of Love

That is not to say that once in love we all behave alike. We do not. Each of us has a set of attitudes toward love that colors what we do. While yours need not match your mate's, you best understand your partner's approach. It underlies how your partner is likely to treat you.

There are six basic orientations toward love, Canadian sociologist John Allen Lee first suggested in 1973. They emerged from a series of studies in which subjects matched story cards, which contain statements projecting attitudes, to their own personal relationships. In 1990 Texas Tech's Clyde Hendrick, along with wife/colleague Susan Hendrick, Ph.D., produced a Love Attitude Scale to measure all six styles. You may embody more than one of these styles. You are also likely to change style with time and circumstance.

Both men and women prefer demonstrations of love to outright declarations of it.

You may, for example, have spent your freewheeling college years as an Eros lover, passionate and quick to get involved, setting store on physical attraction and sexual satisfaction. Yet today, you may find yourself happy as a Storge lover, valuing friendship-based love, preferring a secure, trusting relationship with a partner of like values.

There are Ludus lovers, game-player who like to have several partners at one time. Their partners may be very different from one another, as Ludus does not act on romantic ideals. Mania-type lovers, by contrast, experience great emotional highs and lows. They are very possessive—and often jealous. They spend a lot of their time doubting their partner's sincerity.

Pragma lovers are, well, pragmatic. They get involved only with the "right" guy or gal—someone who fills their needs or meets other specifications. This group is happy to trade drama and excitement for a partner they can build a life with. In contrast, Agape, or altruistic, lovers form relationships because of what they may be able to give to their partner. Even sex is not an urgent concern of theirs. "Agape functions on a more spiritual level," Hendrick says.

The Hendricks have found some gender difference among love styles. In general, men are more ludic, or game-playing. Women tend to be more storgic, more pragmatic—and more manic. However, men and women seem to be equally passionate and altruistic in their relationships. On the whole, say the Hendricks, the sexes are more similar than different in style.

Personality traits, at least one personality trait, is strongly correlated to love style, the Hendricks have discovered. People with high self-esteem are more apt to

The Colors of Love

How do I love thee? At least six are the ways.

There is no one type of love; there are many equally valid ways of loving. Researchers have consistently identified six attitudes or styles of love that, to one degree or another, encompass our conceptions of love and color our romantic relationships. They reflect both fixed personality traits and more malleable attitudes. Your relative standing on these dimensions may vary over time—being in love NOW will intensify your responses in some dimensions. Nevertheless, studies show that for most people, one dimension of love predominates.

Answering the questions below will help you identify your own love style, one of several important factors contributing to the satisfaction you feel in relationships. You may wish to rate yourself on a separate sheet of paper. There are no right or wrong answers, nor is there any scoring system. The test is designed to help you examine your own feelings and to help you understand your own romantic experiences.

After you take the test, if you are currently in a relationship, you may want to ask your partner to take the test and then compare your responses. Better yet, try to predict your partner's love attitudes before giving the test to him or her.

Studies show that most partners are well-correlated in the areas of love passion and intensity (Eros), companionate or friendship love (Storge), dependency (Mania), and all-giving or selfless love (Agape). If you and your partner aren't a perfect match, don't worry. Knowing your styles can help you manage your relationship.

Directions: Listed below are several statements that reflect different attitudes about love. For each statement, fill in the response on an answer sheet that indicates how much you agree or disagree with that statement. The items refer to a specific love relationship. Whenever possible, answer the questions with your current partner in mind. If you are not currently dating anyone, answer the questions with your most recent partner in mind. If you have never been in love, answer in terms of what you think your responses would most likely be.

FOR EACH STATEMENT:

A = Strongly agree with the statement
B = Moderately agree with the statement
C = Neutral, neither agree nor disagree
D = Moderately disagree with the statement
E = Strongly disagree with the statement

Eros

Measures passionate love as well as intimacy and commitment. It is directly and strongly correlated with satisfaction in a relationship, a major ingredient in relationship success. Eros give fully, intensely, and takes risks in love; it requires substantial ego strength. Probably reflects secure attachment style.

1. My partner and I were attracted to each other immediately after we first met.
2. My partner and I have the right physical "chemistry" between us.
3. Our lovemaking is very intense and satisfying.
4. I feel that my partner and I were meant for each other.
5. My partner and I became emotionally involved rather quickly.
6. My partner and I really understand each other.
7. My partner fits my ideal standards of physical beauty/handsomeness.

The Colors of Love—cont'd

Ludus

Measures love as an interaction game to be played out with diverse partners. Relationships do not have great depth of feeling. Ludus is wary of emotional intensity from others, and has a manipulative or cynical quality to it. Ludus is negatively related to satisfaction in relationships. May reflect avoidant attachment style.

8. I try to keep my partner a little uncertain about my commitment to him/her.
9. I believe that what my partner doesn't know about me won't hurt him/her.
10. I have sometimes had to keep my partner from finding out about other partners.
11. I could get over my affair with my partner pretty easily and quickly.
12. My partner would get upset if he/she knew of some of the things I've done with other people.
13. When my partner gets too dependent on me, I want to back off a little.
14. I enjoy playing the "game of love" with my partner and a number of other partners.

Storge

Reflects an inclination to merge love and friendship. Storgic love is solid, down to earth, presumably enduring. It is evolutionary, not revolutionary, and may take time to develop. It is related to satisfaction in long-term relationships.

15. It is hard for me to say exactly when our friendship turned to love.
16. To be genuine, our love first required caring for a while.
17. I expect to always be friends with my partner.
18. Our love is the best kind because it grew out of a long friendship.
19. Our friendship merged gradually into love over time.
20. Our love is really a deep friendship, not a mysterious, mystical emotion.
21. Our love relationship is the most satisfying because it developed from a good friendship.

Pragma

Reflects logical, "shopping list" love, rational calculation with a focus on desired attributes of a lover. Suited to computer-matched dating. Related to satisfaction in long-term relationships.

22. I considered what my partner was going to become in life before I committed myself to him/her.
23. I tried to plan my life carefully before choosing my partner.
24. In choosing my partner, I believed it was best to love someone with a similar background.
25. A main consideration in choosing my partner was how he/she would reflect on my family.
26. An important factor in choosing my partner was whether or not he/she would be a good parent.
27. One consideration in choosing my partner was how he/she would reflect on my career.
28. Before getting very involved with my partner, I tried to figure out how compatible his/her hereditary background would be with mine in case we ever had children.

Mania

Measures possessive, dependent love. Associated with high emotional expressiveness and disclosure, but low self-esteem; reflects uncertainty of self in the relationship. Negatively associated with relationship satisfaction. May reflect anxious/ambivalent attachment style.

29. When things aren't right with my partner and me, my stomach gets upset.
30. If my partner and I break up, I would get so depressed that I would even think of suicide.
31. Sometimes I get so excited about being in love with my partner that I can't sleep.
32. When my partner doesn't pay attention to me, I feel sick all over.
33. Since I've been in love with my partner, I've had trouble concentrating on anything else.
34. I cannot relax if I suspect that my partner is with someone else.
35. If my partner ignores me for a while, I sometimes do stupid things to try to get his/her attention back.

Agape

Reflects all-giving, selfless, nondemanding love. Associated with altruistic, committed, sexually idealistic love. Like Eros, tends to flare up with "being in love now."

36. I try to always help my partner through difficult times.
37. I would rather suffer myself than let my partner suffer.
38. I cannot be happy unless I place my partner's happiness before my own.
39. I am usually willing to sacrifice my own wishes to let my partner achieve his/hers.
40. Whatever I won is my partner's to use as he/she chooses.
41. When my partner gets angry with me, I still love him/her fully and unconditionally.
42. I would endure all things for the sake of my partner.

Adapted from Hendrick, Love Attitudes Scale

endorse eros, but less likely to endorse mania than other groups. "This finding fits with the image of a secure, confident eros lover who moves intensely but with mutuality into a new relationship," they maintain.

When they turned their attention to ongoing relationships, the Hendricks' found that couples who stayed together over the course of their months-long study were more passionate and less game-playing than couples who broke up. "A substantial amount of passionate love" and "a low dose of game-playing" love are key to the development of satisfying relationships—at least among the college kids studied.

YOUR MOTHER MADE YOU DO IT

The love style you embrace, how you treat your partner, may reflect the very first human relationship you ever had—probably with Mom. There is growing evidence supporting "attachment theory," which holds that the rhythms of response by a child's primary care giver affect the development of personality and influence later attachment processes, including adult love relationships.

First put forth by British psychiatrist John Bowlby in the 1960s and elaborated by American psychologist Mary Ainsworth, attachment theory is the culmination of years of painstaking observation of infants and their adult caregivers—and those separated from them—in both natural and experimental situations. Essentially it suggests that there are three major patterns of attachment; they develop within the first year of life and stick with us, all the while reflecting the responsiveness of the caregiver to our needs as helpless infants.

Those whose mothers, or caregivers, were unavailable or unresponsive may grow up to be detached and nonresponsive to others. Their behavior is Avoidant in relationships. A second group takes a more Anxious-Ambivalent approach to relationships, a response set in motion by having mothers they may not have been able to count on—sometimes responsive, other times not. The lucky among us are Secure in attachment, trusting and stable in relationships, probably the result of having had consistently responsive care.

While attachment theory is now driving a great deal of research on children's social, emotional, and cognitive development, University of Denver psychologists Cindy Hazan and Philip Shaver set out not long ago to investigate the possible effect of childhood relationships on adult attachments. First, they developed descriptive statements that reflect each of the three attachment styles. Then they asked people in their community, along with college kids, which statements best describe how they relate to others. They asked, for example, about trust and jealousy, about closeness and desire for reciprocation, about emotional extremes.

The distribution of the three attachment styles has proved to be about the same in grown-ups as in infants, the same among collegians as the fully fledged. More than half of adult respondents call themselves Secure; the rest are split between Avoidant and Ambivalent. Further, their adult attachment patterns predictably reflect the relationship they report with their parents. Secure people generally describe their parents as having warm and supportive. What's more, these adults predictably differ in success at romantic love. Secure people reported happy, long-lasting relationships. Avoidants rarely found love.

Secure adults are more trusting of their romantic partners and more confident of a partner's love, report Australian psychologists Judith Feeney and Patricia Noller of the University of Queensland. The two surveyed nearly 400 college undergraduates with a questionnaire on family background and love relationships, along with items designed to reveal their personality and related traits.

In contrast to the Secure, Avoidants indicated an aversion to intimacy. The Anxious-Ambivalent participants were characterized by dependency and what Feeney and Noller describe as "a hunger" for commitment. Their approach resembles the Mania style of love. Each of the three groups reported differences in early childhood experience that could account for their adult approach to relationships. Avoidants, for example, were most likely to tell of separations from their mother.

It may be, Hazan and Shaver suggest, that the world's greatest love affairs are conducted by the Ambitious-Ambivalents—people desperately searching for a kind of security they never had.

THE MAGIC NEVER DIES

Not quite two decades into the look at love, it appears as though love will not always mystify us. For already we are beginning to define what we think about it, how it makes us feel, and what we do when we are in love. We now know that it is the insecure, rather than the confident, who fall in love more readily. We know that outside stimuli that alter our emotional state can affect our susceptibility to romance; it is not just the person. We now know that to a certain extent your love style is set by the parenting you received. And, oh yes, men are more quickly romantic than women.

The best news may well be that when it comes to love, men and women are more similar than different. In the face of continuing gender wars, it is comforting to think that men and women share an important, and peaceful, spot to turf. It is also clear that no matter how hard we look at love, we will always be amazed and mesmerized by it.

RESPONSE SHEET

for Beth Livermore: The Lessons of Love

1. BD three of the most important lessons, for you, of those that Livermore discusses. (10 pts)

www.ingramcontent.com/pod-product-compliance
Ingram Content Group UK Ltd.
Pitfield, Milton Keynes, MK11 3LW, UK
UKHW051241300926
15471UKWH00015B/1516

9 780787 297251